The Founders of
American Cuisine

The Founders of American Cuisine

Seven Cookbook Authors, with Historical Recipes

HARRY HAFF

McFarland & Company, Inc., Publishers
Jefferson, North Carolina, and London

Library of Congress Cataloguing-in-Publication Data

Haff, Harry, 1946–
The founders of American cuisine : seven cookbook authors,
with historical recipes / Harry Haff.
p.   cm.
Includes bibliographical references and index.

ISBN 978-0-7864-5869-1
softcover : 50# alkaline paper ∞

1. Cooking, American — History.
2. Food habits — United States — History.
3. Cookbooks.
I. Title.
TX715.H1238   2011   641.5973 — dc22   2010046634

British Library cataloguing data are available

Front cover: Horn of plenty and borders © 2011
clipart.com; background © 2011 Shutterstock
Back cover: Lady with cook stove © 2011 clipart.com

Manufactured in the United States of America

*McFarland & Company, Inc., Publishers
Box 611, Jefferson, North Carolina 28640
www.mcfarlandpub.com*

With love to my wife Marilyn Wedig,
who is actually able to put up with me and
sacrificed most weekends of her free time
while I was writing this book.

Acknowledgments

I wish I could remember everyone I talked to about the idea for this book. These are some of the people I especially want to thank.

Mrs. Judith Polk, my former student at Le Cordon Bleu, for testing so many recipes and giving me good ideas about the foods with which she worked.

Mrs. Grace Robinson for her proofreading and suggestions.

Alma, a volunteer with Merced County, for tracking down newspaper articles on Chef Hirtzler, including his obituary.

Gioia Stevens at the Brooklyn Historical Society who sent me some information on Delmonico's and their Brooklyn farm.

Andy Smith for help with Amelia Simmons, Chefs Hirtzler and Ranhofer.

The wonderfully helpful staff at the Forsyth County Library here in metro north Atlanta for securing books from libraries around the state and the Southeast for me.

My feline editorial staff, Mimi, Ronney and Roxy, who spent countless hours with me proofreading, adding interesting keystrokes to the manuscript and generally thinking about the book with eyes closed and feet injected into the atmosphere.

Kelly Chamberlin at the St. Francis Hotel for all her research and assistance.

Table of Contents

Preface

The subjects of this book are seven influential people in American gastronomy, each of whom published an influential cookbook that nurtured and developed what we now call American cuisine. As a food professional for over 25 years I discovered these authors only recently. They need to be recognized for what they accomplished in the United States in the development of our multicultural, ethnic and classically influenced cuisine. Through their biographies and books, we can trace the main culinary influences on American cuisine, from French to West African to Native American, from English to German to Creole. In the time period covered in this book, roughly 1796 to 1919, the dynamism of the growing country and its culture can be seen in its food and expanding national boundaries.

To be sure, there are many recent books available on the history of American food and cookbooks. This book tells the stories of the people who, through their lives and their works, shaped and defined the cuisine of a new nation.

Information about most of the authors has been scarce. Simmons is virtually unknown in the culinary field. Miss Leslie was well known. Mary Randolph has almost nothing written about her by her contemporaries. Lafcadio Hearn is quite well known, more for his work in Japan rather than New Orleans. Without Frederick Starr's recent book on Hearn in New Orleans, there would be very little to go on other than Hearn's own writings on Creole culture and his beloved city. Abby Fisher was a freed slave and was unknown until just a few years ago. She was illiterate at the time her book was published. Although she is credited with one of the first cookbooks by an African American woman, her recipes have languished in obscurity for almost a century. Ranhofer was enormously influential but where he worked disappeared in the first quarter of the 20th century, and his book *The Epicurean* was eclipsed by Escoffier with his *La Guide Culinaire*. Hirtzler returned to France in the 1920s with his name kept alive largely by the St. Francis Hotel and its various owners.

Some of the material for the present work came from books written at the time the authors were alive. And there certainly is ample material drawn from 19th century magazines and newspapers, including the *San Francisco Call*, *The Brooklyn Eagle*, and *The New York Times*, which featured articles chronicling local events, such as the Raisin Bread Contest in Fresno or the charity balls of the French Culinary and Philanthropic Society in New York. But the main part of the story lies within the cook books these authors created. These volumes document, in the recipes themselves, how our nation and its cuisine grew throughout the late 18th, 19th and early 20th centuries.

1

The story of American cuisine is not complete without these recipes and the culinary traditions that created them. The influences of these authors were profound and are ongoing. Their lives and works helped to create and define our national cuisine. It is time to get to know them on a professional and personal basis.

Introduction

In 1796 the first American cookbook, by Amelia Simmons, was designated for women of all stations in society; it relied on mostly English cooking traditions but was the first American-authored and -published book to also incorporate ingredients used by Native Americans in their cooking. As I show later on, while there were earlier cookbooks published in Europe, many of these were mainly for noble or very wealthy households.

Later, Mary Randolph's book *was* geared to the wealthy, but her system of organization and methods of preparation made her book relevant and appreciated by people in all social settings. Certainly not every copy of this exceptional book was purchased by the wife of a plantation owner. Here there is not only an expression of culinary influences, but also the inclusion of a regional (Virginia/Southern) focus that was the first of its kind expressed in a cookbook published in the United States. To be sure there are many tips on how to run a complex household, but what speaks more immediately to readers is the sense of organization expressed by Mary Randolph. Her skills running a large household served her well when she was no longer one of the Virginia landed gentry. The skills and knowledge she shares have kept this book in print since it was first published.

Miss Leslie's book was the largest selling cookbook in the 19th century and influenced an entire generation, maybe more, in how to prepare quality food. A well-known author of books for children and young adults, as well as a magazine editor, her literary reputation paved the way for her cookbooks, from which she said she made most of her money. Here are French, German, Native American and good commonsense influences geared towards the individual household and not the massive estate. She also included important tips on food safety and sanitation. While these topics may not be glamorous or exciting, not paying attention to them could result in dire consequences. In Miss Leslie's time, there were no emergency rooms to receive patients. It was far better to prevent illness than to try to cure it. While this aspect of her book is noteworthy, her cooking skills and insistence on quality of food products speak volumes about her as a person and indirectly shed light on some of the common daily trials of running a successful household in a major city in the still fledgling country.

Mrs. Fisher showed us Southern cooking from the perspective of the slave and the servant. Her remarkable story defies perceptions about what a slave could be and demonstrates what a freed slave could be with sufficient force of will and determination — along with lots of good things to eat, of course. Her adaptations of traditional African ingredients, which ironically came also to be known as Southern ingredients, did much to preserve for us the culinary, hence social, traditions of plantation life from the downstairs side of the business, a counterpoint to Mrs. Randolph's experiences.

With her extraordinary personal circumstance and later her dynamic business venture, Abby Fisher was a person who was able to overcome horrendous odds and create one of the great books in American culinary history. She also lived an incredible story that could be a myopic biopic were it not for the fact that this is a life that was lived in real time by a real person.

Lafcadio Hearn brought Creole cooking to the world outside of Louisiana almost as an afterthought. The man was in love with everything Creole and this cookbook is one part of that intense, ten-year love affair. At first he wanted to publish the book anonymously as he did not want to be known as a cookbook author for fear it would lower his worth and diminish the appreciation of his other works dealing with Creole cuisine. A truly phenomenal intellect, he pursued Creole culture with the same abandon as he did languages, comparative religion and later the myths and culture of Japan. As part and parcel of his cultural interests, he just happened to invent comparative linguistics and ethnography along the way. Seen as an expression of his intellectual pursuits, this book captures the Creole culture in the home as expressed through food, celebrations and folk traditions. His comprehensive knowledge did a lot to have this wonderful cuisine appreciated beyond geographical and temporal boundaries.

Chef Ranhofer, in *The Epicurean*, documented the elaborate food at America's most famous restaurant, Delmonico's. Here Americans had their first genuine experience with what we would now recognize as a restaurant. The innovations present in this century-long establishment had an enormous impact on the creation of what is now commonplace in concept, if not in execution, around the United States. Drawing on the French traditions from which he had developed, he transformed the culinary world of America. In doing so, he was able to influence how people living in other countries saw this country. The wealthy who could afford to travel could afford to eat at Delmonico's. The fame of this restaurant caused Charles Dickens to change his mind about America and American food.

Due to his encyclopedic knowledge of food, service and wines, Chef Ranhofer was in the right place at the right time. The partnership between America's greatest chef and America's greatest restaurateur at that time created a still living legend. Many people are familiar with the name Delmonico's — but how many know the name of the man who was primarily responsible for the success of the restaurant for more than 30 years?

Chef Ranhofer also defined the term "chef" as it is now understood. Prior to his position at the restaurant, great chefs were often in the employ of nobles and supremely wealthy people. In fact, it was not until 1980 here in the United States that the job title "chef" was changed from that of household servant to professional.

His epic culinary book also created quite a stir. It was the first time a professional chef had disclosed the "secrets" of running an haute cuisine restaurant. Amid hysterical cries from the restaurant world, Chef Ranhofer served as a model for future chefs who would write cookbooks based on their restaurant experiences. And by the way, his book was written about a decade before that of one of his compatriots, whose name may be familiar to more readers: August Escoffier.

There is considerable material here on the restaurant as well. With some history as background, Delmonico's is presented in some detail. It may be hard to imagine, but when Delmonico's first started, the fine restaurant business did not exist in the United States. The restaurant as such was even a relatively recent phenomenon in Paris. I felt it necessary to explore this aspect of culinary history as Chef Ranhofer and this restaurant did more to create the idea of a restaurant than any other partnership in history.

Chef Hirtzler established the West Coast as a focal point for fine food and got California cuisine started. As chef for the finest hotel west of Chicago he was in a position of influence and placed American foods and cooking on a par with their European counterparts. What stands out in part in his book is the crediting of food products to a particular place of origin for a specific food. It is useful to know that this is a common European practice. Here in America it seems relegated to "specialty foods," but Chef Hirtzler was at the forefront of professionals who recognized a "specialness" of foods coming from certain areas in the United States. He also placed the foods and their preparations on a par with European classics — a tribute to American cuisine if ever there was one.

Though born and trained in France, as was Chef Ranhofer, Chef Hirtzler became an American chef in that he incorporated American foods almost as a matter of course and saw to it that these items and preparations were second to none in terms of quality and sophistication.

With the authors and their books featured here, we are not focused on food or recipes for an elite fraction of a civilization's population. These were skilled professionals who wanted to share their knowledge with all kinds of people, rich and not so rich. From Amelia Simmons, who wrote her book to be of service to women of all classes, to Ranhofer and Hirtzler, who were writing for the elite of society and their highly-trained chefs, these authors show how our cuisine developed and they invite us into their worlds, if only for a brief time, to share their experiences in the kitchen.

The authors selected for this book are people who were able to absorb and own material from other cuisines and cultures and make them their own. Through their books, a melding of influences created what we call American cuisine.

Reading these books is not just looking at a collection of recipes. Cookbooks serve as windows into the past for the day-to-day concerns of real people. They are still living documents that bring to life the personalities of the authors for us in the 21st century. There is always a snippet of information leaping out at you about how to stoke a fire, keep the coals steady, keep your butcher honest, where to catch your catfish, what to look for as markers of quality. All of these tidbits show us life as it was when the authors were alive.

And here, too, we see a development, a timeline if you will, of the integration of Native American foodstuffs into familiar recipes from the old countries. Or, in the case of Miss Leslie and Mrs. Randolph, the use of classical French cooking techniques show everyday people in the new United States how to adopt these sometimes sophisticated procedures to their everyday cooking chores. It is a compliment to these authors in particular that people were able to learn these "classic techniques" without ever really knowing how classic they actually were. They became techniques of cooking that the readers could absorb and make their own. And is this not the mark of a great teacher: to have people learn and make new knowledge a part of the student?

Get to know these people as you read through their recipes and prepare their food. I was amazed about how easy it was to time travel and be in the kitchen with these wonderful authors.

With the recipes, any changes have to do with scaling of ingredients and updating of cooking methods, rather than with the essence of the recipes themselves. People are more likely to measure in cups or grams rather than in pounds for home use. Also, where a method was not clear, this was added to assist in making the recipes. Food equipment has come a long way since 1796. So some of these changes are molded into the recipe updates as well. But remember, the originals included in the book are in the authors' own words, from their original books. You can certainly try anything the "old fashioned way" if you choose.

Part One

The Cuisine of America

Prologue: The Development of Food and Cuisine

To provide a sense of place and perspective with regard to the major, mostly European influences on American cuisine considered here, it is worth taking a little time to examine some earlier history to see where these influence themselves came from.

Principal influences on American cuisine come from several different sources: Native American (or Indian), British, French and German, and to a much lesser extent, Spanish. Spanish influences were mostly in Central and South America, but Spain also controlled Florida and other parts of the American continent extending through the southwest and up into California. One of the most important facets of Spanish cuisine is wheat.[1] And as we shall see, a key component of Spanish food did much to depopulate the southeastern Indian tribes.

Spanish conquerors had no compunction about using slave labor,[2] which would add to the development of the African slave trade as the availability of field workers declined as the Indians were annihilated.

Indian foods and cuisine are covered in detail in Chapter One. In the time period covered here many culinary influences that are now quite commonplace in the 21st century had not yet made their appearances. So from here on out we will be discussing mostly French, British and German foods and traditions that contributed in significant ways to our cuisine.

Britain's location — surrounded as it is by the Atlantic Ocean and warmed by the Gulf Stream — provides the country with wonderful pasture land for grazing cows and sheep. With ample amounts of rain and a temperate climate, pasture land generally grows on a year-round basis.[3] Many of what are now standard "English" foods were in fact introduced by the Romans by the fifth or sixth centuries, including orchard fruits (which then made their way to the colonies), cattle, sheep, pigs, wheat, rye, barley, culinary and medicinal herbs and winemaking grapes planted in extensive vineyards that were productive until the late 1300s.

The early Christian church also had a significant influence on English foods. Friday was the Saxon Frigga's day and as part of that tradition, fish was a Frigga day staple.[4] This early tradition evolved into the tradition of eating fish on Friday as a commemoration of Good Friday. It was a painless way to give the new religion credibility with the local populace and continued as a commonplace tradition up until the late 20th century.

A further aspect of English cuisine that is often mentioned is its blandness. Apparently

Pope Gregory the Great believed that well-seasoned food led to lusty behavior and he recommended a bland diet. The English seem to have taken this to heart as well as table over the years and too often this tradition continues to have a strong pull on American dining habits.

Some of the basic American cooking utensils were first brought to the colonies by the English settlers, which will be seen vividly in the chapter on Amelia Simmons. These included large kettles or cauldrons, covered bowls and pans for hearth baking, techniques for keeping the fire coals live, griddles and pudding cloth, also found in Simmons' book.

There were also some traditions of foods that carried over from England to the colonies, including pigs raised on nuts (Gloucestershire on beech nuts, Virginia on peanuts), and a drink called flummery, which is made from milk or cream and wine or mead, honey and some type of cereal.

The desire to grow wine grapes in the colonies can also be seen as an extension of an existing English agricultural practice. This effort was not successful due mostly to North American grapes, mostly *Vitis Labrusca,* not being the same species as the European wine grape, *Vitis Vinifera.* Labrusca makes awful wine and the European grape vines that were imported to the eastern states were killed by the louse phylloxera, the same pesky bug that was to decimate European vineyards in the 19th century.

In France, the tradition of food was quite different than in England. As early as the 1300s there was a tradition of professional cooks having the ability to rise socially due to their ability in the kitchen as well as being able to handle the attendant administrative duties such as procurement, purchasing, inventory and variety. A cook and author by the name of Guillaume Tirel, aka Taillevent, is credited with the writing of the first professional cookbook in France.[5] His career was a lesson in serendipity — although not of the overly fortuitous kind. He survived the plague and the Hundred Years' War with England, but many others did not. As the court of Valois needed lots of provisioning and someone skilled to cook the provisions, Taillevent was the man on the spot. In addition to culinary skills he was adept at finding food and making sure that the ledgers were in order and that the court was quite the courtly place, in a culinary sense. He was elevated to *ecuyier de cuisine,* which is akin to an English squire. His coat of arms has three sauce-pots on it so there is no mistaking why he was so amply rewarded. He also garnered lands and a good wage for his troubles, which shows the philosophical differences between English and French cooking.[6]

After the war with England ended, France underwent a centralization of power. The kings apparently wanted to keep the nobles where they could keep a royal eye on them. Especially after Louis XIV built Versailles, the nobles wanted to be at the court and as a social affectation would try to emulate the food and entertaining going on with the royal court. Renown was accomplished primarily through the arts, including cooking, rather than through political success.[7] This was also to lead to employment for many highly trained professional household chefs whose job was to make sure that their employers could always out-cook the Joneses next door.

England was a different story with a less centralized system of royalty and landed gentry. After the English Civil War the power of the throne was somewhat de-centralized. Rather than having a stage for the elite of the country to display themselves as in France, the landed aristocracy was the tradition that held sway and this concept was transported to Virginia and the deep South.

The result of this decentralization was that many of the nobles and ultra-wealthy people who would have been at court in France preferred to reside on their estates in the country. This self-sufficiency and isolation did not lend itself to opulent displays of food as courtly residence demanded in France. A simpler way of eating was called for and provided.

As the English and French rarely got along well, there is an epithet in an English cookbook published in 1747 that refers to French cooking as resorting to "trickery" and ingloriously refers to French chefs as "boobies." This book would be *The Art of Cooking Made Plain and Easy* by one Hannah Glasse. No wonder they were always fighting wars.

The German influences on American cuisine go back to the founding of the country but become especially important after 1848. The European revolutions of 1848 started in Sicily and ended up in barricades and riots in most of Western Europe with France and Germany most severely affected. The unrest started in Sicily, in Palermo, and spread to Naples and Paris. Within a couple of months Munich and Berlin were affected, as were other central and eastern European cities.[8]

One of the results of this turmoil was the immigration of more than 435,000 Germans to the United States by 1850.[9] This influx of people brought a wealth of new food items to many parts of the United States as the settlers spread out across the country with large numbers settling in the Midwest and upper Midwest. Rye bread, sauerkraut, sausages of all manner and lots of beer, established themselves in the pantheon of American foods. The misnamed Pennsylvania Dutch are really Moravian Germans who made large contributions to the culinary as well as the cultural life of the country.

From wonderful Moravian Christmas music to the Bethlehem Bach Festival to shoefly pie to snickerdoodles to most of the large American breweries — Coors, Schlitz, Budweiser, Miller, Pabst, etc.— this immense influx of refugees from Germany was one of the social and culinary milestones of early America. As Andrew Smith points out,[10] this deluge of Germans eventually led to the start of delicatessens, which paved the way for Jewish delis somewhat later on. In a real sense, these establishments started the tradition of take-out or take-away foods. There were also foods like head cheese, pigs' feet, prepared salads and imported foods, which became a huge part of what is now everyday fare in the United States.

These are merely a small sampling of Old World influences that made their way westward. But we shall see how they and others like them were used and adapted to create American cuisine.

CHAPTER 1

Native American Foods

Columbus was certainly not the first European to reach the shores of the Americas. Well documented evidence indicates that Norse settlements in Newfoundland and some other coastal areas of maritime Canada pre-date 1492 by about 500 years.[1]

As a continuation of settlements in Iceland and Greenland, the Norse forays into North America were not successful in the long term with their efforts to inhabit the lands beyond northern Europe. The Greenland settlements did not survive past about 1350, most likely due to a climatic change that turned Europe colder, and the growth of the Hanseatic League in Germany.[2] This group tended to dominate the northern oceans and as the sparse trading in Greenland dwindled to nothing with the mother country of Norway, the settlers were not able to sustain themselves. Only Iceland remained a viable settlement.

There have been stories and legends that Saint Brendan found "the land of promise of the saints."[3] This story relates how St. Brendan, at the age of 71, sailed around the north Atlantic for seven years, landed in Newfoundland and returned to Ireland with wonderful tales.

And although there have been champions of the sailors of Bristol actually finding and fishing in the formerly rich waters off Newfoundland, there are no pieces of hard evidence save for a couple of oblique references in letters of traders of the period. (Some people suggest that the famous Maine coon cat is a direct descendant of the Norwegian forest cats that were left behind when the Norse people went home. So maybe there was permanent settlement after all!)

When speaking of pre-contact then, what many people start with is an examination of what the land was like before the Columbus discovery in 1492. However, the term "new world" is something of a misnomer as dates for other than European occupation keep getting pushed back further and further in time.

Professor Eske Willerslev of the University of Copenhagen stated in a press release from the University of Copenhagen in April of 2008 that fossilized fecal material from eastern Oregon dates to 14,340 BC. This is about 1,000 years earlier than most people postulated for the earliest inhabitants, and about 400 years before the ice-free corridor that was supposed to have made migration from Asia possible. He was able to identify two genetic types unique to North American Indians.

As more discoveries are made there could be older traces of human habitation waiting to be discovered. We are continuing to enlarge our knowledge of pre-contact societies from all of the Americas. There are discussions about whether or not early human inhabitants were responsible for the extinction of the mega-mammals that populated the land at the time of the last ice age. We may learn more about that as well, so the jury is still out on so many aspects of early in habitation of the continents.

A discussion of Native American foods is a complex undertaking. A glance at the geography encountered reveals a landmass of enormous variety encompassing virtually every climate found on planet Earth, from tropical and temperate rain forests to deserts. Elevations in North America vary from 20,322 feet for Mt. McKinley to Death Valley more than 100 feet below sea level. Temperatures range from 134° F in Death Valley to minus 81.4° F in Snag, Yukon. Rainfall amounts vary from more than 200" per year to less than 2" per year.

It is only natural that in such a varied landscape the number of items that the Native Americans relied on for food was enormous. Fortunately, the focus on the eastern part of North America makes the task more manageable. However, in order to appreciate more the diversity of the continent before 1492 we need to consider some relevant information. For just as the foods available were many and varied, so too were the cultures that relied upon them.

The human population was as diverse as the terrain, flora and fauna. Estimates are that at first contact with Europeans, there were somewhere between 1,000 to 2,000 languages spoken in North America. Of these languages, only one developed a written version, and that was the Cherokee language in the southeastern United States — and that not until the 1800s. The lack of written languages makes investigations of Native American foods challenging. Accurate research is reliant on archaeology, anthropology, linguistics, genetics and tribal oral histories to fill in some substantial knowledge gaps.

There is now a wealth of evidence that strongly suggests that the Americas were more populated and complex in organization than previously thought.[4] Although exact population estimates can be hard to ascertain with certainty, there is plenty of recorded evidence to document a depopulation of about 95 percent in the years between 1492 and the late 18th century.

Consider the following two accounts: From around 1539 to 1543 the Spaniard De Soto pillaged a huge swath of territory in Florida, Georgia, North and South Carolina, Tennessee, Alabama, Mississippi, Arkansas, Texas and Louisiana. Accounts of these travels speak of settlements along the Mississippi River in what is now Arkansas. The area was described as heavily settled with great towns and from whatever town one was in several more could be seen from that one spot.

In 1673 Messrs. Marquette and Joliet made an exploratory trip down the Mississippi River and found a land almost devoid of people. The next recorded European visitor was de la Salle in 1682. He found no villages and a land deserted of people. To put a number on these two accounts: The first is estimated to indicate a population of around 200,000 people. The second indicates a population of around 8,000 to 8,500. (In what was at the time Nieuw Amsterdam, the Dutch had exterminated the native Algonquins on Manhattan Island by 1664.)

This enormous population decline occurred throughout the Americas — North, Central and South — as a result of the introduction of infectious European diseases, sometimes spread by man, sometimes spread by animals. Charles Mann mentions in *1491* that the force De Soto led was accompanied by a herd of pigs. They carried a host of diseases that could be transmitted to humans for which the natives had no defenses. (If you have further interest in this aspect of early contact years, definitely see Mann's well-written account.) Given the lack of scientific and medical knowledge at the time, one might suppose that all these infections were accidental. Often that was the case. But there was enough of a functional understanding of what diseases could do that at times infections were deliberately spread to simply eliminate the natives.

The isolation, or rather the location of Native American lands, prevented cross-fertilization of ideas on foods and farming technology with Europe and Asia, at least to any measurable, sustainable degree. blessed with a natural bounty of plants and animals throughout North America, large-scale draught animals were absent. The largest draught animals in the Americas are the llama, vicuña and alpaca, which are native to South America. Large scale tilling and farming, so common in Europe, which was largely dependent on larger animals, was not present in pre-contact America. (This is not to say that there was no large scale farming at all, however, quite the opposite is true.)

Intercropping was common and given the size of pre–Columbian population estimates farming had to have been on a relatively large scale in order to support the large settlements for which there is ample archeological evidence. Mark Cohen states that population drove agricultural innovation and that the integration of farming, gathering and hunting were so well done that there are no "qualitative signs of malnutrition or deficiencies in vitamins and minerals."[5]

One key item of Native American culture was the belief in the interconnectedness of all living as well as inanimate objects. Such an ingrained belief system had Native Americans see food and food production in a way not found in European traditions. This allowed for more than adequate nutrition while still not depleting the land or animals. To be sure, Native Americans cleared land by burning, and in the thought provoking book *1491*, Charles Mann makes a compelling case that Native Americans managed their environment to provide adequate food derived from farming, fishing and hunting and gathering to an extent just now becoming better understood. But this management was done in a way that largely allowed for the natural environment to replenish itself on a cyclical basis.

In the east, Native Americans grew crops, including the loveable giant sunflowers, hunted abundant game (now all but gone), fished with apparent ease from a seemingly endless supply of finned fish and shellfish, and gathered nuts and berries. The tribes along the coast from Maine to Florida were fishing for items from shad to sturgeon to oysters to crabs.

From about 8,000 B.C. on, the evidence for a wide variety of foods tells us that there were trade patterns for centuries and that agricultural development was sophisticated enough to create the crop of our modern corn from its unlikely ancestor teosinte. Looking further into this botanical process shows how disciplined and systematic the agricultural systems were before Columbus. This is not the book to go too deeply into that aspect of Native American foods, but it is a fascinating topic.

To give just a partial list of what was available to Indians in North America, consider the following list. Edible roots: wild onion, garlic, hog peanut, Jerusalem artichoke, Indian cucumber. Condiments and nuts: honey locust, sumac, maple syrup, sassafras, black walnuts, acorns, butternuts, honey, American chestnut. Animals include turtles of a bewildering variety, snakes, quail, passenger pigeons, wild turkey, doves, possum, rabbit, squirrel, two kinds of deer, occasionally black bear, all manner of fin fish and both salt and freshwater shellfish, waterfowl of all kinds as well as water mammals such as beaver, muskrat and otter.[6]

The farming practices were varied as well and used for specific areas and circumstances. We spoke already of intercroppng, but there were also slash and burn and raised fields or beds for growing different crops.

Foods were prepared and preserved by boiling, smoking, drying and even treating corn with wood ash to increase the availability of niacin from the corn.

Stavely and Fitzgerald state simply: "When Europeans arrived in the Americas, nutrition-deficiency diseases were unheard of." This is a direct result of relying on the Three Sisters (corn, beans and squash), a wide variety of domesticated if not cultivated crops, as well as on fishing, hunting and gathering skills. Michael Krondl writes, "It has been estimated that Native Americans were using about two thousand food plants before Columbus came."[7] For some people there may be lingering residues of ideas that Indians were a savage lot and not very sophisticated compared to the European colonizers. Nothing could be further from the truth and as research continues into the composition of Indian societies, there will undoubtedly be more revelatory information about what life was really like before Columbus.

As interactions between natives and foreigners occurred, there were noticeable influences of one group's foods on the other. In New England and Virginia Europeans were shown corn, squash, pumpkins, cranberries, turkeys, beans and maple syrup as well as a variety of fruits and nuts. And when it comes to the most beneficial plants farmed by Native Americans, it can be said that in the pre-contact environment there was a trinity in Native American agriculture. Corn, squash in many forms and beans in many varieties are all but ubiquitous among the Native Americans, which speaks to their value as food products as well as the commercial and social interaction of tribes and nations across the continent. Corn, or maize (according to Stavely and Fitzgerald the Arawak name for corn was "mahiz"), is a member of the grass family that originated in Central America. Most recent research implies that Central America or Mexico was the birthplace of corn around 10,000 years ago. In what is a feat of agricultural technology, the probable ancestor of corn, teosinte, was developed from an unlikely food source to become the most productive agricultural crop in the world. Although initially developed in Central America, maize quickly wended its way northward and by about A.D. 1000 frost-resistant varieties appeared in Native American agriculture as far north as Ohio. As Native Americans interacted and the range of corn spread around the country and the Caribbean, special varieties were developed to deal with specific climatic conditions. Stavely and Fitzgerald rightly state that by continuing this process of specialty corn development, the Native Americans developed a sophisticated type of agricultural science.

Ellen Messer says that cave deposits from Mexico show "evolutionary sequences" for the development of maize extending from 3500 to 1500 BC. This was purposeful agricultural science that also included hybrids of teosinte and more "advanced" maize as early as 1500 BC.[8]

This staple was introduced to Europeans by the Native Americans in what must be one of the most profound agricultural cross-fertilizations in history. Corn today is found all over the world, with over two thirds of the corn raised used for animal feed. Corn is also the basis for the American processed foods industry. It finds its way into all facets of our lives, from take-out food containers to corn sweetener in soft drinks, beers and distilled products, crackers to pastry cream.

One of the most prominent distinctions between Native American and European agriculture was the way the land was owned and farmed. According to Douglas Hurt's book *American Agriculture*, it was mostly women who were responsible for the farming, and in the process they became "accomplished plant breeders" able to develop different varieties of corn and other crops to different climatic conditions. This division of labor was dramatically misunderstood by European settlers. In the north, the Huron tribe developed strains of corn with different ripening times, early corn for eating and later ripening corn for drying and putting by for the long winters. The storage corn was generally air or fire dried and stored in large baskets in the ground.

As women cultivated the land so too did they own the land. Women in the Five Nations held title to all the lands and possessed veto power over male instituted initiatives and could demand reconsiderations of any measure of governance not to their liking.[9] Indians of the Northeast had a degree of liberty totally unknown in European societies. Ben Franklin noted that among the Indians of Pennsylvania there was a level of autonomy not found in supposedly more civilized European countries. There was a basic tenet that said no one had ranking over another.

In her paper "Native American Women and Agriculture,"[10] Joan M. Jensen brings up the fact that among the Seneca, the women were responsible for the agriculture and owned the land and did the trading as well. Women were given high status socially and were accorded a high level of respect. The enforcement of European ideas of individuality, male supremacy and domination of women created havoc with the Seneca and other tribes as well. These so-called "primitive" societies achieved a level of gender equality based on division of labor that is still found wanting in many modern countries.

Given this sense of equality, the farming and storage and land ownership enjoyed by women makes a great deal of sense. The welfare of the food supply was what we might now call vertically integrated, with women having overall responsibility for everything from the health of the farming land to sophisticated crop breeding.

The land cultivated was mostly alluvial bottom land, soft and easy to turn over. Although they did not know the precise scientific reason, they found that clearing by burning brush amongst mature trees produced better crops on the land later on. The burning reduced soil acidity, which resulted in an increase in microbial activity that hastened organic decomposition. The burning also deposited magnesium, calcium, potash and potassium.

Burning did more than nourish the soil. Hilliard that early settlers commented on the almost park-like condition of the forests in the South. When Native Americans "burned" the forest it was more for clearing underbrush than wholesale clearing as is the norm now in many areas of tropical rain forests. The burned off brush allowed for planting of the Three Sisters and other crops, while still maintaining the forest. This is classic example of what Europeans did, and is known as intercropping.

By cultivating the Three Sisters — corn, squash and beans — Native Americans were able to take advantage of how each of these crops grew. The corn leached nitrogen from the soil and this was replaced by the beans. The beans climbed the corn stalks and the squash vines crawled along the ground thereby reducing weed growth. (Maple sugar derived from boiling the sap of sugar maples in the late winter or very early spring provided a reliable sweetener, as the mature trees could exist in conjunction with the cultivated plants.)

Further south, squash and gourds were cultivated from around 2000 B.C., but after A.D. 500–1000 corn was king. Farming the river bottom land worked well because the land was easily tilled and the regular flooding and resultant silt deposits continuously replenished the soil nutrients and aided in moisture retention. By intercropping and producing more crops than were needed, Native Americans replenished the soil and avoided famine.

In addition to the crops grown, all manner of wild berries and nuts and fruits were gathered. Hunting and fishing were the ways in which protein was supplied in the diet. In a spectacularly abundant landscape replete with deer, bear, antelope, bison roaming virtually from coast to coast, abundant fish and seafood, the Native Americans were able to enjoy the bounty of the earth in many ways.

What we know about Native American cooking and foodways and eating habits are generalized observations made mostly by European settlers.

After Contact and Before 1796

When Columbus was in the Caribbean in 1492 and having Christmas dinner with Guananagari, the Taino chief in Hispaniola, Columbus's reactions to native foods at dinner are lost. But Guananagari, the native, who had his thoughts recorded by a friar in attendance, said that the food the Spaniards were eating and he sampled were "almost like human food"—makes me wonder what he thought the Spaniards were, if not humans who would actually eat human foods. This may have been his reaction on being served something made from white flour with sweetening in it, as he does mention several times that it tasted sweet. What was a common native food at this time in Hispaniola was cassava flat bread, which is neither white nor sweet. So it isn't too hard to see how a sweetened bread or cake or cracker could have had a noticeable impact on the local dignitary. This may be a good example of how certain foods endure. In any large American city with a thriving Caribbean population, cassava bread is not all that difficult to find. So what was a common native food at that Christmas in 1492 is still available to modern day shoppers, whether native, Spaniard or otherwise.

As to actual recipes for Native American foods we are looking at a blank slate. While Native Americans had rich traditions of oral history, they did lack written languages and as a result, no detailed period recipes or recordings of food preparation exist.

In her book *Cooking in America, 1590–1842*, Trudy Eden does quote some methods of how the Native Americans cooked. White colonists observing Native Americans in their daily lives recorded these accounts, from the 1500s and early 1600s, including some by the famous Captain John Smith. Sketches exist of villages, farming plots and food preparation techniques; missing are the historical recordings done by the Native Americans themselves.

As the country continued to draw white settlers and later black slaves (the early 16th century saw more Africans in South Carolina than British and French settlers combined) each influx brought something new and different to the table. While early settlers were primarily from Holland and England, countries such as Scotland, Germany, Ireland, Spain, Italy and France were present in differing degrees. In the South, the slaves brought influences from West Africa and the Caribbean, which also found their way into southern regional cooking and Creole cuisine.

The abundance of cheap land also created a pattern of farming that lingers even now. With so much land available there was a large dependence on animal protein. When the land was settled the increase in food animals made meat plentiful and cheap.

As colonists spread throughout the land mass there were bound to be interactions and cross fertilization of ideas regarding food and cooking techniques. In some areas, settlers adopted native foods with traditional European touches. In Rhode Island, Roger Williams compared differing versions of hasty pudding made with cornmeal. Natives used water with the corn and little else, while Williams and friends added butter and milk. (In an early account of cross-fertilization of ideas, as early as the 1690s there was a report of an Indian in Maine "keeping a cow." Cows came to the colonies with the settlers.) As natives became more used to foreign ideas, foods and animals were absorbed as a matter of course into their daily lives. The Cherokee in the Southeast were cultivating European fruit trees, peaches in particular, from a very early time after contact.

Squash was raised domestically around 5,000 years ago, modern corn about 1,000. As settlers arrived, foods did change, but maybe not in the way most people would think. At the Museum of the Cherokee Indian in Cherokee, North Carolina, a series of dinners arranged in the 1950s demonstrated how many native foods became a regular part of what the early colonists ate. Foods prepared included corn mush, pones, dry beans, succotash, ramps (wild leeks), all kinds of berries, squirrel gravy and biscuits, persimmons, a wide variety of native grapes and other fruits. Clearly, the abundance of foods had a profound effect on how the Europeans ate in the mountains.

As might be expected, the most prominent Old World influence in the early colonies was British. And unlike many other ethnic groups settling here, many Brits maintained close ties with their ancestral homeland. As British traditions inculcated themselves more deeply in American society, many traditional food items became naturalized Americans. Traditional items such as roasts of beef, lamb, mutton and game soon became the culinary staples of a large segment of American colonies. This was especially true in New England where there was a strong British culinary influence. One needs to look at the culinary differences of John Adams and Thomas Jefferson to see this demonstrated in high relief.

The surfeit of foods available when colonists got to America made an impact in three principal theaters of daily life; these were family, societal and frontier foods, and eating. Most people were actively engaged in farming and proved to be self-sufficient providers for their families. There is an account of a typical prosperous New England farmer from 1787 spending a whopping $10 per year on things such as salt and nails. Everything else was made down on the farm.[11] Although there were not a large number of cities, the large ones that were in existence, primarily New York, Philadelphia and Boston, were able to provide a wide range of foods that were of native origin, as well as imported foods. The cities were not large geographically, with farms and forests not far away from city centers. But for most of the populace luxuries did not form a very large part of their lives.

But in a seemingly contradictory development, the British love of sweets easily crossed the Atlantic, especially in the otherwise grim culinary tradition of New England. There is still a deep love of all things sweet in the Northeast. There are a couple of reasons for this.

The growth of sugar plantations produced profound effects on the colonial powers. For the first time in history a mostly pure sweetener was readily available and Jeffrey Pilcher says that by 1598 in England there was the wonderfully picturesque condition known as "Blackteeth," which was known as an "English defect." This was apparently due to high sugar consumption.[12]

The other part of the explanation may be due to the Triangle Trade in slaves, sugar and rum that was so prevalent among New England traders. The molasses, a by-product of sugar refining, was shipped to New England where it was distilled into rum. This, along with other products such as wood and timber or other agricultural goods, would be shipped to England. The goods were bartered in Africa for slaves, which were then transported to the Caribbean and American agricultural plantations in the South. There were variations on this theme, but whether the trading ships started in England or New England, the results were the same and the crops and manufactured goods were largely the same.

This was a huge trade. Boston had 25 distilleries by 1750 with an additional ten, at least, in other parts of the colony. Rhode Island was home to 20; New York to 17; Philadelphia alone claimed 14. Some estimates state that there were at least 159 distilleries producing rum in New England alone, and this by 1763. This industry generated lots of rum and lots of money that largely fueled the American version of the Triangle Trade.

Although much of the molasses was used for rum, a cursory look at other New England recipes does reveal that molasses was used quite often as the sweetener of choice.

As a complement to that, when we look at what might be served on a well set table on the "frontier," the folks were doing well, just in a different way than in the cities and on the farms. According to the *Oxford Encyclopedia of Food and Drink*, a well set table might include the following: elk steaks, venison, fried greens in bear fat (mmm — nothing quite like greens and bear fat), corn, potatoes, sweet potatoes, an assortment of desserts and often fresh hot biscuits, all kinds of fruits, berries, honey, cream and, to settle the stomach, some home distilled whiskey.

The natives showed the settlers which wild greens and other plants were good to eat and added valuable nutrition that could be foraged rather than planted and cultivated. Many of these items are still around today for people who seek them. Included were watercress, dandelions, fiddleheads (still an important tradition in New England as a sign of spring after a long winter), ramps and purslane, as well as other wild or field greens. Some of these items are still found in organic spring or field mixes in mainstream food markets. Check out the ingredients in one of these packages next time you are in the market. You may be surprised at what you find. Some of the wealth of native foods is still available, though not of the overall variety that one would have found in the 17th, 18th, and 19th centuries. (See De Voe, Simmons and Leslie.)

As time went by, the idea of scientific eating and eating for the sake of fueling our bodies was introduced, where our bodies were viewed as little more than machines. Flavor and condiments were considered little more than irritants. A look at the wealth of cookbooks related to self-named scientific eating in the 19th century shows how important this idea became.

But this is not cuisine. Cuisine has to do with the use of foods, food prepared in a way that reflects the area in which it is produced. In the case of "foreign" restaurants or food preparation in the home, cuisine seeks to mimic and recreate the food of a specific area. Nowhere in this definition is there mention of machinery, kilocalories, nutrients or mechanical processes. Cuisine is deeper than that. It expresses, at least in part, the soul of the people who live on the land, produce the food, eat the food, drink the wine and have an all-encompassing connection to the land and its offerings that defines who and what they are.

As we look at the authors and works selected for this book, one aspect common to these authors keeps coming back: The people involved here, from Simmons to Hirtzler, understood this primal connection, relished the foods they were working with, and strove to convey how others might feel the same. Read between the lines and behind the words and tell me you do not get a sense of connectedness to and oneness with the foods the authors were writing about.

With Miss Leslie's words from Philadelphia or Mrs. Randolph's words from Virginia the reader cannot help but be struck by how indivisible the people were from their culinary roots and how differing ethnic influences influenced their everyday lives. Their lives were a celebration of the foods they ate even though it was an enormous task to prepare these foods on a daily basis. The warmth and intimacy of sitting down for a meal with family where all could experience the bounty of the earth making itself manifest on the dinner table, the pride the people took in entertaining and putting out a good spread for company — this is not just eating, this is cuisine as an expression of self and one's culture and does, in a very real sense, reflect the soul of a country.

With the expansion of the country there was a huge influence of French cooking in

American cuisine. This influence reached its pinnacle in Delmonico's Restaurant where Charles Ranhofer presided in the kitchen for close to 40 years. (There is more to come about America's greatest chef later on.) The French influence was in the home as well.

Thomas Jefferson, that most well-educated, erudite and inquisitive of all our presidents, lived five years in France. When duties of state were not interfering with his real interests in life — food and wine — he cultivated a garden, sought to unite French and American foods and cooking, hired the first French chef in the White House at the unheard-of amount of $28 per month and apprenticed two of his household staff to Chef Julien. Edy and Fanny, two of Jefferson's culinary staff, would take their newly acquired skills back to Monticello. Patrick Henry excoriated Jefferson for admiring French food so much.

Jefferson was known for the sumptuousness of his dinners both in the White House and at Monticello; he returned from France with list after list of desserts, sauces, pastries, fritters, compotes, custards and cakes. He even took the time to make sure his kitchen staff at Monticello knew the classic vegetable cuts such as hacheé and tourneé and classic sauces such as piquante and Robert, items still staples of French and French-based cooking techniques.

Not confined to an appreciation of food only at dinner, there is a contemporary account by one George Tichnor, who visited Monticello and was duly impressed with the breakfasts that could be included at one sitting: braised partridges, eggs, bacon, assorted cold meats, breads, batter breads, brandy, citron, eggs, milk, cream and even tansy pudding.

Jefferson was one of a long line of Southern aristocracy who enjoyed the pleasure of the table and the bottle. George and Martha Washington in Mt. Vernon were no strangers to good food as well as drink. Martha Washington took pride in her table; her recipes and methods still appeal to modern readers and her cookbook is still available. And although this book reprints many previously printed English recipes, there are many items that are truly Southern and were of great personal pride to her. George Washington also loved food as well as drink. Not only did he have his own brewery where it is reported his best brew was his porter beer, but he owned the largest distillery in the new country, imported Madeira by the barrel-full and never showed his teeth in a smile because, it is now thought, his ivory false teeth were badly stained from drinking so much red wine.

The cuisine that was based in New England owed a great debt to Native Americans and their foodstuffs. It may represent the foundations of the first regional cuisine in the new United States and as such was one of the building blocks of what we now call American cuisine. (See, for example, Simmons' recipes in Chapter 2.) In later chapters on cuisines of the South, especially in Virginia, Creole cuisine, West Coast foods, haute cuisine in New York and foods of the deep South as prepared by former slaves, our American cuisine inherited influences from West Africa to Germany. Our regional cuisines, from New England to Hawaii, depended upon local foods, and that was the true glory of our food and cuisine. Everything is here, in season at least. Defining American cuisine is not possible without taking into account what our culinary leaders used as raw materials for their recipes, restaurants, schools and hospitals.

As a result of a growing population, a focus on foods as commodities, and vast improvements in methods of transportation, Americans have strayed far afield from the regional, local and seasonal foods that historically shaped American cuisine.

There is now the beginning of a return to our culinary roots, after more than a century of industrial farming. After Liebig "discovered" the three nutrients that would guarantee abundant crop yields, there was much industrial-scale food production. And in animal husbandry, factory "farming" is an inherently cruel and inhumane way of raising meat, as it denies the animals the nature of their very existence. By oversimplifying the process of life, we have gone away from life itself.

Over the last century and a half we have striven mightily to over-simplify our food (and as a result, our existence) to the point of absurdity. Three nutrients can no more grow good food than three personality traits can define a person or three "sounds" can define a Mozart piano concerto. Yet this is where we have allowed ourselves to be driven.

The people who were responsible in large measure for our American cuisine were using real food. Amelia Simmons and Ms. Leslie did not go to the supermarket to get good food. Hirtzler founded California cuisine not on food from Iowa or New Zealand, but from the ingredients found in California. Ranhofer did not call nationwide companies for deliveries. Delmonico's started a farm to contribute the finest foods available to the restaurant — the restaurant at which virtually all elite Americans dined and which still has an immense impact on restaurants today.

The specter of vast mono-culture fields stretching for miles on end and factory farms confining animals in hideously cruel environments is not part of American cuisine. In a well-meaning (sometimes) effort to increase food supply, we are destroying the environment that makes food production possible. More and bigger is not better. Gains in food productivity have come at a huge cost to the Earth and our fellow creatures living on the Earth. Perhaps with the increasing awareness as typified by the Slow Foods movement, we can return to a more balanced model of food production. Our predecessors knew what food was. We are slowly getting back to that ideal.

NOTE: *There is a fascinating book of what was for sale in food markets in these cities, called* The Market Assistant *by Mr. De Voe, a butcher by trade in New York City. Ox was considered as a category of beef and part of the domestic animals raised for food. Further on in the section on game, Mr. De Voe mentions wagons coming to the markets with bear, hare, venison and, from close in Sullivan County, an eight-foot-long panther. The market also boasted such* delicacies *as lynx, raccoon, opossum and ground hog.*

CHAPTER 2

Amelia Simmons

By 1796 the United States as a geographical entity possessed a long and diverse past. As mentioned in Chapter 1, the "new world" was reportedly first seen and settled by the Vikings around 900 to 1000 AD. They may not have been the first Europeans to land on these shores but are the only ones who left even a minimal trace of their habitation. The settlement lasted for only a few years and then the "settlers" returned to Scandinavia or other destinations in northern Europe, most probably Iceland or Ireland. They may also have perished here but there is not enough evidence to draw accurate conclusions.

There are two sagas that report on the adventures of the Vikings in this short-term endeavor but no secondary corroboration. The sagas dating from the 12th and 13th centuries relate in writing a much earlier story passed down in the classic Icelandic oral tradition. This does not men that the sagas are inaccurate or made up. We take for granted that oral traditions lack a verity that is to be found in the written word. But with a centuries old tradition and people schooled in the craft of memorization, these oral histories are often times as accurate as their written counterparts, if not more so.

Around 985 Bjarni Herjolfsson, a Norse settler living and trading in Greenland, was apparently blown off course and sighted a "new" continent but returned to Greenland without ever landing. In 1000 AD, the famous Leif Eriksson made the first European exploration of the continent. A settlement was located at Lanse aux Meadows and lasted about ten years.[1]

While there were earlier settlements and conquests by the Spaniards in Central and South America (most well known from the destruction of the Aztec and Inca empires), Florida and into the now American Southwest, for our purposes here the first permanent settlement was at Jamestown, Virginia, in 1607. There were 104 settlers on the small ships *Susan Constant, Discovery* and *Godspeed*. The ships sailed up a wide navigable river and the settlers were struck by the beauty and bounty of the place.[2]

Possibly as a measure of distance, which was an obstacle to British governance, the colony elected its first representative body in 1619, the House of Burgesses — burgess being a person of civil authority. In one of those ironic twists of fate, 1619 saw the arrival of the first black slave in the same year as the continent's first elected European governing body. This dichotomy was to be a persistent thorn in the side of the country, even into the 21st century.

In 1620 the Plymouth Colony was established in Massachusetts and by 1650 the population of the colonies was estimated to be slightly more than 50,000 inhabitants. When the English took control of Nieuw Amsterdam in 1664 and renamed it New York, America became a de facto British colony. In the century between 1664 and 1750 population increased dramatically, mostly in a handful of cities, mostly in the Northeast.[3]

City	1720	1750
Boston	12,000	15,877
New York	7,000	22,667
Philadelphia	10,000	34,583
Charleston	3,500	10,667

While French and Spanish interests were further west and south, most of the traditional lands of the new country, which evolved into the 13 colonies, became British. The French and Indian War was a struggle to assert dominance in what is now Canada and the northeast United Sates, and perhaps, most importantly, along the Mississippi River Valley.[4]

Along with this geographical specification, English was the official language and English cooking traditions, as mentioned in the prologue, held sway until the 1800s. As a matter of a more or less common language, there were British published cookbooks imported into the colonies and reprints were, while not common, certainly available over the years.

During the French and Indian War, many colonists saw parts of the countryside that were new to them. A Virginian by the name of George Washington also acquired some good military experience and achieved an understanding of how the British army functioned. As so often happens, the law of unintended consequences kicked in later on and a good British soldier would prove a nemesis for his former masters.

As most Americans know, the colonies would not remain so for long. The Boston Tea Party followed the Boston Massacre of 1770 three years later. And soon the colonists were in a full-scale war that was to last longer than anyone expected and ended with a result that created a new country.

The Revolutionary War of 1775–1783 concluded at Yorktown, Virginia, in 1781. The formal Treaty of Paris was signed in 1783 and ended the war and ceded all lands east of the Mississippi River to the United States. This treaty, coupled with the Louisiana Purchase engineered by Thomas Jefferson and his ministers, would lead to inexorable American dominance from the Atlantic to the Pacific. The acquisition of the territory beyond the Mississippi also meant that Indian removal east of the Mississippi was inevitable.

Seventeen ninety was the first meeting of the Supreme Court in Manhattan. At that time there was one chief justice and five associate justices and the very first census showed a population of almost four million. These formative years saw the establishment of a functioning three-part system of government still in effect today.

The year 1793 witnessed the invention of the cotton gin by Eli Whitney, which dramatically increased the demand for slaves in the cotton fields. Coupled with the near extinction of Native Americans, this created the impetus for increased demands on the African slave trade and increasing tensions within the fledgling country. As the country expanded, the slavery issue would arise as each new territory and later state was admitted to the Union. The increased demand for African slaves would also impact our national cuisine in significant ways. Not only would the African slaves look to familiar foods to use here in the United States, but for some the cooking skills they possessed would eventually provide an escape avenue from the fields, which led to the kitchen, as was the case with Mrs. Abby Fisher, profiled a bit later in the book.

The country prospered and grew with the population pushing ever westward, especially into the "northwest frontier" areas of what would become Kentucky and Ohio.

At the time of John Adams' election as our second president, a woman working in and around the Hudson River Valley produced what has become known as the first American cookbook. Her name was Amelia Simmons, and her book was first published in 1796 and was to remain a popular book for about the next 40 years. It is a small book in terms of pages and recipes but a large book in terms of the development of an American cuisine.

Who Was Amelia Simmons?

It must ever remain a check upon the poor solitary orphan, that while those females who have parents, or brothers, or riches, to defend their indiscretions, that the orphan must depend solely upon character. How immensely important, therefore, that every action, every word, every thought, be regulated by the strictest purity, and that every movement meet the approbation of the good and wise.

The candor of the American Ladies is solicitously intreated by the Authoress, as she is circumscribed in her knowledge, this being an original work in this country. Should any future editions appear, she hopes to render it more valuable.

> ### PREFACE.
>
> It muſt ever remain a check upon the poor ſolitary orphan, that while thoſe females who have parents, or brothers, or riches, to defend their indiſcretions, that the orphan muſt depend ſolely upon *character*. How immenſely important, therefore, that every action, every word, every thought, be regulated by the ſtricteſt purity, and that every movement meet the approbation of the good and wife.
>
> The candor of the American Ladies is ſolicitouſly intreated by the Authoreſs, as ſhe is circumſcribed in her knowledge, this being an original work in this country. Should any future editions appear, ſhe hopes to render it more valuable.

Simmons is something of an enigma. What we know of her comes from the preface to her *American Cookery* and slight references throughout the book. Simmons first published her book in 1796 in Hartford. After that, there were several other editions apparently authorized by her, published in and around the Hudson River Valley in towns such as Albany, Troy and Poughkeepsie. There were also other, unauthorized editions that sometimes received post publication corrections by Simmons.

Simmons probably grew up in or around New York State in the Hudson River Valley near Albany. Albany was the main area of potash production, which is discussed later in this chapter. In her book Simmons uses the terms cookje and slaw, which were common terms used in Dutch cooking. The single largest concentration of Dutch colonists in America at that time, other than perhaps in Manhattan, was in the Hudson River Valley, centered in the Albany area. A quick look at a map reveals plenty of town names of Dutch origin: Kinderhook, Kerhonkson, Watervliet, etc.

The first edition was published in Hartford but subsequent editions were published in the Hudson River Valley region. Seemingly out of nowhere Simmons appears, is vaguely visible for the reprints of her book and then vanishes. While this may seem strange in a modern world, for a single woman without a family and ancestral locus, records of any given individual would have been scarce to begin with. Add to that the rapid changes in the area over the last decades of the 18th and early decades of the 19th centuries, and it is not hard to see how records could be misplaced, burned in fires or otherwise destroyed.

In her title page she uses the phrase "an American orphan." Early on in the preface she mentions "many hints are suggested for the more general and universal knowledge of those females in this country, who by the loss of their parents, or other unfortunate circumstance, are reduced to the necessity of going into families in the line of domestics." This does seem to indicate that she was indeed alone in a less than hospitable world for single women. As a household servant, the ability to establish an independent persona would be further diminished.

The life of an orphan in New England was not an easy one, to say the least. As early as 1682 an institution called the Boston Almshouse was rebuilt so that "children who shamefully spend their time in the streets could be put to work."[2] In 1720 George Whitfield set up an "orphan house" where there were two-hour shifts alternating between work and schooling. As a founding principle for school, he said, "No time is allowed for idleness or play, which are Satan's darling hours to tempt children in all manner of wickedness."

In the 18th century domestic manufacturing become more commonplace and in 1770 William Mollineux went before the Boston legislature for the purpose of organizing children for domestic manufacturing shops.

In a society with these attitudes towards children and orphans the introduction by Amelia Simmons in her book seems like an understatement as to the living conditions of an orphaned child. If Amelia Simmons showed culinary prowess early on it was probably a good thing as it was a more beneficial trade than working in a manufacturing environment.

A clue to her personality may be found in the sentence, "The orphan, tho' left to the care of virtuous guardians will find it essentially necessary to have an opinion and determination of her own." This says to me that Simmons as a woman was strong-willed and certainly determined. A single woman publishing a book at this time was not an everyday occurrence. It also implies that a woman needs to be her own person and Simmons says so in no uncertain terms.

As a harkening back to England it can also be noted that cookbook authors in England were primarily women and that as part of any respectable cookbook in the 17th and 18th centuries there would be significant mention of preserving as well as cooking techniques. Compare this with the French tradition of cookbooks, which were mostly by either professional chefs or the nobles who employed them.

This contrast as to who authored cookbooks can be seen as a distinct difference between the philosophy of what food and cooking were in France as compared to England. As many of the English cookbooks which served as models for early American books, including Simmons' book, were more geared to cooking with a practical bent and were home-centered, the French authors delved more deeply into flavors and cooking techniques which were to lead to the structure of professional kitchens as well as the refinement of cooking techniques of hâute cuisine. Certainly these distinctions appeared early on with a heavy emphasis on British philosophy, but this focus would later shift towards the more refined French side of the scale, as we will see in later chapters.

Despite Simmons' success in having her book published, she felt strongly enough to mention "It must ever remain a check upon the poor solitary orphan, that while those females who have parents, or brothers, or riches, to defend their indiscretions, that the orphan must depend solely upon her *character*" (author's italics).

What can we glean from this? It seems to indicate Simmons did attend the school of hard knocks but was able to build her character to the point where she was able to overcome her undesirable circumstances. While in the employ of wealthy families, one wonders what "indiscretions" needed defending by a woman's family and what additional trials a single woman would have gone through to achieve a strong, respectable character. Probably the same indiscretions that are around today.

This is an especially appealing aspect of the book. Here is a virtually unknown woman who is credited with the first American cookbook, giving oblique hints as to what her life was like. There are not enough details to piece anything truly substantive together — just enough to have one project what this woman and her life must have been like.

In the edition from 1798, used for reference for this book, the first 17 pages were not authored or authorized by Simmons but were added before publication without her knowledge or approval. In the *Feeding America* article on Simmons it further states that the author believed that "city or country folk, know the difference between good and bad market produce, and do not need a guide in such matters."

That said, Simmons was certainly an accomplished cook. As the noted food historian Karen Hess points out, Simmons calls for a wide variety of ingredients and the use of wine. She is quite explicit about roasting techniques, which although of an English tradition, were "admired by even the French."

A look at her pantry shows a woman of skill and taste who, based on her book, produced some flavorful foods. In the meat department we find: beef, young and old; ox; mutton; veal; lamb; turkey; goslin (an old term for goose); turtle (make sure you hang the turtle no later than 9 o'clock and "hang up your Turtle by the hind fins"); calves head; chickens; and tongue. Herbs and seasoning: thyme, sweet marjoram, summer savory, sage (although it is not "generally approved"), parsley, and penny royal (although it does not seem all too common as Simmons writes that it "might be more generally cultivated in gardens, and used in cookery and medicines").

Her supply of fruit was also impressive: pears, hard winter pears, harvest and summer pears ("a tolerable dessert"), and all kinds of apples. She does advocate planting more trees. In this list we have some items not commonly found in American kitchens anymore: currants, black currants, Malaga, Lisbon and Madeira grapes. Spices and other flavoring agents are legion including cinnamon, mace, allspice, nutmeg, ginger, rose water and cayenne pepper. In the recipe section you can see what a deft cook Simmons was. Although the recipes are adapted to modern cooking methods, adventurous cooks could certainly try some of them if they have large barbecue grills or outdoor fireplaces.

When it comes to her knowing cooking techniques, she is firmly grounded in English traditions but certainly makes a number of "French" dishes as well as recipes that adapted American ingredients and had them appear for the first time in print.

In discussing roast beef, she calls for basting every 15 minutes with rare being the "healthiest and the taste of this age." Lamb is to be "done more gently than beef, and done more." Here she does advocate serving the lamb with "scraped horseradish, and serve with potatoes, beans, cauliflower, watercress or boiled onion. Caper sauce, mashed turnip or lettuce."

Turkey is, of course, stuffed with butter, salt pork, grated wheat bread, eggs, sweet marjoram, summer savory, parsley and sage, pepper and salt "if the pork be not sufficient." A variation of the stuffing calls for thyme and a gill of wine along with beef suet rather than salt pork. This latter version one should "serve up with boiled onions, cramberry sauce [*sic*], mangoes, pickles or celery." This description of what sounds like a modern Thanksgiving dish contains the first mention of cranberry sauce in an American cookbook.

Reading Simmons' directions for the turkey and other items, it seems she would not have the bird in an oven or on a spit. Rather, the bird was suspended over the fire on a "string." Suspended in this way over the open fire, the air currents rotate the bird. Does this distribute juices and flavoring better? There must have been a good reason for this as she states it as well for the roast beef.

Any careful look at the size of a well-made colonial fireplace shows ample room to suspend items over a fire. Yes, there would most likely be baking ovens on the side of the fireplace, but this is not what Simmons specifies in her recipes. Simmons gives directions for an alamode (in the style of) for a beef round: first make a mix of salt pork, marjoram, thyme, cloves, mace and nutmeg, slit the beef and stuff it with this mixture. The next day, put some bones in a pot, add some claret (red wine) and an onion, place the beef on top of these ingredients. Cover with a paste, or crust. Stew it two hours and turn and stew for two more after resealing the crust. When the beef is done, "...grate a crust of bread on the top and brown it before the fire; scum the gravy and serve in a butter boat, serve it with the residue of the gravy in the dish." So after stewing for four hours, she takes the time to put a crunchy, toasted crust on the outside of the beef, removes all the unwanted bits floating on top of the pan juices and serves the au jus on the side. Not bad for a poor American orphan.

There are also instructions for smoking ham and bacon with corncobs, also a first in the history of cookbooks and another uniquely American twist to a traditional preservation method. What with corn being an American food, its European use prior to the arrival of the colonists was not a possibility. Although smoking meat and fish was common enough in Europe for thousands of years, this "new" ingredient was a definite culinary innovation.

Rice pudding includes rice, milk, fresh grated nutmeg, stick cinnamon and rose water; optional is to line the baking pan with puff pastry. Rose water is often found in medieval culinary texts, whether as a simple flavoring agent or as part of a medicinal concoction. This use of rose water was quite common in early America; we find it not only here but in Miss Leslie's writings as well. For those of you not familiar with the product, it lends a multi-layered floral and perfumed aspect to most dishes and has a subtle, lingering aftertaste that can be quite fascinating.

The puff pastry mentioned by Simmons is not a classically prepared paste, but rather a blending of some classical techniques with a more frugal attitude insofar as ingredient cost and time are concerned.

Simmons was savvy in her initial dealings with the original publisher. For the 1796 edition it states that the book was published "For the Author," which indicates that she covered the printing costs and retained profits from all sales. That the book sold well is clear because Simmons says, "The call has been so great, and the sales so rapid that [the Author] finds herself not only encouraged but under a necessity of publishing a second edition."

Whatever Simmons realized from the sale of her book, we are forever indebted to her for writing this first American cookbook. Perhaps one of the reasons the book sold well may be linked to the following. A French traveler to New England in the 18th century remarked that New England food was swimming in fat, grease and lard, people made "half baked bread," "boiled pastes" were caught masquerading as puddings and "sauces, even for roast beef, was melted butter." Sounds like she went to press just in time!

The Book

American Cookery, OR THE ART OF DRESSING VIANDS, FISH, POULTRY, AND VEGETABLES AND THE BEST MODES OF MAKING PASTES, PUFFS, PIES, TARTS, PUDDINGS, CUSTARDS AND PRESERVES, AND ALL KINDS OF CAKES FROM THE IMPERIAL PLUMB TO PLAIN CAKE.
ADAPTED TO THIS COUNTRY AND ALL GRADES OF LIFE BY AMELIA SIMMONS, AN AMERICAN ORPHAN, 1798.

Now *that* is a title for a cookbook. This book is recognized as the first American cookbook because American ingredients are used, American terminology appears and the meaning behind the words is that of an American writing for Americans. Prior to 1796 cookbooks were published in America but these were reprints or rewrites of British, and in some cases, French or German books. The date 1796 is important because the first two editions were printed in 1796 in Hartford, Connecticut. Many later editions, published in and around upstate New York and western Massachusetts, then followed. The copy I cite here is from 1798, printed by Simeon Butler in Northampton, Massachusetts.

As copyright laws were unenforced at this time, there were inevitable knockoffs. Some copies simply republished the book, with or without their own additions, word for word from Simmons' original book. For an egregious example of this, see *New England Cookery* by Lucy Emerson, published in 1808. When issues arose with unauthorized copies, Simmons would sometimes respond to set the record straight. As a person lacking in formal education, Simmons did have some problems with these changes. The second 1796 Hartford edition had a list of changes that were made to her original manuscript. The food historian Mary Tollford, commenting on this edition, states that there was an insertion on a sheet of obviously dissimilar paper which is labeled as an "Advertisement." In this "Advertisement," Simmons rectifies some of the impromptu changes wrought for the first publication. The changes were indicated, but somehow never quite caught up with the subsequent printings of the book.

This edition also included an addition of 17 pages on descriptions of all manner of food products and their selection, which was an addition not authorized by Simmons for which she, Simmons, "does not pretend to be acquainted."

Although lacking a formal education and not having a family for support and advice, Simmons had a good idea and strong business sense when she says the book is "Adapted to the Country and All Grades of Life." Simmons was obviously making her work available for the entire spectrum of American cooks, with a price point that was reasonable: two shillings, three pence ($1.75 in modern prices).

There are some practical aspects that make the book important from the standpoint of American cuisine. We already spoke about this as the first original book written by an American on American food. Original content makes the book important.

Some of the book reprints information from an earlier book published in 1772. In Williamsburg, Virginia, the publisher William Parks published an American reprint of *The Compleat Housewife,* from which Simmons "borrowed," via a 1772 Boston reprint, entire sections on creams and syllabubs. That said, Simmons broke away from simply pirating someone else's book and introduced into print American ingredients not previously noted.

With this book, American foods, those native to the continent, were used and discussed for the first time in a cookbook. Squash, pumpkins, potatoes, corn, cranberries, turkey—all are food items that we now take for granted but were not publicly documented until Simmons authored her book. For example, Native Americans had used corn for centuries. Simmons' book is the first to incorporate this uniquely American item into recipes for ordinary people to use. Hoecakes, slapjacks and Indian pudding were these recipes and variations of these can still be found in many New England cookbooks.

Probably the biggest single impact on American cooking was the use of pearl ash as a leavening agent in baked goods. This practice, native to America, first formally mentioned in a cookbook, forever changed baking around the world, not just in the United States. In order to incorporate air into bakery items, the sponge method, which was most common up until this time, was to whip eggs with some sugar. When flour and liquid butter are added and the item is baked, the air cells whipped into the eggs expand and the product rises. The resulting texture is lighter and has a finer crumb than had the eggs and sugar not been whipped together. Separating eggs and whipping egg whites with some sugar into a meringue, which is then folded into the batter, can achieve additional lightness. The air in the meringue also expands and adds volume, lightness and a finer texture.

Pearl ash is a refined form of potash, a form of potassium carbonate, which is a residue of wood ash. This ingredient was the forerunner of modern American baking powders. Rather than relying on air incorporated into whipped egg cells, using pearl ash is a fast-acting chemical process that is activated by moisture and heat. This process releases carbon dioxide rather than the expansion of air cells held in suspension by the eggs. This innovation written down for the first time in Simmons' cookbook had, and continues to have, an enormous impact on foods all over the world. Many, if not most, commercial sweets and snack foods rely on a type of this product for leavening. A quick glance at bakery product labels will demonstrate how important this technique is. Traditional cakes, muffins, biscuits, quick breads — these are part of the living history of Simmons and her *American Cookery*.

It can be argued that this chemical process creates products less subtle and complex than traditional methods using incorporated air or yeast. Maybe. However, this book, as Simmons states in her preface, is for all walks of life. While a wealthy household may have had access to a large staff, certainly this was not the case for everyone. Making a sponge method cake takes more time and uses more eggs as an ingredient in the total recipe than using a leavening agent. Being able to save time, labor and ingredient cost it is no wonder that chemical leavening became so popular.

In the more settled areas of Europe, where breweries were located, the use of ale yeast was common; however, there were not many breweries in America in 1796. And these would have been located in large population centers. To be sure, many if not most American women knew how to brew beer at home, but a reliable chemical leavening simply made life a little easier and more expeditious. As time went by the ability to make a yeast starter was refined, and then that gave way to yeast that was commercially produced, thereby vastly simplifying the process of baking for the home and in industrial situations.

For a woman in a smaller town or on a farm, Simmons does provide a concoction to take the place of this yeast residue. This is called *emptins* and is essentially a starter of water and maybe some sugar or honey, boiled with hops and left to ferment. Simmons says that sealed in a jar it will last a few weeks. In effect, this is a type of beer cum sourdough starter, but not to be used for drinking. The fermentation would start when the yeast in the air found the mixture and the hops would be a flavoring agent, as well as a much-needed preservative in the days before refrigeration.

Simmons' book was widely popular. In one form or another, it was available for over 30 years. Three editions appeared in the 18th century with an additional ten appearing over the years published in New York, Vermont, Connecticut and Massachusetts.

This book provides a window into the life of 18th-century American cooking. Through the recipes the modern cook can see what a variety of foods were available to our ancestors. The careful reader will pick up on cooking methods, cooking times and invaluable tips on seasonings, sweeteners and flavorings.

In this book one also sees an assumption of a certain level of expertise on the part of the reader. There are good directions, especially for turtle preparation, but much of what Simmons includes in her recipes would have been second nature to the cooks of her time.

Fire temperatures, colorings, cooking times of an indefinite duration — all these are techniques born of experience.

In her recipes and in other early American cookbooks, directions are given for flouring a cloth, and whatever needs cooking to the cloth, tying it securely and boiling in a large pot suspended over the fire in the fireplace.

Boiling a pudding, either savory or sweet, or a piece of meat in a cloth may seem odd. In *America's Founding Food,* the authors make a good case for this type of cooking. It was time consuming and laborious to maintain a fire at a specific temperature all the time. Cooking hearths were never cold. Roasting, baking, grilling, all required a certain amount of "due diligence" as cooking methods. Anyone who has left a burger on a backyard grill too long knows what happens to food if it is left unattended near an open fire.

Boiling a pudding in a cloth (actually a special material made just for this purpose) was valuable for a couple of reasons. Cooking vessels were expensive. Most households would have had a large cauldron suspended over an open fire, maybe a grill plate for setting on a frame over the coals, or what we call now a rotisserie. (This rotisserie would be made of metal with a lateral spit that could turn. The side facing the fire would be open to the heat or have a bed where hot coals could be placed. The side away from the fire would have type of a trap door to open as needed for basting the item that was cooking.) Once the item was placed in a bag and immersed in the simmering water, the woman of the house was free to do other things without worrying about her dinner getting charred or overcooked. Hasty Pudding is sometimes done this way. Indian Pudding as well as whole turkeys and beef and other meats were often cooked in a similar fashion. This method works well and poaching a beef tenderloin can achieve a degree of doneness as accurately as on a grill.

These pudding cloths, suspended in a large kettle, could be used in many productive ways. As long as the water level was maintained, the housewife could go on about her other chores without worrying about the pudding.

In her recipe "To Roast Beef" it says from the start that the rules presented here are general rules: brisk fire, hang down, "baste with salt and water," tender beef versus older beef, "pricking with a fork to test for doneness. The cut of beef is not indicated. Is this a top round? A bottom round? (Not likely as Simmons would know a bottom round would need moist cooking.) Beef shoulder? Sirloin? If so, bone in or out? Ribs of beef? Bone in or out? Probably in as it would retain its shape better. Beef tenderloin? Would a tenderloin have been cut out of the loin to begin with? What temperature is a brisk fire? 350°? 375°? Maybe 450°? The ambiguities here speak to the cooking method that was to eventually disappear as homes acquired metal stoves, whether fired by coal, wood, gas or electric. But in Simmons' day temperatures were often gauged by sight and informed guesses based on years of cooking experience. In professional kitchens, chefs will often open an oven door and put a hand inside to see how hot the oven actually is, as more often than not, temperature dials on commercial stoves become all but functionally useless after a short time. So maybe we are not so far from Simmons' techniques after all.

The doneness is tested with a fork; now, many recipes suggest a thermometer telling the cook that 125° is when the meat is rare. As to rare being the healthiest, that may not be true, but for many it certainly tastes the best. And remember that is the "rare" of 1796 or 1798. Is that the same "rare" as today?

How about "baste with salt and water?" What is the dilution of salt? Does it simply flavor the meat or does it help create a nice crust to add to the textural appeal of the finished product? All these directions would be spelled out in a modern cookbook. For Simmons, it was common knowledge.

In her directions on roasting a turkey, also on a string, we are now dealing with a solid fire rather than a brisk fire. Anybody want to take a guess? We are told to "add a gill of wine." Well, a gill is four ounces, that part is easy. What kind of wine? In many modern recipes the name of the recipe can be determined by such a detail; for instance, roast turkey with herb and gewürtztraminer stuffing. This seemingly simple step will yield a vastly different result depending upon the choice of wine used. Color and flavor of the stuffing will be affected as will the compatibility of the stuffing with the other dishes served with the turkey. One of the most commonly found and appreciated wines in colonial times was Madeira. So would this have been a default choice as most people would be familiar with it?

For making a Stew Pie we are told to use a shoulder of veal. How large? Does it matter? Slices of raw salt pork. How many or how much by weight? "Make a layer of meat and a layer of biscuit dough into a pot, cover close and stew half an hour in three quarts of water only." The shoulder is pre-cooked then used for the pie. No biscuit recipe and no additional seasonings are indicated. "Cover close and stew half an hour in three quarts of water only." Were seasonings and herbs added to the original cooking of the veal? How thick is a good thickness for the dough? This sounds an awful lot like making chicken and biscuits. The seasonings here would have been used whether indicated or not. Simmons and her contemporaries would know which seasonings would be used for what kinds of meat.

For the biscuit dough, would it be sweet or savory? Would it be rolled thickly or thinly? Would it be marked into portions, such as a drop biscuit? Or would it be rolled and simply layered on top of the meat as one would do for a cobbler?

For the filling in the "Pompkin No. 1" pie recipe, there are quantities for the pumpkin, cream and eggs; nothing for sugar, mace, nutmeg and ginger. And the dough is to be crossed and chequered with a spur. Although dough three or seven is specified, there are no directions for rolling, thickness or method present. Also, note the absence of any indicated temperature. Modern cooks would most likely need a specific instruction as to temperature along with time. But for Simmons and her readers, the baking of a custard pie would be so commonplace as to not need any further elaboration.

Quite often in colonial homes there were ovens built into the side of the fireplaces. When the fire was really hot, the oven would be used for baking bread, other unsweetened items or even fruit pies or game pies. As the fire cooled, the bricks would hold the heat and something like a custard pie could be baked in a much slower oven.

There are also short cuts in the instructions in many recipes because Simmons would expect a reader to know how to do certain things. Especially in the pastry dough recipes, general instructions for rolling are severely abridged if the cook is to achieve the desired end product of the recipe. These shortcuts speak more to the knowledge of early American women as cooks than to oversights on the part of Simmons.

In the Tongue Pie, which is roughly similar to a mince pie served around Thanksgiving time, we are told to "bake in paste No. 1, in proportion to size." In a modern cookbook the total amount of dough would most often be specified, as would techniques for rolling the paste. In addition, the specific size of the dish would, in modern books be specific. Not here. Also, is this a two-crust pie? Is this a one-crust pie? Not an issue in Simmons' day as she expected that her readers would know.

This says a couple of things. It suggests that Simmons' readers knew the techniques required for making these abridged recipes — otherwise the book would not have been such a big seller. If people could not understand or reproduce the recipes, they would not have purchased the book. It says much about the skill level and cooking knowledge of the American housewife that these techniques could be so abridged and still be understood by a wide audience. In today's cookbook we are more accustomed to painstaking detail for every step of a recipe; and at times it makes reading a recipe almost impossible. Too many words spoil the broth. It is amusing to think that with all our modern gadgets and conveniences our recipes need so much more explanation to be understood, whereas in Simmons' book, a few words went a long way.

For example, look at the size of the recipes. Either Simmons was cooking for large households — likely — or she worked from a substantial *mise-en-place,* which allowed her to save time by always having certain items on hand.

To look at this issue, where we asked about the cut of beef used for the roast beef, even a small top butt, a portion of a top round, would be around 13 or 14 pounds; with an entire top round the weight would be substantially more depending upon the size and age of the steer. How many of us routinely purchase a roast beef of that size?

In Simmons' day, there would have been larger families, especially in rural areas. Add to that the way people ate and there are some good reasons why the quantities of the recipes would be so large. More often than not the main meal of the day would be at mid-day. After that, the leftovers would be eaten for supper, the evening meal. The reasons for this are due to the fact that there was no refrigeration anywhere. Keeping any type of leftover food that was not subject to standard preserving techniques was risky at best, with exception of bread products and non-dairy sweets such as fruit pies and cookies. Yes, many houses would have had keeping cellars or root cellars, but these would generally be around 50 degrees most of the year, prime temperature for the growth of bacteria. And although no one knew what bacteria was, people would still have gotten sick from eating contaminated food, which could easily have been a life threatening process of trial and error where only one mistake could be a big one.

In her recipe for Plumb Cake she calls for six and 21 eggs along with a pound each of citron and currants, one quart of ale yeast and no quantities specified for salt, orange peel or blanched almonds. The Plain Cake is hardly less impressive, calling for nine pounds of flour, three pounds of sugar, three pounds of butter, a quart of emptins along with a quart of milk and nine eggs. Take a look at any favorite cake recipe in your files and what will most likely be there is a quantity of flour expressed in cups, with one cup roughly weighing four ounces!

Remember, too, that all fuel had to be cut or dug by hand. Timber would need cutting on a regular basis and adequate dry storage provided for its seasoning. Burning green wood is not very efficient and is also more dangerous than using dry wood. This effort translates into many hours of labor to simply provide the basic heat source to accomplish any cooking or baking. In short, cooking fuel was expensive because of time and labor. The large colonial fireplaces would require large amounts of wood to generate enough heat to be able to simply boil water.

A long-cooking item such as a large roast or boiled beef, a large meat pie, a stew or even bread, would of necessity be made in quantity in order to make best use of a difficult to come by fuel. In her recipe "To alamode a round," Simmons uses a full round for braising the meat. Placed on bones in the pot "to keep from burning," Claret, red Bordeaux wine, water and onions are added. The pot is hung on the fire "in the morning" and stewed for four hours, which would make it the mid-day meal. Notice here as well that the pot is stopped tight "with dough." Either it would have been completely covered with a pastry dough or the dough would have been used around the edges of a lid for the pot. Cooking utensils were expensive and hard to come by. A lid for a large pot would have seemed like a veritable luxury, maybe even an extravagance. A pastry lid would be more practical, less expensive and could have served as a sop for the gravy. If we think about the size of a pot that could be hung on a spit or hook over a fire, the amount of dough to cover it would be substantial.

The combination of expensive fuel, the very nature of open hearth cooking, which is inefficient for heat retention, the need to supply "home grown" fuel and lack of keeping options for leftovers, made the production of food in large quantities a practical adaption to the above conditions.

Simmons' book is geared to American women in all social classes, generally using traditional British cooking techniques but with the inclusion of American ingredients for the very first time. It is a cookbook and a social treatise. Simmons gives other orphans and women who did not have the needed support and protection of families the ability and knowledge to make themselves more valuable to others and hence also to themselves. In a harsh world for single women she offered a level of security and knowledge that could serve others.

That she was the author of the first truly American cookbook places Simmons in a unique position in the history of cooking and the history of America. Although some would say that Simmons' incorporation of large segments of other, previously published works negates her volume as the first American cookbook, this misses the mark by a wide margin. In earlier times, the use of non-original material as part of an author's or composer's works was not uncommon. Going back to Shakespeare and moving forward in the written word and music, authors and composers would often turn to other material as a part of or inspiration of a reworking of that older material. In the 1700s J.S. Bach would borrow material from other composers and his own earlier compositions to create a new work. Much of Shakespeare is made up of "quotes" from the plays of other authors, especially Marlowe.

Does this alter or diminish any of these later works? I think not.

Add to this the fact that Simmons clearly defines herself as American and states that the book is for Americans; these may be clues that this is an American book. And when we add to these considerations the fact that Simmons did record the first uses of many items and techniques that would become integral parts of what we now call American cuisine, the case becomes much clearer. In the case of American ingredients, the ingredients can be followed all the way up until the time of Chef Hirtzler in the 20th century as being integral parts of our national culinary heritage. As the book continues this will become apparent to even a casual reader of the text and recipes.

Reading the recipes in her book is to return to Simmons' time and experience her kitchen and cooking. First of all, there are the antiquated letters, spelling and phraseology. Remember, at this time written English still had two different characters for "s": one which appeared in the beginning and middle of words (the "s" that looked like an "f") and one which appeared at the end of words (our modern "s").

Her style of writing reaches across the centuries to enfold the reader in the atmosphere of an old-time kitchen and society. Along with her recipes, her observations on people and the place of an orphan female in society carry the reader into daily life in early America.

The recipes themselves, reprinted in the latter part of this book, are in their original form and format. If needed, there are comments about the recipe itself defining unclear terms or phrases. Then follows a "modern" recipe transcription for the reader to try at home. If ratio adjustments are needed to have a recipe work or to add some cooking information that may have been taken for granted by the author, this material is added and so noted.

The selection of the recipes later on in this book illustrates some of the important contributions made by the author or otherwise illustrates important aspects of this historical work that are still in practice today. When taken as a whole, the contributions of Simmons started to inform and shape our American cuisine. Her adaptations of various English and Native American foods and cooking techniques started us on a road to national cuisine, shaped and informed by the various ethnic and national traditions that came to America through her immigrants. These facets of cooking were made American by their usage, change of available ingredients and regional variations in foodstuffs that, taken as a whole, gave us a national cuisine.

Simmons gives us new foods: cranberries, corn meal, potatoes and pumpkin and makes them useable for the reader of her book. Roasted meats and fowls are initially included for two reasons: First, they show how English cooking traditions played a huge role in colonial cooking; Second, they demonstrate how Simmons could use Native American ingredients to enhance traditional dishes with local ingredients.

There is no doubt that with Simmons' book, American cuisine started on a journey that is still ongoing over 200 years later. There have been influences that came and went and food products that have appeared and disappeared (especially since 1900). But what is key is that whether dealing with Native American foods or applying French classical cooking to imported and domestic foods, American cuisine is a cuisine of adoption and adaption. Yes items were borrowed, techniques were borrowed and terminology was adapted. With all this energy, a cuisine took shape that was marked by the inventiveness of American cooks as much as by the foods they were preparing. It is my intent in the succeeding chapters to show how our remaining authors sprang from Simmons' starting place to develop our cuisine.

Thanks, Amelia Simmons, for getting us started in the right direction.

CHAPTER 3

Mary Randolph

How the Country Looked in Mrs. Randolph's Time

Mary Randolph was a young woman in 1797 when John Adams was inaugurated as president with Thomas Jefferson, another Virginian and relative of Mrs. Randolph, as his vice president. It is worth noting that the president and vice president were of different parties: Adams was a Federalist and Jefferson was a Democratic-Republican. While they had differing views on the role of government in society, they were lifelong friends and correspondents and died within six hours of each other on July 4, 1826.[1]

Adams served in Congress from 1774 to 1778 and through 1785 was at times foreign minister to France, the Netherlands and England. At this time the two biggest vote getters were the winning president and winning vice president, hence the odd two-party administration.

In a country that was growing rapidly, the Louisiana Purchase had a measurable impact on the foods Mary Randolph knew and cooked, and would continue to do so quite quickly when Jefferson became president. The United States was still getting its feet wet in the world of diplomacy. In 1797 there was a strange-sounding crisis called the XYZ Affair. It involved French anger at America, American anger at France, and a shooting war of sorts that lasted for about two years without a formal declaration of war. It was known as the Quasi War and was settled in 1800 by a treaty with France.[2] It may be remembered that France was the principal ally of America in the Revolutionary War and that Thomas Jefferson served as ambassador to France and that Mary Randolph was a member of his extended family, and that all these events would meld together over the years to help create our American cuisine. Jefferson's love of French food and wine and the society he and Mrs. Randolph were part of influenced not only the cuisine of Virginia and the South, but would eventually feed the larger context of a national cuisine.

In 1798 the Alien and Sedition Acts were passed, but were repealed when Jefferson became president. These were among the first laws that attempted to limit free speech in the United States in time of war, even though no war had been declared. These acts were the 1798 equivalent of the modern day Patriot Act, designed to protect America from "alien citizens of enemy powers" and to stifle dissent with the party in power.

The government was literally just getting started and among the notable achievements at this time was the creation of the Library of Congress, which was largely restocked by books from Jefferson's personal library after the original building suffered a catastrophic fire. The first presidential election that went to the House of Representatives for resolution

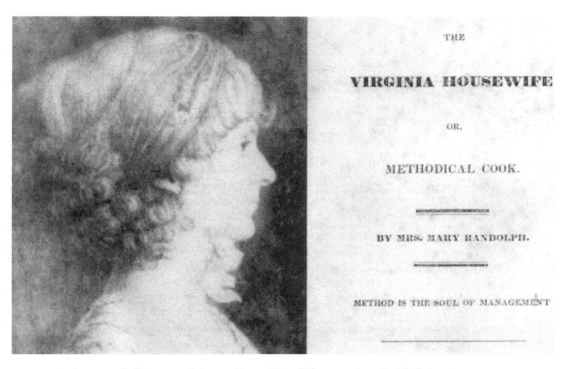

THE

VIRGINIA HOUSEWIFE

OR,

METHODICAL COOK.

BY MRS. MARY RANDOLPH.

METHOD IS THE SOUL OF MANAGEMENT

was a tie between Jefferson and Aaron Burr. The difference that decided the victor was one vote.

As the Supreme Court was also getting started, the justices would serve as circuit judges as well as a complete Supreme Court. The court handed down one of its monumental decisions at this time: In 1803 it ruled on *Marbury vs. Madison*.[3] The Supreme Court decision upheld the constitutional process of judicial review and ruled for the first time that a law passed by Congress was, and could in the future be declared, unconstitutional.

In what is probably the most far-reaching land transaction in the history of our country, the Jefferson administration concluded the Louisiana Purchase. This was such an immense area of land that no one knew really how large it was. Prior to the actual purchase, Jefferson funded the Lewis and Clark expedition to find out as well as they could just what was actually involved as far as land area was concerned.[4] This single purchase transferred land to America that stretched from the Mississippi River to the Pacific Ocean, and from Canada down to what is now Texas. With one transaction it defined the United States as a bicoastal country, secured territory that would create what is now our Midwest and Pacific Northwest, and in practice made Spain not much more than a babysitter for California waiting for America to come home and claim this area as well. Here there is another of those wonderful contradictions that define Jefferson. Allegedly a proponent of limiting government and its influence over the people, he was responsible for the government making the single largest purchase of land for the new country and for subsidizing one of the most famous exploratory expeditions in American history. In this act the stage was set for ensuing events that would unite the east and west coasts of the United States and define the stage for our national cuisine. Without this purchase and with a much stronger Spanish colonial presence, there is a good possibility that the United States could have stopped at the Mississippi River and that our modern southwest and California and Texas would have remained part of Mexico.

THE

VIRGINIA HOUSEWIFE:

OR,

METHODICAL COOK.

~~~~~~~~~~~~~~~~~~~~~~~

BY MRS. MARY RANDOLPH.

~~~~~~~~~~~~~~~~~~~~~~~

METHOD IS THE SOUL OF MANAGEMENT

STEREOTYPE EDITION,

WITH AMENDMENTS AND ADDITIONS.

BALTIMORE:
PUBLISHED BY PLASKITT, & CUGLE.
218 *Market Street.*

. . . . .

1838.

This was a real estate transaction that may very well have avoided a long string of wars, large and small. The strategic victory of this purchase was the fact that at this time France was much more powerful than Spain. There were concerns about having a Napoleon-led France as a western neighbor to the fledgling country. This was a more immediate issue than a Spanish presence in the now southwest and California. As time progressed Napoleon's dreams of a large, dynamic presence in America waned — due in no small measure to the fact that he needed money to finance his European adventures. In play here also was the slave revolt in what is now Haiti. The occupying force was decimated by yellow fever and could not sustain itself. This slave revolt was a significant factor in forcing Napoleon to sell Louisiana to the United States. It not only showed how impossibly expensive it would be to maintain a needed level of security on the North American continent in terms of men and money, but created the modern country of Haiti to which Hearn would later travel to explore the Creole language and foods. The cost of having troops occupy all of the Louisiana territory was perceived as prohibitive, and Talleyrand made the formal agreement to sell the property, including the city of New Orleans, where Lafcadio Hearn was later to write his seminal book on Creole cookery, for $15 million. This transaction doubled the size of the United States.[5]

It was a time of rapid growth and the beginnings of the industrial revolution in America. Some of the notable achievements of this time were: the invention of the steamboat; the first federal highway, the Cumberland Road[6]; the opening of the Erie Canal, which opened up trade from the Great Lakes to New York City; the continuation of the presidential election system; nine states admitted to Union by 1837; the founding of Harvard Law School; and the United States stretching its legs in foreign policy with the Monroe doctrine.

As the country grew in size, there were more and more possibilities for regional foods and cuisines to develop. And develop they did, as explained later in this chapter. Without the events that shaped the country, it is reasonable to imagine that the foods discussed later on in the book might not have contributed to the development of American cuisine in the way they did.

The Cumberland Road made trade and travel, if not easy, at least achievable from the western frontier of Kentucky and Ohio, to the eastern part of the country. This led indirectly to the creation of another American classic: bourbon whiskey, as it was easier to transport the corn in the form of whiskey than as corn, which could rot before reaching market.

The Erie Canal opened western New York state to barge traffic, which led to increased grain shipments, which allowed a larger population to be economically provisioned. All this increasing trade and wealth led to more textile production in the northeast, which could have mills powered by water. And much of the cotton for these mills came from the South, including Virginia, where Mary Randolph and her husband lived. It also created more demand for tobacco as a domestic crop as well as an export commodity. This also greatly increased wealth, especially in Virginia and the Carolinas.

With the immigration of French Huguenots to the Charleston area and the growth of the plantation economy, Abby Fisher's mother was brought to America as a slave. Such a tangled web. Everything is vitally entwined with everything else.

In the 1830s, the Oregon Trail opened, providing a way for settlers to move from the Mississippi River all the way to the Pacific Ocean. (Parts of the Trail are still visible with wagon ruts worn into the ground.) This was later to have an effect on one of our other authors: Abby Fisher, again, as she and her family headed west after the Civil War and left for the West Coast, most likely from around St. Louis.

Eighteen thirty saw the infamous Indian Removal Act, which in 1838 to 1839 forced the Cherokee to walk to Oklahoma from their homelands in the Appalachian Mountains, a walk aptly named the "Trail of Tears." This truly "removed" all traces of Indians east of the Mississippi River with the exception of some supremely resistant Cherokee in North Carolina.

In 1835, De Tocqueville published his epic *Democracy in America,* a book still quoted in modern times. This was to become a tradition of sorts as all manner of European and Asian elite were to travel to the new country to see for themselves this great experiment. Dickens, Brillat-Savarin, and Anthony Trollope were among the most notable concerning the world of cuisine. After the French Revolution there were many skilled private chefs who were looking for work, and many came to the United States.

In 1838 *The Virginia Housewife,* the cookbook of our second author, Mrs. Mary Randolph, was published in Baltimore, even though Randolph had died at a young age in 1828. The book was originally published in 1824, and the 1838 edition used here continues a long line of reprints. This book is a landmark in American cuisine: It is the first regional cookbook published, and it is still in print. It shows the wealth and diversity of foods and cooking styles available to a wealthy household. Even for those people less well off, the increasing international trade and use of products foreign and exotic would eventually find their way into mainstream cooking.

Mrs. Randolph had the advantage of not having concerns about money

DISTRICT OF COLUMBIA, TO WIT:

Be it remembered, That on the twenty-ninth day of January, in the year of our Lord one thousand eight hundred and twenty-eight, and of the Independence of the United States of America, the fifty-second, WILLIAM B. RANDOLPH, of the said district, has deposited in the office of the Clerk of the District Court for the District of Columbia, the title of a book, the right whereof he claims as proprietor, in the words following, *to wit:*

"The Virginia Housewife; or, Methodical Cook. By MRS. MARY RANDOLPH. Method is the soul of management."

In conformity to the act of the Congress of the United States, entitled, "An act for the encouragement of learning, by securing the copies of Maps, Charts, and Books, to the authors and proprietors of such copies during the times therein mentioned"—and also to the act, entitled, "An act supplementary to an act, entitled, 'An act for the encouragement of learning, by securing the copies of Maps, Charts, and Books, to the authors and proprietors of such copies during the times therein mentioned,' and extending the benefits thereof to the arts of designing, engraving, and etching historical and other prints."

In testimony whereof, I have hereunto set my hand, and affixed the public seal of my office, the day and year aforesaid.

EDM. I. LEE,
Clerk of the District Court for the District of Columbia.

and her exquisite cooking reflects this in her book. Not only do we find food items common to Virginia, many items from around the country and around the world were staples in her well-run and supremely well-organized kitchen.

Who Was Mary Randolph?

Mary Randolph was of the Old South. Born into a family of Virginia landed gentry, she was related to some of the best known, wealthiest and most well regarded families of her time. We spoke briefly of her relationship to Jefferson, but that was only a small part of her aristocratic heritage.

Born in 1762,[7] Mary Randolph was the eldest child of Thomas Mann and Ann Cary Randolph. Thomas Jefferson's parents raised her father, an orphan, as they were distant cousins. Thomas Mann served in the House of Burgesses, the constitutional conventions of 1775 and 1776, and later in the Virginia legislature.

Mrs. Randolph's mother was the daughter of Randolph Cary, a wealthy plantation owner, and her brother, Thomas Mann Randolph, served as governor of Virginia and in the United States Congress.

While Mrs. Randolph was growing up and being educated in the ways of a lady of stature, the rapid expansion of American territory continued. In her too short lifetime, Mrs. Randolph was to do much to define our national cuisine. By making use of the already large number of national cuisines and regional foods, she led the way for so many other authors who were to write their own cookbooks.

As befitting a child of her family's stature, her education was provided by private tutors and included reading, writing, music, mathematics and household management.

Mary Randolph. Courtesy the Library of Virginia.

It was a given that a woman of her upbringing would run the household of her future husband. This was a complicated task, involving building and grounds management, oversight of dozens of slaves and servants, accounting and other administrative duties that went with being in a wealthy and socially prominent family.

As part of her household duties, the lady of the manor was expected to know all about food preparation, preserving, menu planning and etiquette in the planning of formal and informal social functions. Over the years, Mrs. Randolph acquired a vast knowledge of Southern cooking simply as part of her regular duties. To her credit and our benefit, in her later years this knowledge was compiled in her only book, *The Virginia Housewife*.

First published in 1824, four years

before her death, it offers a glimpse of daily life in the South through the prism of a woman highly skilled and proficient in her life's work. The title page includes a phrase that suggests how Mrs. Randolph accomplished her very complex tasks: "Method is the soul of management."

David Meade Randolph became her husband in 1780. On her side of the family, she was a cousin to George Washington Park Custis, godmother to Mary Randolph Custis, who later married Robert E. Lee. George Washington appointed David Randolph federal marshal for Virginia, whereupon the family moved to Richmond. Here in their home in Richmond, Mrs. Randolph achieved a reputation as a well-known hostess who was especially noted for her food.

The local society families coveted invitations to her events and her reputa-

David Randolph. Courtesy the Library of Virginia.

tion grew to the point that, ironically, she was well regarded by the slaves around Richmond. During a slave insurrection in 1800 near Richmond, the leader, "General Gabriel," stated that her life should be spared so that she could become his personal cook![8]

As often happens to political appointees, Mr. Randolph was at odds with the new president, Thomas Jefferson. Politics trumped family and he was removed as federal marshal. After this the family fortunes suffered a decline. Tobacco prices collapsed and a recession ensued.

Lots and rental houses were sold in Richmond in an attempt to recover financially, but this was not entirely successful. They were forced to sell their Richmond home and much of their plantation lands.

Ever the resourceful and commanding lady, Mrs. Randolph opened a boarding house in 1807. The boarding house acquired the name "The Queen" after the distinguished lady who owned and operated the establishment. Apparently the skills and knowledge that made her such a renowned socialite were transferrable to the world of public hospitality.

The new business was advertised in 1808 as a boarding house for ladies and gentlemen. Members of her family were not convinced it would succeed. Mary's sister-in-law Martha wrote her father stating that she thought the family fortunes, Mary's family, were continuing to decline and that the venture would ultimately fail.

Remember that restaurants as we now know them did not as yet exist to any extent in the United States. (This is discussed in much greater detail in the chapter on Charles Ranhofer.) This was a new venture for a heretofore independently wealthy lady. The very concept was almost unheard of to begin with. For members of her family to have reservations was only natural, but it does seem they underestimated her skills and strength of character.

Her boarding house became a vibrant center for refined social intercourse in Richmond. A contemporary chronicler, Samuel Mordecai, stated that "there were few more festive boards" found in the social setting of Richmond.[9]

It may seem unusual for a wealthy landowning family to delve into the realm of hospitality on a commercial basis. But remember, Mrs. Randolph, as mentioned earlier, had quite an existing reputation for her social skills before her family had their financial troubles, and it was not a stretch of her impressive abilities to go from what was really a director of operations for a large agricultural plantation to adapting those very skills to a much smaller commercial venture.

Consider the long-standing tradition of hospitality in Virginia of which Mrs. Randolph was one of the leading ladies in the early 19th century. This tradition was famous long before Mrs. Randolph. There actually was a law in the Virginia colony that stated "everyone shall be reputed to entertayne those of Curtesie with whome they make not a certaine Agreement." In *London Magazine,* in 1746, a traveler wrote, "All over the Colony, an universal Hospitality reigns; full Tables and open Doors, the kind Salute, the Generous Detention, speak somewhat like the old Roast-Beef Ages of our Fore-Fathers and would almost persuade one to think their Shades were wafted into these Regions." With such a longstanding tradition of

hospitality in Virginia and having been responsible for their own estate, it is perhaps not so surprising in hindsight that Mrs. Randolph would select this type of occupation.

After closing the boarding house in 1820, the family moved to Washington, D.C., where Mrs. Randolph published the first edition of her book in 1824, just four years before her death. One of her sons was made an invalid as the result of an accident and Mrs. Randolph became his caregiver, which was the reason she and her husband moved to Washington.

The book she penned in 1824 was so successful that another edition appeared in 1825, two editions were published in Baltimore in 1831 and 1838, another in Philadelphia in 1850. All told, there were more than 19 editions published before the Civil War and the book is still in print.

The book shows the incredible variety of foods available to well-heeled families in the early

This is Mary Randolph's grave. Related to the Lee and Custis families, she asked to be buried on the family estate, which later became the home of Robert E. Lee and Arlington Cemetery. Image courtesy of Findagrave.com.

This is the cover stone for Mary Randolph. The inscription reads in part, "died the 28th of January, 1828 in Washington City, a victim of maternal love and duty." Image courtesy of Rachel Cooper, About.com, Inc.

1800s. Her recipes, *receipts,* feature a wealth of fruits, vegetables, meats, fish and herbs. It is very much like a time capsule that makes the social and culinary world of ante-bellum Virginia come alive once again, and it demonstrates the culinary influences that shaped the food of one America's leading cookbook authors.

A scant four years after publication of the first edition, Mrs. Randolph died and was buried according to her wishes in what is now Arlington Cemetery, which was at that time the home of her cousin George Washington Custis. Her gravestone is still visible and bears in part the inscription "a victim of maternal love and duty."

A touching remembrance of Mrs. Randolph was published in 1829 and shows what sort of lasting impression Mrs. Randolph made as a person on her contemporaries[10]: "Nature was bountiful to her ... endowing her with a gentle disposition, and infusing into her temperament, modesty, goodness and genius; and she was beloved by her intimates and admired by all who were acquainted with her."

The Virginia Housewife— The Book

This book is considered by some to be the first truly American cookbook. (*Pace* Amelia Simmons.) It is regarded by virtually everyone who knows it to be the first regional American cookbook. Southern food has long had a reputation for being among the finest regional cuisines in the United States, with Virginia noted as one of the best culinary locations in the South.

An abundance of seafood from the Chesapeake Bay and the Atlantic Ocean was one highlight of Virginia cuisine. The mild climate made possible the growing of a large variety of food crops, at times bringing forth two crops a year. Vegetables and fruits of all kinds, from berries to orchard fruits, were routinely staples of Virginia households.

Pigs were generally allowed to roam the woods as was the tradition in England, and when harvested would have a singular taste that created a reputation that still exists, although today it is more a marketing ploy than an actual distinction of taste. In their free-range adventures, the pigs could eat a wide variety of tree and groundnuts, berries and grapes, as well as wild greens that were also comestible for humans. This combination of foods gave Virginia hams their distinctive taste and created a pinnacle ingredient of American cuisine.

What Mrs. Randolph relates in the book is a lifelong knowledge of how to make good food by using a system of organization that "lies in three simple rules — Let everything be done at a proper time, keep everything in its proper place, and put everything to its proper use." This reflects the professional creed of *mise en place*.

She goes on to describe how a successful mistress must organize her day, see to the minutiae of the daily food preparation and table setting, attend to a regimented schedule of household management, and overall make sure everything is run in an economical manner. Included here is the "Preface" in its entirety. In a nutshell, this gives a look at the character and organizational skills of this woman and how she went about the running of her personal household or her business.

An oddity about the preface is the date at the end. Mrs. Randolph died in 1828. The date is 1831. So unless she had some really exceptional powers, this is the time of the reprint of this particular version of the preface, which was also used for the later 1838 reprint.

Mrs. Randolph states that immediately after breakfast, "When the kitchen breakfast is over, and the cook has put all things in their proper places, the mistress should go in to give her orders. Let all the articles intended for the dinner pass in review before her: have the butter, sugar, flour, meal, lard, given out in proper quantities; the catsup, spice, wine, whatever may be wanted for each dish, measured to the cook."

The "Introduction" is included in full because this essay demonstrates how Mrs. Randolph saw her responsibilities as household manager and key member of a family. The ethos in this introduction comes out in the recipes.

This dictum refers to the preface of the 1838 edition, where Mrs. Randolph states that she had numerous difficulties when she started running her own household. As a means of improving and organizing her job, she says: "[Difficulties] compelled me to study the subject, and by actual experiment to reduce everything in the culinary line, to proper weights and measures."

That she was successful in sharing her experiences is evidenced by the fact that so many editions appeared in the 30 years following publication.

Reading the table of contents for this book is a revelation as to how well our forefathers ate in wealthy homes.

Soups that specifically included "Southern" foods include soups made with oysters, okra, rabbit, catfish, turtle and mock turtle made from calf's head. (It is interesting to think of okra as being "Southern" when it was of African origin.) The African influence is felt throughout the South, due in no small measure to the fact that slaves were divided into field slaves and household slaves. As part of some household slave duties, cooking for the household would be high on the list of daily tasks.

But we also are treated to Soup with Bouilli, which is a decidedly French term for a broth that has both meat and vegetables and is often thickened, which leads to a French tradition of also having it mean a type of a stew.

Beef is presented à la mode, which means in the fashion of or a dish that is "in fashion"; stewed, in a fricando (a type of stew made with sliced meat, vegetables and a thickened gravy). Depending upon whom one asks, this is either a French inspired type of braised item with veal or beef, or a version of a traditional Spanish or Italian dish of the same type. Beef à la daube is another French item traditionally made with lots of garlic and red wine and stewed with assorted vegetables. Mrs. Randolph tones it down a bit and refines the sauce by clarifying it with eggs whites as for a consommé. A Hunter's Style beef is really a type of a cured dish rather than a classical chasseur, and the English traditions come forth in beef hash, pie and steak.

For veal, there are almost two-dozen different recipes as well as directions for "the pieces in the different quarters of veal." She tells the reader about chops, knuckles, heads, feet, heart, breast and filet, among others. In a flavorful and somewhat novel twist, veal cutlets are fried as a schnitzel, but then a sauce is made and finished with curry powder, preserved lemon (a north African specialty), and white wine. The meat is then reheated in the sauce and served with fresh lemon. This is quite an array of flavors.

Another cutlet preparation uses the same pan-fried veal that is first poached with parsley, pork trimmings, garlic, thyme and nutmeg. The dish is finished with the reduced poaching liquor, a large amount of butter, browned flour, and mushroom catsup. So here is a dish with a condiment of oriental origin, and a French-style reduced liquid and white wine or Madeira. This is an awful lot of flavors to keep a tongue happy!

Fillet of veal is stuffed and braised; veal collops (which is of Scandinavian origin indicating a stewed piece of meat) with fried parsley and skewers of thick bacon; a ragout, veal olives, which is a version of the Italian *Saltimboca* made with Virginia ham; several recipes for calf's head and calf's feet; broiled liver and a stuffed calf's liver served with a white wine sauce.

Lamb is not prominent but mutton shows recipes for steaks, chops, breast and how "to harrico mutton." This involved cutting single rib chops from the rack, pounding and seasoning them; then grilling and finishing in rich gravy with diced vegetables.

A Virginia specialty, shote was a young fatted hog and instructions are here for how to roast it, make cutlets, prepare the head and corn it. One of the interesting methods of preparation is the feeding of the hogs at least six weeks before slaughter, and then making sure that "the shorter distance they are driven to market, the better will their flesh be."

There are directions on how to make bacon and ham. Smoking after salting different meats for different lengths of time is done with a cold smoke. In other words, the curing with salt, now known as dry curing, would take care of the moisture and the smoking would finish the process of preserving the meat. But to smoke with heat, "be careful not to have a blaze," which would make the hams hard. And do not forget to "hang the hams and shoulders with the hocks down to preserve the juices."

These procedures would be done during the winter and starting in April with the hot weather "it [the ham] should be occasionally taken down, examined, rubbed with hickory ashes, and hung up again." This would be a check for mould, which would be scraped off and the ashes would both flavor and help sterilize the meat.

The shote as mentioned above gets special mention. In a footnote she says:

Shote being a Provincial term, and not a legitimate English word, Mrs. R. has taken the liberty of spelling it in a way that conveys the sound of the pronunciation more clearly than shoat, the usual manner of spelling it.

Shote has a special butchering process in that it is quartered, with each quarter weighing around six pounds if the shote is of proper size. There follow recipes for barbecuing or roasting the forequarter; making cutlets from the hind quarter; corning a hind quarter; and making a stew from the head and brains.

We are treated to recipes for sausages, black pudding and "bologna sausages." Clearly, despite her wealth, Mrs. Randolph did not allow any waste in her kitchen!

Featured fish and seafood include: herrings, sturgeon, shad, rockfish, perch, oysters, catfish and salt cod, among others. Showing a northern European tradition adapted to Virginia, herrings are pickled, but are caught and thrown while still live into the brining liquid and then processed with alum and saltpeter. Be careful to use only fat fish and after salting and brining, soak and scale them, place in buttered paper and broil.

Sturgeon was a plentiful fish in the eastern coastal states, so much so that sturgeon caviar would be on bars in towns along the Hudson River for free as it was salty and would cause patrons to drink more beer! This ancient fish is baked, made into cutlets and steaks and boiled or poached.

Shad, a fish of the herring family, which is found on both sides of the Atlantic, the Mediterranean Sea, and Black and Caspian Seas, was an important fish during the 1700s and early 1800s in the eastern United States. Pollution of rivers, where shad spawn, has drastically reduced their numbers, but they were always valued as a fine, well flavored fish on par with or superior to salmon. Mrs. Randolph has them broiled, baked and stuffed "with a forcemeat."

"Matelote of any kind of firm fish" shows again the prevalence of the influence of French cooking in Virginia. (Matelote is a French fish stew with wine.) And to show an example of "fusion cuisine" we have a "curry of catfish."

There is a recipe "to caveach fish," which is a type of fish and onion stew with vinegar, eels, carp and cod tongues! This is a cooked hot version of an escabèche or ceviche of fish that would be "cooked" by the acid in the vinegar or a citrus juice with no heat applied.

Eels, oysters, carp and jellied fish that could be used as a buffet dish round out her seafood recipes.

Poultry appears boiled, roasted, stewed, curried "after the East Indian manner," in a gumbo, "a West Indian dish." Turkey has a prominent place in Mrs. Randolph's book, including that quintessential American creation, "turkey with oyster stuffing," served with oyster sauce. This is boiled or poached, the meat and skin remain perfectly and it is wonderfully juicy. What some people consider a Philadelphia dish is included—"pepper pot." In her words we also have "chicken pudding, a favorite Virginia dish."

There is a "Spanish Method of Dressing Giblets," which is actually an omelet made by boiling the giblets, with onion, and then frying to a "nice brown" in butter or pan drippings. As they are frying, beat six eggs, add to the pan, stir a little and serve.

Mrs. Randolph tells how to make polenta, macaroni, mock macaroni (crackers) and a "Dish of Rice to be Served Up with The Curry, in a Dish by Itself."

"Ropa Vieja—Spanish" is a dish of tomatoes with any leftover meat or fowl and we also have "An Ollo—a Spanish Dish" that is a stew made with pork, beef, fowl and mutton.

Sauces, vegetables, puddings, ice creams, curds and creams, preserves, cakes and cordials—for someone to master this repertoire would require a strong sense of organization.

Displayed here, as well as the focus on Virginia cooking, are the breadth of Mrs. Randolph's education and her battery of cooking techniques. As mentioned, we have curries,

Spanish foods, French-inspired dishes, down-on-the-farm procedures for preserving foods and preparations for elegant and festive dinners.

Some of what might be called contemporary food today was also in her domain. For example, she displays a wealth of vegetable dishes, including 17 different tomato recipes in the various editions of her book. (This at a time when tomatoes were sometimes considered poisonous.) She also prefers that vegetables be cooked just until done, which is a far cry from what many of us consider a "Southern" way of cooking vegetables, especially beans and greens.

Potatoes are here in various incarnations along with the American Jerusalem artichoke, which was never in Jerusalem and is not an artichoke. All manner of root vegetables, beans, cabbages of many varieties, our old friend the pumpkin, the sweet potato, cimlins (young squash), salsify and a Johnny Cake made with rice.

Mrs. Randolph was particularly known for her ice creams, which is no mean feat considering where she lived. In her general directions she takes "indolent cooks" to task for being lazy in the freezing of ice cream. (This is covered in more detail in the recipe section.) Through simple statements such as these, we can get a hint of the personality of the person writing this book. Clearly, Mrs. Randolph would suffer no fools in her kitchen. It was to be done correctly, that was the only option. What she counsels here is a well known fact in pastry kitchens: Ice cream must be frozen quickly for best results, and she hits the nail on the head — if not, the ice cream will crystallize.

Her advice to keep the freezer going, maintaining as cold a temperature as possible, is as true now as it was then. And in the midst of her professional quality observations, she also cautions against wasting ice by having too large a freezing tub. This also gives another glimpse to the resources of a plantation owner at this time — there were no commercial ice freezers in the 1820s. Ice, harvested in the winter by sawing frozen ponds and lakes, was wrapped to prevent melting and packed into insulated wagons or rail cars later on; it could be transported great distances. Clearly an expensive commodity, it was readily available in Mrs. Randolph's home.

Pies, puddings, "Indian Meal Pudding," "Pumpkin Pudding" — all speak to the growth of American cuisine and how items that were once new or looked at with suspicion by early European settlers had become a large part of our culinary heritage. As in any good American cookbook there are many dessert recipes: ice creams, custards, trifles (showing her English heritage), floating island (a French dish of poached soft meringues), the medieval blanc mange, fools, creams. Not to mention some of the best breakfast items ever created.

Here is a woman who was born into wealth and gentility and educated to execute the demands of her social standing. When times turned sour, she took her "method" and applied a life of learning and organizing into a profitable business. The business itself turned out to be one of the most successful examples of an early American "boarding house" that served food and drink, and provided a social setting for the public. This is almost what is now called a boutique hotel.

In the course of her cooking directions she was able to use and adapt cooking techniques from many different cultures and styles, incorporate these disparate elements and create a harmonious whole that not only made these techniques crucial elements of our American cuisine, but in utilizing local ingredients constituted our first truly regional cuisine.

In the 1838 edition of her book, starting on page 26, Mrs. Randolph has some observations that ring as true today as when written in the early 1800s. "Beef and mutton must not be roasted as much as veal, lamb or pork." A tendency to enjoy beef and lamb more medium rare to rare holds true today. Pork was often afflicted with trichinosis, a parasite that would also infect those who ate the less than completely cooked meat. Veal is not served with more than a touch of pink. This is for texture, sanitation and taste.

Her admonition, "You may pour a little melted butter in the dish with the veal, but all the others must be served without sauce, and garnished with horse-radish, nicely scraped," reflects the English side of her culinary training and heritage. This was something that would undergo a change as our cuisine was more and more influenced by French cuisine, and French-trained chefs.

"A loin of veal and a hind quarter of lamb, should be dished with the kidneys uppermost; and be sure to joint everything that is to be separated at table, or it will be impossible to carve neatly." Kidneys are not often served now, but are a staple of British cuisine and often found in French cooking as well. However, they are invariably served with some type of sauce or moisture added with the meat. A classic preparation is with a Madeira sauce. Also, kidneys have a layer of fat for insulation on their outside which would melt during roasting but in English style would also add moisture, or, more properly, richness, which would partially alleviate the need for a separate sauce. However, the melting fat would also impart an even stronger taste to the organs.

"For those who *must* have gravy with these meats, let it be made in any way they like, and served in a boat." Mrs. Randolph's indicates by her italics that this was not something she approved of very much. The almost dismissive tone of her voice comes through the years to make her point clearly. The idea of serving sauce on the side is now quite common but maybe not quite so common in her time.

"Nice lard is better for basting than butter for basting roasted meats, or for frying." With no refrigeration at the time, it is not hard to imagine butter getting sour. And although other works refer to washing salt out of butter, lard would have been more reliable. It also creates a finer crust on roasted meats and turns out fried food with an unsurpassed crisp delicate texture. Remember, this is fresh lard, not the processed material available in stores now with stabilizers and preservatives. Fresh lard, rendered pig fat that is cloud white, is a delicate fat and actually has less cholesterol than butter.

"To chose a butcher's meat, you must see that the fat is not yellow, and that the lean parts are of a fine close grain, a lively color, and will feel tender when pinched." Mrs. Randolph is looking for a young cow, white fat. A lean close grain indicates a cow not too old. The prescription for good quality meat still applies today. The color of fat is a good indication of the age, hence tenderness and gaminess, of beef or especially lamb.

"Poultry should be well covered with white fat; if the bottom of the breast bone be gristly, it is young, but if it be a hard bone, it is an old one." Mrs. Randolph is looking for what now is called a broiler or a fryer, a young bird rather than an older laying hen or rooster. Size would also come into play here, but her guidelines are sound and hold true today. For quick cooking or roasting a young bird would be required. If a fowl or rooster were used, it would need moist, slow cooking, e.g. braising or stewing, in order to have tender meat.

"Fish are judged by the liveliness of their eyes, and bright red of their gills." This is what every professional chef in the world knows and is how Mrs. Randolph judged her fish. The standard gauges for quality in modern professional kitchens were in play in Mrs. Randolph's kitchen 150 years ago. Mrs. Randolph was fortunate that most of her fish and seafood would have been local — either caught in local streams and rivers or shipped live from the coast. Even in restaurants now it is not uncommon to have fish and seafood more than a week old coming in the back door and listed as "fresh fish."

"For broiling, have very clear coals, sprinkle a little salt and pepper over the pieces, and when done, dish them and pour over some melted butter and chopped parsley — this is for broiled veal, wild fowl, birds or poultry; bed steaks and mutton chops require only a table-spoon of hot water to be poured over." Here Mrs. Randolph indicates a little added fat for leaner meats while the beef and mutton would naturally be fattier, and would need just a little moisture to make the meats shine for table presentation. This is similar to what is done in restaurants now, save for the fact that items are normally brushed with melted butter rather than water. Some professional chefs will also nappé an item before serving, which means to cover with a sauce.

"To have viands served in perfection, the dishes should be made hot, either by setting them over hot water, or by pouring some hot water in them, and the instant the meats are laid and garnished, put on a pewter dish cover." Again, this is a standard type of professional presentation. Always serve hot food on hot plates and serve hot food hot, cold food cold. Pre-heating plates and taking them into the dining room with covers is almost universally accepted. Remember that there was also no central heating in Mrs. Randolph's day and that throughout the fall and winter this elegant technique was based on practicality: a cold room will take carefully prepared food and ruin it if the food arrives to the guest cold or lukewarm rather than hot.

For the final excerpt, listen to Mrs. Randolph speak for herself:

"Profusion is not elegance — a dinner justly calculated for the company, and consisting for the greater part of small articles, correctly prepared, and neatly served up, will make a much more pleasing alternative to the sight, and give far greater satisfaction to the appetite, than a table loaded with food, and from a multiplicity of dishes, unavoidably neglected in the preparation, and served up cold."

What you just read above is so well ingrained in professionally trained chefs that the advice could have been written last year. The message is the same, the effect on food and guests remain the same as they were in 1824 when Mrs. Randolph wrote this wonderful book and the same good advice is practiced on a daily basis in professional restaurants and kitchens around the country whose aim is to serve quality food beautifully presented. More and bigger are not better; they are simply more and bigger.

When called to minister to her son, Mrs. Randolph devoted herself to the task with zeal. However, she took the time to save for us the wealth of knowledge and experience she acquired over a too short lifetime. Mrs. Randolph is truly one of America's leading ladies.

Recipes

The recipes selected and reproduced herein in Chapter 11 are an attempt to show several things:

- the wealth of food available at this time;
- Mrs. Randolph's cooking techniques and organizational skills;
- the breadth of cuisines and seasonings which were available in America as a whole.

When talking about an American cuisine there are so many influences present that it is too easy to believe that this is a recent trend. Many of the elements of "ethnic foods" were present over 200 years ago and were regular preparations for experienced cooks.

A look at some of the recipes chosen will show there were African, Creole, Native American, English and French influences when Mrs. Randolph wrote her book. Add to that the foods available in Virginia and prepared on a regular basis, and there is now a varied and sophisticated Virginia cuisine, as a regional cuisine of American cooking.

For the most part, Mrs. Randolph is writing in "modern English" with an easily understood type. The "translations" that were needed for Amelia Simmons are not needed here. When there are unfamiliar words or directions they are covered in the updated versions of the recipes.

Mrs. Randolph takes a lot for granted as far as the cooking skills of her readers. Maybe we modern folks have forgotten how much someone needed to know in earlier times. If you do not know Mrs. Randolph, you should. She was a caring person with impeccable standards of hospitality and represents what the best of American cuisine can be. If ever we had a "first lady" in our kitchens rather than the White House, surely Mrs. Randolph was she.

CHAPTER 4

Miss Leslie

In the 1840 presidential election, William Henry Harrison was elected and served for one month. The White House web site states that Harrison was the son of a wealthy Virginia plantation family, who gained fame by serving as a soldier and governor in the then northwest, which is now Ohio and Indiana. One of his victories generated the campaign slogan, "Tippecanoe and Tyler, too." This northwest frontier would be settled by people from Pennsylvania and other points east, many of whom would likely have taken Miss Leslie's book with them.

Well educated as a young man, Harrison had his inaugural address edited by none other than Daniel Webster. Unfortunately, inauguration day was cold and rainy; he caught a cold that developed into pneumonia and was dead a month later. He was succeeded by his running mate, John Tyler, of the above political slogan fame.

Although not a landmark case in the sense of the abolition of slavery in the United States, the Amistad Case of 1841, argued before the Supreme Court by none other than John Quincy Adams, garnered increased attention on the condition of slaves and slavery on an international as well as a national basis. The court ruling in favor of the "slaves" on trial angered the then president, John Tyler. The specter of slavery would continue to intrude into American life, including its food. Abby Fisher was a slave in South Carolina who was able to transform her knowledge of cooking before the Civil War into a highly successful career after the war. More about her later on.

The decade of the 1840s saw the annexation of Texas in 1845, the election of James Polk as the 11th president the same year, and the first mention in print of the idea of Manifest Destiny. The doctrine espoused the idea that America was all but pre-ordained to continue her westward expansion. As a result of this, the Oregon Trail was an important route for migration of settlers, probably including Abby Fisher, and definitely led the way for the transcontinental railroad. The railroad opened up the West coast and helped create the "Paris of the West," San Francisco, where Victor Hirtzler was to establish a new standard of quality in cuisine west of Chicago at the St. Francis Hotel. In this way, the railroad made possible another block in the foundation of the building of a national cuisine. (See the chapter on Hirtzler.)

The border between the United States and Canada was established as the 49th parallel with the Oregon Treaty.[1] This was a settlement that defined the northern boundary of the United States all the way to the Pacific Ocean while still granting British citizens right of ownership of all property if they were already settled in the new area defined by the treaty. (Oregon itself was acquired in that same year, 1846.)

DIRECTIONS FOR COOKERY,

IN

ITS VARIOUS BRANCHES.

BY

MISS LESLIE.

" ————————

TENTH EDITION,

WITH IMPROVEMENTS AND SUPPLEMENTARY RECEIPTS.

————————

PHILADELPHIA:

E. L. CAREY & A. HART, CHESTNUT STREET.

————

1840.

The Treaty of Guadalupe Hidalgo, signed on February 2, 1848, had Mexico cede California, Utah, Nevada, most of New Mexico, and Arizona, along with parts of Colorado and Wyoming. The boundary between the United States and Mexico was set as the Rio Grande River; all this for only $15 million. Needless to say, this huge swath of land is now home to a vibrant set of regional cuisines that form parts of our culinary tapestry.

In 1848 gold was discovered in California, and miners and settlers heading to California brought clippings of the zinfandel grape which were planted in California and zinfandel remains California's signature wine grape variety.

Zachary Taylor became our 12th president in 1849 and Harriet Tubman escaped slavery and became instrumental in the underground railroad.

In this decade the states that were admitted to the union range from Florida to California and the United States became a truly bicoastal country with defined borders also in the north and south. What this did for American cuisine is hard to overstate in that the geographical boundaries were set that defined the continental United States. This meant that food products either raised in or imported to the United States were fair game for the development of a national cuisine.

Some of the notable inventions and scientific advancements in the decade included Justus Liebling's artificial fertilizer that attempted to reduce all agricultural nutrients to three items — potassium, phosphorous, and nitrogen — thereby ushering in industrial agriculture. For the richly fertile lands of the Midwest this discovery would start the slide towards industrial agriculture, which was to have an enormous effect on the food supply of all of the United States in the coming century. The increased production was a benefit. The monoculture agriculture that defines modern agriculture was not.

The national population jumped from 17 million in 1840 to over 23 million in 1850. Many of these people would settle in Pennsylvania and the upper Midwest. New brides would look to our next author for advice and guidance to the extent that this book became the largest selling cookbook in the United States in the 19th century.

In Philadelphia, a woman who found her literary and culinary voice becomes our third person who profoundly influenced American cuisine — Miss Eliza Leslie.

Who was Miss Eliza Leslie?

Eliza Leslie was born in 1787 to the former Lydia Baker and Robert Leslie. Mr. Leslie was quite a capable man who was a watchmaker, owned an export business and for a time was an international businessman, moving his family to England to further his commercial enterprises. Miss Leslie was the eldest of five children and spent her early childhood in England, voraciously reading every book she and her father could acquire.

In *Female Prose Writers of America* there is an autobiography Miss Leslie penned to her friend, Mrs. Alice B. Beal. In Miss Leslie's words, "My father was a man of considerable natural genius, and much self taught knowledge." She goes on to describe his talents as a scientist, writer, "draughtsman," and musician, playing both flute and violin. His intelligence and love of learning was transmitted to his daughter and under his tutelage Miss Leslie became well read, learned to be a respectable artist and ended up as one of the most important female authors of the 19th century.

When the family moved from Elkton, Maryland, to Philadelphia, Mr. Leslie became quite a successful watchmaker. As Philadelphia was at that time the nation's capital, his success as a craftsman brought him into contact and friendship with some of our most famous historical personalities including Jefferson, Franklin, Robert Patterson (who was to become president of the mint), and Charles Peale, the artist who painted many of the leaders of the American Revolution.

In 1792 the family relocated to London where Mr. Leslie was intent on building an export business focused on clocks and watches. The family lived in England for about six years, and although Eliza had little formal education, Robert Leslie encouraged his daughter to read, write and develop her artistic skills.

As a child, she recalled later in life, there was a dearth of children's books. So after a brief period reading what juvenile literature there was available while living in England, Miss Leslie moved on to reading all kinds of literature, writing poetry and making copious drawings. Writing poetry at an early age, she did get discouraged. But, as she later wrote, "I then for many years abandoned the dream of my childhood, the hope of one day seeing my name in print." If she only knew then what she was to accomplish later in her life!

The family returned to the United States in 1799. Mr. Leslie's business partner died and had lost a lot of money while Mr. Leslie and his family were in England. Miss Leslie simply states that her father "lived until 1803," and says that they "were left in circumstances which rendered it necessary that she (her mother) and myself should make immediate exertions for the support of those who were yet too young to assist themselves, as they did afterwards." In essence, Mr. Leslie's partner ran the business into the ground. And what should have been a time of prosperity and prestige for the Leslies ended up being a time of living in survival mode. One cannot help but wonder but that these financial setbacks were instrumental in the early death of Mr. Leslie.

According to Sarah Hale, the editor of the 1853 *Women's Record* (p. 171), Miss Leslie and her family encountered some hard financial times. Apparently, the family was able to deal with these circumstances well as Miss Leslie states that "we lived on cheerfully, and with such moderate enjoyments as our means afforded; believing in the proverb that, 'All work and no play make Jack a dull boy.'"

In an effort to keep things together, Mrs. Leslie opened a boarding house. Here we have a situation that roughly parallels that of Mrs. Randolph. Miss Leslie was the eldest child and worked with mother in their boarding house to keep the family together, with Miss Leslie learning about hospitality and food and cooking as a matter of course.

Apparently Miss Leslie and her mother did a good job of raising the family despite whatever hardships they encountered. Her younger siblings, as well as Miss Leslie, made names for themselves. One brother, Thomas Jefferson Leslie, became a career Army officer after graduating from West Point. Her other brother, Charles, became a well-known painter. He was born in London and returned with the family to Philadelphia, then found himself gravitating towards art and drama even though he was training to become a book seller. He showed talent and was introduced to some notable artistic personages in London, attended the Royal Academy and was successful as a painter who focused on bringing literary characters to canvas. He later taught at the Royal Academy and was known as an author as well, with perhaps his best known work being a biography of the painter Constable. Both sisters, Anna and Patty, did well later in life, with Anna becoming a painter of skill who "has been very successful at copying pictures."[2]

Did Miss Leslie start her culinary training in an effort to improve the food at the boarding house? That we do not know. What we do know is that she enrolled in the first cooking school in the United States, Mrs. Goodfellow's cooking school in Philadelphia, which was essentially a school for "finishing" upper-class ladies in the domestic arts, and American cuisine was never the same after that.

Her Writing Career: Cooking, Fiction and Advice

After a time, Miss Leslie compiled her first culinary book, *Seventy-Five Receipts for Pastry, Cakes and Sweetmeats* (1828). The book was successful to the point that her publisher, Munroe and Francis in Boston, asked for a work "of imagination," i.e. fiction.

What followed in 1829 was *The Young Americans or Sketches of a Sea Voyage*. This was published anonymously but was so successful that she decided to sign her name to her next book in 1831, *The American Girl's Book*. Apparently if there was a dearth of juvenile literature, Miss Leslie was about to take care of that herself. Time and again she would write books for children, both fiction and books on advice, especially for young girls.

For the next 25 years Miss Leslie was not shy about signing her own name to her cookbooks, etiquette books, children's stories, magazine articles and works she edited. Her childhood dream to see her name in print was realized dozens of times during her lifetime.

Her best selling book, *Directions for Cookery in Its Various Branches* (1837), was one of the most influential cookbooks published in the 19th century. Sales of over 150,000 copies made it a book that could be found in homes all across the country. In the decade after its first edition, eight more states were added to the United States, stretching from Florida to

California. And in that same decade the population of the country expanded by more than six million people — from 17 million to 23 million. That this book Miss Leslie authored would have a profound influence on American cuisine is in part related to these contemporary developments. For a family heading west, one of the important items taken along would be a cookbook, or rather a book on domestic management that was heavy on recipes but also contained the latest advice on home remedies, spirits, often brewing, and care of household items. It would be a treasured family possession.

Miss Leslie wrote in her preface, "The author has spared no pains in collecting and arranging, perhaps the greatest number of practical and original receipts that have ever appeared in a similar work; flattering herself that she has rendered them so explicit as to be easily understood, and followed, even by inexperienced cooks."

In an appeal to reach across all socio-economic strata, she wrote the book "in the hope that her system of cookery may be consulted with equal advantage by families in town and in country, by those whose condition makes it expedient to practice economy, and by others whose circumstances authorize a liberal expenditure, the author sends it to take its chance among the multitude of similar publications...." Just as Amelia Simmons strove to have her work useful for the widest possible audience, so too did Miss Leslie, with similar but much more large-scale results.

It should be remembered that when a family left the East and migrated to a new area of the United States, this was most often a permanent move. Travel was not easy and homesteading was harder still. When new territories opened for settlement there were many farming families who moved to Ohio and other parts of the Midwest where farming promised to be easier and much more productive. Farming was never easy, and in Vermont where the only reliable crop was rocks, the idea of three or four feet of topsoil without rock must have been quite a temptation. It was such a life-changing event that when farmers in New England would move to the Midwest for farming, they routinely burned their houses to the ground in order to sift the ashes to save the nails. Near where I lived in Vermont and across the river in New Hampshire, it was easy to find cellar holes where farmhouses had been, and in one case, there was an entire town that had just moved away. Unlike the ghost towns of the West, these places left no buildings — merely holes in the ground.

For a homesteader, a reliable book that could help with day-to-day living was an invaluable item, and many of the migrating families would have had Miss Leslie's book with them.

Her choice of recipes and her methods are still in evidence today. Her selection of recipes serves multiple purposes for us a century and a half after publication. Historical cookbooks not only compile recipes, they offer glimpses into a time and place far removed from our own. The cooking techniques and advice on product selection demonstrate facets of everyday life that would not find their way into more conventional history books. Reading her prose and her recipes is like being invited into her kitchen and getting to know her, at least on a professional level. Consider: "Designing it as a manual of American housewifery, she has avoided the insertion of any dishes whose ingredients cannot be procured on our side of the Atlantic, and which require for their preparation utensils that are rarely found except in Europe." Clearly this shows a practical bent and allows the reader to experience quality food preparations without breaking the bank.

In this modest sentence, Miss Leslie makes a case for the strict American-ness of her book. This is an American book, written in America for use by Americans whose boundaries are set by what is available here in the United States. In the next sentence she further states that recipes do not include foods not "considered good of its kind" as well as recipes not "worth the trouble and cost of preparing."

These two paragraphs express a continuity of purpose, whether intended or not, shared by our first three authors, Simmons, Randolph and Leslie. The emphasis on things American for Americans firmly established a genre and a culture of quality that these authors lived by and which is transmitted to our own time. Yes, there is lots of junk food in what has become known as American food, but these authors established a dedication to quality, using native ingredients and making the recipes available across the spectrum of American households, that established a true American cuisine. All three emphasize the quality aspect of fresh seasonal local ingredients as the basis for any quality preparation. This is a long denied notion that is finally making a return to American food in general.

When foreign recipes are encountered in these books there is a certain Americanization of the recipes; this was so with Mrs. Randolph and Amelia Simmons. As we shall see it is also true of Miss Leslie.

The book is crafted "as if each receipt was to stand alone by itself, all references to others being avoided." The user of the book need not spend time learning the entire volume or worry about being a skilled professional cook. The ease of having exact measurements and making each recipe a world unto itself would certainly have made the book accessible to almost everyone who would buy it. This is still true today. Miss Leslie's painstaking exactitude makes her receipts virtually foolproof. I cannot help but think that the exactitude of writing baking formulas in her first book are, of baking and pastry, carried over into her approach to this volume.

In a further effort to make the book useful to everyone, Miss Leslie has some helpful hints that may seem too commonplace for words. But when read by a person learning to cook and run a household for the first time they were probably nothing short of revelations. Even in professional kitchens, we continually go "back to basics" and focus on "*mise-en-place*," everything in its place. Ninety percent of good cooking is getting oneself organized, and this is something Miss Leslie covers simply and thoroughly. Sound like anyone else we know from Virginia?

"We recommend to all families that they should keep in the house a pair of scales, (one of the scales deep enough to hold flour, sugar, &c., conveniently,) and a set of tin measures as accuracy in proportioning the ingredients is indispensible to success in cookery."

Any experienced baker will tell you that accuracy in measuring is critical in achieving desired and consistent results. What Miss Leslie is saying intuitively is that all good cooking depends upon percentages of ingredients and a balance of these percentages to be successful.

Professional recipes are typically written for a certain batch size, say ten portions. And somewhere there is also a column stating the percentages of ingredients by weight for the total recipe. In baking, the weight of the flour is generally pegged at 100 percent, with other ingredient weights expressed as a portion of the flour. For example, if we have five pounds of flour, that equals 100 percent. Then when we make our bread we have three pounds of water. This is 60 percent of the weight of the flour.

In cooking as opposed to baking recipes, often the entire recipe is considered 100 percent with each ingredient making up a portion of that 100 percent. If we have a stew made with five pounds of meat and the total weight of the stew is ten pounds, then the percentage of meat for this recipe is 50 percent. In modern professional kitchens and bake shops both of these methods are used. Some chefs say they do not measure anything, but that is not true. And for maintaining a budget to run a household, or turn a profit in a restaurant, knowledge of ingredient amounts determines recipe cost.

Miss Leslie gives these professional techniques to her readers even though they would not necessarily be aware of what they were learning. As an experienced cook and teacher, she was able to distill this knowledge into one simple sentence.

Look at her summary of common volume measurements as opposed to weights measurements.

> Let it be remembered, that of liquid measure —
> Two jills are half a pint
> Two pints — one quart
> Four quarts — one gallon.

Some explanation here:

- Jill is also known as a gill, or four ounces.
- Four tablespoons are two ounces by volume, or ½ ounce per tablespoon.
- A common wine glass is two ounces.
- A large coffee cup is eight ounces.
- A quart by volume of flour weighs about 16 ounces.
- A quart of volume of sugar and butter weigh in at two pounds.
- Ten eggs to a pint, 20 to a quart, about the size of our modern large eggs of two ounces each, of which ¼ ounce is shell.

As we go through the recipes included, adjustments are made for the above calculations.

Her Literary Reputation

In a book entitled *Female Prose Writers of America,* written by John S. Hart, Miss Leslie is one of the authors included. It helps to remember that she was an accomplished and popular author, writing children's books and magazine articles and editing the works of others. Mr. Hart includes an autobiography Miss Leslie penned for a close friend that details some of her accomplishments as a writer: after several books for children, a story based on Mrs. Washington Potts won a prize in a contemporary literary publication called *Godey's Lady's Book.* Monthly and weekly articles for various magazines and newspapers and one attempt at a full-length novel, *Amelia, or a Young Ladie's Vicissitudes,* had her state that were she to start writing all over again, novels would be her forte.

I am not a literary historian. So let me relay to you some of what Mr. Hart has to say about our Miss Leslie. "Her tales are perfect daguerreotypes of real life; their actors think, act, and speak for themselves." Further on he says simply, "Her writings are distinguished for vivacity and ease of expression...." Her recipe writing seems to me to be in that same style of ease of expression and clarity.

"In her juvenile tales the children are neither 'good little girls, or bad little boys,' but real little boys and girls, who act and speak with all the genuineness and naïveté of childhood."[3]

I read a number of her stories while researching this book and I enjoyed them immensely. For anyone who likes 19th-century writing, try reading some of Miss Leslie's works. There always seems to me an underlying sense of good humor and good naturedness in her stories. But she does not pull any punches — if a point needs to be made, Miss Leslie writes in no uncertain terms what that point is. This clarity of expression helps her characters live and breathe as if they are in the room with the reader.

She does say that her greatest financial successes came from her "three books on domestic economy." The book we are examining here, *Domestic Cookery Book* (1837), by 1851 had received 41 editions with "no edition having been less than a thousand copies."

She certainly was a woman of extraordinary talents and became a magnet later on in her life for people from all over the United States. On the Feeding America web site, it states that she was *the* Philadelphia celebrity who had a "sarcastic wit" but was generous to those in need.

She died in 1858 in New Jersey. Her books are still with us and through them we can get to know her a little and appreciate what a profound effect she continues to have on our American cuisine.

Foods Used in Her Book

Miss Leslie covers such a range of foods! The variety of foodstuffs available, from produce to seafood to game to domesticated livestock, is striking. A sobering statistic from the Slow Foods movement states that since 1900, the United States has lost 97 percent of the variety of food available since the start of the 20th century. In these cookbooks, the reader can get some sense of what we have lost in the name of progress. Fish and seafood in Miss Leslie's book include salmon (fresh, smoked and pickled); halibut, cod, shad, mackerel, rockfish, sea bass, perch, trout, carp and sturgeon. Oysters, clams, crabs, lobster — all are here.

Her soup recipes were especially renowned and in reading through her recipes one can see why. The variety of soups — everything from "family soup" to "mulligatawny," offer a variety that speaks to the wealth of foods available as well as American and non–American influences common in Philadelphia at this time.

Veal is used for a variety of soups where long simmering to extract the flavor and gelatin is followed by adding a variety of ingredients depending upon the occasion.

Included here is a soup using powdered almonds with cooked egg yolks and cream and then seasoned with nutmeg and mace. These ingredients could have been used in the middle ages, and were.

Mock turtle soup is substituted for real turtle as "when that very expensive, complicated, and difficult dish is prepared in a private family, it is advisable to hire a first-rate cook for the express purpose." Interesting job, that: turtle cook! Already by Miss Leslie's time what was once a commonplace and everyday food item was becoming increasingly scarce. Demands of population were affecting what was available even in the 1830s and 1840s.

Miss Leslie presents us with a true American classic, the soup known as Philadelphia Pepper Pot. Similar to what Mrs. Randolph gave us, this has become more the traditional definition of what a Pepper Pot is. Where the recipe appears herein in Chapter 12, I have modernized it a bit as most people simply do not have easy access to ox feet. The effect of cooking the tripe with the ox feet is to make a broth at the same time that the feet are cooking; remember how Miss Leslie was cooking in a large pot in a wood fired open hearth. It is now possible to use a large soup pot and cook the tripe in a pre-made beef broth. If you are more of a purist, use beef soup bones, which are readily available in most markets. If you have a real butcher shop nearby, you can probably order in some beef shins cut up.

This recipe with ox feet is what Escoffier called for when he wrote his legendary book,

La Guide Culinaire. And although his recipe is for Tripe à la Mode de Caen, the flavor and texture precepts are valid for the soup as well. He states that the feet are considered part of the tripe along with the honeycomb and all the stomachs. When Miss Leslie learned how to cook tripe for this American classic soup, it is fundamentally the same as Chef Escoffier documented later in the century.

Soups with ingredients native to America, including okra, catfish, lobster, and several kinds of beans, give indications of what a well versed household cook was expected to prepare on a daily basis.

Fish appear in the form of salmon, halibut, mackerel (a fish not much appreciated in our own time), salt cod and shad. As mentioned in Mrs. Randolph's chapter this was a mainstay of early American fish cookery, not least because of its availability throughout the East in rivers that drained into the Atlantic Ocean. Shad roe was also highly sought after and gave increased importance to this now uncommon fish.

The uniquely American soup, chowder, is here presented as a fish chowder made with alternating layers of onions and salt pork with layers of "firm white fish." Open hearth cooking was still common and the soup is to be "set on hot coals." As an aside Miss Leslie states clams may also be used for this all time classic American soup.

Shellfish were still relatively common. Remember that Chesapeake Bay is not far from Philadelphia, and until close in oyster beds became spoiled with polluted water, these were generally available without much trouble or expense.

Terrapins are here, distinct from turtles, lobsters abound, and our unique soft-shell crabs here are "soft crabs."

Many of these staples of American cuisine have become increasingly scarce and expensive. Seeing Miss Leslie's recipes makes one appreciate the bounty of ingredients that was present when our national food traditions were being created. That many of the historical foods are rare or non-existent now sometimes makes these everyday recipes almost prohibitively expensive.

All manner of beef parts are here: tripe, brisket for corned beef, smoked beef, and, of course, steaks. Miss Leslie says that the best beef steaks are cut "from the ribs or from the inside of the sirloin" (p. 74).

Miss Leslie gives almost eight pages of tips on beef—from how to judge fat ("white rather than yellow"), color of the meat ("the élan should be of a bright carnation red") and texture of the flesh ("it will feel tender when squeezed or pinched"). She cautions against discolored meat — a sure sign of severe bruising or meat that is spoiling.

Meat purveyors do not get off the hook at all. "See that the butcher had properly jointed the meat before it goes home." The fact that Leslie and her readers would be familiar with the commercial "jointing" of beef indicates how much knowledge a housewife had to have.

Her adherence to quality is expressed as to uses of certain cuts of beef.

- "Sirloin, fore and middle ribs": roasts.
- "Sirloin — it is the piece most esteemed."
- "The best beef-steaks are those cut from the ribs, or from the inner part of the sirloin." This is what we now call beef tenderloin. Anyone who enjoys a porter-house or t-bone steak gets both sirloin and tenderloin, one on each side of the bone.
- "The round is generally corned or salted, and boiled."

Directions for roasting beef are meticulous, with instructions about the fire, the use of a tin kitchen, washing and seasoning of the meat, distance from the fire, fat for basting, and the allowance "of about twenty minutes to each pound of meat ... for roasting." Her terminology here can be a bit confusing for a modern reader, as she labels as gravy what we would call juice from the meat.

Using only pan drippings diluted with hot water, she recommends serving the beef with horseradish with vinegar. Pickles and French mustard are also indicated as excellent condiments for roast beef.

Miss Leslie specifically makes a distinction between roast beef and a "baked beef." The baked beef is put in a pan with some water and potatoes, "either white or sweet ones." The meat is baked well-done and served with degreased pan juices and potatoes served in a separate dish from the meat. She cautions, however: "This is a plain family dish, and is never served for company."

Also included in the beef section is a mention of Yorkshire pudding, which may be used in place of the potatoes. Place the batter in the pan under the meat, which is elevated on a trivet. Miss Leslie advises to make the pudding thin as a thick layer will need turning in order to cook well. In a modern kitchen, we are more apt to heat melted beef fat in a muffin or popover tin and pour in a thin batter and bake separately from the meat. The best popovers are almost paper thin, crisp on the outside and moist on the inside. Not so far really from what Miss Leslie recommends and another way in which she still has influence on modern American food.

As an ingredient beef is here as stew, bouilli, hashed beef and beef cakes. Most are reflective of the English traditions with the exception of the bouilli. Miss Leslie gives recipes for tongue, heart and tripe; directions on how to corn beef; smoking and drying of beef along with beef pie, "a-la-mode," which is somewhat similar to Mrs. Randolph's and is made with a stuffing placed from where the bone was before the cook boned and pounded the meat until tender. Lots of fresh herbs, marrow, bacon in the pot, some water or wine for moisture and, "cover the pan closely, set it in an oven and let it bake for at least six hours."

Judging by the amount of beef recipes using beef as a main ingredient, this protein was already a staple of our national cuisine as far back as Miss Leslie's time.

Miss Leslie is on the money when giving tips on how to judge veal: "The flesh of good veal is firm and dry, and the joints stiff. The lean is of a very light red, and the fat quite white." The light red indicates a farm-raised calf who lived old enough to be grazing for a time, and the "quite white" fat is an indication that the calf was young.

What follows are things to look for when buying a veal head (make sure the eyes "look full, plump and lively"), and veal feet ("endeavor to get those that have been singed only and not skinned; as a great deal of gelatinous substance is contained in the skin"). Having a veal with sunken eyes indicates it "has been killed too long," and in the case of the feet, one of the principal uses for calves feet is for the gelatinous stock produced. This, when cooled, jells for making headcheese, fancy hors d'oeuvres and anything lined or coated with aspic. Now most cooks, even professional, used boxed gelatin, powder or sheets. "Veal should always be thoroughly cooked, and never brought to the table rare or under done, like beef or mutton. The least redness in the meat or gravy is disgusting." While modern diners may prefer a little bit of pink in their veal, remember that we are talking about animals raised in a totally dissimilar way to today. Also, tastes change over time.

Concerning roast veal, Miss Leslie simply states, "The loin is the best part of the calf." Still true today. When talking about her technique, she is talking about roasting an entire loin. Her serving suggestions state clearly, "In carving a loin of veal help everyone to a piece of the kidney as far as it will go." She also recommends that just before the veal is done, put a little flour on the roast and baste it with butter to give a nice crunchy crust to the meat.

Further on are directions for breast of veal, veal tenderloin (which sounds like an entire double rack) and the option of stuffing a veal shoulder with sausage meat. Veal shoulder is hard to find now, but is quite flavorful and makes wonderful stews and braised items and is the ingredient for the classic Blanquette de Veau.

Veal is presented in several ways, and as cutlet it is quite interesting. After frying the cutlets, which are cut from the leg of filet, Miss Leslie instructs the cook to make a pan sauce by removing most of the fat, adding a little flour and then the gravy. What is most interesting is that she suggests that one "mix with the breadcrumbs a little saffron." Evidently this most expensive spice, linked with cuisines in Spain and North Africa, was sufficiently available to deserve mention in her recipes.

Mutton takes pride of place with a dish of French origin, Cutlets à la Maintenon, prominent in this chapter. Our old friend Mutton (Chops) Harico makes its appearance again, showing that this dish was popular from the North to the South.

Mutton and lamb are grouped together; lamb is generally under one year of age, mutton is older. Depending upon the country, definitions change. Miss Leslie's tips for quality still apply. "The flesh of good mutton is of a bright red, and a close grain, and the fat firm and quite white." The same can be said of lamb. A more yellow fat indicates older age.

In an indication of fireplace cooking and cooking for a large family: "Lamb is always roasted; generally a whole quarter at once." For most people now, a leg or a loin or perhaps a shoulder would be as large as anyone would go outside of a professional kitchen or a festive event.

For serving, "always have some currant jelly on the table to eat with roast mutton. It should also be accompanied by roast turnips." If you are not sure about the turnips, try using a mix of ¾ mashed potatoes and ¼ mashed turnips seasoned with salt, pepper and whole butter, swirled together like vanilla fudge ice cream. "Pickles are always served with mutton," and Miss Leslie also suggests stuffing the leg with chopped lamb.

Her cooking times are longer than what we would expect now, but remember she was using a fireplace and not an insulated oven. But the meat is always to be well done although many people now prefer lamb with a goodly amount of pink, especially lamb rack and loin.

If there is a universal meat, pork must be it. Except where forbidden by certain dietary laws, pork is a staple in most cuisines around the world, wherever it is raised. This section of her book is larger than the veal and lamb sections combined, and that reflects the overall importance of pork in the cooking of her time. Fresh or preserved as ham or sausage, roasted or stewed, it has a prominent place here as it did with Mrs. Randolph.

As might be expected, pork appears in the guise of roasts, stews, hams, corned pork, "Pickled Pork and Pease Pudding," pork cutlets (aka schnitzel), New England Pork and Beans, and pork and ham pies. There are explicit directions on how to cure a ham. These types of directions would be valuable not only to settlers moving west, but to residents wherever they lived. Remember there was no refrigeration other than an ice-house stocked with frozen lake water every year. Curing and smoking were vital in Miss Leslie's time as a means of having enough to eat throughout the year. Transportation before railroads was not easy and if someone lived 10 or 15 miles outside of center city Philadelphia, or center city anywhere, they ate what they made and produced themselves. A trip of 10 or 15 miles could take a day or more.

Included here is a section on pig roasting, including "The pig should be newly killed, that morning if possible," and how to wash and prepare the pig for its roasting. She advises to save the heart and liver as well as the freshly cut off feet for making the "gravy." An example of her detailed instruction on the cooking itself: "The fire should be largest at the ends, that the middle of the pig may not be done before the ends." The "ends" of the pig have lots of fat and will remain juicy with a higher cooking temperature, more so than the middle, which is the rack and loin. They have less of a fat covering and if the heat were the same in front of the fire for the entire length of the pig, the center parts would be too dry and not up to her standard.

In Miss Leslie's time there was no shortage of game to use as a main ingredient for dinner or lunch. There were still professional hunters to supply city markets with all manner of game from venison to hare as well as different types of feathered game. Miss Leslie is talking about wild hunted venison, which was abundant and hunted by professionals along with a variety of other game animals, birds and waterfowl. Much of what was available then is not now, and all venison sold in markets is farm raised. In the case of New Zealand venison, the deer are free range in the truest sense in that they are unconfined, freely roam a large area, are killed and inspected before dressing and shipment. Venison is lean in comparison with domesticated animals, has a wonderful dark color and can be roasted, grilled or done to the same degree as beef or lamb. It tastes like "game" and has a firmer texture than other animals.

Venison bones make a rich, flavorful stock of which Miss Leslie makes good use. Her directions for roasting a saddle or haunch of venison are extensive. Miss Leslie advocates covering the loin with a paper covered with a rolled paste of flour and water and the fat side facing the fire. She specifies a spit for roasting. If that option is available, use it. Otherwise, roast venison in an oven preheated to 350°. (As it is roasting, baste it with clarified butter or rendered and strained bacon fat. Venison does not have a thick fat coating like a sirloin or a prime rib and benefits from basting often.)

It would take another few decades before this constant hunting would deplete most game stock to the point of scarcity. But game was always a large part of American cooking, from Native Americans to now, where "game" is farm raised.

When Miss Leslie is talking about meats, fish and seafood it is obvious she is concerned with quality and proper cooking. What is not so obvious is that reading between the lines, one can imagine some of the issues that would have confronted less well-versed housewives. And something else that is often overlooked in most recipe collections is that Miss Leslie was keenly aware of food hygiene and safe eating practices. Many of her directions are concerned with sanitation and proper food handling practices that now seem almost unnecessary. Proper cooking of uninspected meats and seafood along with temperature recommendations for storage of uncooked and cooked items helped insure that her readers would be preparing safe fresh as well cooked food.

To anyone who pays attention to the news, safe food handling is still a concern. Miss Leslie was concerned before people knew what caused sickness and took prudent steps to have her food be safe. This would have been a huge influence on her readers without their even knowing it. She was not aware of why certain procedures were better than others; she just knew it. And when a modern reader takes the time to read her directions clearly, this knowledge is obvious. When we talk about her influence on American cuisine, it does not hurt to think about her influence on the people who were cooking the food. If they followed many of her directions exactly, how many would have been spared the tragedy of a child dying of food poisoning, or a family member getting horribly sick from the contaminated food?

Miss Leslie gives good tips here on selecting poultry, and in the second paragraph makes an interesting point: Often if an animal is slaughtered the muscles need time to relax from the trauma suffered. And in the second sentence she makes a great point regarding food safety in that "all food when inclining to decomposition being regarded by us with disgust." This is in reference to the European tradition of hanging game until it started to rot before cooking due to the fact that there was no refrigeration anywhere. Meat that has begun the process of putrefaction is not fit to eat.

Referring to the previous comments about food safety, the following paragraph on frozen poultry and its method of thawing largely applies today. Poultry is to be thawed under cold running water or over time in the refrigerator. Again, here is a sound health practice in place before people knew why they were doing it.

In the poultry section are all manner of chicken dishes, including classic French fricassee along with croquets and what Miss Leslie calls "rissoles." The rissoles are the same meat preparation as for croquets but are placed on a circle of dough which is then brushed with egg and folded over to make a half-moon shape. Depending upon who is reading this, it is a chicken pasty, turnover or empanada!

There is also an interesting dish made with a "standing crust." The cook lines a form with a dough, bones a goose, a fowl, a piece of tongue and some ham and some other small birds, including bones. The birds are stacked inside the crust, which is sealed on the bottom and top, and baked for four hours in a "regular oven." This was a traditional English Christmas dish and is quite similar in concept to a trendy dish known now as "Turducken" for turkey, duck and chicken.

Small game birds include partridge, ortolans, snipes, woodcocks and plovers, most available now only to those who still hunt.

People today sometimes seem to think that our forefathers subsisted on gruel, bark and twigs. But when a reader looks at Miss Leslie's section on sauces nothing could be further from the truth. There are about ten pages of sauces here: anchovy, celery, nasturtium, white onion, brown onion, mushroom (stewed in veal gravy or cream), egg made with hard cooked eggs, bread, mint, caper, parsley, apple (for roast pork, goose and duck), cranberry, peach (made with dried peaches where she states "those are richest and best that are dried with the skins on"), wine sauce which is actually a dessert sauce, cold sweet sauce, cream sauce also for desserts and oyster sauce, not for desserts! Ingredients and tastes we may think of as modern or contemporary are in Miss Leslie's recipe folder a century and a half ago.

As a glimpse into Miss Leslie's era, there are 137 pages devoted to sweetmeats, pastry and puddings, syllabubs, cakes and warm cakes for breakfast. Certainly the American sweet tooth was alive and well in Philadelphia and shows how important high calorie foods were in the bad old days. While the recipes show a good knowledge of cooking techniques on Miss Leslie's part, such a large selection of bakery items would make the book valuable for persons of even modest means. Items such as flour, sugar and eggs are relatively low cost items compared to fresh meats, game, fish and seafood. A housewife need not worry about her family suffering simply because of their economic state.

Fruit was plentiful as most people farmed for a living, so pies, cobblers, and all manner of fruit desserts would naturally be a large part of most people's diet.

And for the complete household, there are recipes for beer, wine, shrubs and cordials, preparations for the sick, perfumery and a guide to "Animals used as Butchers' Meat."

The Recipes

Starting with the soups for which Miss Leslie was famous, she lays down some strict guidelines for how to make quality soup. In her "General Remarks" she starts off by saying, "Always use soft water for making soup, and be careful to proportion the quantity of water to that of the meat. Somewhat less than a quart of water to a pound of meat, is a food rule for common soups." Hard water is replete with minerals that can adversely affect the taste of the finished product. Her suggested quantity of meat will deliver flavorful results. She further states that soup should always be made from fresh, uncooked, un-chilled meat. Soups are not to be made from leftovers, as these leave the soup "indigestible and unwholesome, as well as unpalatable." Did I not say she does not mince words?

In a nod to the French influence on her cooking, she states, "*good* [her italics] French cooks are not, as is generally supposed, really in the practice of concocting any dishes out of the refuse of the table." Remember she did live in England for some time and was well acquainted with French and continental influences on food. And at the time of this book, there were quite a few French household chefs who came to the United States after their patrons in France succumbed to the Revolution.

Mrs. Randolph was on the cusp of a long lasting French influence on food in American kitchens, domestic and commercial, that was to last well into the 20th century and beyond. And Miss Leslie was also part of this admiration society for French food.

One of the best pieces of advice in the very next paragraph states: "Soup, however that has been made of raw meat entirely, is frequently better the second day than the first; provided that it is re-boiled only for a very short time, and that no additional water is added to it." This is good cooking common sense as it allows the flavors to meld and develop overnight. By reheating without overcooking or adding excess liquid, Miss Leslie guides the cook to preserve the quality of the finished product. It does not get overcooked and the flavor intensity is actually enhanced by serving the soup the second day.

Quality! "Every particle of fat should be carefully skimmed from the surface. Greasy soup is disgusting and unwholesome." Guess what happens in good professional kitchens? We learn a technique called "*depouiage*," which is to remove the grease from the soup. With a nod to health and nutrition Miss Leslie is on the money when she states that ingestion of excess fat is "unwholesome," something that could be stated in any modern cookbook.

Reflecting on a balance and simplicity of flavors harkening to the English side of her cooking, Miss Leslie states: "The cook should simmer the soup but very lightly with salt and pepper. If she puts in too much it might spoil it for the taste of those that are to eat it." The statement behind the words is that if a cook uses quality ingredients and makes her soup properly then a high level of seasoning is not needed; quality preparation speaks for itself.

Stating a technique from classical cooking: "Long and slow boiling [simmering] is necessary to extract the strength from the meat." When making a stock of veal or beef bones the stock slowly simmers in excess of eight hours to extract flavor, nutrients and texture. Even for a chicken stock, the simmering time is over four hours. Here as in our previous chapters, I take boiling to mean slow simmering and poaching as well as boiling. The recipe determines the technique, and someone who is familiar with good cooking will discern for him or her self that this crucial distinction is more a matter of syntax from a previous century rather than an incorrect application of a technique.

A little further on a recipe for a consommé is referred to as "rich veal soup." In a modern version, this is a brown veal consommé clarified with egg whites, as Miss Leslie indicates, with a change of technique: starting with a cold stock, we now slowly simmer the egg whites with a raft of ground meat, in this case veal, and *mirepoix* for about 45 minutes to clarify the soup. Her result is about the same with a note: "But it is better to have the soup clear by making it carefully, than to depend on clarifying it afterward, as the white of egg weakens the taste." If a stock is well made it is clear. This reveals a lot about how Miss Leslie worked, indicating that if a cook does not make her broth properly, than clarification will be needed. My guess is that she made her broth properly.

In a further nod to classical cooking (French) she calls for soupe à la Julienne. Julienne is a vegetable cut where items are cut in identical strips or, as she says, "Cut some turnips and carrots into ribbands, and some onions and celery into lozenges or long diamond-shaped pieces." These classical vegetable cuts are cooked separately, and added to the clear soup which then has small croutons floated on top, "taking care that they do not crumble down and disturb the brightness of the soup, which should be of a clear amber color."

Here again is the ultimate commitment to quality, accuracy of technique and the careful attention to detail that influenced more than one generation of American cooks. Miss Leslie instructs them in using a number of classical techniques used by professionally trained French chefs, and they did not know it. Miss Leslie has the ability to explain clearly what is needed in the production of her recipes, whether classically based or not.

In a final introductory nod to classical cooking techniques properly executed, Miss Leslie says that the practice of thickening a soup with flour is not a good one as it "spoils the appearance and taste." This is known as a whitewash, where flour is mixed with water or broth and stirred into a simmering soup. It adds little flavor and if overdone does spoil the appearance of the product. A well-made stock has flavor and texture from the gelatin extracted from long slow simmering.

Concerning fish and seafood it is clear from Miss Leslie's writing that both quality and hygiene were paramount in her kitchen. In the "Remarks" section she states clearly what to look for in selecting fish for the kitchen and then how to ensure quality and safety once there. "In choosing fresh fish, select only those that are thick and firm, with bright scales and stiff fins; the gills very lively red, and the eyes full and prominent." These are the basic qualities still sought for use in professional kitchens, and, hopefully, by the retail shopper as well.

She further states the fish must be cleaned and iced and insulated as soon as possible, cautioning that "even then do not attempt to keep a fresh fish till next day." This is reflective of quality and health concerns.

Details are given for mackerel and oysters specifying that oysters may be kept for a week "to a fortnight." To do this, "cover them with water, and wash them clean with a birch broom." Scrape away the sand and change the water daily in a cool place and sprinkle them "well with salt and Indian meal." Make sure the tub is well covered "with an old blanket, carpeting, or something of the sort." This flushes any remaining sand from the oyster and the "Indian meal" will actually work to fatten the oysters.

"It is customary to eat fish only at the commencement of the dinner. Fish and soup are generally served up alone, before any of the other dishes appear, and with no vegetables other than potatoes; it being considered a solecism in good taste to accompany them with any of the other productions of the garden except a little horse-radish, parsley, &c. as garnishing." This instruction combines both the English tradition of horseradish with fish and the French of serving steamed or boiled potatoes with fish.

Here as with Amelia Simmons and Mrs. Randolph, boil is a somewhat generic term that would now be refined by using words such as simmer or poach. Boil typically refers to a rapid rolling of bubbles at 212°F, whereas poaching is a more gentle 160–180°, simmering generally a little hotter. Overcooking of fish is the greatest problem most people and professionals have now.

However, Miss Leslie emphatically states regarding fully cooked fish, "It must however be thoroughly done, as nothing is more disgusting than fish that is underdone." Our modern conventions of seared tuna and rare salmon? Sashimi? Miss Leslie would not have approved!

Miss Leslie states that "potatoes are a part of every dinner," which is a far cry from the novelty of potatoes when Amelia Simmons was writing her book. This was in keeping with the ever-expanding role of potatoes in the kitchens of Europe as potatoes were emerging from being considered animal fodder into being perceived as a highly nutritious food for people. Here we also find sweet potatoes served as a side dish or used in a pork stew.

Vegetables in her recipes are legion: cauliflower; broccoli; spinach, which "requires close examination and picking, as insects are frequently found among it"; root vegetables, including turnips and carrots; summer and winter squashes; pumpkin; hominy, "Indian corn"; and eggplant, stewed, fried and stuffed. There is a recipe for fried cucumbers. "They make a breakfast dish."

Giving up the concept in American folklore of tomatoes being poisonous, she gives us recipes for "stewed and baked tomatas [sic]."

Eggs are represented in abundance. Again speaking to the skill of everyday cooks we have omelets, omelet soufflé, fricasseed eggs, which are boiled for about six or seven minutes, chilled and peeled. They are then breaded and fried and served for breakfast with fried parsley.

Dozens of pickling recipes are in the book, including pickled tomatoes, onions and cauliflower. We also have a recipe for "Tomata soy," which is salted tomatoes, boiled for a full day, cooled and strained for another day of cooking with cloves, mace, black pepper and cayenne. Small bottles are then filled and sealed with melted rosin. Miss Leslie's version of tomato catsup. She does say if made according to her directions and properly sealed, this concoction will "keep for years."

Slaw also makes a cameo appearance — two actually — as cold slaw and warm slaw. East India pickle and pickled oysters round out the recipes here.

A Few Words About Catchups

As you may remember from the chapter on Mrs. Randolph, catchups, now spelled catsups or even ketchups, were common seasonings prepared in the home kitchen from a variety of ingredients. These were not sweet; rather, they were savory to the point of spicy. What we have now available is a rather bland mutation of traditional American catchups. An oyster catchup might sound strange but think about an oriental oyster sauce which is a savory sauce of a similar nature and you see that we simply need to make a few adjustments and we are back in the flavor world of traditional American cuisine. Two are included in the recipe section, a real tomato (tomata in Miss Leslie's book) catchup and an unusual lemon catchup. Do not expect these to be sweet.

Recipes in the category of "Sweetmeats; including preserves and jellies" occupy about 140 pages. Many of the recipes are for the service of fresh fruits and, as may be expected, many for jams and jellies. Peaches, raspberries, cranberries, red currants (rarely seen fresh anymore), apricots, quinces (a sorely neglected fruit), apples, crab apples both green and ripe, green gages, purple plums, pears, gooseberries (when was the last time you saw fresh gooseberries?), black currants, strawberries, cherries, barberries, rhubarb. All these are preserved, made into jam or jelly or marmalade, or brandied. The bounty of summer would be available in the winter via all these recipes that showed the housewife and cook how to put food by.

Sweets were a big part of American food from the time the first fire was lit. Miss Leslie has custards, including an apple custard, custards in pies (as in pumpkin), all manner of puddings, including a sweet potato pudding with white potatoes (not sweet potatoes), sugar, butter, cream, rose water, wine, brandy and eggs along with lemon and spices. This is not to be confused with her sweet potato pudding, which directly follows her potato pudding. For anyone who lives or has lived in the Southeastern states, sweet potato pie is still a staple. So why not white potatoes as well?

There are some traditional items here — suet pudding, which uses melted suet in place of butter in what is a baked custard bread pudding; hasty pudding, which is boiled milk flavored with peach leaves thickened with flour "till it is about the consistence of a boiled custard." It is then optionally enriched with eggs or a little butter and covered with brown sugar. Looking to already established traditions, there are four types of "Indian" puddings as well as a surfeit of fruit-based desserts.

Syllabubs and trifles mingle with floating islands (a poached meringue famous in French cooking), charlottes, creams, ice creams and blanc mange.

Pages 334 to 391 are devoted to cakes: "Various sweetcakes and gingerbread" with a separate section on "Warm cakes for breakfast and tea; also bread, yeast, butter, cheese, tea, coffee, &c."

The cakes run the gamut from classic sponge and almond cakes to jelly cakes (a type of a seven layer cake), Bath Buns with saffron, the already traditional Election Cake and a Washington Cake that is leavened by the addition of pearl ash. As there were many German settlers in the Philadelphia area it is probably no surprise to find Moravian Sugar Cake here as well. After reading this recipe for the first time I realized this was a staple that my German grandmother made when I was growing up, even though we lived in New Jersey and not Pennsylvania.

Apees (a type of cookie flavored with caraway), marmalade cake, Secrets, Kisses, Crullers, dough-nuts, waffles, New York Cookies (which are similar to sugar cookies but with the addition of pearl ash); all manner of confections and gingerbreads round out the first 30 plus pages.

The breakfast section has pancakes galore, including the now famous Johnny Cake; rolls, French rolls and a large section on breads, stretching from page 374 to 379.

Do you want to know how to make: baker's yeast, butter, cheese, Stilton cheese, cottage cheese? Ask Miss Leslie. Do you not know how to make hot chocolate, tea or coffee? Ask Miss Leslie. Cordials, wines, beers, a cherry flavored whiskey concoction called "Cherry Bounce" that is more likely to make you lie down than bounce; punches, mulled wine and cider, egg nog and sangaree, which is watered down wine or porter with sugar added, are all available for the new homemaker.

Further on Miss Leslie included sections on "Preparations for the sick" and "Perfumery" along with two more sections of recipes.

This is a large book and would have served as an indispensable household volume whether a person lived in the city or was headed westward or lived in an outlying area away from any large towns. Not only did Miss Leslie include what by her time had become staples of American cooking, she delved into assorted foreign cuisines, most notably that of France, to augment her native recipes. We can see that by this time ingredients that were almost unique to Amelia Simmons were by now mainstream food items. Many of them still are.

And something not to be overlooked is her experiential knowledge of proper food handling, an issue that can still be a vexing one in the 21st century.

She was a skilled and talented writer who made her fortune by her well selling cookbooks, but her other books, especially her children's books, deserve more notice and certainly paved the way for this popular form of literature.

Through her recipes she documented the development of American cuisine and influenced countless numbers of home cooks. Her books give us a detailed picture of domestic life in the early 1800s in America's then largest city.

Her reputation endures but definitely needs some light shed on it for what she accomplished and contributed to American cuisine.

CHAPTER 5

Mrs. Abby Fisher

The birth of Mrs. Fisher in South Carolina as a slave and her rise to culinary prominence in San Francisco was the end result of a long process that started when Europeans first came to America. Native Americans, who were largely unable to survive European diseases, succumbed in staggering numbers throughout the then colonies. According to Charles Mann, fully 90 to 95 percent of Native Americans perished as a result of the horrendous European diseases — smallpox and typhus — to the mundane — measles and chicken pox.

With large swaths of the country virtually denuded of native population, labor was sought outside of the continental United States, particularly for agriculture in the South. The growing plantation economy of the South relied on slave labor, and the triangle trade that already existed between the United States and Britain, Africa and the Caribbean made the African continent the natural place to look for more of that needed labor. The trade was highly profitable and was a mainstay of North American seaborne commerce for centuries.

Molasses is a by-product of sugar cane refining and the Caribbean Islands experienced increasing amounts of sugar cane production after Europeans found out that the area was a nigh ideal place for this much in demand crop. As sugar refineries grew, their molasses was shipped to New England for distillation into rum, the preferred early American spirit. Traders would then proceed to Great Britain for manufactured goods and thence to various areas on the West African coast to pick up cargos of slaves destined for the sugar plantations. The triangle trade continued to earn large profits for sugar growers, plantation owners and New England merchants and shippers.

In what Mann cites as a devastating irony, maize made its way from Mesoamerica to Africa, where it became a staple food crop due mostly to its high per acre yields. This high yielding crop allowed populations to increase and this increase in population in West Africa made more Africans "available" for the slave trade.

In the American South the slave markets were busy, sending thousands to work in fields of cotton, tobacco and rice. The climatic and topographical features of the coastal South Carolina coast are well suited for the growing of rice and tea. Both of these crops are labor intensive and with the invention of Whitney's cotton gin at the end of the 18th century, plantation owners had the ability to produce increasing amounts of cotton. Hence, there was a ready market as well as a perceived need for the slaves imported from Africa.

French Huguenots fled in large numbers to different regions of America, including South Carolina. (An ancestral branch of my maternal family settled in northern New Jersey. And in New Paltz, New York, there are some historic houses still standing built by Huguenots in the 17th century.) Perhaps when coupled with the societal turmoil in France in the late 1700s and the ongoing persecution of French Huguenots, it is not surprising to have our Mrs. Fisher born of a slave mother and a French father in coastal South Carolina. In *The Huguenots of South Carolina,* Arthur Hirsch gives a detailed recounting of their influx and influence in the state. Their presence led to one of the great women of American cuisine, Mrs. Abby Fisher.

Throughout the time between Miss Leslie and the publication of Mrs. Fisher's book, the country struggled and suffered. Slavery was the impetus for much debate and legislation. An example of the continuing debate over slavery, territory gained from the war with Mexico allowed California as a free state, Utah and New Mexico were left undecided and subject to popular sovereignty and the slave trade was prohibited in Washington, D.C. But as part of the compromise legislation, the fugitive slave law was made stricter.

Uncle Tom's Cabin was published in 1852 and in 1857 the Dred Scott decision stated that Congress did not have the right to ban slavery in the states and that slaves were not citizens. This could lead to a freed or escaped slave being forced by law to be remanded to a slave state from a free state.

In 1860, while Mrs. Fisher was still a slave, Lincoln became president and South Carolina seceded from the Union that December, which set in motion a chain of events that led to the formation of the Confederate States of America, the Civil War and eventually the freeing of the slaves.

Eventually, the 13th, 14th and 15th amendments to the constitution were ratified, setting Mrs. Fisher free and guaranteeing the "inalienable rights" that heretofore had largely been reserved for white males.

The westward trend of population growth and land occupation continued apace and was to entice our author to remove with her family from the deep South of Alabama to the San Francisco area. In what can only be considered a profound irony, many of Mrs. Fisher's patrons who were responsible for the publication of her book were originally from the South. Although illiterate, Mrs. Fisher was able to work with the Women's Cooperative Printing Office in San Francisco to see her book created and published in 1881.

Not only was this the first cookbook published by an African American woman, but also it gives a glimpse into the culinary ethos and actual recipes that were prepared by Mrs. Fisher while a slave on various plantations. Indeed the book,

WHAT MRS. FISHER KNOWS

ABOUT

Old Southern Cooking,

SOUPS, PICKLES, PRESERVES, ETC.

Awarded Two Medals at the San Francisco Mechanics' Institute Fair, 1880, for best Pickles and Sauces and best assortment of Jellies and Preserves.

DIPLOMA AWARDED AT SACRAMENTO STATE FAIR, 1879.

San Francisco:

WOMEN'S CO-OPERATIVE PRINTING OFFICE, 420, 424 & 430 MONTGOMERY STREET,
1881.

What Mrs. Fisher Knows About Southern Cooking, is remarkable in many ways, not the least of which is the author herself.

Who Was Mrs. Abby Fisher?

Mrs. Fisher was born in South Carolina sometime in the 1830s to a French father and African mother. Her mother was a slave before her and San Francisco census records in 1880 note Mrs. Abby Fisher as a "mulatto." (The fact that she had a Frenchman for a father would surface many years later when Mrs. Fisher lived in San Francisco. In the 1900 census she identified herself as "white," as opposed to her previous status as a mulatto. This would most likely have been a boon to her business as a cook and pickle manufacturer.) Her duties as a kitchen slave revolved around the household and by slave standards, the owners favored her. It is likely that her years were spent as a companion, cook and general household servant. There is no mention of her being a field hand or doing anything other than household duties.[1] As a slave who spent most of her time in the kitchen, Mrs. Fisher would be the recipient and practitioner of cooking traditions and recipes passed from generation to generation.

In her cookbook she adds some personal information that is remarkable. By her own word she states simply, "I gave birth to 11 children and raised them all, and nursed them with this diet. It is a Southern plantation preparation." (Here she is referring to one of her creations, Pap for Infant Diets.)[2] For any woman to accomplish the feat of raising so many children to maturity was almost unheard of, let alone for a slave woman. Enslaved women were generally not allowed to keep their children and would often have them sold away from their care. A periodical article from 1862, originally published in the *Hartford Press* by an "officer in a New England regiment, now on service with Burnside," illustrates how a slave woman gave birth and was told by her master that he did not care what she did with him. Later on, as she narrates, "Massa Green com'd in and say 'Dis boy sold,' and dey take him away."[3] This seems to have been the norm for slave children; and the fact that Mrs. Fisher was able to retain, raise and see all her 11 children to adulthood is amazing, and speaks volumes about her personality.

PREFACE AND APOLOGY.

———— • ————

The publication of a book on my knowledge and experience of Southern Cooking, Pickle and Jelly Making, has been frequently asked of me by my lady friends and patrons in San Francisco and Oakland, and also by ladies of Sacramento during the State Fair in 1879. Not being able to read or write myself, and my husband also having been without the advantages of an education—upon whom would devolve the writing of the book at my dictation—caused me to doubt whether I would be able to present a work that would give perfect satisfaction. But, after due consideration, I concluded to bring forward a book of my knowledge—based on an experience of upwards of thirty-five years—in the art of cooking Soups, Gumbos, Terrapin Stews, Meat Stews, Baked and Roast Meats, Pastries, Pies and Biscuits, making Jellies, Pickles, Sauces, Ice-Creams and Jams, preserving Fruits, etc. The book will be found a complete instructor, so that a child can understand it and learn the art of cooking.

Respectfully,

MRS. ABBY FISHER,
Late of Mobile, Ala.

————

I take pleasure in referring, by permission, to the following of my friends, namely:

WM. F. BLOOD...................415 California Street, San Francisco
E. M. MILES ....413 Montgomery Street, San Francisco
WM. O. GOULD...................512 California Street, San Francisco
MRS. CHARLES S. NEALE ....1814 Sutter Street, San Francisco
MRS. JOHN HARROLD..............416 Chestnut Street, San Francisco
MRS. W. H. GLASCOCK............ ... .Oakland
MRS. G. H. COY .. .. .431 Geary Street, San Francisco
MRS. JOHN C. FALLS. .... San Francisco
MRS. LOUIS H. VANSCHAICK....... .....129 Page Street, San Francisco

During the 1850s, there was a move to Alabama where she met her future husband. In 1859 Mrs. Fisher married Alexander Cochet Fisher, also a slave, two years younger than she. The reason for the move is not known, but census records of 1870 tell us that three of her children were born in Alabama.[4]

In 1877 the Fisher family decided to move to California, perhaps in search of a more promising future. On the way to, probably, the Oregon Trail, Mrs. Fisher gave birth to her youngest child in Missouri. With all the attendant hardships faced by westward moving people, this must have been a daunting task. For two former slaves and 11 children, 13 mouths to feed during a hazardous trip two thirds of the way across the continent, this was quite a feat. It says much about Mrs. Fisher and her husband and their resiliency that they were able to survive plantation life, the Civil War, a good part of Reconstruction in Mobile, and such a perilous journey in search of a better life.

After her arrival in San Francisco, she established herself as a caterer in demand. The city was maturing, and wealth from the gold rush, the trans-continental railroad and shipping created a wealthy urban elite. In keeping with their status, these people hosted lavish dinner parties, and Mrs. Fisher was much in demand.

In what surely is an ironic twist of fate, many of her ardent devotees were émigrés to San Francisco from the "old South."[5]

While her reputation as a caterer continued, she and her husband started what we now call a specialty food business, manufacturing preserves, sauce and condiments learned in her 35 years experience as a plantation cook. The 1880 census listed Mr. Fisher as a "Pickle and Preserve Manufacturer" and Mrs. Fisher as a "cook." But it seems apparent that the driving force behind the business, from a production and client standpoint, was Mrs. Fisher.[6]

In this context, Mrs. Fisher was able to document through her food and home remedies the types of foods eaten in a low country plantation. These recipes reflect an almost unbroken connection between the foods of West Africa and the New World, and show how these two traditions came together to produce what we now call Southern food. What is also on display in this work is Mrs. Fisher's sense of style and her dedication to quality food production.

For example, in her beaten biscuit recipe is the phrase, "Put the dough on a pastry board and beat until perfectly moist and light." Nowhere does she mention the amount of time or work this actually takes; depending upon who is performing this task, it can take over half an hour. Her directions for roast beef say to baste the meat with lard or butter before roasting and then the cook must baste with pan drippings "every two or three minutes until done." This classic French technique assures a constant replenishment of moisture and fat to produce the finest roast possible. Her lemon pie recipe instructs the cook to roll the lemons, as this breaks the membranes in the lemon and releases the maximum amount of juice for the pie. For the apple pie, "the best of apples to be used."

But how did Mrs. Fisher, an illiterate former slave married to another illiterate former slave, come to write this remarkable book?

After moving to San Francisco, Mrs. Fisher was able to support her family by doing what she did best, which was cooking. By 1879 Mrs. Fisher was awarded a diploma at the Sacramento California State Fair and two medals at the San Francisco Mechanics Institute Fair in 1880. The prizes were awarded for pickles, sauces, preserves and jellies. Following these triumphs, Mrs. Fisher was able to dictate her recipes for her book and have it published by the Women's Co-Operative Printing Office in 1881. (The co-operative was listed in the 1900 San Francisco telephone book as Women's Co-Operative Printing Office, Mrs. L G

Richmond and Son propos, 424 Mont Street.) This organization was a century ahead of its time in promoting the rights of women in the workforce and society, with a special emphasis on having women employed in aspects of the printing business.

The cooperative was founded in San Francisco where there were a number of similar offices in the 1870s and 1880s. The Woman's Co-Operative Printing Union was founded in 1868 by Mrs. Agnes Peterson and continued under Mrs. Lizzie Richmond in 1873. It was a diversified operation producing everything from invitations to books to corporate reports to legal briefs. Women authored many 19th-century cookbooks and were moving into positions as editors and writers; some of the subjects that spurred this growth in professional opportunities were as diverse as spiritualism and women's suffrage. Some of their titles were *The Nature of Spiritual Existence and Spiritual Gifts* by Mrs. Cora Richmond and *Healing Power of Mind* by Miss Julia Anderson.

In a taste of what was to come, a book entitled *Clayton's Quaker Cookbook* by H.J. Clayton starts indentifying food products by place of origin, a trend that was continued and expanded upon by Victor Hirtzler at the St. Francis. Clayton also advocated buying directly from famers so consumers could be sure of quality and freshness, an idea that has resurfaced in recent times with locavores and Slow Food enthusiasts.

In her book, Mrs. Fisher lists her "friends," who were likely the women and men who had such enormous respect for her and her food that they took the time and made the effort to record her recipes and publish the book. To these generous people we owe a debt of gratitude, for without their dedication to Mrs. Fisher we might not have this singular book.

Her journey continued in San Francisco; in the 1900 U.S. Census she is listed as 68 years old, her husband 66. Both were able to read and write by that time; Abby had no occupation listed and Alexander, her husband, was listed a janitor. Certainly they were prosperous, as they owned a mortgage-free house on Twenty-Seventh Street in San Francisco. They also no longer listed themselves as mulatto, but "rather as white."[7]

Her recipes and parlance tell much about the life on a plantation, from meats selected for cooking to how to cure all manner of ailments without recourse to a doctor. Mrs. Fisher was at the opposite social pole from Mrs. Randolph in Virginia. Yet each of their books shines a spotlight on their respective places in society and the foods they cooked, the ethnic and cultural influences of these foods and how these items remain with us in the 21st century.

In the case of Mrs. Fisher, we see a woman of skill and dedication, one who is socially savvy to rise from literally the lowest rung of society in the antebellum South, to a respected and admired professional woman in the blossoming city of San Francisco a half century later. As a mark of her stature, her book is still with us. She is represented in The Henry Ford Museum/Greenfield Village and her reputation is solidly entrenched in our American cuisine. That she was for so long unknown to us is now a thing of the past and we can prepare her food and share her story more than a century later.

The Recipes

The numbers by the recipes that appear in Chapter 13 are the numbering from the book. Mrs. Fisher's page sequence is followed here even though, by modern standards, the book may seem to skip from place to place with numbered recipes out of sequence. Mrs. Fisher organized her book as follows: Breakfast Breads, Broiled Meats, Croquettes, Cakes, etc., Pickles, Sauces, etc., Pies, etc., Puddings, Preserves, Spices, etc., Roast Meats, Salads, Sherbets, Soups, Chowders, etc., Miscellaneous. The recipe numbers themselves are not in sequential order to coincide with page numbers. The table of contents is organized more like what is now called an index, with items listed alphabetically.

Recipes for the book were selected to demonstrate a wide variety of Mrs. Fisher's skills, to show what influenced her cooking and, in turn, what influences are with us still. In these recipes we are looking at a history, a still living history, of plantation life in the antebellum south and the foods that so impressed the people of San Francisco almost a half century later. If you try them, they will also impress you.

The organization of the book is by recipe number but not in consecutive order. For example, the first section, "Breakfast Breads," covers recipes one through ten. The next section, "Broiled Meats," are recipes 11 through 14. The third section, listed as "Croquettes," are 28 through 35; "Cakes, etc.," go from 60 to 72 and so on. There are 13 recipe sections in the book for a total of 160 individual items.

Taken as a whole they demonstrate Mrs. Fisher's skill as a cook, which she was later to parlay into a successful career. She shows a wide range of foods and cooking traditions, ranging from French to West African. There are numerous caveats about quality and correct procedures that were meant to create the best possible food regardless of whether the cook was making pancakes or pepper mangoes.

Breakfast items range from Maryland Beaten Biscuits to Sally Lund (Lunn) to Plantation Corn Bread or Hoe Cake. Broiled Meats includes roast meats from pork to venison, beef to birds (directions for birds are "In the same way," referring back to chicken which in turn referred back to turkey.)

Her directions for broiling a beefsteak are interesting. Mrs. Fisher says to turn it over after two minutes, remove it from the fire and stick it "through and through with a fork so as to let the blood run out." After her "twelve minutes" on a hot grill this would produce a steak well done, which may have been a personal preference or simply the way steaks were traditionally prepared in the plantations where she lived. Certainly it is a direct opposite of Amelia Simmons advocating rare as the best way to serve beef.

Eight different croquettes are listed with one called Veal or Lamb Vigareets. These, too, are a type of croquette but with veal or lamb brains replacing about half the meat in the recipe. Mrs. Fisher instructs, "singe all pin feathers off over the fire," when getting ready to make fricasseed chicken; her fried chicken is crusted only with flour and done "when the fork passes easily into it."

Soups are varied, with both real and mock turtle soups; both oyster and okra gumbos; corn and tomato soup and a soup for the sick which is, of course, chicken soup, that all purpose remedy for what ails you!

Her pies (probably the best known is her sweet potato pie) are to be made only with the best fruit available and her directions for pie pastry are extraordinary: Use of butter and lard in equal amounts, use of cold water until the pastry just "holds together." In her words,

> Sprinkle flour very lightly on the pastry board, and roll pastry out to the thickness of an egg shell for the top of fruit, that for the bottom of the fruit must be thin as paper. In rolling pastry, roll to and from you; you don't want more than ten minutes to make pastry.

The section on cakes makes me want to work in her kitchen: Gold Cake, Silver Cake, Almond Cake, Feather Cake.

On page 35 we switch to condiments and start with Chow-Chow and then a Creole Chow-Chow; there is a spicy cherry chutney that has no sweetening added to it. Mrs. Fisher has her version of a tomato catsup entitled "Compound Tomato Sauce, which contains tomatoes, onions, black and cayenne peppers, salt, allspice and cloves. After a night of standing to drain off the water, the batch is cooked in vinegar and cooked all day. You may want to know it will keep better in a demijohn than "in bottles when first made." In a note that sounds like an afterthought, she does note that if you do not like it spicy, reduce the pepper. "If you like it very hot use double the quantity."

Pickles, brandied fruits, preserves (quince again), jellies, blackberry syrup for children infected with dysentery are here; and in talking about her dysentery remedy she says, "This recipe is an old Southern plantation remedy among colored people."

Her soups are interesting and include recipes for fish and clam chowders, specifying that the clam chowder is made the same as fish chowder, except that tomatoes must be used.

There are several pudding recipes, vegetable preparations, and a Ladie's Custard. We have her recipes for Circuit Hash, Suet Pudding, Stewed Tomatoes, Oyster Pie and Yorkshire Pudding.

She shares the formula for infant pap that kept her children alive so that all 11 made it into adulthood — an amazing feat.

We may not have any photographs or other likenesses of Mrs. Fisher, but we can still "see" her through her work and life. With the recipes and remedies that Mrs. Fisher left us we get a glimpse into a vanished way of life — one that was transformed by Mrs. Fisher into an exercise in determination and steadfastness. She was an exceptional mother, an accomplished cook and a woman who shed a unique and wonderful light on our American cuisine.

CHAPTER 6

Lafcadio Hearn

Hearn's Introduction to *La Cuisine Creole:*

La Cuisine Creole [Creole cookery] partakes of the nature of its birthplace—New Orleans—which is cosmopolitan in its nature, blending the characteristics of the American, French, Spanish, Italian, West Indian and Mexican. In this compilation will be found many original recipes and other valuable ones heretofore unpublished, notably those of Gombo file, Bouille-abaise, Courtbouillon, Jambalaya, Salade a la Russe, Bisque of Cray-fish a la Creole, Pusse Café, Café brule, Brulot, together with many confections and delicasies [sic] for the sick, including a number of mixed drinks. Much domestic contentment rests upon the successful preparation of the meal; and as food rendered indigestible through ignorance in cooking often creates discord and unhappiness, it behooves the young housekeeper to learn the art of cooking.

It is the author's endeavor to present here a number of recipes all thoroughly tested by experience, and embracing the entire field of the "Cuisine," set forth in such clear, concise terms, as to be readily understood and easily made practible, thereby unveiling the mysteries which surround her, upon the entrée into the kitchen. Economy and simplicity govern "La Cuisine Creole"; and its many savory dishes are rendered palatable more as

LA CUISINE CREOLE

A COLLECTION OF CULINARY RECIPES

From Leading Chefs and Noted Creole Housewives, Who Have Made New Orleans Famous for Its Cuisine

SECOND EDITION

NEW ORLEANS:
F. F. HANSELL & BRO., Ltd.

the result of care in their preparation than any great skill or expensive outlay in the selection of materials. The Creole housewife often makes delicious morceaux from the things usually thrown away by the extravagant servant. She is proud of her art, and deservedly receives the compliments of her friends. This volume will be found quite different from the average cook-book in its treatment of recipes, and is the only one in print containing dishes peculiar to "la Cuisine Creole."

Of the authors presented in *The Founders of American Cuisine*, Lafcadio Hearn was perhaps the least likely, from a culinary standpoint, to produce an iconic text that not only defined and made known a dynamic and flavorful cuisine, but also did much to actually create a perception and definition of a major American city. As S. Frederick Starr has written, Hearn "virtually invented the notion of Louisiana, more specifically New Orleans, as idea and symbol."

As the country expanded westward after the Louisiana Purchase, the southern Louisiana port city of New Orleans grew and became a center for what we now call cultural diversity. With Arcadians, Americans, Caribbean natives, Spanish and French immigrants, slaves and black freemen, New Orleans truly became a microcosm of what many Americans would later come to call a "melting pot."

With New York, Boston and Philadelphia maintaining their importance as centers of immigration, there were rapidly expanding choices as to where the new immigrants could settle. States were being added to the Union on a regular basis — Nebraska, Colorado, North and South Dakota, Montana, Washington and Idaho — and as more and more people took advantage of the opportunities presented by great farmland and lots of it, seemingly endless tracts of forests and an entire west coast, other cities were seeing rapid expansion as populations grew in more westerly areas of the country.

Along with the growth of territory and population, the late 19th century was a period of great technological innovation. The first transcontinental railroad was completed in 1869 and this meant that it was easier than ever to "go west." For a relatively modest fee, a person could go from Omaha to Sacramento for $111 first class, which is roughly $1500 in modern currency. Second class was about half of that and third class about half of second class. In June of 1876 the Transcontinental Express travelled from New York City to San Francisco in 83 hours and 39 minutes, compared to about six months on the Oregon Trail.[1] This was a profound event for the country, truly linking and uniting east and west.

With blacks being granted the right to vote and citizenship via the 15th and 14th amendments to the Constitution, they could travel across the entire country, as evidenced by Abby Fisher. The increased ease of travel with a westward flow was also the impetus for both native-born Americans and immigrants to choose where in this vast country to live. Surges of national immigrants would settle in certain areas of the country — Scandinavians in the upper Midwest, lots of Germans and Bohemians in the Midwest — and many cities took on ethnic flavors when a certain ethnic group had a large population in the area.

Milwaukee had a reputation for brewing beer; most of the great breweries were founded by German immigrants.

In the area around Spillville, Iowa, there were so many Bohemian settlers that Antonín Dvořák spent several months there when he visited the United States in the late 1800s. There is still a Czech music festival in the town.

One of the distinguishing features of New Orleans is that in some of the areas mentioned above, cultural and ethnic homogeneity was what drew certain people to a certain area. In New Orleans, although there were definite social and racial barriers amongst the residents, the cross cultural mix created a kind of self sustaining energy where each group brought something to the table. Languages, dialects, foods, dress, family structures, religions — kind of a crazy quilt hodge-podge that enveloped Hearn in its magic and mystery.

As a world refugee, our man Lafcadio Hearn came to America via New York City, then after about four years relocated to Cincinnati where he started his writing and translating in earnest. He then relocated yet again to New Orleans. He remained there for ten years and in those ten years became enraptured with the Creole culture, language and dialects, produced the first cookbook highlighting this uniquely American cuisine, defined a city, made Creole culture known beyond the confines of New Orleans and invented comparative linguistics and ethnography along the way.

Who Was Lafcadio Hearn?

Patricio Lafcadio Tessima Carlos Hearn was an international journalist, author, comparative linguist, translator, educator and wanderer whose career and life imbued him with a sense of wonder, astounding knowledge and a love of cultures as disparate as New Orleans and Japan. He had a penetrating eye for what constituted the essence of a society's culture and was able, through his skill as writer and journalist, to make these traits available and understandable to a wide audience.

The cosmic cultural mishmash in Hearn started before his birth when his father met his mother. Charles Bush Hearn was a surgeon of Irish ancestry serving in the British Army in Greece when he met his future wife, Rosa Tessima, who was born on another island, Leukas.

Rosa was the daughter of a well-to-do family who would have nothing to do with their daughter marrying an officer in the army of occupation. They eloped, Hearn was born shortly thereafter and his father was transferred to the Caribbean but left the family behind on Leukas. The family could not remain there and were relocated to Dublin to live with a distant aunt.

Things went downhill from there, however. Charles Bush Hearn was an infrequent visitor to his family's home; he remained distant and was found out by Rosa to be living with another woman in the Caribbean. She divorced him and went back to Greece with a rescuing cousin and left the young Lafcadio with the aunt.

The man who invented New Orleans.

The aunt apparently was a woman of means and sent Hearn to a Jesuit school in France where he learned to hate the Jesuits, the Catholic Church and organized religion in general. The religious schooling did seem to imbue him with a long-lasting interest in the occult, the macabre and stories concerned with superstition and myth, which was to influence his writing later on. After changing schools a number of times, Hearn was sent back to France from England, where he promptly ran away from school to immerse himself in the Latin Quarter in Paris. The aunt suffered a reversal of fortune and Hearn found himself on the way to America.

After two years in New York, Hearn travelled to Cincinnati where a printer, Henry Watkin, befriended him. Hearn learned proofreading and typesetting and started writing articles and translating French novels on a regular basis.

Hearn, who was an avid reader and writer, submitted a story to the *Cincinnati Enquirer* and was hired as a reporter. Always the mutli-culturalist, he did reporting while continuing his translating of contemporary French authors' works into English. He achieved a reputation as a reporter who specialized in gruesome or bizarre crimes, and presented the stories in a vivid, personal style while still being able to write factual accounts.

His writing is penetrating and objective, yet atmospheric at the same time. In 1877 Hearn was in New Orleans, where, after a slow start and a bout with dengue fever, the "lite" version of yellow fever, he began writing for a minor fringe paper called *The Item*. His assignment was to write about what he wanted to write about, which in his case were everyday stories about New Orleans and tales bordering on the gothic. These collected stories he wrote were like germinating seeds in the creation of the idea of New Orleans.

He continued his French translations while turning out an impressive amount of work and soon got noticed by the editor of the *New Orleans Times-Democrat,* which was the primary paper in New Orleans.

New Orleans, being a city of varied cultures, was a virtual paradise for Hearn. He became engrossed in Creole culture, the high end of French and Spanish traditions and influences of the upper classes, and the everyday culture of African and Latin working people.

Hearn spent a lot of time *being* in New Orleans, recording the people, traditions, superstitions and daily life of the city. Many of these observations were published in his newspaper articles and drew portraits in words of the essence of the city and the people as surely as a painter would depict the scenes on canvas. Learning the Creole patois, he was able to mingle with the populace and become one with the city he was helping to create.

The following years were the happiest of his time spent in America and in 1882 he published his first book, called *Cleopatra's Nights and Other Fantastic Romances.* This was a translation of stories by Gautier, and in 1884 he authored a book, more of an anthology, of folktales and stories from a wide variety of cultures including Inuit, Hindu, Arabic, Jewish and others; it was the result of an intense study of world religions and cultures and this penetration into the mythic worlds of human culture and the psyche would travel with him for the rest of his life.

This fascination with culture and myth led in 1885 to two seminal studies of Creole culture. One of these is *Gombo Zhebes: A Little Dictionary of Creole Proverbs.* This landmark book of comparative linguistics notated and translated tales taken down in six different Creole dialects, all of which Hearn mastered, from New Orleans and the Caribbean. In *Lafcadio Hearn's America,* discussing "Creole patois," Hearn said, "Creole is the maternal speech." It is the language of the home and family and all the attendant events that orbit around the home. Reflecting on the physical and sound and emotional feeling of the Creole language and its dialects, Hearn referred to them as "lingual caresses."

In a recently released book of his writings entitled *Inventing New Orleans,* the editor S. Frederick Starr succinctly portrays how Hearn was, indeed, largely responsible for how New Orleans and Creole culture are viewed, even in our own time.

> In ten years of serving as a correspondent and selling his writing ... he crystallized the way Americans view New Orleans and the its south Louisiana environs.

With his study and observations of Creole life in all its facets — from the death of its most famous voodoo practitioner, Marie Laveau, to séances, sexual debauchery, home life, medical remedies, partying, corruption and its overall sensation of strangeness, frivolity and "otherness" — Hearn set New Orleans apart from all other areas of the United States. In reading his work, one almost feels as if Hearn is writing about a city and a culture in an entirely different country than the United States. The culture of the city was created by its remarkable diversity of ethnic sources, which expressed themselves in its social rituals, mystery, language and food.

Hearn was also mesmerized by the climate found in New Orleans, a mixture of subtropical heat and humidity coupled with occasional bouts of cold weather and cataclysmic hurricanes, one of which he wrote about in his novel, *Chita.* This was an unnamed, late 19th-century hurricane that was similar to Katrina in the havoc it wreaked upon the area and the city.

His love for the city in all its seamy guises and wonder, its degradations and grandeur of its architecture, held sway over him to such an extent that he wrote "It is better to live here in sackcloth and ashes than to own the whole state of Ohio." (Remember he came to New Orleans from Cincinnati.) That he was able to recount the many contradictory facets of his city still can move people who take the time to read his works. Two modern authors, Louis Maistos (Hearn could tell so much of the daily reality of the city)[2] and Susan Larson (commenting on his "portrayals of the French Market")[3] both remark on how, over a century after he left New Orleans, his perceptions and powers of description still resonate in the city.

His perceptions and descriptions of the Creole culture and its people proved a valuable resource for inspiration in his writings about the city and its people. And these same perceptions and insights live with us today, over a century later, in how we as Americans see the city and Creole cuisine.

The other seminal volume in the exploration and exposition of Creole culture was *La Cuisine Creole,* which for the first time set down the culinary traditions and artistry of the people of the city. It may seem strange to have a person who did not cook for a living, or even very much for himself, write a cookbook. But food is an integral part of Creole culture and it had Hearn's full attention the whole time he was in New Orleans. He published the book anonymously, in part because he did not want to be known as a cookbook author.

The publisher, Will Coleman of New York, tacked the book of recipes onto the publication of *Gombo Zhebe* in an effort to sell more books by including recipes with the more esoteric parts of the book. Timing was not good, and the books came out too late to be money generators for the 1884–85 World Industrial Exhibition. But the cookbook sold well anyway and was reprinted within a year by a New Orleans publisher, F.F. Hansell.

As the first printed collection of Creole recipes, this book helped preserve a tradition that is still living and vibrant in the 21st century. *La Cuisine Creole* set down and helped define this unique aspect of our American culinary heritage and made it known beyond the confines of New Orleans. It served as the inspiration for the 1901 Creole cookbook published by the *Times-Picayune,* and it is still considered the most authentic sources for this cuisine anywhere.

The recipes in Hearn's book document the domestic aspect of Creole life, and his "Introduction" begins to correct the frequent misunderstanding of Creole cuisine. It is not a cuisine of searing heat and flashy preparations. Rather, it reflects the lives, customs and traditions of the people Hearn came to love and from whom his affection was returned. His is a cookbook documenting a culture through its food. A careful reading of his introduction will give many hints as to the day-to-day living of the Creole housewife, cook, family and culture. His statement concerning how a Creole housewife "often makes delicious *morceaux* from the things usually thrown away by the extravagant servant" speaks to the fact that Creole cuisine as Hearn experienced it is truly a cuisine of the people and hence, the city itself; a dynamic part of the culture as a whole. The tone is one that speaks of frugality and creativity and the ability to produce exquisite food without having the resources of a wealthy household at one's disposal.

Anyone can produce great food with the best ingredients and a large budget. Indeed, if a cook could not do that, then there would be something very wrong with his or her culinary acumen! The real test of a skilled cook is to take what is available and make these ingredients into a dish that transcends its component parts. As Hearn's book shows, this was part and parcel of a Creole cook's bag of tricks and was responsible for the building of a cuisine from the ground up: being able to use the local ingredients with the complex influences of cuisines from around the world, along with some classic cooking techniques, home-style cooking traditions and innate sense of good taste. *La Cuisine Creole* served as a microcosm of the nature of American cuisine itself. The blending of ingredients, domestic and imported, and various national cooking traditions to make something new and vibrant — Creole cuisine is both model and component of the larger American cuisine.

Hearn's first paragraph states the dishes that most people are familiar with in Creole cuisine: Jambalaya, Cray-fish Bisque, Gombo file. But beverages also play a large part in this cuisine. The mixed drinks and the service of the drinks as described in the book create an atmosphere that can transport the reader to a Creole bar or a spooky Creole séance. What would be missing from New Orleans if Pusse Café, absinthe and Café Brule were not in existence? All aspects of this cuisine speak not only of individual recipes — taken as a whole they show a culture, a cuisine and a life of colorful clothes and people, dark voodoo and occult mysteries and the thriving acceptance and inclusiveness that encompass so many of our world traditions into one cuisine and one city. And it is this presentation of the totality of *La Cuisine Creole* that served to define the culture and existence of a people and a great city.

In 1887 Hearn left New Orleans and published a collection of legends and folk tales as well as his first novel, *Chita.* In 1890 his *Two Years in the West Indies* was published while he was living in New York. He published a second novel, *Youma,* about a slave rebellion, and received a commission from *Harper's Monthly,* the publishers of his first novel, to travel to, and write a book about, Japan.

This was a fateful event for Hearn: He left America in 1890 and never returned. Shortly after arriving in Japan, he started teaching English in Matsue, later moving on to Kyushu. Always a prolific writer, his constant stream of articles was syndicated and became well known. His marriage to Setsu Koizumi in 1891, and the subsequent births of their four children, anchored Hearn in Japan for the remainder of his life.

Hearn legally changed his name to Koizumi Yakumo after his marriage to Setsu Yakumo and became a Japanese citizen. A planned lecture series that Hearn was to present at Cornell University was cancelled due to a typhoid epidemic and he never did return to America after that. He died at the early age of 54, apparently of heart disease, on the island of Honshu. Honshu, when Hearn lived there, was a bit of relic in that it was still a feudal city. It is now a "New Industrial City," so designated by the Japanese government, but Lafcadio Hearn's house is wonderfully preserved and is treated as a bit of a shrine. His influence is still present in Japan, as school children find themselves reading about their country from this unique author.

While in Japan, he authored 12 books on Japan and made the country known around the world. Considered the world's leading authority on Japan, he translated many legends and stories and wrote original works which possess an almost other worldly, misty, haunting intensity.

His work and his heritage combined to make him a true multi-culturalist. His writing gave voice to his penetrating perceptions and understanding of cultures that were all but unknown in America and Europe at that time. Indeed, a unique facet of all his writing is its ability to delve into the meaning and the spirit of a topic, whether a folk tale or a crime story, and search out the emotion and verity behind the surface appearance of the story or event.

His writing in Japan made this culture known to Americans and Europeans on a scale not achieved before or since. His depth of perception, and the validity of his conclusions, retains a freshness and immediacy more than a century later.

Hearn displays an understanding of people, language and culture that asserted itself in whatever culture he chose to immerse himself. From Inuit mythology to Japanese folk tales to Creole language and cooking, we see a man of great understanding and acceptance who still has the ability to shine the light of profound understanding on people around the world. His life and works reflect his fascination with and gift for portraying the most grotesque and gruesome aspects of life along with some of its most worthy and heart-felt sentiments. His perceptions of cultures and languages gave rise to new academic disciplines that thrive in our time.

It seems he is more well known and appreciated in Japan than here in the United States. In Japan his house is a museum and children are introduced to his writings in the early years of their schooling. His cookbook gives modern readers the opportunity to learn the city and Creole cuisine from the man who "discovered" the culture.

The Recipes

La Cuisine Creole is a large book of over 250 pages with a table of contents at the end. Foods are arranged by category and are presented this way herein in Chapter 14. As in other chapters, some suggestions are made in the recipe section to allow for modern appliances and products but the recipes are true to form. What is to be remembered is that these recipes are from the homes of the people in whose culture Hearn immersed himself for ten years, and the food he presented was both an expansion of his love for the culture itself as well as a method for the food to become better known on its own terms.

The discussion of the recipes starts with Hearn talking about soup. "Nothing more palatable than good, well-made soup, and nothing less appetizing than poor soup." What

Hearn says here is similar to what Charles Ranhofer believed as well. A well-made soup is the hallmark of a good cook. (See the chapter on Ranhofer and remember that Ranhofer also spent some time in New Orleans.)

Hearn states that cooking should be considered a science, and an understanding of ingredients a requisite for making good food. He also states that most female cooks do not think of this but that "men with their superior instinctive reasoning power are more governed by law and abide more closely to rule." This is given as the reason men get paid more than women. A creature of his times was this Hearn — able to penetrate in some areas of understanding and utterly lacking in others.

The general precepts here talk about the heat of the fire, the desire to keep one pot for soup only, detailed cleaning instructions on its care and sanitation, and a list of how to proportion ingredients to make a good soup. Certain ratios and relationships defined what a good soup could be and they are clearly stated here.

For example, Hearn states "Soup must have time to cook." This seems self evident, but then the explanation makes clear that the soup needs to "boil gently" (simmer) to achieve tenderness of the meat and extract all the juices. His directions for ratios are simple: one quart of water and one teaspoon of salt for one pound of meat, 1:1:1. In directing that "soup meat must always be put down in cold water," he affirms a classical French technique whereby the impurities of the meat are extracted as the temperature slowly rises in the pot and the surface must be skimmed of the resultant scum. This is done in making a stock and even though Hearn is actually making a broth for his soups, the same principle applies.

The Creole cook would use a variety of mixtures of vegetables depending upon the soup. "One large leek, two carrots, one bunch of parsley, two turnips and a potato, will be enough for one pot of soup." For a soup to be served twice the amount goes up but the ratio stays the same. A different style of soup calls for peeled and seeded tomatoes, leeks, parsley and potatoes replacing the first style. "Okra alone is vegetable enough for a gombo, unless onion is liked with it"; more on gombo and okra later. Making a soup with spring lamb? Then "green peas, lettuce and new potatoes" will fit the bill.

Directions for minimizing prep time, how to peel and scrape carrots, and how to peel and seed tomatoes, some of the first things a culinary student learns, are included here. This is significant because it speaks to the high skill level of Creole cooks and the techniques they employed on a regular basis to the extent that said techniques were considered important enough to describe the cuisine to non-residents of New Orleans.

For his stock pot, economy rules and as in many commercial kitchens Hearn advocates that "all cooks know that the most economical plan is to have a general stock pot," which serves as a receptacle for bones, meat trimmings, ham, turkey, any manner of fowl with the addition of seasonings and herbs. His key point that a Creole cook would understand in a practical sense is that "anything that will become a jelly will assist in making stock." This is because the texture of a soup or sauce is largely determined by the gelatin content in the basic stock. This is also how an aspic is made — with a clarified, highly gelatinous stock. For a better quality soup the Creole cook would use "the jelly from a cow heel" to impart a more luxurious texture to the finished product. As if teaching in a culinary school, Hearn carefully specifies the removal "of every particle of fat" from the stock after it has cooled.

There is a section on clarifying a stock for a crystal clear presentation. This is especially important for clear soups, consommés and aspic. His stock is clarified with egg whites alone and strained through cloth and a sieve. This is in contrast to his stock for gravies, which is veal knuckle and lean beef, which are covered and simmered with salt and pepper, then strained but not clarified. Generally a gravy is thickened with a roux or flour or some other starch and does not need to be as clear as a clear soup or consommé.

In a decided break from some other authors Hearn simply says, "Always keep a pot or stewpan in which to throw all nice pieces of meat left from dinner, also any steak, bines, chicken wings, etc. This makes a reserve stock with very little fresh meat. It is useful and economical, and, being without vegetables, never sours." I am not sure about the last part, but this is similar to the way many professional kitchens still make stock.

He also provides details on how to color a soup — spinach for green and burnt sugar or browned flour for a richer appearance; pureed tomatoes for red, okra for pale green and carrots if amber is desired.

Soup was to be the start of a good meal. But it could also serve as a medicinal preparation. The universal chicken soup makes its appearance in a Creole cookbook as a "young fowl" boiled slowly and gently, skimmed and enhanced by the "white heart of a head of lettuce and a handful of chervil." Pearl barley would complete the Creole penicillin to make "it quite a nourishing soup." Folk remedy? The broth, which is skimmed, would be fat free and easy to digest with the proteins leached from the meat into the broth. The addition of hearts of lettuce and the wonderfully fresh and delicately aromatic chervil makes the broth appeal to the taste buds and the barley would provide starchy calories as well as added protein and trace nutrient.

The "Cray-fish Broth for Purifying the Blood" is similar in that it uses lean veal and cray-fish as protein sources and the appealing aroma and delicate taste of chervil again. Often when people are ill, their nutrient intake suffers because food prepared for them is tasteless. The Creole cooks obviously knew that if a broth were to aid a sick person, it would have to taste good enough that they would eat it — common sense that is not always practiced today when it comes to food for sick people.

We have plain beef soup, which is made by simmering beef shin or leg meat with vegetables for "four hours and a half." It is a soup, a broth really, made with the meat and a slew of vegetables that are all strained out before service. It is optional that if the cook wants to serve the meat with the soup for dinner, about two pounds out of five pounds of meat be taken out of the pot about two hours before service. The remainder of the soup would be "strained through a hair sieve before service." It is really a long simmered beef broth with added nutrients and flavors from the vegetables served as a plain broth.

Soup et bouilli is more flavorful with the addition of garlic and served with vegetables, "previously boiled and cut into shapes." In modern parlance we would say the vegetables were tournéed or cut paysanne or julienne to more accurately describe their shape. The soup is made more substantial by thickening with a roux and served in a tureen with a French roll in the bottom. Hearn also suggests adding a "spoonful of French mustard."

There are broths in haste, soup maigre for lent; rich soups including a Scotch Barley Broth, "Cheap and substantial."

There are soups that are baked (all the meat and vegetables are put in a pot or pan that Hearn calls a jar, seasoned, covered and baked until done and strained), clear, with vermicelli, and made from peas (Queen Victoria's Favorite Green Pea Soup followed immediately by Economical green pea family soup with egg dumplings). Why Queen Victoria? Hearn gives us a clue later on in this chapter. There are soups made of green corn ("very delicate"), oysters ("delicate" or "very strengthening" depending upon the version selected), turtles, more mock turtle soups than "real" turtle soups, and then he adds in ox-tail and rabbit soups.

"Remarks on Gombo of Okra or Filee" gives detailed instructions for the use of two of the seminal ingredients most often associated with Creole cuisine: okra and filee, or gumbo filee. The gombo part is the soup itself and as Hearn says "is an economical way of using up the remains of any cold roasted chicken, turkey, game or other material to make the soup." After simmering the soup and removing the bones, "add okra or a preparation of dried and pounded sassafras leaves, called filee. This makes the difference in gombo." By implication the gombo must use either of these ingredients to make the quality soup he sought. In addition to the left-overs, gombo could be made with oysters, crabs and shrimp if seasonal, and the soup was never to be strained but could be served with "plain boiled rice." Some specialized instructions for crab and shrimp versions follow, but it is interesting to see that these seafood gombos are made with a beef broth and heavily flavored with bacon, bacon fat or lard — items modern cooks do not usually associate with seafood soups, but that are one of the hallmarks of Creole cooking.

A "simple okra gombo" relies on beef bones as well as cubed veal brisket along with the requisite okra pods and onion being cooked brown before the addition of any water. These recipes produce a hearty, nourishing soup with multiple layers of flavor. Mixing seafood and beef broth thickened with filee or okra creates a complex, flavorful and multi-textured soup that, while it may have been a staple of home cooking, displays remarkable sophistication and complexity. Flavors in well-made soups and sauces reveal themselves in layers, often depending upon the temperature of the soup at the time of its tasting. Flavoring compounds in sauce work the same way and in order for this to happen, ingredients must be selected to create the layers of flavor. This is what the Creole cooks knew by experience.

There are gombos with chicken and oysters; oysters and chicken; maigre oyster gombo; maigre shrimp gombo for lent; crab gombo; a seemingly endless set of variations on a theme that is presented as a simple and everyday component of home cooking that ends up displaying how accomplished a good Creole cook needs to be.

The "Crayfish Bisque — A Creole Dish" shines with the flavors of this cuisine and shows a seamless integration of a classic French compound roux with a myriad of flavors that combine beef stock, crayfish, ham, sage, butter, thyme and bay leaf.

Fish cookery talks of Fricassee of Fish where large fish are to be used. Although not a classic fricassee, it is a type of fish stew with onions, tomatoes, garlic and parsley; very Mediterranean in concept. Maybe that needs a little qualifying as Hearn says in the last sentence, "Add catsup if liked."

Fried fish is to be fried in salt pork or bacon as it will produce a much better product than lard. Hearn also shows that the Creole cook knew how to get a well browned and crispy fish by removing all surface moisture and using enough fat to "float the fish," which allows for even browning and maintains frying temperature so that the fat is not unduly absorbed into the flour that coasts the fish.

Fish that is baked and stuffed and a flavorful Trout à la Venetienne that is stuffed with parsley, butter, lemon, thyme, basil and chives, covered with oil, then coated with "chopped sweet herbs" and broiled. (The book actually says boiled but that would produce a mess and broiling makes better culinary sense.) Although it has an Italian name the dish shows classic French herbs used in a traditional French way.

Spanish mackerel is seasoned with salt and pepper and grilled, still the best way to cook this fish. Flounder is broiled and offered up fried with mullets, which "are very fine when fresh from the waters of Lake Pontchartrain."

Snapper appears as snapper or red fish and is boiled, although not really boiled at all.

Hearn says to "cover it with soft water and throw in a handful of salt. As soon as it begins to boil, skim and let it simmer; hard boiling breaks the fish." The Creole cooks here would be poaching the fish; sometimes these recipes need a more in-depth reading if one is to deduce what was actually meant in the recipe. As cookbooks evolved the directions tended to get more and more specific.

In another nod to French traditions in Creole cooking we find Red-fish à la Provencale. This is an intensely flavored preparation that uses a fish marinated with carrots, onions, parsley, bay leaves, garlic, lemon salt, pepper and oil. It is then baked while being basted with butter and wine. The sauce is finished with additional wine, reduced and seasoned with cayenne pepper and garnished with capers and lemon.

Oysters appear in a stuffing for turkey, a stew made with champagne and stewed with milk as a "nice little dish for a luncheon or a late supper." Oysters are fried, scalloped, pickled, made into a pie with sweetbreads and with beef. The scalloped oysters are a simple dish — oysters and some of their liquor in a baking dish, covered with breadcrumbs and "served hot with tomato or walnut catsup poured over them." American condiments in a Creole household being used in a French style of cooking — talk about fusion cuisine!

One of the more interesting dishes here is a "Beefsteak and Oyster Pie." While we may not think of these ingredients as compatible, it seems the Creole cooks found a tasty way of combining them to produce a mix of a traditional English-style savory pie with a true Creole twist.

There is a fairly gruesome recipe for a "Fricassee of Crabs" that demonstrates how terminology of food preparation can change from one culture to another. A classic fricassee is made by stewing veal or chicken that then uses the cooking liquid as a base for the sauce. The meat is not browned at all and the sauce when finished is a white sauce, generally enriched with cream and egg yolks, what is called a liaison.

In this Creole version, Hearn directs us to take "fat crabs" and cut off their legs while still alive, clean them while still alive and set them aside for a while. A couple of onions are then browned in butter and lard with flour added to make a brown roux. Parsley, green onions and boiling water are added to make "the gravy." The still live crabs are then added to the boiling "gravy" and simmered "in the gray for half an hour." these are then served with boiled rice and Hearn admonishes, "Parboiling the crabs destroys their flavor; they should be alive to the last minute." This recipe is a good example of how an idea is carried over from one cuisine to another with local adaptations creating an entirely new dish, albeit based on a centuries-old model.

The crab fricassee uses a hallmark of Creole cooking, the browned roux as thickening and flavoring agent. Why a brown roux? It adds a lot of color and a nutty taste to the liquid as it thickens. On a more subtle level, a browned roux has less thickening power than a white roux, pound for pound, which was often used in a more traditional fricassee. The result is a more colorful and flavorful dish that is not as heavy as a more traditional roux-thickened sauce.

Detailed directions for cleaning a turtle, preparing terrapin and frog's legs round out the seafood. Note here that turtle and terrapin are listed separately even though a terrapin is a turtle. We can attribute its frequent appearance in recipes of early American cooks to the fact that terrapins are native to coastal marshlands along the eastern seaboard.

Following is a section on cold meats, a spice preparation for "meat pies, etc." and some truffles used in stuffing recipes for pig and turkey. These must have been locally harvested truffles or canned, as fresh truffles from France or Italy would have been almost impossible to ship to New Orleans without rotting.

Sauces include tomato sauce; cranberry sauce; and Sauce Piquante for cold meat, which is made with sweet herbs, carrots and vinegar, all rubbed to a smooth paste. There are several incarnations of Sauce Piquante that all have the acidic snap of a good vinegar. The acid will balance any richness in the item to be sauced as well as help to cleanse the palette, which will make the food taste better.

The French influence is shown by a group of sauces bound with a roux — "Butter and flour sauce or white sauce" — followed by variations or derivative sauces that use capers, parsley, lemon, or lobster roe for Sauce à l'Aurore, for fish. Later on there is a recipe, Sauce number 21, that is a "savory jelly for cold turkey or meat." It is a highly gelatinous sauce, well seasoned, clarified and further seasoned with mace and wine or lemon juice and strained. This produces classic French aspic with the addition of a more traditional American spice, mace. Hearn says, "When well made it is delicious with cold turkey and under the name of 'aspic jelly,' figures in the finest French cooking."

Although not much used in modern cooking, a good aspic, well made, flavorful and crystal so that it sparkles like jewels, is always a test of a cook's skill. What surprised me here was how many recipes make use of this sophisticated preparation.

Sauce Robert, Cream Sauce, Piquant Tomato Sauce which combines fresh tomatoes with brown sauce and tarragon vinegar — all show decidedly French roots that are included with traditional American favorites such as Cranberry Sauce, Apple Sauce, a variety of sauces made with mustard, peaches, fried apples, lemons and even a traditional English hard sauce. One of the most interesting is a sauce made with peaches, "not fully ripe," that are sliced and sautéed in the pan drippings from a roast pork, more of a fruit compote than a sauce.

A Creole version of Soubise Sauce, made by slowly sautéing onions without browning until the sugars develop and then adding them to a Béchamel, calls for first boiling the onions until soft and then adding milk enriched with butter and flour.

There are a variety of oyster sauces: brown, white and oyster sauce for turkey. There is a Creole version of a Sauce Robert, essentially a demi-glace with added prepared Dijon mustard.

Hearn also includes a section on how to make a "good vinegar," "another way to make vinegar," "good vinegar for pickles" and "good and cheap vinegar."

Entrees are diverse, ranging from Kidney and Mushroom Stew to Irish Stew; Pigeon Stew to Tripe Stew. We have "veal hash for breakfast" as well as beef hash, sandwiches, directions for making French mustard, veal and ham pie, sweetbreads, veal loaf "for lunch," along with "calves' feet and pig's feet fried in batter." Many recipes in older cookbooks make use of items we Americans no longer eat — pigs' feet, snout, calves' head, brains — all these items were staples of our forefathers and can still be found in cuisines of other countries. Part of this has to do with the increasing wealth of the majority of the population and the removal of food production from local to remote sources. When people grow their own food or have local suppliers who do, these items are more likely to remain in the cook's repertoire.

Meats appear in all manner of ways including a Fricandellons of Cold Veal or Mutton — very similar to what Mrs. Randolph might have made in Virginia. Mrs. Randolph may have chosen simple melted butter to serve along with this item but in the Creole tradition Hearn serves it up with a sauce or gravy, as he calls it, made with a browned roux.

Here it also worth noting that on page 59 the page heading is for "Mutton, Beef and Hams." Once again lamb is relegated to a second place finish with mutton, which is now almost impossible to find in the United States. Leaning in a French direction there is a cold "Daube glace of beef, for cold supper." This is a dish of beef round into which slits are cut, a stuffing inserted and then the beef is braised, chilled and covered with the jelly when cold, i.e. the stock is gelatinous and starts to set into an aspic when cold. This would also have been decorated as it served primarily as a focal point for a cold buffet; classic French. A Round of beef Bayonne is braised in red wine reflecting, as its name suggests, a dish from the Basque region of France.

Welsh rarebit and New England-style baked beans with pork add a New England touch to the Creole cook's repertoire, and along with some meat pies, shows a residual English influence in the most un–English of cities.

There are many variations of beef and one I find interesting, as it straddles two worlds of cooking technology. "To Roast a Beef in a Stove" states the following: "A fine roasting piece of beef may it be properly managed, be baked in a stove so as to resemble beef roasted before a large, open fire." This phrase gives a hint as to how some cooks may have still been using an open fireplace or pit for roasting. Self contained metal stoves started appearing around the 1840s but were still fairly expensive. I also wonder if Hearn was saying that a roast could be as good using this new technology as in the "good old days" of open fireplace cooking.

In a seeming throwback to colonial times, we have a Boiled brisket of Beef, Stuffed. Hearn directs the reader to make a stuffing with "bread crumbs, pepper, butter, salt, sweet herbs, mace and an onion, all chopped fine and mixed with a beaten egg." The stuffing is placed between the fat cover and the meat. The cook then flours a cloth (the traditional English pudding cloth also found in Amelia Simmons' recipes) and then boils the packet for about six hours. So here in the midst of this worldly, cosmopolitan city there is an ancient cooking technique still being practiced.

"Fowls and Game" includes a fried chicken recipe that makes a good point. The chicken is seasoned and dredged in flour. When the time comes for frying, Hearn says to "drop in a few pieces of the chicken, always allowing room in the pan for each piece to be turned without crowding." This helps ensure a quality cooking in two ways. First, the flour coating will always be exposed to hot fat and all will cool evenly. The other positive effect is that with only a few pieces added at a time the temperature of the fat will remain hot enough, so that the coating does not absorb excess grease. This is how to make a crispy fried chicken that is not heavy and greasy.

Chicken Marengo is sautéed for 20 minutes. Then the cook adds truffles, parsley, chives or shallots, garlic, pepper and salt. Excess fat is drawn, a roux is made in the saucepan and a brown gravy sauce is added along with some button mushrooms, and when finished cooking, the dish is garnished with fried croutons and crayfish. Most other recipes call for tomato and eggs. The brown sauce seems to be a reflection of Creole preference.

Curried chicken is made with "a dessertspoonful of curry powder or paste," tomatoes and veal stock. A nice touch here is that along with the onions and chicken, sliced apples are sautéed and then stewed together with the fowl and curry paste.

Chicken with oyster sauce, plain broiled chicken, Chicken pie, à la Reine, with white sauce thickened with hard cooked egg yolks, all speak to cross cultural influences in Creole cuisine and the skill and accomplishment of Creole cooks.

There is a challenging recipe for a boned turkey: the cook makes forcemeat with veal, mushrooms, egg yolks, bacon and herbs. This is set aside while she prepares a pound of peeled truffles, smoked tongue and then a choice of bacon, calf udder or veal. "Bone the turkey" is the only direction the cook gets here, because the Creole cook would know how to do that already. The skin laid onto a cloth as "it is now limp and boneless," slices of breast meat are made and placed where the meat "seems thin." Once the meat is evenly distributed over the skin and seasoned, the forcemeat is spread on the meat, truffles, tongue, bacon and veal are added. All are sewn up tightly with "the ends tied, like a cushion, or roly-poly." Once tied it is added to a large pot with its bones, veal or poultry trimmings, two boiled calf's feet, two onions stuck with cloves, parsley, green onions, two blades of mace, basil, thyme, peppercorns and a half-pint of brandy or wine. The bird is poached, cooled and will set up nicely so it can be sliced as needed. If this sounds familiar, it is a Galantine of Turkey, which Hearn calls Gelatines. He says that this is its first incarnation in an American book and comes from "one who was Chef de Cuisine to a crowned head of Europe." Remember Queen Victoria's favorite soup? We are getting there.

Wild turkey, curried turkey, canvas back ducks, teal ducks, wild geese, game from venison to squirrel, Carolina rice birds to partridge, pigeons to suckling pig — all the staples of the Creole cook are here including a "Goose, with Chestnuts à la Chipolata," which features the all American chestnuts coupled with a citrus reduction sauce sweetened and thickened with currant jelly. Although the traditional sausages are not present in this recipe, it certainly shows some Spanish influence in the name and in the use of citrus fruit, longtime staple of Spanish agriculture. As in a modern kitchen, the sauce is reduced really to a glaze and poured over the goose just before serving.

Hearn states in the next recipe that "Venison is the finest game we have (in the) South," and it is featured as roasted, fried or broiled steak and as a traditional English or New England "Venison Pasty."

Vegetables run the gamut from Irish Potatoes to green corn and succotash, to Okra and Corn Fricassee. This is a dish made with sautéed okra to which is added corn off the cob, a compound roux is made and then milk is added along with seasonings; we might call this creamed okra and corn.

Asparagus and eggplant, artichokes, snap beans, lima beans, squash, cabbage and lots of other vegetables are here. A clue to supplies of fresh dairy products that were available in a large city may be inferred form Hearn's statement that Asparagus with Cream should be made "when cream is plentiful." This would most likely be in early spring before the weather got too warm. Remember there was very little commercial refrigeration, and the transport of non-pasteurized dairy products was always an issue.

Also we have "Pumpkin with salt meat." This is a dish that could take us back to New England of the 1700s. Pumpkin is sliced and roasted with either brown sugar or molasses; "some smoked meat" is laid in the roasting and the dish is served when the pumpkin is fully cooked. Hearn says, "It is better than many things with more reputation."

Egg dishes show a high degree of skill, in that many of the omelets are made with egg whites folded into the yolks and soufflés are included as well as savory (Spanish, with oysters, with parmesan cheese) and sweet baked omelets (omelet with sugar, Omelette Soufflé with powdered sugar and fresh lemon zest), and a wonderful concoction, Omelette Souffle in a Mold, which is separated eggs, yolks beaten with rice flour and orange flour water, mixed with melted butter and baked. Quite a repertoire for the Creole cook, and it demands a keen understanding of ingredients and some advanced cooking techniques. It stands to reason that eggs would feature prominently in a household book, as many people then as now would "keep" chickens.

As befits a warm weather climate, there is quite a selection of salads here in Hearn's

Creole kitchen, from chicken to potato salad, tomato salad with or without shrimp, Jambalaya of Fowls and Rice — all of which are preceded by a variety of ketchups and other condiments. Harkening back to the Dutch influence in New York, there are two recipes for "cold slaw," one with what we now recognize as a boiled dressing, and one with vinegar and hard cooked eggs.

Pickles of all sorts are here — made with tomatoes, peaches, oysters, walnuts, onions, lemons, just about anything that would lend itself to preserving throughout the growing season, an important consideration in a warm climate before in-home refrigeration. One of the most interesting is Peach Mango, where peaches are partially preserved, the pits removed, a stuffing made, the cut slice replaced, tied securely and then boiled and stored in a brining liquor.

It can be hard to imagine but often people needed to make their own yeast in order to make bread. Some of the recipes are quite similar to what might be found going back to Miss Leslie, Mrs. Randolph and Amelia Simmons. Here we have yeast and bread recipes galore, including a recipe for a Graham Bread that was made known by Sylvester Graham, one of the early dietary reformers who promoted vegetarianism and temperance. Graham flour is a type of whole-wheat flour as Mr. Graham was a champion of whole grains and did not have much good to say about white, refined flours. Also making a visit from New England is the famous Boston Brown Bread, which when served with the aforementioned beans and bacon will give a Creole cook a traditional Saturday night "supper" still found in New England.

There are also recipes for Muffets and Crumpets with Yeast, probably better known now as English muffins, Graham Muffins for Dyspeptics, and the ancient traditional English Sally Lunn. The famous Pain Perdu shows up here right next to Indian Breakfast Cakes, Italy's Buckwheat Cakes, and traditional egg noodles, more often associated with German cooking.

As if showing how cosmopolitan New Orleans was, as well as Miss Leslie's still vibrant reputation, we are treated to Miss Leslie's Tea Rusk, a yeast raised, pan fried biscuit meant to be served with tea, piping hot from the griddle. They could also be left to cool and could serve as a type of New Orleans-Philadelphia-New England Johnny Cake, especially if twice baked like a biscotti.

Sweets play a large part in *La Cuisine Creole,* from beignets or crullers, to all manner of cakes and frostings, to Charlotte Russe and traditional English Fruit Cake. Bride's cakes, Madeira Cake (Miss Leslie?), Portugal cakes, several types of sponge cakes and pound cakes, and what may be original recipes for Cup Cakes (not the little cakes we may be familiar with, but cakes made by measuring ingredients by the use of cups, i.e. one cup of butter, three cups of sugar, five cups of flour and so on). There are German Ladies Fingers, Ring Jumbles, Citron Cake, a wonderfully named Louisiana Hard-Times Cake, classic Genoise, a trifle, Silver and Gold cakes, six different "cocoanut" cakes, and a fabulous Tipsy Cake, made by placing a sponge cake in a bowl, pouring over it a cup of mixed Madeira and Sherry, studding it with almonds and then pouring a rich custard over the entire cake in the bowl.

Desserts are in a separate section from the cakes, a distinction that does not much happen any more, where cakes are considered the same as desserts. Classic desserts such as Charlotte Russe, Blanc Mange, almond macaroons, what is now known as a lemon meringue pie, here called a lemon custard. There is a dish called Francatelli's Lemon Pudding, which again shows the scope of Hearn's learning as well as what a sophisticated city New Orleans was. Francatelli was a chef who was born of English and Italian ancestry in England. He trained in France under Carême and was one of the most famous European chefs in Victorian England. He cooked at some of the most fashionable clubs in London, was chef to Queen Victoria and Prince Albert and authored four cookbooks, including one on pastry, two on elegant cooking and one on cooking geared to the limited resources of England's working classes. Bearing in mind that *La Cuisine Creole* is a book that showcases primarily the food of the Creole populace and not elegant society, it makes it all the more remarkable that such a high level of cuisine was practiced side by side with literally world famous recipes and down home food, and was taken as a matter of course. So it probably should be no surprise that a little later on in the book we find Prince Albert's Pudding.

Following is a litany of puddings and preserves, brandied fruits, wines (fruit wines), cordials, and preparations for the sick and convalescent. Coffees, teas, candies and a section on wines round out the recipes for the food.

The next section is one of the earliest recordings of cocktail recipes, covering, among other items, fizzes and punches, different ways to serve absinthe, pusse cafes and other spirituous libations!

There are hints on cooking and cleaning that round out the book, with the index giving but a skeletal outline of the wonders within. In this book is an edible sketch, if you will, of a culture that enraptured Hearn, and his other writings in conjunction with *La Cuisine Creole* presented a glimpse of this unique culture that made it known beyond the boundaries of New Orleans and Louisiana. Creole cuisine has become a taken-for-granted part of American cuisine in many ways, but it was not always well known outside its birthplace.

What I trust the reader and cook will get from *La Cuisine Creole* is a sense of the diversity, uniqueness and dynamism of Creole food and Creole culture. Anyone interested in either should cook with this book and read Hearn's writings on the Creole culture.

The first *La Cuisine Creole* cookbook is still young and vibrant, waiting to be devoured by readers with a passion for Creole food and Creole culture.

This vibrancy, the exotic spices in a sub-tropical climate, voodoo, language — all things Creole captured the soul of Hearn and this cookbook is only one of the ways he chose to share his love and knowledge of this unique culture. He was later to move on to Japan where he astutely studied and absorbed Japanese culture to an extremely high degree.

Hearn influenced the development of two fields of social science, comparative linguistics and ethnography, which have shown us the beauties and wonders of hitherto unknown cultural and linguistic traditions. A remarkable man was Lafcadio Hearn, who left an indelible mark on American cuisine and American culture.

CHAPTER 7

Charles Ranhofer

From the Preface to *The Epicurean:*

In publishing this work I have endeavored to fill a much needed want, viz: — the best and most effectual manner of preparing healthy and nutritious food.

This edition contains innumerable recipes which I have simplified and explained in a comprehensive manner so as to meet the wants of all. It suggests, also, many useful and important hints to those about entering the profession.

The book is illustrated and contains instructions how to prepare, garnish and serve according to the traditional rules of our most able predecessors, and now followed by the principal chefs of France and the United States.

In some instances, where it was deemed necessary to differ from the standard rules and methods in order to cater to the various tastes, changes have been made.

The book is divided into twenty-four chapters: Table Service, Bills of Fare, Supplies, Elementary Methods, Supplies, Stocks, Hot and Cold Sauces, Garnishings, Hot and Cold Side Dishes, Shell Fish, Crustaceans, Fish, Beef, Veal, Mutton, Lamb, Pork, Poultry, Game, Miscellaneous Entrées, Cold Dishes, Vegetables, Cereals, Hot and Cold Desserts, Pastry, Bakery, Confectionary, Ices, Fruit, Wines and Preserves.

Not relying solely on my experience and knowledge, I have quoted from the most illustrious modern author, my much beloved friend and colleague, Urbain Dubois, ex-chef at the Court of Germany, and it gives me sincere pleasure to thank him for his generous assistance.

The profession will acknowledge its indebtedness to the Messrs. Delmonico for the interest shown by them in developing the gastronomic art in this country.

Many will recall the business receptions given to distinguished guests under the supervision and direction of Delmonico.

Mention may be made of the following dinners: to President U.S. Grant, to President A. Johnson, to the Grand Duke Alexis of Russia, to Gen. Prim, to Charles Dickens, to Sir Morton Peto, to Aug. Belmont, to Giraud Foster, to Gen. Cutting, to Luckmeyer, the so-called "Black Swan Dinner," to Admiral Renaud, to Prof. Morse, to Bartholdi, to De

THE EPICUREAN

The Epicurean

BY

CHARLES RANHOFER

OF

DELMONICO'S

THE EPICUREAN

A COMPLETE TREATISE OF

ANALYTICAL AND PRACTICAL STUDIES

ON THE

CULINARY ART

INCLUDING

Table and Wine Service, How to Prepare and Cook Dishes, an Index for Marketing, a Great Variety of Bills of Fare for Breakfasts, Luncheons, Dinners, Suppers, Ambigus, Buffets, etc., and a Selection of Interesting Bills of Fare of Delmonico's. from 1862 to 1894.

MAKING A

FRANCO-AMERICAN CULINARY ENCYCLOPEDIA

BY CHARLES RANHOFER,

CHEF OF DELMONICOS'

MADISON SQUARE.

Honorary President of the "Société Culinaire Philanthropique" of New York,

ILLUSTRATED WITH 800 PLATES.

NEW YORK :
CHARLES RANHOFER, PUBLISHER,
681 WEST END AVENUE
1894

Lesseps, to the Comte de Paris, also the ball given to the Russian And Fleet and the Greek dinner.

I have entitled this work The Epicurean, and have justly dedicated it to the memory of Messrs. Delmonico, as a token of my gratitude and sincere self esteem.

Their world-wide reputation continues to be maintained by Mr. C.C. Delmonico.

In conclusion I feel that my experiences will be useful to those seeking information in the gastronomic art.

Hoping the public will appreciate my efforts,

I remain respectfully,
CHARLES RANHOFER.

"The turn-of-the-century Delmonico's chef spills everything he knows about cooking. Ranhofer's work was unprecedented — and was considered high treason by his peers at the time. A fascinating and imposing tome and an important piece of culinary history."

Anthony Bourdain, America's culinary "bad boy" writing in the *Guardian Newspaper* on the ten most important cookbooks ever written.

From an article written on April 8, 1894, in the now defunct *Brooklyn Eagle Newspaper* entitled "Floating Literature-Books on Many Subjects of Present Interest":

The Epicurean claims to be a Franco-American culinary encyclopedia. It consists of 1200 hundred pages, has 800 illustrations and is published by Charles Ranhofer, New York. Charles Ranhofer has at his back thirty-five years' experience as chef of Delmonico's, Madison Square, New York. The volume may be regarded as a complete and exhaustive treatise of analytical and practical studies on the culinary art, the best manner of preparing and supplying enjoyable, healthy and nutritious food economically and without waste appears to be the leading feature of the book. It contains nearly 4,000 recipes. It shows 218 different ways of cooking fish, 200 for soups, 165 for beef, 224 for poultry, 163 for game, 101 for eggs, 279 for pastry, 172 for vegetables 189 for ices and ice creams, etc. It has a variety of bills of fare for each month in the year for all occasions, and for invalids. The 64 pages of index adds great value to the work.

From the *Omaha Bee Newspaper* of May 26, 1891:

Culinary literature has never before made so valuable an acquisition as in Charles Ranhofer's publication, *The Epicurean....* This teeming, massive volume contains a complete and exhaustive

ESTABLISHED 1827

Delmonico's

BEAVER & SOUTH W. STS
22 BROAD STREET
MADISON SQUARE

Office Beaver & South W. Sts

New York, Feb'y 24th 1893

Chef
Charles Ranhofer Esq.
Dear Sir;

In my opinion after looking over your Mrus It so very worthy of the reputation you have in my estimation for editing a work of this character, and It so with much pleasure I recommend It to the attention of those to whom It is most directly addressed.

A perusal will I think give one an appetite —

Yours truly,
Charles Delmonico —

CONTENTS.

treatise of analytical and practical studies on the culinary art, and is beyond doubt the as well as the latest work of the kind extant.... Chefs, cooks, stewards, caterers, private families, confectioners, ice cream makers, restaurant keepers, hotel proprietors, managers of sanitariums and hygienic institutions and hospitals, all are interested and can benefit by possession and use of this voluminous and exhaustive work.

With the above words the general public was made aware of one of the towering achievements in the world of culinary literature. Written at the end of an illustrious career to help provide for his wife and family after his death, which was in 1899, Chef Ranhofer stood the then professional culinary world on its collective head. With his detailed instructions on methods and ingredients and how they were used in a professional kitchen came a storm of dire warnings about the end of restaurants and the craft of the professional chef. The 19th-century culinary Cassandras ranted and raved that with this information made available to everyone there would no longer be a reason for anyone to go to a restaurant to eat or to entertain, and this only about 80 years after the concept of what we now know as a restaurant developed in the United States. Never mind that it was Delmonico's Restaurant that all but created the concept of elegant dining and that Charles Ranhofer was the first to actually define and live the idea of being a chef. Never mind that the partnership of Delmonico and Ranhofer would create the idea of what a restaurant is, what a chef is and what wonders of culinary artistry can be produced in a restaurant kitchen.

This restaurant and this incredible chef, America's greatest on both accounts, would reshape how Europeans and people around the world would view the United States as a country and American cuisine. In a very real sense, the maturation of the country would be experienced not only by the elite of American society, politicians and businessmen, but by foreign heads of state and other dignitaries and celebrities whose perception of the entire country would begin to be shaped by having Chef Ranhofer prepare their dinner at Delmonico's Restaurant.

The irony of this situation is that now the restaurant lives on in memories generated long ago and the name of its greatest chef, Charles Ranhofer, is largely unknown even among culinary professionals. While the name of Escoffier is well known to the point that many non-professionals recognize it and may be vaguely aware that there is a book written by Escoffier, there is no such familiarity with Chef Ranhofer and his treatise.

Chef Ranhofer penned his work a decade before Escoffier. But whereas Escoffier had an ongoing professional relationship with Cesar Ritz, who was a genius in his own right, after Chef Ranhofer died Delmonico's lasted only little more than an additional quarter century before closing its doors. The Ritz name garnered continuing fame with standard bearing hotels around Europe and now the world. The Delmonico name lived on only in legends of a bygone era. Escoffier's name blossomed due to its association with Ritz, and Chef Ranhofer's reputation gathered dust as part of a never to be recreated culinary experience.

And we owe so much to Chef Ranhofer. My hope is that with this chapter more people will come to appreciate his skill, professionalism and dedication to his art and fellow human beings. It is time.

Where Restaurants Were at This Time

Chef Ranhofer and Mrs. Fisher were of the same time period, roughly speaking, which spanned the latter part of the 19th century. From a culinary standpoint these two seem at opposite ends of the culinary universe in regards to birth, training and professional careers. Chef Ranhofer was a traditionally trained chef who grew up in France from whence he emigrated and went to live in the United States. He served in a number of different positions before accepting employment with the Delmonico family at their eponymous restaurant, where he remained on and off, mostly on, for almost 40 years.

This is a good time to take a look at the institution of the restaurant — now so ubiquitous that it is hard for many people to conceive of life BTO (before take out), or living in a society where eating away from home was a highly unusual experience. (I have students who, when I tell them that the Food Channel did not always exist, are absolutely stunned.)

Many people are surprised to learn that restaurants are a relatively recent phenomenon in European and American society. Certainly, in ancient times people were able to purchase food outside of the home. Especially in Ancient Rome with the games, it is hard to imagine such a dynamic city without street vendors or stall owners supplying food and drink to the vast crowds who would watch entertainment that went on for hours at a time.

Patrick Faas states that Rome "had countless bars, restaurants, inns" throughout the city, as in modern times often located where the traffic was — near bathhouses, libraries, sporting arenas and so on. Restaurants had bars, cooking facilities, sometimes tables and chairs and in larger establishments may have enjoyed cellars for keeping food and drink. Some even had separate rooms for kitchens.[1]

In the evening, street vendors, food stalls and more elaborate venues supplied a need as well as a safety feature: The majority of Romans lived in simple tenements and thousands of cooking fires would have posed a catastrophic risk on a daily basis. Imperial Rome had over 1 million people, and the sheer number of fires would have created conflagrations on a regular basis.

Depending upon the sumptuousness of the establishment, there would be quite a variety of food offered: sausages, beets, different types of lettuce, eggs, ham, fish of all sorts, game, yogurt and, since the water was not safe to drink, wine. (It was in Rome that wines started achieving reputations for place of origin and vintage as well as degree of ageing.)

After the fall of Rome there were crude establishments that could cater to travelers, and monasteries that would offer shelter for a night. By the time of Shakespeare, food was readily available in many places of entertainment. Sometimes the food served a dual purpose when sold in a theater or other entertainment venue: If the performers were lousy, a theater-goer could always send an airborne apple or pear or a handful of nuts at the actors who were on stage.

After the French Revolution, the time was at hand for something new, and what we now know as restaurants made their debut. The nobles who had enormous wealth and employed skilled culinary professionals lost their lands and often their heads. So there were a number of what we would call chefs, well-trained and experienced, looking for work.

Paris is generally regarded as the city in which the first "modern" restaurants opened, with a couple of establishments in the running for the distinction of being the "first restaurant." During the Middle Ages there were a variety of guilds whose products and services were restricted to members of each specific guild, e.g. brewers, silversmiths, cobblers, etc. The guilds prevented an establishment from serving food items under one roof that may have been the traditional domain of more than one guild. In the *Oxford Encyclopedia of Food* the Parisian food scene is described thusly: "For a genuine meal one had to look either to a good inn or go to a rotisseur or traiteur (caterer, from the Italian trattorie). In France, these two guilds, together with the charcutiers, had been granted a monopoly on all cooked meat other than pates."

An urban legend says that in 1765 a merchant by the name of Boulanger, which means baker, offered for sale "restoratives fit for the gods." This was actually a dish of lamb's feet in a white sauce. He was challenged in the courts by the traditional guilds but won his case and was permitted to continue operating. (The next time you enjoy some white-sauced lamb's feet in a restaurant, thank Mssr. Boulanger.)

Following shortly were two men named de Chantoiseau in 1766 and Beauvilliers in 1772. The latter operated the first restaurant to actually have a stated menu with food served individually and at fixed hours of operation.

In the United States restaurants came into existence in the late 1700s. With the aid France provided during the Revolution there lingered an affinity for things French, including food. A man by the name of Baptiste Gilbert Payplat, who found himself in Boston, opened what may truly be the first restaurant in the United States, called Jullienne, which was his personal nickname, as well as a classical cut for vegetables.

A restaurant then as now depended upon a good location and substantial population in order to prosper. At the end of the 18th century with a total population of around four million people, only about five percent of which lived in cities, there did not exist large numbers of potential customers to support free-standing restaurants. But after 1800 the population grew rapidly and the cities grew as part of this expansion. It was more and more feasible for a restaurant to prosper in this environment.

As the population grew in the cities so to did commerce and societal wealth. Living conditions in these cities were challenging to say the least. Pigs would roam in the streets eating garbage that had accumulated during the day. Slaughtering shops and businesses roasting and selling meat sprouted all over due in part to the lack of sanitary food handling and preservation techniques. This meant that if an animal were slaughtered, there was very little time in which to butcher and cook the meat before it spoiled. Refrigerated food transport was still a century in the future. Add to that the fact that there was no municipal service for removal of animal waste in a city that was filled with horses and oxen, both alive and dead, and it may become clear why "eating out" could be hazardous to your health.

Public eating was fast and furious and it was not until the Tremont House in Boston started offering French service in its dining room that people sat at individual rather than communal tables and were able to order food from a menu. This was 1828. At about the same time, two other Boston landmarks also opened their doors, Durgin Park and the Union Oyster House. Both are still in operation.

In Manhattan in 1827 Giovanni Del-Monico opened the first of the famous restaurants that displayed the name Delmonico in Lower Manhattan. Starting initially in a pastry shop, this name and the restaurants with which it was associated were to become the locus of elegant dining for well-heeled customers from around the world for over a century.

The Delmonico family was originally from Ticino, the Italian part of Switzerland. In 1825 John opened a wine import and distribution business in New York for Spanish and French wines. After a few years, his brother Peter joined him and together they opened a café, Peter being a trained confectioner. The quality of food sold made the business prosperous, and they soon opened a full-fledged restaurant next door on Williams Street.

Lorenzo made his appearance a short while later and was brought into the business. John died in 1842, Peter retired in 1848, and Lorenzo took over the business of operating the restaurant. He remained in charge until he died in 1881. Under his stewardship the restaurant reached the peak of hospitality and culinary excellence, unsurpassed, perhaps, in the entire history of the United States.

It was Lorenzo who hired Charles Ranhofer, a French trained patissier, to be the chef de cuisine. This was in 1862 and Ranhofer ran the show in the kitchen, with a couple of brief interruptions, almost until his death in 1899. The family members maintained control of the business for almost 100 years.

Delmonico's Restaurant broke new ground by being the first American restaurant to use table linens, provide menus written in French and English and offer a separate wine list. In a city replete with elegant restaurants in an elegant era, Delmonico's was the standard for the country and for the world. According to an article by Christopher Gray early version of the Delmonico's menu "11 pages, with 47 kinds of veal, 12 kinds of boiled beef, 50 fish dishes and 21 red Bordeaux — but only one kind of coffee."

At the height of its business Delmonico's owned a 200 acre farm in remote agricultural Brooklyn as the quality of vegetables and fruit they could produce was superior to Phat was available in the market. They maintained an international wine cellar on the premises and were

Lorenzo Delmonico, exact date unknown. The man who hired Chef Ranhofer to lead Delmonico's Restaurant. Image courtesy of Print Collection, Miriam and Ira D. Wallach Division of Art, Prints and Photographs, the New York Public Library, Astor, Lenox and Tilden Foundations.

noted for stupendous catered events around the city. Try to imagine what it would have been to attend this event as related in *Around the American Table*[2]:

> Edward Luckemeyer, a successful import-exporter, received an unexpected windfall in the form of a ten thousand-dollar rebate from the government and decided to blow it all on a single meal at Delmonico's. He gave the management a completely free hand to do whatever they wanted, and Delmonico's responded with its masterpiece. The seventy-two guests were ushered into a sylvan wonderland. In the center of the giant table was a good-sized lake, some thirty feet long, complete with its own waterfall. The lake itself was surrounded by gently rolling hillocks and rafts of flowers, while songbirds twittered sweetly in gold cages suspended overhead. The star attraction was four swans on loan from Prospect Park that swam up and down the man-made waterway. The only graceless note of the evening was that the swans spent much of the dinner either fighting or mating. There is some confusion on this point on the part of the contemporary observers, who quite possibly had never before seen swans doing either.

Most, if not all, notables of the late 19th century dined at Delmonico's. The guest list reads like a Who's Who of Victorian era history: Jenny Lind, Mark Twain, Theodore Roosevelt, Lillian Russell, Diamond Jim Brady, Charles Dickens, Oscar Wilde, Napoleon III, Nikola Tesla, Edward VII, to name a few. Every United States president from Monroe to Franklin Roosevelt dined there.

Charles Dickens made two visits to the United States, one in 1842 and one in 1868. On the first it may be said that he was underwhelmed by America: its food, manners, people and general lack of civility. He mentions that while staying in New York there was a dinner bell custom. Someone would ring, or rather smack, an "awful gong which shakes the very window frames as it reverberates throughout house and horribly disturbs nervous foreigners."[3]

Delmonico's Restaurant, renamed the Café Martin. Dated 1908, after Delmonico's moved uptown to 44th Street. Image courtesy of Picture Collection, the New York Public Library, Astor, Lenox and Tilden Foundations.

Other European visitors related that blinds were kept shut on a permanent basis, both for keeping out the flies and to prevent the guests from too closely examining the furniture, especially the upholstery. I would be remiss if I did not mention men sitting and smoking cigars with feet propped up on marble balustrades and happily spitting on the floor the whole while.

It was especially vexing to European travelers that there were no real restaurants in the United States. Now a staple of Continental life having flourished since 1782, restaurants were apparently nowhere to be found in the new country. Where Beauvillier served all manner of game, terrines, broiled kidneys and copious quantities of champagne, there were simply none of these real restaurants to be found here. Beauvillier was apparently so successful that he had a real house specialty: one could have a champagne breakfast, a Dueler's Breakfast, before going out for one's morning duel. One had the opportunity to fill one's stomach before having one's head blown off or getting oneself hoisted on a petard just the same as one's breakfast meats.

When workers in cities headed off to work, it was usually what they could stuff in their pockets that would serve as their lunch. The idea of "doing lunch" was just not available in a public forum.

During Dickens' first visit he also commented on the quality of the food he endured while visiting. His words for American food? "Piles of indigestible matter." Not what one would call a ringing endorsement for outstanding quality.

However, on his second visit he found a vastly different country. By the 1860s restaurants had become much more common and there were some fine ones. Hotels had greatly improved and one hopes guests were no longer spitting on the floor.

Dickens was fêted at Delmonico's while Chef Ranhofer was running the kitchen. The menu, which is included in *The Epicurean,* was impressive by any standard. First courses were oysters, soups, beef filet, stuffed lamb, braised lettuce, grilled tomatoes; these items were starters and then the real dinner started. With more than 30 dishes following that brief warmup, Dickens offered to retract his earlier comments about American food and hospitality.

This sea change was brought about, literally, by the Delmonico family, especially Lorenzo, and the iconic Delmonico restaurants. (Once the family got rolling there were usually no fewer than two Delmonico restaurants at any one time.) In the middle of the 19th century this landmark of civilization changed the dining habits of Americans, along with their table manners, and was powerful enough to have a man like Dickens revise his opinion of the entire country by the experiences he had at Delmonico's. This seems almost like a fantasy but it is actually true.

The Fourteenth Street restaurant was demolished in 1879. At this time there were three principal Delmonico family members involved with the restaurant: Lorenzo, Siro and Charles. They oversaw four different operations on William and Broad Streets, Broadway and Fifth Avenue.

The Fourteenth Street operation was the site of Charles Dickens' dinner where he altered his opinion of America and, thanks to Chef Ranhofer, American food. It was also the site of the most expensive dinner they prepared: one Sir Morton Peto gave a party for 100 people with entertainment and the best the restaurant had to offer on all accounts. (Mr. Peto was a high roller who made great show of attending churches, giving to charities and generally living the life of a "model Christian merchant." Unfortunately, when he went to England he was busted for financial fraud along with assorted investment scams and barely escaped going to jail.) The singer Clara Louise Kellogg received $1,000 plus some diamond jewelry. Wines were an outrageous $25 per bottle. The total tab for this event was $20,000.[4]

The restaurant, or rather restaurants, became the gathering places for all manner of society events, including the non-modestly named Patriarch Balls. These were for the self-proclaimed best of society. Held at Delmonico's, they served to showcase the most desirable people to know and be seen with. In the social season of 1872 to 1873 these were the elegant soirees of the ultra wealthy.[5]

Although it was the restaurant of society, like any other restaurant there was always something going on apart from drawing rooms and exclusive enclaves, especially in New York. As a restaurant it was subject to the everyday events of any well-established restaurant.

There was a waiters' strike in April of 1893 at the Twenty-Sixth Street and Fifth Avenue location. The restaurant had a party booked for 200 people and the waiters presented their demands. *The New York Times* of April 28, 1893, wrote, "Mr. Delmonico waxed wroth." They wanted $30 per month, wanted to wear mustaches and also wanted one day off every other week. They also asked for $1 extra per day for every day spent out of town on restaurant functions.

Delmonico refused, saying, "I am running this business to suit myself and not you. I can tell you right here that I won't yield an iota to your demands ... if you don't like it, well you know what you can do."

The waiters walked out led by their spokesman, Alphonse, who said, "That is monsieur's final decision, I so presume ... then I have the greatest of regrets in unison with mes camarades to bid Monsieur 'Adieu.'" Delmonico was left with five waiters but contacted a group called the Columbia Club and got at least some replacements. Apparently they also brought waiters from their Beaver Street restaurant to serve the dinner.[6]

Throughout its lifetime, Delmonico's was known as the standard bearer for exceptional food, décor, wine, service and extraordinary catered events. The combination of family management that did not manage well in the early part of the 20th century, World War I ripping society apart like a scythe through wheat and that peculiar institution of prohibition eventually sealed the restaurant's fate. Family members sold the restaurant in 1919.

It is also noted that Lorenzo, perhaps the essential force behind the empire of cuisine, ended badly. He apparently suffered from a form of dementia, disappeared for several days, was found wandering in the wilds of the Oranges in New Jersey and ended life as a mental invalid. Sad ending for such a titanic personality.

Delmonico's always employed highly talented and skilled chefs: John Lux, Felix Delice, Charles Lallouette, the renowned Alessandro Filippini and the most prestigious chef of his age, Charles Ranhofer.

Who Was Charles Ranhofer?

In 1836 Ranhofer was born in St. Denis, France, Saint Denis being the patron of France. Chef Ranhofer came from a culinary family: His grandfather was a cook and his father owned a restaurant. Following the European tradition of apprenticeship, at the age of 12, Charles was apprenticed to a pastry shop where learned his craft over a three year period.[7] After completing his training he was employed as either a baker or chef in a Parisian restaurant — accounts differ. Wherever he found employment, he must have been impressive, because only a year later he was cooking for nobility, one Prince Henin of Alsace.

In this position he had good exposure to elaborate banquets that would serve him well later on. He was soon *chef de cuisine*, but he chose to relocate to America in 1856. At the ripe old age of 20 he was hired as a chef for the Russian consul in Washington, D.C. He spent some time in New Orleans and returned to France in 1860. For a season he was employed at the Tuilleries Palace, principally in charge of balls and special parties for the court of Napoleon III.

In 1861, Chef Ranhofer returned to New York to assume the position of chef de cuisine at Maison Doree, which was Delmonico's prime competitor. Just one year later, he was hired away by Lorenzo Delmonico to be the chef at the restaurant, which in this incarnation was on 14th Street and 5th Avenue.

Here is what Lorenzo Delmonico had to say: "He was perfect in dress and manner, and his attitude was such as to make me feel that he was doing me a great favor by coming into my employment. He gave me plainly to understand that he would be 'chief' indeed. 'You are the proprietor,' he said. 'Furnish the room and the provision, tell me the number of guests and what they want, and I will do the rest.' That was the way it was. And it has been a good thing for Charles, and for me, too."[8]

Why is this quote important? Among other things, the conversation relates a dialogue between two equals, not a boss and an employee, or a master and servant. Remember that until the French Revolution, chefs were the servants of wealthy patrons and nobility. After the revolution, the people made their way into a more roustabout world. Ranhofer says it all: "You are the proprietor. Furnish the room and the provision, tell me the number of guests and what they want, and I will do the rest." This is the modern concept of a chef as we now know it, at least in independent restaurants. Setting the chef as an equal who considers whether or not he chooses to work for the owner was a seismic separation from the history of the position. And as Lorenzo stated, the arrangement worked well for both of them.

For 36 years, Chef Ranhofer set the standard for elegant dining in America. Everyone ate there and guests from outside the United States would make Delmonico's a stop on their travels, from Charles Dickens to Napoleon III to the heir to the Russian throne, the restaurant was the showpiece of what could be done with great food and a superb chef in a kitchen whose standards were set and upheld by a titanic talent.

Although Chef Ranhofer led the kitchen and had final say over everything that left the line for the dining room (it is said that he tasted every dish or plate that went out), he nevertheless was intensely responsive to the wishes of his guests. He states, "It is a mistaken idea that everyone, willy-nilly, is compelled to take or go with the particular style of cooking that commends itself to the chef."

He is the chef but is ultimately responsible to the guest, which is one reason why the parties that Delmonico's catered were so extraordinary. Consider:

- In November 1863, a banquet was around 14 courses, each course of which had several choices. This added up to 46 separate dishes listed on the menu.[9]
- Chef Ranhofer was in the kitchen for the above-mentioned dinner for Charles Dickens. Afterwards Dickens publicly revised his opinion of America based on this dinner.
- Ranhofer, who reputedly earned $6,000 per year, a princely sum in the latter part of the 19th century, catered the Peto dinner mentioned above that cost $20,000. (Ranhofer was also proud of the fact that for around $12 six people could enjoy a good dinner, with an acceptable wine.) An article in the June 22, 1910, *University Missourian* entitled "High Salaried Cooks" reported that when Chef Ranhofer died he left an estate of over $100,000 plus the rights to his book.

Thomas also states in his book that Chef Ranhofer's crew held him in high esteem and had "unbounded respect" for him. But rather than being a tyrant, he seems not to have overstepped his authority or "overrate[d] his powers."[10] Such was his reputation that in New York it was said Charles Ranhofer was the first chef in the city, and there was no second. (It is interesting to note that Ranhofer always made his own soups, considering a fine soup the mark of a great restaurant. This seems to be a pattern with our authors and their high regard for soups. How the genre has suffered!)

Chef Ranhofer left New York to retire in France in 1876, but returned in 1879. This time he was chef at the restaurant in Madison Square on 28th Street. Lorenzo Delmonico died in 1881 and a younger Charles Delmonico took over the restaurant business. In 1894 *The Epicurean* was published, a massive summation of the art and craft of a truly professional chef.

In 1898 Chef Ranhofer oversaw the final move of the main restaurant kitchen to its ultimate location on 44th Street and 5th Avenue. When he retired again, for the final time, he was succeeded by one M. Grevillet, as chef de cuisine of Delmonico's.

From 1862 until 1898, Charles Ranhofer established the art of fine dining in America. His tenure at Delmonico's ensnared a newly wealthy society and set their expectations of what food could be at the hands of a master chef. His mastery was complete: from operating the country's finest kitchen on a daily basis to planning and crafting spectacular functions; to refining service to go along with the world's finest food to creating the modern position of chef; to being involved in numerous professional as well as charitable organizations; to writing his exemplary *The Epicurean* a decade before that other guy, Escoffier, compiled his own version of Ranhofer's book. (Maybe a slight exaggeration, but I'm in Ranhofer's corner on this one.)

Like many chefs he was active in professional organizations and would often show off his art and skill at professional shows, what we now call trade shows, and benefit dinners. The American branch of the L'Union Universelle de l'Art Culinaire presented such a show at the Lexington Avenue Opera House with all manner of food and provisions displayed as well as booths for the demonstration of culinary art. Chef Ranhhofer was one of the exhibitors at this first ever show of its kind.[11]

Chef Ranhofer was honorary president of the Société Philanthropique Culinaire and represented Delmonico's at the 29th charity ball and exposition where one of the displays was a fanciful bridge over the Atlantic Ocean forecasting what might be possible in future international travel. It was made entirely of sugar and complemented the displays of savory foods such as Pain de Gibier Diane, Galantine de Dinde à la Bergére, Galantine de Volaille à la d'Orleans and a nougat show piece, Le Phare.[12]

A year earlier he represented "Delmonico uptown" in the same philanthropic event. *The Times* stated Chef Ranhofer had 16 exhibits alone with the crowning achievement of a nougat piece called the Grand Nougat Parisien. In addition to this showpiece he made assorted desserts, sugar flowers shielded by a red sugar umbrella, and an array of savory buffet pieces, all for a charity benefit.[13]

As mentioned before, Chef Ranhofer was somewhat of a celebrity (recall the period expression to the effect that Ranhofer was New York's first chef and there was no second) and his reputation was not confined to the New York area alone. In April of 1898 the *St. Paul Globe* did a feature article on cooking eggs for Easter and Chef Ranhofer contributed what may be called the centerpiece of the articles. He described a dish quite similar to Eggs Benedict but served with a Colbert Sauce rather than a Hollandaise Sauce.[14] (This is a sauce named after the chief minister of Louis XIV and consists of demi-glace with shallots, tarragon and lemon.)

Another example of his renown comes from further west.[15] In 1894 he was solicited for a trendy set of recipes for Thanksgiving time. He spoke of a new item called oyster crabs, little crabs that apparently were actually inside the oyster shell. All the rage in New York high society, the paper quoted Chef Ranhofer for the recipe, which cooked the crabs in cream and was then finished with some Madeira.

He could also be used as a source for business and regulatory issues, as he was even in 1907, eight years after his death, when heated discussion took place over the legal definition of ice cream, with hearings held in a variety of locations. As "proof" that there could never be a definition of what quality ice cream really is, especially insofar as butter-fat is concerned, a Mr. Cutler referred to the ice cream section of *The Epicurean* to show that even an illustrious professional such as Chef Ranhofer had a variety of recipes ranging from 2 percent to 17 percent butter fat that he prepared at the Fifth Avenue location.[16] And by implication, how could anyone supersede the quality standards of such a legendary chef?

He invented and made popular preparations that are common today, such as Baked Alaska, Lobster Newberg (originally Wenberg, but that's another story), Delmonico Steak, Delmonico Potatoes, and many others. He was able to take his classical French training in pastry and cooking and use those skills to adopt and adapt "American" food products such as sweet potatoes and avocados, which were introduced by Ranhofer to New Yorkers in 1895.

There was no aspect of culinary art that eluded him and he was master of all. He died in 1899 of what was then known as Bright's Disease, now known as kidney disease, and is buried in the Historic Woodlawn Cemetery in New York City. His obituary in the *New York Times* of October 11, 1899, led with the banner, "Charles Ranhofer Dead — He Was for Many Years Chef at Delmonico's." He died at his home at 782 West End Avenue after an illness of two months.[17]

The obituary goes on to mention his early training in France, his work at the Russian Consulate in New York and stints in Washington, D.C., and New Orleans. His first return to France was to organize the grand balls of Napoleon III and his second return was to own the Hotel American in Enghien-les-Bains near Paris. He eventually returned to America and ended his career in New York City.

His professional and philanthropic associations were the aforementioned chef societies, the French Benevolent Society, the French Orphan Asylum, the Chefs' Gastronomic Club of Chicago and the Epicurean Club of Boston.

The funeral was held at St. Vincent de Paul's Church on Twenty-third Street not far from Seventh Avenue. He left a considerable financial estate as well as the rights to *The Epicurean* to his wife, three sons and two daughters. The greatest chef America has ever known passed into history after a lifetime of service as a chef after actually inventing the profession, as we now know it. His life was marked by outstanding culinary technique, a command of his art, an encyclopedic knowledge of all things culinary. Respected by the premier restaurant family at the country's greatest restaurant, he inspired respect, admiration and affection from those who worked in the kitchen with him. Quoted as a food authority even after his death, his influences are all around us all the time. His book was the first of its kind and rather than spelling doom for the nascent American industry served as a beacon of knowledge for those who would take the time to know this incredible book.

It is simply not right, and so sad, that this great man should be so neglected after what he gave to American cuisine. He was a Frenchman who became, by his tenure in America, an American. He was America's greatest chef. Period.

Ranhofer Dinner Menus

Avril, 1867
DINNER DE 175 COUVERTS,
EN L'HONNEUR DE CHARLES DICKENS,
MENU
Huitres sur coquilles,
Potages

Consommé Sevigne

Crème d'aspereges à la Dumas
Hors d'Oeuvre Chaud
Timbales à la Dickens

Saumon à la Victoria

Pommes de terre Nelson,
Relevés.

Filet de Boeuf à la Lucullus

Laitues braises demi-glace.

Agneau farci à la Walter Scott

Tomates à la Reine.
Entrées.

Filet de brants à la Seymour
  Petit Pois à l'Anglaise,
    Crustades de ris de veau à la douglas
     Quatieres d'artichauts Lyonnaise
      Epinards au veloute
     Cotelletes de grousse à la Fenimore Cooper
        Entrées froides,
        Galantines à la Royale
       Aspics de foie-gras histories
        Intermede
       Sorbet à l' Americaine
       Rots

Bécassines   *Poulets de grains truffes.*

       Entrements Sucrés
     Peches à la Parisieanne, (chaud)
  Macedoine de fruits   *Muscovite à l'abricot*
  Lait d'amandines rubanes au chocolat
             Charlotte Doria
  Viennois glace à l'orange
    Corbeile de biscuits Chantilly
     Gateau Savarain au marasquin
    Glacés forme fruits Napolitane
      Parfait au Café
      Pieces Montees.
  Temple de la Litterature
    Trophée à l'Auteur
  Pavillon International   *Colonne Triomphale*
  Les Armes Britannique   *The Stars and Stripes*
  Le Monument de Washington   *Le Roi du destin*
  Fruits   *compotes et peches et de poires*
       Petits fours
       Dessert
  Fourteenth Street and Fifth Avenue

                   Delmonico

It should be added that the "pyramids of pastry" were great confections which featured sweet, sculptured likenesses of Lincoln, Alexander II, Washington, and Peter the Great on "pedestals of variegated sugars," as well as replicas of famous monuments and symbols of plenty. Not even the visit of the Prince of Wales a few years earlier had called forth such a conspicuous display of extravagant hospitality.

*   *   *

DINNER GIVEN BY SIR MORTON PETO
at
DELMONICO'S, OCT. 30, 1865
MENU

Barsac   *Huitres*
            Potages
Xeres F.S. 1815   *Concomme Britannia*
         Purée à la Derby
         Hors d'oeuvre
    Cassoulettes de foie gras   *Timbales à l'ecariate*

Poissons

Steinberger Cabinet   *Saumon Rothschild*

Grenadins de bass, New York

Relevés

Champagne Napoléon   *Chapons truffes.*

Entrées

Chateau Latour   *Faisan à la Londonderry*

Cotelettes d'agneau Ptimatice.

Cromesquis de volaille à la purée de marrons

Aigullettes de canards a la bigarade

Rissolettes à la Pompadour

Entrées Froides

Cotes roties   *Voliere de gibier*

Ballotines d'anguilles en Bellevue

Chaufroid de rouges-gourges à la Bohemienne

Sorber à la Sir Morton Peto

Rotis

Clos-Vougeot

Selle de chevreuuil, sauce au vin de Porto groseilles

Bécasses bardées

Entrements

Choux de Bruxelles   *Haricot Verts*

Artichaut farcis   *Petit pois*

Sucrés

Pouding de poires à la Louisiannaise à l'ananas

Madison   *Pain d'abricot à la vanille*

Tokai Imperial

Gelée de fruits   *Gelée Indienne*

Moscovite fouettee   *Cougloff aux amandes*

Mazarin aux peches   *Glases assorties*

Caisses jardiniere

Fruits et Desserts

Pieces Montées

Madere Faquart   *Cascade Pyramidale*

Corbeille arabesque   *Ruines de Poestum*

Le Palmier   *Trophée militaire*

Corne d'abondance   *Nougat à la Parisienne*

Fourteenth Street and Fifth Avenue   *Delmonico*

Chef Ranhofer almost off-handedly mentions in his preface a dinner for Prince Alexis of Russia. This came about apparently by the unannounced visit of the Russian fleet to New York. After arriving over the course of several days, the fleet was based in Brooklyn. New York always being New York, this visit was taken up in a New York minute and the entire fleet, from the prince to the officers and sailors, were feasted and fêted for the length of their stay.[18] New York was visited by dignitaries from the Northeast, all eager to mingle with the Russians, and the parties, it seems, were endless. And one of the affairs took place at the New York Yacht Club.

The size of this party that Chef Ranhofer oversaw at the New York Yacht Club was probably not routine, even for Chef Ranhhofer and Delmonico's. The reported amount of victuals served up for one dinner:

Twelve thousand oysters —10,000 poulette and 2,000 pickled.

Twelve monster salmon — 30 lbs. each.

Twelve hundred game birds.
Two hundred and fifty turkeys.
Four hundred chickens.
One thousand pounds of tenderloin.
One hundred pyramids of pastry.
One thousand large loaves of bread.
Three thousand five hundred bottles of wine.

The Epicurean

A look at the table of contents reveals something unique, to my knowledge, in a cookbook: The author starts with service of wine and food and the menus are crafted with a very noticeable nod towards seasonality and local origin.

But more than this, he also relates the different types of service, French, American and Russian, for breakfast, lunch and dinner. In Chef Ranhofer's own words:

The success of a dinner depends upon good cooking, the manner in which it is served, and especially on entertaining congenial guests. The American service is copied more or less from the French and Russian, and remodeled to the tastes and customs of this country; as it varies somewhat from all others, a few instructions may be found useful to those desirous of learning the difference existing between them.

He then writes three pages on the finer points of this service, stating that, as with Russian service, the food must be served quickly and served hot. Specifying a 14-course meal served "of ten minute intervals," the chef can accomplish this in only two hours and 20 minutes; with an eight minute interval, a mere one hour and 52 minute time period is all that is required. For example (he provides nine separate "cards" or menus, each with ten and eight minute intervals), Chef Ranhofer lists the following for a 14-course meal:

Course 1: Oysters
Course 2: 2 Digestifs, hot and cold
Course 3: 2 soups
Course 4: 2 different fish with potatoes
Course 5: Remove with vegetables (something served from a service cart)
Courses 6, 7, 8: One entrée each with vegetables
Course 9: 1 punch
Course 10: 1 or 2 roasts
Course 11: 1 or 2 colds, salad
Course 12: 1 Hot sweet dessert
Course 13: 1 or 2 Cold sweet desserts
Course 14: 1 or 2 ices or additional desserts.

There then follow some smaller meals with fewer courses and reduced serving times as well. It is interesting to note that every single dinner, large or small, starts with oysters. The smallest dinner is whittled away to practically nothing, with a mere five courses and only two entrées for the third course.

Also of note is the instruction on beverage service to go with the dinners. Remember that Delmonico's was the first restaurant to actually have a separate wine list. Oysters rate sweet wines more than anything else: Sauterne, Barsac, Graves, Mont Rachet (Montrachet) and lastly Chablis. After the soup comes Madeira, Sherry or Xeres. With fish, Rhine wines: Johannisberg, Marcobrunner, Hochheiner, Laubenheiner, Liebfraumilch, Steinberger.

Should the guest or host prefer a Mosel, Brauneberger, Zeltinger, and Bencasteler were available.

With removes come Côtes St. Jacques, Moulin-à-Vent, Macon, Clos de Vugeot, and Beaune, which indicates the remove would most likely be a fowl or light meat such as veal.

With the entrées come St. Émillion, Medoc du Bordelais, St. Julien or possibly a dry champagne "for certain countries." Iced punches and sherbets rate rum or Madeira.

With roasts are the Burgundies: Pommard, Nuits, Corton, Chambertin, Romanée Conti. Cold roasts go lighter and less expensive with Vin de Paille or Steinberger.

Interestingly the desserts also rate wines we normally think of as accompanying non-sweet foods: Château Margaux, Léoville, Lafitte, Château Larosse, Ponter-Canet, St. Pierre, Côtes du Rhone, Hermitage and Côtes-Rôtie. Chef Ranhofer also allows for red champagne: (Bouzy or Verzenay), and only one Porto.

He goes on to list other wine selections as well as beers (Bass Ales, Porter, Tivoli, and Milwaukee) and cordials (Curaçau, Kirsch, Cognac, Chartreuse, Maraschno, Prunelle, Anisette and Benedictine). Sweet wines as separate from cordials include Muscatel, Malaga, Alicante, Malvoisie of Madeira, Lacryna Christi, red and white Cape, Tokay, Constance, and Schiraz [sic].

Some of this may not seem remarkable, but remember this was the first American restaurant to have a separate wine list and to indicate which wines were suitable accompaniments for which courses. This was a level of professionalism not seen before in a restaurant. Yes, there were other places that served wines, beers and spirits. But to take food and wine together to this level set a standard that is still followed in modern, 21st-century restaurants. And the idea that the chef is the one who takes responsibility for this and addresses service and beverages in such detail in what would have simply been a high-end cook book by the world's greatest chef, set a standard that has rarely been matched, if ever.

This book largely defines how restaurants *are* today.

The next section details how the selection process would differ depending upon the clientele being served.

BILLS OF FARE FOR DINNER

Should the menu be intended for a dinner including ladies, it must be composed of light, fancy dishes with a pretty dessert; if, on the contrary, it is intended for gentlemen alone then it must be shorter and more substantial. If the dinner be given in honor of any distinguished foreign guest, then a place must be allowed on the menu to include a dish or several dishes of his own nationality; avoid repeating the same names in the same menu. Let the gravies be of different colors, one following the other.

Also vary the color of the meats as far as possible from one course the other. Offer on the menus all food in their respective seasons, and let the early products be of the finest quality (consult a general market list to find the seasonable produce), and only use preserved articles when no others can be obtained.

If the menus are handwritten, they must be very legible.

The comments on who is attending may strike a modern reader as anywhere from quaint to sexist, but reflects the society in which Chef Ranhofer was living. Remember this was a time of Victorian sensibilities and excess of American wealth and consumption. The caveats on colors of sauces, repeating the same names, the color of the meats — these are still standard precepts when planning a menu.

Different menus for different nationalities speak to the international flair Chef Ranhofer brought to the restaurant.

THE EPICUREAN
WINES AND LIQUORS USUALLY CALLED FOR (Vins Et Liqueurs Généralement Servis)
A DINNER OF AMERICANS
RECEPTION ROOM
Sherry   Bitters   Cocktails
DINNER WINES
Haut Sauterne   Amontillado   Sherry   Barsac   Pontet-Canet
Perrier-Jouet Brut   Liquors
A DINNER OF FRENCHMEN
RECEPTION ROOM
Sherry and Bitters   Vermouth   Absinthe
DINNER WINES
Graves   Xerres   Lafaurie   St. Pierre   Yellow Cliquot
Beaujolais Liquors
A DINNER OF GERMANS
No wines or mineral waters in the reception room.
DINNER WINES
Niersteiner   Sherry   Hochheimer   St. Espéphe
Pommery Sec   Beaune   Liquors

He was the chef but his knowledge and duty had him address service issues and protocols along with knowing preferences in food and wine for specific national tastes at that time. A close look at the beverage list reveals subtle but very real refinements of beverage offerings.

It is not always so that chefs have the knowledge or experience to handle this side of catering. The situation is getting better but precious few had, or have now, Chef Ranhofer's encompassing knowledge of food, confectionery and beverages.

His experience extended to the actual service as well, and large parts of his book are devoted to this aspect of fine cuisine. In fact, the book starts with a section on service and wines, not an everyday format by any means.

The following list states in great detail what is required for "French Service for 24 persons" and "Necessary Material for 24 Persons."

24 soup plates	24 dessert knives and forks
24 side dish plates	72 large forks
72 dinner plates	72 steel knives
48 dessert plates	24 silver or gilt knives
24 soupspoons	24 side-dish knives and forks
24 coffee after dinners cups	24 coffee spoons
Small salt cellars and pepper casters, one for each person	
12 radish dishes for 24 persons	2 shelved stands
A glass or silver knife rester for each person	2 silver baskets for fruits
8 silver toothpick holders	2 drums for fancy cakes
24 wine decanters and water bottles	2 dishes for jellies
2 soup tureens	2 dishes for cheese
2 chafing dishes and covers for removes	4 compote stands
4 chafing dishes for entrées	4 dishes and covers for vegetables
2 chafing dishes and covers for roasts	2 dishes for cold entrees
24 water glasses	24 sherry glasses
24 Chablis glasses	24 Burgundy glasses
24 Bordeaux glasses	24 punch or sherbet glasses
24 Champagne glasses	

Fine baccarat glass is the handsomest; keep in reserve glasses of all kinds in case of an accident.
The oil and vinegar caster, as well as the mustard pot, are to be passed around according to necessity.

Chef Ranhofer covers each course for dinner, luncheon "for ladies and gentlemen, or for ladies only, or for gentlemen only." Each of these had its own specific requirements.

While the above menus were for specific private parties, Chef Ranhofer did serve as chef in a restaurant that offered à la carte meals throughout the day and night. With these menus we see what was required of the staff in the kitchen led by the world's best chef. Bearing in mind the conditions in professional kitchens in the mid–19th century makes one realize how fortunate we are in our own time for conveniences such as gas stoves, electric refrigeration and modern ventilation equipment. In the time of Chef Ranhofer most stoves were coal fired and often had tanks affixed to them for hot water. Electrical refrigeration was just becoming known, but many operations relied upon ice deliveries to provide for their refrigeration. Add to that the lack of industrial strength ventilation systems, and what remains is a kitchen where stoves had to be maintained constantly to keep the heat sufficient for the demands of the menu. Stoves needed to be banked at night and re-fired in the very early morning for bakery and breakfast service. (This was sometimes a job for a young commis or assistant.)

It is not surprising that we have the expression, "If you can't stand the heat, get out of the kitchen." Given the crude ventilation systems available, the kitchens would have been incredibly hot and sometimes toxic. As the coal burned, if there were not sufficient windows or a powerful fan system in the kitchen, air could actually become saturated with carbon dioxide from the burning of the coal.

Early on in the book Chef Ranhofer also has "Tables of Supplies" which list items and seasonality of availability. Beginning with "Fish and Shell Fish" the reader can find a selection in excess of 45 fish along with eight shellfish and "Divers" items including cod tongues, crab oysters, frogs, milts, terrapin, turtle (green), and prawns. Still looking for something else? He also offers salt fish and smoked fish.

Fruits, game, meats, vegetables and legumes follow poultry items. There is still to come a "Model Market List" that breaks down each individual item listed in the tables above as to individual cuts in the case of meats and fish, to size of packages for fruits and vegetables.

Through page 164 we are regaled with menus, "bills of fare," for parties that range in size from 20 to 24 to over 300 guests for all manner of occasions, from breakfast, lunch and dinner, to picnics and grand buffets and "informal" sideboards.

Following the extravaganza of culinary knowledge come four restaurant bills of fare, breakfast, lunch, dinner, buffets or standing suppers, coliations (which would be a lighter, less substantial meal often times following a period of fasting as during Lent), hunting parties, garden parties served ambigu (informally or impromptu), sit-down suppers and dancing parties including the refreshments and supper.

Menus are composed by the month and each item is listed with its recipe number in the book, something Escoffier was to replicate. What is unique and groundbreaking is that the wine for each course is specified to accompany each individual preparation. For example: Tomate Grillées sauce mayonnaise chaud (recipe 2838) requires Vin de Moselle. Perdreaux rôti piques au jus garnis (2102) is served with Pontet-Canet.

The next section is devoted to breakfasts, where there are no wines recommended, although based on the size of the breakfasts, there certainly could have been.

There is a page titled: "Bill of Fare for Invalids" whereon Chef Ranhofer lists items suitable for people who have digestive and nutritional problems. The list includes Bavaroise, which would supply high quality protein and gelatin. All manner of broths, or clear soups, would extract nutrients from the principal ingredients including vegetables that would be used along with meat for production. Items are puréed for ease of eating and digestion: chicken, oatmeal, partridge, grouse, roebuck and frog broth and purée.

Luncheon menus are again listed by month with suitable wines. In the mood for Écrevisse vinaigrette (782)? Well, then you get to enjoy a nice Barsac. Would you like a Côtelette d'agneau và la Clémentine (1673) avec Pommes de terre fondants (2799) et Asperge à la sauce Hollandaise (2692), then the St. Estephe is on the way.

Delmonico's was noted for its wine list, which offered around 60 different wines and beverages. While that may seem small by today's standards, remember that many restaurants had no lists, and served bulk wines, cask beers or fortified wines. Delmonico's was the first to offer a wine list as we now know it.

For this reason the wine list is presented as it was in 1894 when Chef Ranhofer wrote *The Epicurean.*

Note the presence of both absinthe and vermouth as aperitifs, something not often found on menus anymore. Aperitifs in general are severely under appreciated in the United States, and for a century absinthe was illegal. Although it is once again legal to distill and sell absinthe, it will take a while before it is a staple in most American restaurants.

The sherries and Madeiras that follow display some familiar names and a surprising number of vintage dated wines. Madeira was well known in America for many years, was beloved by Washington and Jefferson and was so common it was known as the wine of America.

Moselle and Rhine wines display many places of origin still familiar as well as an interesting sparkling Moselle and a rare red wine from Assmannshausen. This illustrates how common German wines were in former days. What is heartening now is that Riesling-based wines are growing in popularity again. These wines were good matches for the game and seafood items in Delmonico's.

Looking at the balance of the white wines, it is instructive to note that the sweet wines are comfortably integrated with the still, or dry, wines. Bordeaux and Burgundy are heavily represented with reds and a sparkling Montrachet! The champagnes are mostly still easily recognized, a testament to the tenacity of the producers over the last 200 years.

Missing are the distinctions in port between ruby and tawny and the inclusion of a white port, again a bit unusual. Note that Delmonico's had a private label brandy listed as "Private Importation." There were also private label rye and bourbon. Beers, ales, cider and mineral waters round out the list.

Rounding out the discussion on wines in the book is a short section that includes instructions on how to clarify a cask of 225 liters, a barrique, which would have been shipped directly from Europe. Shipping wines in casks was still common throughout the 19th century and into the 20th. With the exception of certain specialty restaurants, this custom is all but extinct. It does shed light on how quality restaurants provisioned themselves in Victorian times.

To reiterate what was said before, this was new and groundbreaking territory for a restaurant and a chef and still influences the way restaurant and catering menus are composed today — not to mention book after book on food and wine pairing. Chef Ranhofer did that already!

Reading through these à la carte menus gives a new appreciation for what Chef Ranhofer

(3709). DELMONICO'S WINE CELLAR LIST.

Absinthe.   Vermouth.

SHERRY.
From the De Renne Estate.

Duff Gordon.

Première.	G. S., 1815.	C. Old around the cape.	Peter Domecq Jerez Med.
Imperial.	J. S., 1815.	Peerless Cape.	1818.
Brown.	Pale Gordon.	Choice Amont'ado 1857	Montilla xxxx.
Pando.	Suarez Superior.	P. G. Old, No. 5.	Wellington, P. Domecq.
Amontillado, Dry.	Suarez Pasto.	Dry Soleras, 1828.	Jerez, 1730.
Amontillado, 1834.	Suarez Oloroso.	Solera Cape.	P. Domecq £100 Royal,
Old Mantilla.	Pale Pemartin.	Harmony.	Pale.

MADEIRA.
From the De Renne Estate.

Imperial.	L. I., 1815.	Agrella Madeira, 1818.	F. Amory Imported, 1806.
Green Seal.	Thompson's Auction.	L. C. Madeira.	Y. Amory Dom Pedro,
O. S. Y., 1820.	Old Reserve.	Thorndike A, 1809.	1791-92.
		N. G., 1798.	F. Amory, Imported, 1811.

MOSELLE.

Scharzberg Muscatel.	Brauneberger.	Scharzhofberger.	Piesporter.
Berncasteler Doctor.	Zeltinger.	Sparkling.	Josephshofer.

RHINE.

Johannisberger Red Seal.	Steinberger Cabinet.	Geisenheimer.	Rüdesheimer.
Johannisberger Gold Seal.	Steinberger Auslese.	Marcobrunner.	Rüdesheimer Berg.
Johannisberger Schloss.	Steinberger Cab. Imp'l.	Marcobrunner Aus.	Rüdesheimer Berg Aus.
Rauenthaler Berg.	Bocksbeutel.	Domdechaney.	Rüdesheimer Berg Cab.
Hochheimer.	Deidesheimer.		Laubenheimer.
Liebfraumilch.	Assmannshauser (Red).		Niersteiner.

HUNGARIAN.

Budai.	Tokay Imperial (White).	Somlyai (White).
Villanyi.	Tokay Cabinet (White).	Budai Crème.

BORDEAUX.
White.

Château Yquem.	Graves.	Sauterne.	Lafaurie.
Château Yquem Crème de	Haut Sauterne.	Sauterne 1re.	Latour.
Tête.	Barsac.		

BORDEAUX.

Pichon.	Pontet Canet.	Larose.	
Château Lagrange.	Rauzan.	St. Julien.	Château Léovillé.
Batailley.	Léoville.	St. Julien Supérieur.	Château Larose.
St. Pierre.	Mouton Rothschild.	Château Couffran.	Château Margaux.
Château Langoa.	Haut Brion.	St. Estèphe.	Château Latour.
Château Pontet Canet.	Magnum Bonum.	Château de Pez.	Château Laffitte.

BURGUNDY.

Nuits.	Macon.	Clos de Vougeot.	Beaujolais.
Corton.	Macon Vieux.	Romanée.	Volnay.
Chambertin.	Pommard.	Romanée Conti.	Beaune.

BURGUNDY.
White.

Montrachet.	Chablis.
Montrachet Mousseux.	Chablis Vieux.

RHONE.

Hermitage.	Côtes Rôties.
Hermitage (White).	

CHAMPAGNES.

Cook's Imperial.	Pommery.	Moët, White Label.	Krug Sec, 1880.
Jules Mumm Grand Sec.	Pommery Vin Nature.	Moët, Imperial Brut.	Perrier Jouet, Special.
Deutz & Geldermann Sec.	Clicquot.	Piper Heidsieck Sec.	Heidsick Brut.
Dry Monopole.	L. Roederer.	Delbeck. Extra Dry.	Perrier Jouët, Brut.
Monopole Club, Dry.	Ruinart Brut.	Delbeck. Brut.	Mumm's Extra Dry.
Giesler.	Royal Charter.	Delmonico.	Irroy.
Giesler Brut, 1884.	Montrachet Mousseux.	Krug Sec.	Irroy Brut.

MALAGA, OLD.
PORT.

Première.	Very Old (White).	Osborn.	Sandeman's Old.

BRANDY.

Renault & Co.	Vierge.	Martell.	Private Importation.
Jules Robin & Co.	Renault, 1858.	Martell Old.	Very Old English Brandy.

WHISKEY.

Delmonico's Private Stock-Rye.	Delmonico's Private Stock-Bourbon.	Irish.
Bourbon.	Hollywood.	Irish (Powers).
Rye.	McGrath.	Old Cabinet Rye.
		Scotch.

MISCELLANEOUS.

Old Tom Gin.	Holland Gin.	Old Rum.	Very Old Jamaica Rum.

LIQUEURS.

Noyau.	Kümmel.	Bénédictine.	Curaçoa.
Prunelle de Bourgogne.	Kirsch.	Chartreuse (Yellow).	Curaçoa Sec.
Crème de Menthe.	Eckau.	Chartreuse (Green).	Anisette.
	Maraschino.		

ALES, ETC.

Scotch.	Kaiser Beer.
Porter.	Yuengling's Tivoli Beer.
Ginger Ale (Imported).	Milwaukee Lager.
Beadleston & Woerz's Imperial Lager.	Bass—McMullen.
St. Louis Lager.	Bass Dog's Head.
Ind. Coope & Co. Pale Ale.	Cider, Jericho.

MINERAL WATERS.

Apollinaris.	Clysmic	Juliushaller.	Vichy (Imported).

and his crew were able to accomplish on a daily basis. The most important aspect of a restaurant's food is its consistency. The ability to produce the meals required on a day-to-day basis while maintaining the operational standard of quality is the real test of a chef and the crew in the kitchen and in the dining room. Anyone can produce a spectacular meal from time to time for a private party with a big budget. The mark of a true professional is the ability to replicate daily the demands of the menu so as to be able to satisfy the guests each time they come in for breakfast, luncheon or dinner. When we reflect that Chef Ranhofer was leading the kitchen at various Delmonico locations around New York City for over three decades, this herculean feat becomes all the more impressive.

One of the fascinating aspects of this book, and all the books here as well, is how it documents the most intimate and conversely public social customs of the times: how people ate. It is possible to chart the changing tastes and requirements of society through the foods and how they were consumed.

As with some menus shown later on in the chapter on Victor Hirtzler, the chef at the St. Francis, dining trends have markedly changed. Breakfast menus no longer offer items such as clams, sandwiches, Arles sausage, Mackerel, mortadella and olives. Gone from the breakfast menus are the eight choices of fish ranging from red bass to porgy with Chablis. While breakfast meats now are a simple matter of bacon and breakfast sausage with an occasional steak or pork chop, the breakfast crowd no longer can select hot items ranging from pig foot to chateaubriand, from beef palate à la béchamel to mutton cutlets. It is rare for any restaurant to offer cold meat preparations on a breakfast menu, but dining habits for Chef Ranhofer's kitchen required the availability of such items as red beef tongue with jelly to roast chicken, pressed corned beef to aspic of foie gras.

When was the last time we saw breakfast salads on modern menus? Or breakfast vegetables from broiled sweet potatoes to succotash? Add to this the more or less still common fare of hot breakfast cereals and waffles and an assortment of fresh fruits, and there are probably more items on Chef Ranhofer's breakfast menu than most restaurants now offer for dinner!

Luncheon menus were similarly gargantuan, offering eight soups, eight different fish items, roasts listed on the menu as "ready," 12 items listed as cooked to order from veal cutlet to squab à la Briand. And don't forget the cold items (19), salads (6), vegetables (11), dessert (11), along with assorted cheeses and fruits.

For a guest to enter into Chef Ranhofer's culinary world at dinner, it could take until breakfast the next morning to read through the menu, which, by the way, was printed in French and English, also a first. (That's a surprise.) On any given day there would be around 11 or 12 soups, nine or ten salads, eight or nine entrées, roasts, cold items, a bewildering array of more than a dozen vegetables, hot dessert items, cold dessert items, ices, ice creams, sorbets, fruits served fresh and preserved, cheeses and coffees. To execute this variety of menu items required a huge staff and a world-class manager of purchasing, receiving, production and financial acumen: Charles Ranhofer.

The supper menu would be what we might now call late night dining. Please note the absence of chicken fingers and zucchini sticks! This menu was to round out the day for people who were at the opera or the theater or ballet, or were maybe attending a gala somewhere. As such it required the same attention to detail as breakfast, luncheon and dinner menus, but it was at least more concise. There is a smaller selection of soups and hot items, a fair amount of salads and, perhaps not too surprising, a focus on the dessert and sweet side of the kitchen.

A careful reading of these menus, breakfast, lunch and dinner, illuminates what it took on a daily basis to execute their demands while maintaining a restaurant quality of such a caliber that it created the idea of an entire new industry and shaped the world's perception of the United States.

BILLS OF FARE

BREAKFAST
JUNE

Coffee   chocolate   Arabian racahout   English breakfast tea
SIDE DISHES
Clams   Gherkins   Sandwiches   Radishes   Olives   Caviar
EGGS
Boiled   Fried à la Eugène   André Scrambled à la Columbus   On a dish
Fried turned over à la sole   Hard boiled, Russian style
OMELETS   Argentine   With clams   With bacon   Cocottes
Soft eggs with purée of sorrel   Poached eggs with gravy
FISH
Red bass water fish   Pike perch à la Durance   Whitebait
Black bass à la Narragansett   Mussels à la Poulette
Kingfish à la batalière   Porgy with Chablis wine   Bluefish à la Barnave
HOT
Pig's feet à la St. Ménéhould   Veal cutlets   Mutton cutlets
Beefsteak   Pork chops   Spring lamb cutlets   Roast squabs
Beef palate à la Béchamel   Chateaubriand
Escalope of veal à la Habirshaw   Mutton breast broiled
Stuffed breast of lamb, Velouté tomato sauce
Frogs' legs à la Poulette with mushrooms   chicken sautéed, half glaze
Squabs à la Carolina   Delmonico sirloin steak, Spanish style
Porterhouse steak
COLD
Corned beef, pressed   English ham with jelly
Red beef tongue with jelly   Ribs of beef Bellevue
Boned turkey   Calf tongue à la Macédoine   Lamb pie
Beef à la mode   Aspic de foie gras   Roast chicken with beef tongue and jelly
SALADS
Tomato   Watercress   Celery   Macédoine   Chicken mayonnaise
Russian
VEGETABLES
Potatoes fried   Mashed in snow   Broiled sweet potatoes   Saratoga
Beets with butter and fines herbes   Boiled asparagus with Hollandaise sauce
Succotash
BREAKFAST CAKES
Brioches   Wheaten grits   Hominy   Oat meal   Muffins
Corn bread   Indian cake   Flannel cake   Waffles
DESSERT
Darioles with orange flower water   Fresh fruits
Apples   Oranges   Bananas   Pears   Watermelon   Peaches
Cheese: American   Brie   Stilton   Roquefort   Chester
Glass of cream or milk
LUNCH
JULY
Clams

SOUPS
Consommé in cup   Pea purée with croutons Julienne faubones
Fish broth with clams   Clam chowder   Chicken okra
Mock turtle thickened   Cream of corn à la Hermann
FISH
Fresh mackerel maitre-d'hôtel   Fried soft shell crabs
Striped bass à la Bercy   Baked codfish Duxelle
Kingfish à la Batalière   Fillet of spotted fish English style
Porgies à la Manhattan   Eels à la Maréchale
READY
Leg of mutton à la Bordelaise   Sirloin of beef à la Dauphiness
Sausages with cream potatoes   Loin of veal with gravy
Bacon with spinach   Chicken fricassee à la Bouehard
Poached eggs with purée of chicken supreme
TO ORDER
Veal cutlet maître-d'hôtel   Small steak plate
Mutton cutlets with purée of chestnuts   Chicken croquettes exquisite
Squab à la Briand   Chicken cocotte
Noisettes fillet of beef à la Berthier   Frogs' legs à la d'Antin
Mutton breast with tomato Andalouse sauce   Squab sautéed à la l'Impromtu
COLD
Pickles   Radishes   Olives   Caviare   Celery
English ham with jelly   Anchovies   Sardines in oil   Lyons sausage
Mortadella   Sandwiches   Mackerel in oil
Stuffed olives with anchovy butter   Marinated tunny   Spring lamb
Red beef tongue   Lobster with mayonnaise   Boned turkey
Goose liver pie
SALADS
Russian   Tomato   Chicken mayonnaise   Potato Macédoine
Watercress
VEGETABLES
Potatoes fried   Saratoga   Hashed with cream   Lyonnaise
String beans à l'Albani   Boiled asparagus with hollandaise
Lima beans with thickened maître d'hôtel   Green peas, French style
Green corn on the cob   Stuffed truffles
Tomatoes broiled with mayonnaise sauce
DESSERT
ICE CREAM: Toronchino   Proeope   Pistachio   Asparagus
Nesselrode pudding with chestnuts   Vanilla   Chocolate
Tutti frutti Tortoni cups   Neopolitan
Banana cream   White coffee
WATER ICE: Raspberry   Orange   Lemon
PUNCH: Roman   Kirsch   Lalla Rookh   Maraschino
Bucket made of Chantilly waffles   Charlotte russe
FRUITS: Watermelon   Muskmelon   Peaches   Bananas   Apples   Grapes
CHEESE: American   Roquefort   Edam   Camembert   Pont l'Évéque
French coffee   Turkish coffee

DINNER

MAY
Clams
SOUPS
Consommé Caréme   Rice à la Rudini   Sherman

Bisque of crawfish à la Batalière   Cream of sorrel with stuffed eggs
Julienne Mogul   Pea purée with croutons   Croûte au pot
Chicken okra   Chicken okra strained   Small individual soup pots
SIDE DISHES COLD
Radishes   Olives   Caviare   Celery   Sardines in oil   Lyons sausage
Marinated tunny   Gherkins   Mortadella
Stuffed olives with anchovy butter   Mackerel in oil
SIDE DISHES HOT
Cromesqui of sweetbreads, Rabanine
FISH
Mussels with shallots   Eels broiled with tartar sauce   Planked shad ravigote butter
Spotted fish Livernaise   Weakfish à la Brighton   Fried soft shell crabs
Blackfish à la Sandford   Lobster à al Camille   Sheepshead Buena Vista
REMOVES
Roast sirloin of beef with brain patties
Rump of beef Boncieault   Pullet in surprise
ENTREES
Mutton pie Canadian style   Sautéed chicken florentine style
Mushrooms crust with truffles   Minions of tenderloin of beef à la Stanley
Hot plover pie   Breast of turkey   Donovan Squabs à la Crispi
Frog shells   weetbread à la St. Cloud
SORBETS: Lalla Rookh   Kirsch   Maraschino   Rum
ROAST
Leg of mutton à la Roederer   Leg of yearling lamb with gravy
Beef ribs, American style   Squabs
Duckling   Partridge broiled English style   Chicken in the saucepan
COLD
Galantine of chicken   Trout, tartar sauce   Terrine of duck livers à l'Aquataine
SALADS: Lettuce   Water-cress   Macédoine   Chicory
VEGETABLES
Purslain à la Brabançon   Lima beans with thickened maître d'hôtel
Potatoes Parisienne   Potatoes, ANNA Potatoes half glaze
Green peas, English style   String beans with butter
Boiled asparagus with Hollandaise Sauce   Succotash
Cèpes baked with cream   Stuffed cauliflower à la béchamel, baked
Fried eggplant   Spaghetti macaroni à la Lawrence
Asparagus ops à la Mantenon   Corn on the cob   Spinach with cream
Macaroni à la Birgnoli   Whole artichokes boiled with white sauce
Macédoine à la Montigny   Sweet potatoes roasted
SWEET ENTREMENTS
HOT: Pancakes with lemon sugar   Glazed apple marmalade
COLD: Blanc mange with strawberries   Bain marie cream molded
Charlotte Russe   Cream Malakoff
DESSERT
FANCY CREAMS: Biscuit Excelsior   Basket filled with oranges
Nesselrode pudding with strawberries biscuit glace
Neopolitan Plonmbière with chestnuts
CREAMS: Vanilla   White coffee   Pistachio
WATER ICE: Lemon   Raspberry · Pineapple
Assorted cakes
Preserved fruits   greengages   peaches   pineapple   quinces
Marmalade   Jelly   Dundee, peaches ginger   Guava Bar-le-duc
Stewed fruits: Pineapple, peaches, pears, prunes, apples, with jelly, bananas, cherries,

chestnuts, oranges, orange salad, strawberries, raspberries
Brandy fruits: greengages, pears, oranges, strawberries with cream
CHEESE: *Stilton, Brie, Strachino, Gorgonzola, Gruyere, Chester, Gervais, Port Salut,*
Holland
French coffee   Turkish coffee

There are some items here that require special mention as to how Chef Ranhofer continued the development of American cuisine at the very pinnacle of 19th-century restaurants.

First, the breakfast menu: The use of an American fish with an American place name appears in black bass Narragansett. This is followed by Squabs à la Carolina and the eponymous Delmonico steak. The "Cold" section features the native American turkey which leads to the vegetable medley of succotash. Note that sweet potatoes had made their entrance into the highest levels of cuisine, which shows how the African influence made its way from the slave cooking in the South all the way to the "top" of the food chain. And of course, the "Breakfast Cakes" section features two corn preparations, corn cake as well as corn bread, also via the Southern foodway.

The lunch menu: The inclusion of an American genre of soup, the chowder, shows how accepted this soup became for even the most sophisticated diners, both American and foreign, who patronized Delmonico's. Perhaps as a sign of decreasing availability we see a mock turtle soup. These animals were slaughtered relentlessly since the Europeans made their way here, and it seems to be showing already by the 1860s. Again with a nod to the cooking of slaves and the African influence there is a chicken okra soup as well as a cream of corn to showcase this native vegetable. The "Fish" section features striped bass, a denizen primarily of the northeastern states. The Hudson River at one time was a leading fishing ground for this species. Is there any seafood item more idiomatic to American cuisine than soft-shell crabs? From the Native Americans via Tidewater cooking, they too made the big time. There is also the use of Manhattan in keeping with the European tradition of place name designations. Turkey makes its appearance again in the "Cold" section and in the vegetables we see the newest fad, Saratoga potatoes, an American vegetable created in and named after Saratoga, New York. Tomatoes and lima beans round out the section. The "Desserts" section features the then ubiquitous American chestnut along with the traditional Pennsylvania Dutch Nesselrode pudding. American cheese makes its way to the "Cheese" section on equal footing with some classic European varieties.

For the dinner menu: Bisque of crawfish reflects the time Chef Ranhofer spent in Louisiana along with the chicken okra soup in two versions. Displaying an early example of American fusion cuisine, the seasonal east coast fish shad is cooked using a method made famous by the Indians of the Pacific Northwest. Here again the soft-shell crabs make their appearance along with blackfish. Lobster in this context implies a lobster from American Atlantic waters. "Entrees" and "Roasts" also showcase items of American cuisine in the Beef ribs, American style and Breast of Turkey now named after one Mr.(s) Donovan. The "Vegetable" section features American purslain, lima beans, potatoes, succotash, eggplant, sweet potatoes again and the all American corn on the cob. Once again Nesselrode pudding makes its appearance along with our chestnuts and exotic fruits such as guava, pineapple and the then not so rare quince. While the tropical fruits may not be native to American soil, they do show how Chef Ranhofer was able to incorporate items from all over the world and meld these items into his version of American cuisine based on French cooking. His kitchen was a perfect blend, reflecting French traditions and techniques and training with American heritage ingredients along with the never-ending search for the unusual items that found a place in our cooking many years ago.

SUPPER

AUGUST

Clams

HOT

Welsh rarebit   Consommé in cups   Golden buck

Stuffed lobster tails, deviled   Ramequins

Deviled mutton kidneys on skewers   Stuffed hard shell crabs   Carolina style

Chicken legs in paper   Croustades à la Castalane

Bondons of woodcock à la Diane   Chicken breast à la Chevreuse

Squabs á la Briand   Minions of tenderloin of beef à la Baillard

COLD

Sandwiches   Caviare   Radishes   Mortadella   Anchovies

Marinated sardines   Celery   Tunny   Lyon's sausage

Boned turkey   Caviare canapé   Goose liver pie

SALADS

Lettuce   Cucumber   Water-cress   Celery

Macédoine   Cos lettuce   Lobster American style

Chicken mayonnaise

Russian   Torcato

DESSERT

Ice Cream

SHERBET: Kirsch   Lalla Rookh   Prunelle   Maraschino

WATER ICE: Raspberry   Pineapple   Lemon   Orange

FANCY: Pudding Cavour   Banana in surprise   Plombiére à la Rochambeau

Vanilla   Chocolate   Coffee   Pistachio

Charlotte russe   Madeira jelly   Apricot flawn

FRESH FRUITS: Bananas, pineapples, apples, oranges, Niagra grapes,

huskleberries, currants, msukmelon, watermelon

CHEESE: Stilton, Gruyere, Cream, Strachino,

French coffee   Turkish coffee

Many of the items here are obviously borrowed from the earlier breakfast, lunch and dinner menus, something that is still a common practice in many modern restaurants. For a menu running at this time of night, it is impressive. Many of our modern day menu items are either deep fried or hastily assembled sandwiches or salads. It is, I think, instructive to notice that while the late night menu was indeed considerably shorter than the main meal menus, it in no way compromised the variety or quality of the preparations. A diner after the theater could go in for a late night supper and still be afforded the quality and variety for which Chef Ranhofer was justifiably famous.

Chef Ranhofer tells us that all the menu items' recipes follow in the main body of the book. Here are items that may be beyond any household kitchens, and most professional kitchens as well, save for restaurants that have cooks at the skill level that Chef Ranhofer expected from his crew. Also, many of these items are of another age, but some are quite modern in concept.

Going beyond the lists of menus, there is a section called "Elementary Methods," which discourses on borders for platters, almond milk, and types of garnish for larger items such as a leg of lamb or mutton or ham. There are directions on how to make buchées, or tartlet shell of puff pastry, instructions on how to properly cook by technique, are carving instructions for birds and beef ribs, tenderloin (which is larded by the way), ham, mutton leg and saddle, goose, duck and turkey.

Pastry cream recipes, how to prepare forcemeats and quenelles, straining and filtering aspic jelly to techniques for larding and barding meats — all are here in the basic methods.

There are some wonderful illustrations of labor-saving kitchen tools here as well. These were probably state-of-the-art at the time and should make any modern chef or cook appreciate the little things in life, like electricity and high speed stainless steel blades for making purees. One of the most clever tools is a vegetable cutter that had interchangeable dies for cutting vegetables and root vegetables into highly decorative shapes.

Chef Ranhofer included a wonderful illustration of a roaster/spit with three different spits for different purposes. What is most interesting is that on page 224 there are pictures of a rotisserie that would be placed in front of an open fire as in colonial times, a type of rotisserie cum contained fireplace of metal so that a leg or a large bird could be suspended form a string, hook or wire as we found in Amelia Simmons' book.

Other wonderful illustrations include a singeing apparatus, an early steam table, a salamander as well as a bain-marie with inserts. Much of the equipment would look familiar in a modern kitchen, including a range/broiler, a transportable heater for off-premise catering, a double-jacketed steam kettle, sautoie, sauté pans, soup pot and braziers. There are different molds for savory and sweet items, poaching pans, sieves, knives (some things never change), cleavers, sugar thermometer, chinois, a meat chopper; the list goes on and gives a remarkable picture of what a cook would have used in Chef Ranhofer's kitchen.

Not to be ignored are the refrigerator, icebox and cold room.

The Recipes

As stated above, elementary methods are given for essential skills such as: making almond milk, borders for platters made from metal to gum paste, brine, liquid caramel, how to carve. The reader can learn how to carve a turkey, coat aspic molds, make dozens of different dessert items, and make forcemeats and stuffings.

The section on professional kitchen equipment, most of which has not changed all that much since Chef Ranhofer's time, probably changed the most in how stoves are heated. Now most ranges are fired by gas or electricity. In Chef Ranhofer's kitchen gas was something new, with many kitchens using wood or coal for the stoves. But many restaurants still have grills fired by wood or charcoal.

In the recipes that appear herein in Chapter 15, if there are references to many items a professional kitchen would have had on hand in Chef Ranhofer's day, some adjustments have been made to accommodate our more modern methods of cooking.

But how to select some representative items? Chef Ranhofer's incredible book has around 3,500 different items. The recipes in Chapter 15 were selected to demonstrate how the fusion of classic French training, paired with some American ingredients and some surprisingly modern touches, made Chef Ranhofer's kitchen the palace of culinary excellence it was. What follows here is a brief summary of the sections of the book sans recipes.

As with other great cooks, Chef Ranhofer has the highest regard for soup: "Soup is the prelude of the dinner." And as with the prelude to an opera, a good, well composed prelude will set a mood or a tone for the composition to follow, whether musical or gastronomic.

Realizing that it is not possible to have good soup without a good stock, here called a broth, he writes, "it is on this article that one's whole attention must be borne."

His soup categories are somewhat different than in today's kitchens, with two basic types — fat or lean — divided into thick or clear. There is a further distinction made in classifications in the chapters on soup:

Those two kinds of soups are divided into six chapters: First Bisques; second, Consommé and Garnishings; third, Creams; fourth, Cosmopolitan or Mixed; fifth, Fish; sixth, Purées.

The first section is concerned with the preparation of the basic broths to be used for all the soups that follow. The section on bisques states that modern bisques are to be purées thickened with rice, thick stock or wet crusts of bread. They are always made with shellfish in five categories, specifically clams, oysters or mussels; crabs; shrimps; crawfish; and lastly lobster. They should be well seasoned and accompanied by "small, simple garnishes."

Consommé is clear although it may be thickened with fecule (potato starch) or arrowroot and finished with Madeira or Xeres, which is a sherry. If thickened, they are then called clear thick soups. All must be well seasoned and served very hot. Consommé may be made with any type of stock or broth but must be made with a specific broth for a specific consommé. For example, Consommé Caréme is made with chicken stock, thickened with arrowroot. For the experienced chef or experienced diner, many of these consommés will be familiar, with the name generally derived from the garnish.

The cream soups are to be made with "fresh vegetables" and thickened with a liaison of egg yolks and cream. Purée soups may be made with vegetables, most game birds or rabbits, even beans. Purée soups made with game meats are a mixture of egg yolks and meat tempered with the hot, lightly thickened broth and garnished.

Chowders are included with the fish soups and there is also a Gumbo with Hard Crabs as well as one with softshell crabs. Terrapins, dried and green turtle and mock turtle soup made with calf's head are here and the soup section is concluded with "Soups and Different Preparations for Invalids."

The next section is divided into three parts: "Stocks," "Essences" and "Auxiliaries." Pages 289 through 320 are devoted to all manner of stocks, essences and sauces, hot and cold, basic and derivative. Chef Ranhofer writes in the book, "A sauce is thick, essence is not. Essence is an extract from the most nutritious parts of meat. Fumet, or flavor, is a steam which rises from certain cooked or raw meats, imparting a most agreeable smell and taste; it is the same preparation as essences, but less watery and reduced with Madeira. This defining paragraph is attributed to a Messr. Becherelle. From the basics are derived glazes, gravies, half-glazes, veloutés and all manner of what we call derivative sauces; i.e., sauces based on what *mise-en-place* is always available in a classical kitchen. Stocks and essences evolve into glazes and demi-glazes with sauces being made with some of the above with added flavorings and each with a specific name.

Butter sauces are cooked step by step and after "proper reduction" are finished with whole fresh butter, a type of sauce-finishing technique still in use.

Cold butter sauces are what we might now call herb butters, but Chef Ranhofer regales us with 20 of them, from gooseberry to crab coral. Cold sauces, such as apple sauce, boar sauce and green Spanish sauce, to name a few, are for everything from serving with game and roasted meats to mayonnaise for mixing with chicken and shrimp salads.

The section on garnishings starts with a preface:

All the following garnishings may be served for removes by arranging them in clusters and making them either larger or smaller, according to the dishes required to be garnished. For large pieces of meat that are intended for removes they must be larger than for those intended for entrées, in the latter case they should be mixed together instead of being dressed in separate groups.

A large item, say a roast venison loin served as a remove, on a cart and carved at tableside would require garnishings not only of certain flavors and textures but size as well. If an entrée were plated the size of the garnish would diminish accordingly. Pages 332 to 354 are exclusively for garnishing. Very often the name of a preparation would depend upon the garnish. For example: A roast of mutton or pork might be called Pork with Tongue Andalusian on the menu. The garnish is neatly trimmed, thinly sliced beef tongue mixed with a demi-glace that is ladled around the meat. An Andalusian Tomato Sauce is then poured over the roast. These two separate items are the garnish for the roast.

The side dishes are both hot and cold and range from relatively uncomplicated vegetable purées to crustades, pastry shells to ornately decorated timbales. Chef Ranhofer again:

Hors-d'oeuvres, or side dishes, signifies out of the work, they having no place on the bill of fare. They are certain appetizing dishes placed on the table before dinner, remaining on in the Russian service, until the dessert; in the French service they pass round a few hors-d'oeuvres after the soup, such as melons, olives, radishes, celery, figs, artichokes, canapés, etc.

Chef Ranhofer continues on a bit about the Russian service and how these little items are served with choice spirits such as "kümmel, brandy, vermouth, absinthe, gin, etc." What is of note here is the inclusion of alligator pears (avocados), which Chef Ranhofer was instrumental in bringing into mainstream American cuisine. These little items may be "outside the work" but run to 45 pages with often five or six individual preparations per page. An awful lot of work for something not even included on a menu!

Mollusks and crustaceans take up the next section with clams, soft clams, crabs (both soft- and hard-shell), the aforementioned oyster crabs, crawfish, snails and frogs' legs. Of frogs' legs Chef Ranhofer says, "Refreshing broths are made with frogs' legs analogous to those composed of chicken or veal." He said it first: They taste like chicken! Lobster and spiny lobster are here, including Lobster Creole, which he probably first encountered when he was working in New Orleans and which impressed him enough to take the dish and put it in his book. As might be expected Lobster Newberg or Delmonico is here as well. Chef Ranhofer created this dish, originally named for a sea captain by the name of Wenberg. Apparently there was some bad blood later on and the name was changed but the recipe become world famous.

Mussels and oysters are offered in more than 20 different ways, followed by scallops, shrimps and terrapin. Ever the professional, Chef Ranhofer gives a reference table with costs for terrapins by size with a reckoning as to size, weight and price per dozen. In the late 1890s, small ones, five to six inches, cost an average of $15.70 per dozen, while the big ones, eight inches and over, were an average of $81.08 per dozen. It is more than understandable why so many cookbook authors had recipes for mock turtle soup.

Fish (poisson) follows crustaceans and what a variety of fish there are. Pages 428 to 469 list no fewer than 218 different preparations for fish, ranging from angel to whitebait. Native fish such as striped bass receive American-named recipes, as in Striped Bass Long Branch (a shore town in New Jersey) to Striped Bass à la Massena. The Hudson River was long a fertile fishing ground for striped bass, salmon and sturgeon.) Classic French recipes such as Parisian Bouillabaise are next to Buffalo Fish à la Bavarian.[19] Buffalo fish is a North

American freshwater fish most heavily concentrated in the southeastern states.) Throughout this section there is almost every kind of fish imaginable, including a large section on trout.

Beef in all its variety is here, including the first mention of a hamburger on a menu: Salisbury Steak, Beef Steak Hamburg Style and Hamburg Steak à la Tartare. The first two are made only from ground beef tenderloin and the last from "lean and tender beef, wither the tenderloin or sirloin." The eponymous Delmonico Steak, which was a 24-ounce rib-eye steak named by Chef Ranhofer, is here as well. As with many recipes written about earlier, there are quite a few recipes named for the garnish appended to them as well as some items no longer seen, such as a whole larded tenderloin of beef à la Chaney. Something also unusual for our day is braised beef tenderloin. Normally this style of cooking is for less tender cuts of meat.

Veal follows with some items also relegated to the dining room of history: brains, breast and calf's head. Veal cutlets are more often than not a modern day veal chop, sometimes larded, sometimes studded with truffles. Veal kidneys, liver, shoulder, sweetbreads — all the organ meats that are now rarely seen on restaurant menus — receive the same care and expertise as the finer, more expensive cuts.

Mutton, which is rarely served in restaurants anymore, has recipes that occupy 15 pages of the text. When reading through these recipes, one is struck by what a wealth of flavors were available from Chef Ranhofer's kitchen. As with other chefs of the period, all parts of the mutton were prepared, ranging from the breast to the leg. Cutlets (chops), fillet, kidneys, leg of lamb that is roasted and even boiled, leg of mutton that is minced or done on a spit; many of the larger dishes were also larded, another practice long since gone.

Lamb, or Agneau, receives 20 pages which may indicate that tastes were becoming a bit more modern, with mutton starting to recede in the public eye. Many of the dishes are similar to mutton as the cuts are the same. What stands out are how many preparations there are for cutlets and their variety: from lamb cutlets giralda (cooked with onions and peppers, covered with a reduced velouté and then served with another velouté enriched with a shrimp butter), to lamb cutlets murillo (which are chops sautéed on one side, covered with a duxelle, sprinkled with Parmesan cheese and finished in the oven, served with a demi-glace). Epigrams of lamb, lamb fries, kidney and loin — all staples of Chef Ranhofer's kitchen.

Pork receives a relatively modest 11 pages; there is a recipe for Black Blood Pudding as the second of the section, which ends with a type of a ham that is a brined pig foot with a large section of the shank left attached, served on a bed of green beans and carved at the table. Chitterlings are here, but listed as Andouillettes de Troyes; about 90 percent of the recipe is devoted to proper cleaning for, as Chef Ranhofer says, "In fact it must be remarked that the quality depends entirely upon the proper cleansing of the bowels."

There is a diagram showing the cuts of the hog and this is then followed by several recipes for cutlets, pigs' feet, and ham — Virginia ham being especially mentioned. Sausages, hams, pork rack, tenderloin, all prepared in a variety of ways including minced, stewed in a blanquette, smoked and roasted and broiled.

Poultry in its myriad of forms consumes a whopping 52 pages starting with capon, which is one of the most succulent birds but rarely seen in restaurants or even in markets. Traditional chicken dishes of French origin, cocotte, maître-d'hotel, Volnay, are interspersed with preparations named à la Harrison (prepared with terrapin and truffles) to chicken fillets Mexican style in paper (cooked and served in the paper with vegetables and white wine). Chicken fricassee is curried, served with carrot balls and eggplant croquettes (à la Favorite) and served with two sauces and mushrooms cooked and flavored with butter, meat glaze and lemon juice. There are recipes for chicken Maryland garnished with corn fritters and à la Marengo along with à la Nantaise and Parmentier, two classic French staples.

There are numerous recipes for duck including still current menu items ranging from Bigarade Sauce (although Ranhofer actually makes a type of haggis with the stomach of the duck) to Jerusalem artichokes.

He mentions goose but says that, "A goose is usually served at unceremonious dinners." He does not say why, but he apparently did not consider this staple of English Christmas feasting and traditional German bird on the same level as duck and other poultry.

Guinea fowls and pigeons follow, and here there are so many recipes for pigeons that is not hard to see why passenger pigeons became extinct after less than a century of intense hunting. A resource that was nurtured by the Native Americans came to an abrupt end in a very short time. Interspersed with these recipes are illustrations of various display pieces for grand buffets, including pigeons with olives, pigeons garnished with Montglass Cases-Stuffed, an impossibly ornate and multi-component platter.

Squab recipes include a dish that always seemed strange to me, Squabs Crapaudine, which is squab cut and shaped to look like a toad. Served à la Flourens, American style stuffed, English style, New York style, fried, as fritters Carolina or with tarragon, these little birds were obviously all the rage along with the pigeons.

Turkey is here, of course, American style, French style, with olives, oyster sauce, à la Jules Verne, chestnuts and with an artichoke purée.

Game runs the gamut from blackbirds to boar, to woodcock, quail, plover, snipe, grouse and ptarmigan — these last six with their own pictures. Wild ducks — blackhead, brant, canvasback, mallard, redhead, ruddy, and teal, all were available to restaurants as they were so plentiful they were still commercially hunted. All these are now the sole domain of individual hunters in what remains of existing flyways. Rabbit and all manner of venison complete the game section.

The entrée part of the book concludes with "Miscellaneous Entrees," far too numerous to go into here. The section ends on page 802.

Salads are cooked and made with a variety of meats and seafood, cooked vegetables, raw vegetables, and salad greens.

There follows a section on vegetables proper that consists of 31 pages, followed by eggs with another 16 pages.

This is such a large comprehensive book that even a brief perusal starts to sound like a laundry list after a while. In an effort to avoid a disservice to Chef Ranhofer, the remaining contents will be briefly summarized. One could easily write a book about this book, it is such a monumental, important work.

Farinaceous products — rice, corn meal, pasta in all sorts of shapes and preparations — have a fairly small section. In reading these recipes, despite pasta being an inexpensive ingredient, the dedication to making each dish memorable is readily apparent. One dish, Risot with Piedmontese Truffles, is a rice pilaf enriched with cheese and butter, placed in a baking dish then covered with white truffles warmed in butter and served with a "clear gravy."

Sweet entrements are next, with a fabulous selection of hot desserts that have largely disappeared from modern menus. There are hot fruit desserts and charlottes, twice-baked "crusts" made of sliced brioche used to line pans and then filled with an assortment of fillings. The Mundane Fritters are listed with a wonderfully contemporary sounding fritter, "Celeriac, Pear and Quartered Apple." Traditional American pies — peach, apple, rhubarb — are in league with Lombarde Pears–Stuffed and Richelieu Peaches.

Puddings baked in dishes and pudding cloths, still a viable cooking method, are listed with soufflés and Zephyr of Rice with Pineapple.

Cold entrements include Bavarians, cold Charlottes, creams, custards, fruit rings and "flawns." Cold puddings and molded desserts and all manner of special jellies round out the section.

Pastries are large cakes and meringues which are then followed by a section on breakfast cakes, including brioche, biscuits, English muffins and hot cross buns, buckwheat pancakes, flannel cakes, "Indian Cakes"—even Wheatties served hot!

Cookies, tartlets, bread items, ices abound, with wonderful illustrations of a machine for freezing ices and ice creams. Ice creams, ice creams, ice creams. One finds caramel, chocolate, nougat, peach, rice milk, black coffee, white coffee, parfaits, frozen mousses, punches, Stanley Punch served in a glass accompanied by a heron and cattails made of gumpaste. Frozen desserts take the shape of dice, cards, swans, ears of corn pyramids, lemons filled with a lemon maraschino cream. There are literally too many items to even list, let alone describe. It is no wonder that this chef and his cooking, presented in this book, revolutionized American cuisine and the entire restaurant industry.

The remainder of the book is given over to some tips on chilling champagne, menus for private parties and a recipe index.

In this book Chef Charles Ranhofer was at the cusp of the restaurant industry in America. By the end of the 19th century there were certainly many restaurants of high quality. In this book we have a historical record of the food served at America's first restaurant, prepared by America's first chef. This restaurant and this man defined what we now as those two segments of our culinary heritage.

Thankfully, the Delmonico family and Charles Ranhofer worked together for so long that they became fixtures of American culture, society and the history of food in America. Through the influence and excellence of Chef Ranhofer, haute cuisine was written down and codified for future generations of cooks and people devoted to the very best that is possible in the creation of food.

Escoffier gets all the press, but Chef Ranhofer came ten years before and was every bit as exhaustive as Escoffier. Also included in *The Epicurean* are American food items and creations that became standards of the cuisine of America. A look at the foods he created and presented for the first time reads like a who's who of American food, both haute cuisine and casual cuisine.

Reading through this book is to experience a world of flavor and elegance unfolding in front of the reader. It is truly a "time machine" that whisks the reader to an elegant and opulent age where, at least in the case of Chef Ranhofer and the Delmonico family, cost was no object in the pursuit of excellence.

Menus, display pieces, directions for making coffee, preserved and brandied fruits. A culinary masterpiece from a culinary master that made an entire industry and created a profession while creating an image of America that spread around the world.

This man truly was America's first chef and the finest that has graced our country.

Charles Ranhofer, America's greatest chef.

CHAPTER 8

Victor Hirtzler

Following the elegant Delmonico's restaurants of New York, restaurants and fine hotels rapidly crossed the country. With the completion of the transcontinental railroad in 1869 the country was now linked by high-speed transportation from the Atlantic to the Pacific. (The actual name of the railroad that completed this feat was the Pacific Railroad.)

This linking of the coasts made further population expansion easier and far less time consuming than walking or using a wagon. From New York City to San Francisco in 1870 was a scant seven days. The fares were close to what air travel is today: $136, or about $1100–$1200 in modern currency, for first class — but this fare also included a sleeping berth and all meals. Come to think of it, it was a much better deal than first-class airfare today! To be sure, these fares were not feasible for all people, but second-class fare was a doable $65, which is around $700 in modern currency. Third class was called simply "immigrant class," which indicates the fluency of movement achieved by this railroad.

The railroad was there and served as a catalyst for increased trade of all sorts. And two types of food products readily utilized this miracle of transportation: beer and regular comestibles. Augustus Busch was the first of the great American beer magnates to see and seize the potential that the railroads presented for brand expansion. And Victor Hirtzler, who had come to the United States via an interesting culinary route, to say the least, used this transportation technology to help define Ameri-

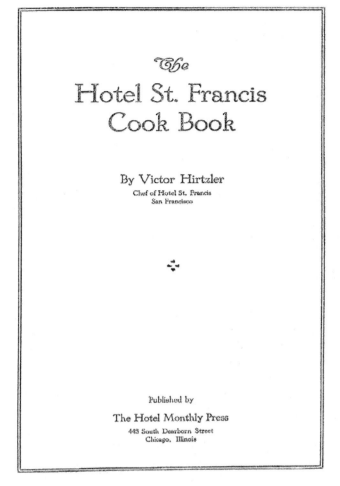

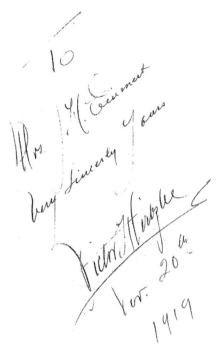

can cuisine by identifying certain foods by name on his menus. These were foods noted for their quality as coming from certain specific areas in the country. The often-used place names of origin covered the entire United States, from oysters of Cape Cod and ham from Virginia, to a myriad of distinctive foods from the West Coast in general, and California in particular. By so doing, Chef Hirtzler was the founder of California cuisine and a major contributor to what we now call American cuisine.

Who Was Victor Hirtzler?

Chef Hirtzler was born in Alsace probably in 1875. In the traditional European method, he apprenticed under Chef Emile Feypell, who possessed a reputation as one of Europe's finest chefs.[1] In *The St. Francis Cookbook*, which is arranged as a menu for each day of the year, Chef Feypell earned a dish in his honor for March 12. The dish, which is artichoke bottoms filled and coated with a stuffing made of artichokes, mushroom puree, cheese and egg yolk, baked with bacon on top and served with a Madeira or tomato sauce, certainly shows a high degree of culinary skill in its preparation and presentation. (The combination of flavors and cooking methods required for its execution are complex and varied.) Further service at the Grand Hotel in Paris and positions in and around France and Germany

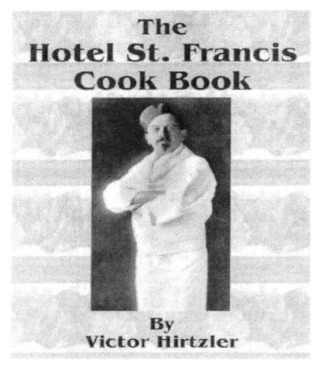

The Hotel St. Francis Cook Book

By Victor Hirtzler

PREFACE

In this, my book, I have endeavored to give expression to the art of cookery as developed in recent years in keeping with the importance of the catering business, in particular the hotel business, which, in America, now leads the world.

I have been fortunate in studying under the great masters of the art in Europe and America; and since my graduation as Chef I have made several journeys of observation to New York, and to England, France and Switzerland to learn the new in cooking and catering.

I have named my book The Hotel St. Francis Cook Book in compliment to the house which has given me in so generous measure the opportunity to produce and reproduce, always with the object of reflecting a cuisine that is the best possible.

The recipes in my book calling for wines and liqueurs for flavoring may be followed by those whose legitimate supplies are not used up; and where these cannot be had there are non-alcoholic substitutes available with the flavor near perfect. The juice of lemons will serve in many cases to give agreeable flavor.

The spaces left open in the pages of the book are for the purpose of affording convenient place for writing in additional recipes. The paper on which the book is printed is specially selected for this purpose.

VICTOR HIRTZLER.

garnered a stellar reputation for Chef Hirtzler. In an article from the *San Francisco Call,* one M. G. Maury interviewed the chef about his life and career. "He is an artist. A composer with a soul for the music of the sputtering roast or the delicious staccato of the broil. A man full of the artistic possibilities in an entrée or a sauce or the rich blending of harmonies in a masterpiece from the soup pot."[2]

Maury states that almost everyone, from hotel guests to hotel workers, knew and addressed him as simply Victor. "Little, but with broad shoulders, a Vandyke beard and sparkling eyes, Victor is far from being the sort of person usually pictured by that word — cook." He goes on to say he was a man with extreme artistic sentiments and was always looking for the possibilities of a dish. After decades in the business, Victor was the first one to admit, despite his exalted career and position as chef one of the finest hotels in the world, and his celebrity status in "the Paris of the West": "Thirty years I have been at it, and I know it all not yet." Still, with the knowledge he did have, he was considered well worth the $10,000 yearly salary paid by the Crockers, who owned the hotel.

Victor's favorite story was the one about the pheasant mousse for the King of Portugal, which at that time, Victor said cost $180 per serving. When he was the chef to King Carlos I of Portugal, he created a dish that became the favorite of the king to such an extent that it had a major impact on the country's treasury, and was, at least in part, responsible for the overthrow of the king. The dish was entitled La Mousse Faisan Lucullus and was composed of a mousse of Bohemian pheasant and woodcock breast, studded with truffles and served with a Madeira Sauce enhanced with cognac and champagne).

Apparently Don Carlos was always in Victor's office talking about food. And along with the love of food went expensive tastes to match. Such love of food and attendant expenses all but bankrupted the Portuguese treasury and led in part led to Carlos' assassination and the later establishing of democratic rule in Portugal.

With rumors and plots rampant in the royal court, Victor's foods were inspected before and after cooking by King Carlos' majordomo, a sort of exalted butler. At one point, after having his kitchen creations poked and prodded into a culinary train wreck, Victor reported he finally lost his temper and let the majordomo know that how could he, a master of the kitchen, "do his best" for the king when his efforts were "rendered futile by the poking and prying of make believe chemists?" Victor was definitely not shy and retiring when it came to his food and his profession.

It seems his tirade did little good, however, and when his employer was blown to bits by assassins Victor took the hint and left town for the United States.

Another story from his early career as a chef to royalty relates that he worked as chef for Kaiser Wilhelm I of Germany. He goes on to describe a banquet for the royal heads of state in Germany that employed 50 cooks in the kitchen and 80 waiters, not including wine servers and other sundry attendants. He says further that "it was very quiet — almost solemn, that dinner. Maybe it was the fact that they were afraid to say too much."

With his rarefied position in the world of chefs, he managed to see his patrons and his work for them in a realistic perspective; consider, as Maury states, "To him a king or a grand duke is simply a man who needs his victuals three times a day" — and presumably puts on his pants one leg at a time!

As one of the royal food tasters for Czar Nicholas II in Russia, Victor also talks about stringent security in the Czar's kitchen — constant food inspections before and after cooking, searches coming into and leaving from the kitchen, examination of displays. One gets the feeling he thought it was all a bit tedious.

With the reflections of Victor in this article we can certainly see his personality coming through. It also offers us a little known or appreciated aspect of a world that largely vanished after World War I. One can almost see the kitchens and smell the food while envisioning assembled groups of royalty around massive tables waiting for the food. As a counterbalance to those visions, consider that Victor also related how when he worked in Portugal, if a servant spoiled a dish or broke a plate, it was charged against his or her wages — penny pinching in the midst of luxury and opulence.

At the same time, as often still happens in modern day kitchens, after dark many of the local caterers would bring their empty wagons to the back door of the royal kitchens to be loaded with food supplies for private catering events. Kind of a high end version of collecting food falling off the back of a truck!

Victor also recalled that when he worked for Grand Duke Ferdinand in Baden in Germany there was another majordomo type, referred to as the *haustofmeister,* who, as Victor called him, was "a crook." He would actually prepare foods from the royal kitchens and sell them to his friends who had private catering businesses. Apparently, as Victor recalled with enjoyment, "he overreached" and actually ordered food and had the kitchen staff prepare an entire separate menu for a caterer in Karlsruhe. The kitchen staff loaded the wagons with the stolen, fully prepared foods, wines included, and had them deliver the feast to the *haustofmeister's* friend the caterer. When Victor joined the grand duke's staff a short time later, the affair was discovered, the *haustofmeister* and a number of chefs and kitchen staff were thrown in jail.[3] Victor clearly was able to appreciate the humor in the mundane daily events that took place in royal households.

This article is one the few references that gives a sense of the personality of the man who had such a worldwide reputation. There seems to be precious little extant about this extraordinary man: a newspaper ad for new gas and electric appliances endorsed by him; a photo and articles about the judging of the California Raisin Bread Competition, but not much else. Even the photo below is missing a big section as it was reportedly taken in the kitchen at the St. Francis.

In the *Oakland Tribune* there is a small glimpse into Victor and his interests.[4] The article states he was interested in collecting menus and had amassed more than 1,000 from around the world. Among the more interesting was a menu in the shape of a coffin adorned with skulls. There was no mention of what was served at the dinner that had featured this unique menu format. Another menu of sorts was a "coupon book" for a train passenger who would clip a coupon for each stage of the journey for a specific item of food.

Later in the article Victor talks about pastries and says he has become a fan of the American pie, providing of course that he supervises the making of said pies.

After the nasty incident that befell his patron King Carlos, Victor moved to America and

served in a number of New York establishments: he was chef at the Old Brunswick Hotel, second chef at the Waldorf-Astoria and chef at Sherry's Café, the restaurant that was to be a significant player in the demise of Delmonico's Restaurant. In these positions we can also see how the growth of the grand hotels was to play a major role in fine dining in the United States. And as the country continued to prosper and expand, it was one of the grandest hotels that lured Victor to San Francisco.

Victor went to California in 1904 where he was the opening chef for the splendid new St. Francis Hotel. This hotel was the original truly first-class hotel west of Chicago and was a monument to the rapid growth and prosperity of the Bay Area. The hotel was built by the Charles Crocker family with the idea of transforming San Francisco into the Paris of the West. It is said that it cost $2.5 million to build and was designed by the firm of Bliss and Faville. It was originally two wings but was subsequently enlarged.

An article published on February 20, 1904, mentioned that the hotel was due to open in "the middle of March."[5] The manager, Allan Pollock, "confidently stated" the hotel would formally be opened at that time. "All the heads of the various departments of the new hostelry" were on site getting ready for the opening. "Prominent among these attachés of the St. Francis is Victor Hirtzler, the chef, who comes directly from Stasbourg. He was formerly chef of the Hotel Steffany and Hotel de l'Europe in Baden Baden and the Balis Royal of Nice."

Picture of the original lobby of the St. Francis Hotel. Image courtesy of St. Francis Hotel/Starwood Resorts, Kelly Chamberlin.

The article goes on to list pastry chef Gaston Renen, who came to the St. Francis via Paris and New York as pastry chef, and Prosper Retter as maitre d'.

On March 20th an article showed a photo of the completed hotel and went on to talk about this splendid new addition to the city.[6] The opening would dazzle with the display of 13,000 electric lights. It was said it took two years to build and there was no hotel "more modern, more handsomely furnished or more beautiful in interior or exterior than the St. Francis"—marble columns, 30-foot ceilings—"The restaurant, 150 × 50, flanked with rows of fluted Tuscan columns, is the most beautiful room of the hotel. Its treatment of grey and gold, and the myriads of cut glass crystals in electrollers and side brackets, multiplied by many mirrors reflecting 958 electric lights, render it brilliant in the extreme."

The café was described as a palm garden with English oak paneling and more fluted columns, marble floors, and windows draped with green silk velour. A library of 4,000 volumes contained walls of leather panels; "the grill has an air of a hunting lodge" with the electroller being made of deer antlers. And the ladies' reception room with its own "English oak" had elevator access so the ladies would not have to traverse the entertainment rooms of the hotel.

The article continues with the description of what we would now call a public relations and travel office that "will be in touch with every hotel in this country" and will supply

The original St. Francis dining room. Image courtesy of St. Francis Hotel/Starwood Resorts, Kelly Chamberlin.

guests with information about California. The office would also link to other states "to promote this State's advancement through this medium."

The final paragraph states that it is "almost superfluous to add that the cuisine of the St. Francis will be a distinguishing feature." It goes on to mention the chef, Victor Hirtzler; the pastry chef, Gaston Renon; and the maître d'hotel, Prosper Retter of Strasbourg, Germany — all professionals of impeccable reputation "selected for the definite purpose of placing this department far in advance of anything ever attempted on this coast."

The St. Francis opened on March 21, 1904; the opening was a huge event and the line to get into the hotel reportedly stretched for more than three blocks. It was immediately and immensely popular, so much so that after only six months construction plans were being considered to add another wing and two floors of apartments, as well as a grand ballroom.

The opening was worthy of a large article and photograph in *The San Francisco Call* of March 20, 1904. There is a good description of the hotel itself, the opening time, and, in the last paragraph, mention of the culinary staff, including Victor.

The hotel boasted its own theater with a resident theatrical director to aid guests in creating and performing their own productions. There was a resident orchestra as well as an in-house school where guests and residents could have their children study French, music and manners.

The public spaces were always grand and impressive, and meeting "under the clock" became non-secret code for meeting one's friends in the lobby of the St. Francis under the famous clock. From there lunch would be enjoyed in the Mural Room.

The St. Francis before the quake. Image courtesy of St. Francis Hotel/Starwood Resorts, Kelly Chamberlin.

The lobby after the earthquake. The building was still standing but sustained considerable damage. Image courtesy of St. Francis Hotel/Starwood Resorts, Kelly Chamberlin.

In 1906 the hotel survived the earthquake but was eventually damaged by the fire that ravaged the city. The morning after the earthquake, Victor and his staff cleaned up the kitchen and provided a breakfast for hotel guests, including Enrico Caruso who was performing at the opera house. John Barrymore was also a guest at the time but was apparently too drunk to notice the earthquake. The story was that Barrymore staggered through the lobby shortly after the actual quake and simply went to his room to sleep it off.

Ever the professional that created the theatrical personality, Victor and his staff created a breakfast menu of chilled rhubarb stew, southern hominy with cream and eggs with truffles in puff pastry! This menu was recreated in 2006 to commemorate the centenary of the quake and fire. It was a tradition that on the day commemorating the quake the St. Francis would recreate the breakfast for the quake survivors.

Within less than two months a temporary hotel was erected by the Dewey Monument and the hotel proper re-opened in 1907, almost doubling its size from 250 to 450 guest rooms.

As seen in the picture at the beginning of the chapter, Victor was at home in this theatrical and flamboyant milieu. Always known as one of the world's best chefs, he cultivated the image of "chef" to the utmost. Wearing a fez and purple robes, sporting a waxed and curled mustache and forever roaming about the hotel, he was truly one of the first celebrity chefs in California, if not the first. In fact, he was known as the chef who would not stay in the kitchen and when guests were present spoke in a wildly exaggerated French accent, laying it on pretty thick in his role as the stereotypical French chef.

His food is rooted in classic and traditional French cooking with assorted international touches throughout. After working in several different countries before coming to America, his range of artistry was impressive, to say the least.

This photograph after the 1906 earthquake and fire gives a good impression of the devastation. Image courtesy of St. Francis Hotel/Starwood Resorts, Kelly Chamberlin.

In Europe, foods as well as wines and some spirits can be identified with place names. Easily recognizable would be Roquefort cheese, Gruyere cheese, Cognac, wines of Burgundy and Bayonne ham. This has not been the case for the most part in the United States. But when Victor was reigning at the St. Francis, he became a champion of using certain foods from certain locales and placing these names on the menu. He was an avid user of various California foods and was not shy about it. He also used specific West Coast foods and identified them as coming from Oregon, Washington or Alaska. When a specific East coast item was required, that would also be recognized on the menu as a mark of distinctive quality.

In reading through Chef Hirtzler's book, first published in 1910 as *L'Art Culinaire* and republished in 1919 as *The Hotel St. Francis Cook Book,* it is impossible for even a casual reader not to notice certain place names and foods appearing time after time. What is now so common on restaurant menus and found in food articles and cookbooks everywhere is the result of Victor focusing on the unique quality a certain region lends to its food products. Their methods of preparation, also focused in a specific area, were recognized by Chef Hirtzler as creating unique culinary traits that needed to be credited on his menus.

The book itself is organized with menus starting on January 1 and going throughout

Top: Despite all the destruction and the obvious damage to the hotel, Chef Victor served breakfast to more than 5,000 people the morning after the quake—no small testament to his skill and dedication to his profession and his city. Image courtesy of St. Francis Hotel/Starwood Resorts, Kelly Chamberlin. *Bottom:* A refugee from the quake with what little he was able to save of his home. Image courtesy of St. Francis Hotel/Starwood Resorts, Kelly Chamberlin.

the year to December 31. Breakfast, lunch and dinner are there for each day with selected items given a recipe or a manner of preparation below. The back of the book lists pages of private party menus as well as a couple of à la carte menus for the hotel dining room. Victor was noted for the impressive number of items on his menus, and the reader can see this is a reputation well deserved.

Victor's book is organized in a unique manner. Not all of the menu items are paired with recipes on the page, and all the recipes are written in paragraph form. Sometimes the directions are more precise than others. For example, on January 3, the Potage Normande is simply a "velouté with Julienne of carrots and turnips." And of course everyone knows how to make a velouté. Right?

The Sirloin of Beef Clermont has instructions for the garnish items, which are chestnuts, tomatoes, boiled cabbage and stuffed onions. The meat itself is simply listed as "Roast sirloin of beef, sauce Madere."

On January 5 there are recipes for baked apples with cream, fried hominy, fried smelts, broiled spareribs, and sauerkraut, sauce piquante or savarin Mirabelle. Remember each page has menus for breakfast, lunch and dinner.

In some ways this is a type of bridge cookbook in that some dishes are clearly explained while for others the author expects the reader to know what is contained in a myriad of dishes from cuisines around the world.

Also, quantities can be given in a general manner. In one of the dishes he thought of as his best, Chicken Edward the VII, the entire recipe is "Boil the chicken in stock and stuff with rice as for Chicken Diva. Add small squares of truffles and goose liver natural. Serve with curry sauce."

Most of the directions are for individual plating with the exception of soups (sometimes), roasts (sometimes), salads (sometimes) and desserts (sometimes).

Even though these are more small-scale incarnations of his food, a quick look at the banquet menus in the back of the book shows that any item could be prepared for one or for hundreds. In fact, the day after the earthquake in 1906 with the city in ruins and fires raging that would eventually consume the St. Francis, which survived the actual quake, Hirtzler and his crew cooked breakfast for 5,000 people both in and out of the hotel. Within a matter of a few hours the hotel was in ruins.

Certainly what stands out here are the identifiers of foods originating in certain places in the United States, and, especially, California. His recipe titles include place-names — by doing this Victor placed traditional American foods and preparations on a par with the best other countries and cuisines had to offer. His food was both elegant and refined as well as simple and basic. While he was working in the finest hotel in the West he certainly had ample opportunity to display his skills as a cook and as a showman. He became what we now call a celebrity chef and was enrolled for judging cooking and baking contests and doing celebrity endorsements for products geared to the general public, most of whom would have known his name even if they could not have been regular or even occasional guests of the hotel.

His championing of local foods and American food items reaches into the homes and professional kitchens of our times. We are now experiencing a resurgence of this type of food supply through Slow Foods and the phenomenon of locavores.

The man who cooked for royalty wanted to be known by his first name by his staff and all other people with whom he came into contact. Exacting standards were encased in a personality of genuineness that is sometimes not found in well known professional chefs.

He was able to add considerably to the reputation of San Francisco as the Paris of the West by being chef of the leading hotel of the West. His tenure did much to validate American cuisine in a truly international venue.

Victor, as mentioned before, was born in Alsace which at the time was part of Germany; he was classically trained, worked in various locations in Europe and with different cuisines. Alsace itself is an amalgam of French and German cuisines, language and wine production. His menus are showpieces for standard classical preparations: Eggs Oudinot; Noisette of Lamb, Cendrillon; Hollandaise Sauce; Vol a Vent Tolouse; Salade Thon Marine. (For his 1914 book, Clarence Edwards asked Victor for his best recipe. Victor produced two: Sole Edward VII, and Celery Victor.)

But along with these classically-named menu items, Victor clearly establishes that he is in America and in California. His menu choices reflect the beginnings of California cuisine and the West Coast as a special place where outstanding and unique foods are produced, so much so that these items are listed by name and put on equal footing with their European counterparts.

Not content with using West Coast names and California places of origin, Victor reaches into the historical trove of American foods and produces menus that truly reflect American cuisine. In the course of one year's worth of menus, the following items and categories of foods appear consistently and with a frequency that leaves no doubt as to where the guest is dining: in America, more specifically California, on the west coast of America, enjoying local foods and what had become traditional American dishes as well. The guest is also in a splendid hotel with these items prepared by a certain celebrity chef who left no doubt as to who was responsible for this wonderful food. Witness these items on a one-year menu cycle.

- Sand dabs, a deep-water fish found in the waters of California, appear no fewer than 16 times on the menu.
- California oysters and Lake Tahoe trout are found at least 61 times in versions from oyster cocktail to Hangtown fry to classic trout recipes Victor had prepared in Europe. Also singled out as descriptors are raisin cocktail with ketchup, shad with California raisins, California marmalade, California olives, green and ripe, Sierra cheese, Petaluma cream cheese, chicken with California raisins and cactus fruit.
- West Coast–produced foods include Oregon cream cheese, Toke Point oysters from Washington and Alaska reindeer and black cod.
- Cooking on a wooden plank, a hallmark of Native American cuisine on the West Coast, is used for steaks as well as seafood.
- The designation "St. Francis" on menu items is found at least 17 times, from canapés to potatoes to desserts. This style of naming dishes for the St. Francis Hotel helped to establish the hotel as a world-class operation.
- Items created by Victor and listed with the appendage "Victor" appear at least ten times, probably the best-known recipe being "Celery Victor."
- Menu items that use American place names or have the name America in their name appear on the menu at least 117 times. These items include sweet potatoes in a variety of preparations, Boston baked beans, Virginia ham, assorted Creole dishes, hominy, corn cakes, oysters from the East Coast including Sea Point, Cotuit, Blue Points, and Lynn Haven.
- Also designated are ruddy duck, nesselrode pie and all manner of dessert pies, ter-

rapin, catfish, Brown Betty, Clam Soup Salem, Potage Honolulu, cobblers, chow chow, pumpkin pie, stewed and scalloped pumpkin, American cheese, planked striped bass (a combination of an East Coast fish and West Coast Native American cooking style), Saratoga Chips (a new-fangled thinly sliced potato deep fried and salted), Philadelphia ice cream made without a traditional custard, Philadelphia Pepperpot, mince pie, and roast turkey with cranberry sauce.

- Also to be found are Salade Americaine, Potage Americaine, Maryland beaten biscuits, succotash and Hare Soup Uncle Sam.
- That newly imported fruit from South America, the alligator pear, first placed on a menu by Chef Ranhofer, makes its appearance no fewer than nine times.
- Dishes created by Chef Ranhofer at Delmonico's include Delmonico potatoes, Lobster and oysters Newburg, baked Alaska and Hamburg steak.
- With a nod to his past we also find Pompano Café Anglaise, Spaghetti Caruso, strudel and sauerkraut. Pompano is an American fish and the Café Anglaise was one of the best restaurants in Paris. Hello fusion cuisine!
- In a look at what was in the future for American food there are also hothouse berries and farm-raised trout.
- Another aspect of Victor's cuisine was that he had a reputation for providing guests with extensive menus, and was able to provide dozens of different preparations for the same item.

Reproduced below is an à la carte menu from the hotel kitchens, a luncheon menu for August 14, 1913. Notice several items here: the length of the menu, the variety of oysters and seafood, the intermingling of American cuisine with classical cuisine and the number of items that are distinctly in the realm of American cuisine.

Following is a dinner menu from two years later, April 9, 1915. The same incredible variety in all food categories, the intermingling of American cuisine on a par with classical cuisine, the designations of place names for specific California and regional foods — they are all there. Note, too, that items are à la carte, including bread, rolls, and butter, and that entrees are served alone with extra charges for potatoes or starch, vegetable and side sauces beyond the specific preparation of the item as listed on the menu.

Not to be outdone by the luncheon and dinner menus, Victor ran a monumental breakfast menu to match the size and quality of the others. Of particular interest are the variety of fruits, the number of egg dishes and the long gone tradition of fish and meat other than bacon and sausage for breakfast.

The breakfast menu incorporates the same point-of-origin nomenclature as the luncheon and dinner menus: California grapefruit, sand dabs, Virginia ham as separate from diced ham, Yarmouth bloater, a type of smoked herring, St. Francis potatoes, Saratoga potatoes (aka potato chips now), and teas from around the world.

The advantage of working in a large hotel is that most of these products would appear regularly on luncheon and dinner or banquet menus. But the execution of such large menus is still a tour de force for any highly talented and professional chef.

396   *THE HOTEL ST. FRANCIS COOK BOOK*

HALF PORTIONS SERVED STRICTLY TO ONE PERSON ONLY

OYSTERS AND CLAMS

Blue Points 35	Stewed 50	Fried Tokelands 60	Little Neck Clams......35
Tokelands 40	Stewed Tokelands......60	Fried Californias 50	Fried Clams 60
Californias 35	Stewed with Cream....60	Newburg 65 1 25	Clam Fritters 60
Cocktail 35	California Fancy Stew..60	In Cream 65 1 25	Stewed Clams 50
Pan Roast 50	Fried Eastern 60	En Brochette......65 1 25	Clam Cocktail 35

RELISHES

Canapé St. Francis 75
Canapé Rothschild 50
Canapé d'Anchois 30
Canapé Riga......50
Canapé Lorenzo ..40
Canapé Regalia 30
Canapé of Astrachan
   Caviar 75
Astrachan Caviar.....
   ......1 25 2 50
Hors d'Oeuvres
   Varits 50
Smoked Goosebreast
   ......45 80
Sardellen Ringe....40
Anchovies 40
Fillet of Herrings 40
Sardines 40
Carciofini 75
Antipasto......50
Lyon Sausage 50
Pickled Walnuts.. 40
Stuffed Mangoes..40
Olives......25
Pim Olas 25
India chutney 25
Pickles 25
Sweet Pickles....25
Chow chow......25
Celery 25
Salted Almonds....40

Luncheon Specialties
Thursday, August 14, 1913.

★Little Neck Clams 35

★Veal Broth, mulligatawney 30 50
★Consommé, Tortellini 25 40
★Cream of Artichokes 30 50

★Lake Tahoe Trout, with salt pork 65 1 25
★Broiled Sand Dabs, maître d'hotel 45 80
★Fried Tomcods, rémoulade 40 75

Omelet with Ham (for one) 35
Eggs, à l'Allemande (1) 40

★Oyster Patties 40 75
★Hot Game Pot Pie (for one) 45
★Deviled Turkey's Legs, with chow chow 45 80
★Chickens' Livers Brochet, Lima beans 45 80
★Ox Tail Braisé, à la Schweitzer 45 80
★Shoulder of Lamb, Brésilienne 45 80
★Escargots, Bourguignonne 45 80

★Fresh Succotash 30 50
★Summer Squash 35

★Dishes Indicated by a Star are Ready

SOUPS

Consommé 25 40
Purée of Peas 25 40
Mock Turtle..30 50
Green Turtle..50 90
Tomato 25 40
Petite Marmite 35 60
Chicken Broth 35 60
Clam Broth ..30 50
Beef Tea 30 50
Beef Juice (cup) 1 00

FISH

Boiled Salmon 50 90
Broiled Salmon 45 80
Broiled Striped Bass
   ......50 90
Halibut 40 75
Sand Dabs 45 80
Pompano....60 1 00
Fillet of Sole..40 75
Smelts 40 75
Tomcods 40 75
Smoked Salmon 50 90
Salmon Belly 40 75
Finnan Haddie 45 80
Salt Mackerel 45 80
Herring......40 75
Terrapin 1 00 2 00
Frogs' Legs......2 50
Bouillabaisse 60 1 00

ROAST AND COLD MEATS.

Ribs of Beef......50	Cold Ham......40 75	Assorted Meats....45 80	Smoked Tongue....40 75
Lamb, Mint Sauce..50 90	Virginia Ham 75 1 40	Assorted Meats with	Boned Capon....60 1 00
Young Turkey....65 1 25	Westphalia Ham Served	Chicken......65 1 25	Paté de Foie Gras......1 00.
Imperial Squab......1 00	on Board 50	Kalter Aufschnitt 65 1 25	

CHICKEN, ETC.

Stuffed Chicken 100 2 00	Chicken in Casserole 2 50	Chicken, Marengo ½..1 25	Squab Guinea Hen.....2 50
Squab Chicken......1 25	Chicken à la King 90 1 75	Sliced chicken....75 1 40	Imperial Squab......1 00
Fricassee of Chicken½ 1 25	Chicken, Maryland½..1 25	Spring Turkey ½ 2 00	Whole Duckling 2 50

STEAKS, CHOPS, ETC.

Sirloin (for 1)......85	Tenderloin (for 4) 3 00	Rump Steak 60	Veal Chops 40 75
Sirloin (for 2) 1 50	Porterhouse (for 2) ..2 00	Hamburg Steak......60	Ham 40 75
Sirloin (for 3) 2 25	Porterhouse (for 3) ..3 00	Filet Mignon......65	Bacon 35 60
Sirloin (for 4) 3 00	Porterhouse (for 4) ..4 00	English Mutton Chop ..75	Kidneys, brochette 60 1 00
Tenderloin (for 1)......85	Club Steak (for 5)....4 00	Mutton Chops (2) 60	Calf's Brains......50 90
Tenderloin (for 2)......1 50	Steak à la minute......70	Lamb Chops (2)......60	Liver and Bacon....50 90
Tenderloin (for 3)......2 25	Entrecôte à la minute ..70	Lamb Chop, Virg.Ham 60	Sweetbreads 65 1 25

Garniture—Plain in Casserole with Potatoes 25, with vegetables 50
Mushroom, Béarnaise or Bordelaise Sauce, for one 25

THE HOTEL ST. FRANCIS COOK BOOK

VEGETABLES

Green Corn 30 50	Lima Beans............30 50	Fried Egg Plant........35	Onions 35
Fresh Asparagus.....40 75	Red Kidney Beans...... 35	Boiled Rice............25	Squash 35
Artichokes...........35 60	Flageolet Beans 50	Succotash..............35	Stuffed Pepper (1)......35
New Peas 30 50	Stewed Corn............ 35	Spinach................35	Macaroni or Spaghetti..35
French Peas 50	Stewed Tomatoes 35	Carrots............30 50	Spaghetti, Milanaise 45
New String Beans..30 50	Stuffed Tomatoes (1) 40	Beets..................35	Cauliflower au gratin....50
French String Beans.. 50	French Asparagus 1 25	Mashed Turnips 35	Cauliflower, Hollandaise 50

POTATOES

Boiled or Baked 20
Fried 20
Mashed...............20
German Fried.........30
Saratoga 30
Sautée 30
Lyonnaise 30
Croquettes 30
Delmonico 30
Au Gratin 30
Julienne 30
Duchesse.............30
Parisienne 30
St. Francis...........30
Maitre d'Hotel 30
Sybil 30
Browned Hashed......30
Soufflée 40
Alsacienne 35
Bénédictine 35
Sara Bernhardt.......35
Anna 40
Stuffed (1)...........30

Specialties, Continued

BUFFET DISHES [for one]

☆Larded tenderloin, of beef, stuffed tomato 75
☆Cold duckling and tongue, vegetable salad 65
☆Curried Lobster, with rice 50
☆Alligator Pear (½) 60

☆ Fruit Salad, Chantilly 30
☆German Date Tart 25

☆Apple Dumpling, hard and brandy sauces 40
☆German Prune Cake 20
☆Peach Pie 15

☆Neapolitan Sandwich 30
☆Grenadine Sorbet 30

Fancy California Fruit in Basket 50

☆Dishes Indicated by a Star are Ready

SALADS

Fruit 50	
Celery Victor... 30 50	
St. Francis (1) 50	
Waldorf (1) 50	
Alligator Pear (1)... 60	
Endives	
Lettuce or Romaine 30	
Watercress	
Escarole or Chicory 30	
Potato................30	
Cucumber 40 75	
Tomato 40 75	
Lettuce-Tomato 40 75	
Artichoke.........45 80	
Chiffonnade 40 75	
Combination 45 80	
Celery Root, Field and	
Beet Salad 40	
Chicken 65 1 25	
Lobster.........65 1 25	
Crab 65 1 25	
Cosmopolitan 60 1.00	
Pepper or Egg, extra 15	

DESSERT

Wine Jelly 30	French Pastry (each).....10	Caramel or Cup Custard 25	Marrons Glacées.........40
Charlotte Russe 30	Macaroons 30	Sponge or Pound Cake...25	Omelette Surprise 1 25
Assorted Cakes 25	Lady Fingers 25	Fruit Cake 30	Omelette Soufflée......1 00

ICE CREAMS AND ICES

Coupe St. Jacques 50	Biscuit Tortoni or Glacé 30	Café Parfait.............30	Peach Ice Cream 25
Peach Melba............60	Lalla Rookh 30	Sorbet au Marasquin..30	Vanilla Ice Cream........25
Baked Alaska (for one) 60	Viviane Cup 40	Lemon Water Ice......25	Chocolate Ice Cream ...25
Meringue Panachée....35	Roman Punch...........30	Raspberry Water Ice....25	Coffee Ice Cream 25
Meringue Glacée.......30	Nesselrode Pudding......40	Neapolitan Ice Cream...30	Pistache Ice Cream......25

FRUIT (Portions for One)

Strawberries, Blackberries or Loganberries 30   Raspberries 35   Fresh Figs 35

Grapes 40	Apples 15	Baked Apples 25	Preserved Fruits 35
Cantaloupe 30	Bananas 15	Compote of Fresh Fruit 30	Marmalade 35
Watermelon 30	Bananas with cream.......30	Stewed French Prunes 30	Guava Jelly 30
Peaches................35	Oranges 15	Apple Sauce 25	Bar le Duc Jelly.........60
Apricots 30	Sliced Oranges 25	Brandied Peaches 40	Honey 25
California Grapefruit ..25	Orange Juice....20 40 60	Stuffed Dates 30	Honey in Comb 30

CHEESE (Portions for One)

Camembert 25, Import. 30	Roquefort...............25	Gorgonzola 25	Chester 25
Oregon Cream..........25	Schloss 25	Mac Laren 25	English Cheddar 30
Neufchâtel 25	Brie or Edam..........25	Gruyère 25	Stilton 30
Port de Salut 25	Pont l'Eveque..........25	Limburger 25	Assorted Cheese.........25

COFFEE, ETC.

Pot of Coffee or Tea with Cream, for one 20   Chocolate or Cocoa 25   Demi Tasse 10   Café Turc 25
Special Coffee 25   Malted Milk, cup 25   Special Bottled Milk 15   Cream, small pitcher 10

Butter, Sweet or Salted, with Rolls or Bread, per cover, 10 cents.

INDIVIDUAL PORTIONS. SERVED TO ONE PERSON ONLY

OYSTERS AND CLAMS

Blue Points 35	Stewed 50	Fried Tokelands 60	Little Neck Clams......35
Tokelands 40	Stewed Tokelands......50	Fried Californias 50	Fried Clams 50
Californias 40	Stewed with Cream 60	Newburg 75	Clam Fritters 50
Cocktail 40	California Fancy Stew..60	In Cream 65	Stewed Clams 50
Pan Roast 50	Eastern, Fried 60	En Brochette 65	Clam Cocktail 35

RELISHES

Canapé St. Francis 75
Canapé d'Anchois 40
Canapé Riga......50
Canapé Regalia 30
Canapé of Astrachan Caviar 75
Astrachan Caviar..... 1 25
Hors d'Oeuvres Variés 50
Smoked Goosebreast 45
Sardellen Ringe......40
Anchovies 50
Fillet of Herrings 50
Sardines 40
Carciofini 75
Antipasto 50
Lyon Sausage 50
Pickled Walnuts..40
Stuffed Mangoes..40
Olives......25
Pim Olas 25
India chutney 25
Pickles......25
Sweet Pickles......25
Chow chow......25
Celery 25
Salted Almonds....40

Specialties for Dinner
Friday, April 9, 1915

★Canapé P. P: I. E. 75

★Terrapin Soup, au gourmet 30
★Cream of Endives 30
★Consommé, royal 25
★Clam Chowder 30

★Broiled Brook Trout 60
Frogs' Legs, Michels 1 25
★Scallops, marinière 75
Pompano, meunière 50

★Loin of Lamb Chops, haricots panachés 60
Squab Chicken Sauté, Sutro (for two) 2 25
★Roast Pheasant, bread sauce 1 50
Breast of Squab, Nivernaise 1 10
★Bouillabaisse Marseillaise 50
Sweetbreads, Eugénie 80
Lobster, cardinal 1 00

★Postrano with Spinach 45

★Dishes Indicated by a Star are Ready

SOUPS

Consomme 25	
Purée of Peas ..25	
Mock Turtle 30	
Green Turtle 50	
Tomato 25	
Petite Marmite 35	
Chicken Broth 35	
Clam Broth 30	
Beef Tea 30	
Beef Juice (cup) 1 00	
Bellevue 40	

FISH

Fried Scallops 60
Striped Bass 50
Halibut 40
Sand Dabs 45
Pompano 50
Fillet of Sole 40
Smelts 40
Tomcods 40
Smoked Salmon......50
Salmon Belly 50
Finnan Haddie 45
Salt Mackerel 45
Herring 40
Terrapin 1 00
Frogs' Legs......1 25
Bouillabaisse 60
Salt Cod, cream....45
Fish Cakes 40

ROAST AND COLD MEATS.

Ribs of Beef 50	Bohemian Ham......65	Cold Ham 40	Assorted Meats 50
Lamb, Mint Sauce 50	Virginia Ham 75	Assorted Meats with Chicken......75	Smoked Tongue 50
Young Turkey 75	Westphalia Ham Served on Board 65		Boned Capon 60
Imperial Squab......1 00		Kalter Aufschnitt 75	Paté de Foie Gras......75

GAME AND POULTRY

Stuffed Chicken ½ 1 00	Chicken in Casserole 2 50	Chicken, Marengo ½..1 25	Squab Guinea Hen......2 50
Squab Chicken......1 25	Chicken à la King 90	Sliced chicken......75	Imperial Squab......1 00
Pheasant 3 00	Chicken, Maryland½..1 25	Spring Turkey ½ 2 25	Whole Duckling 2 50

STEAKS, CHOPS, ETC.

Sirloin (for 1)......90	Tenderloin (for 4) 3 25	Rump Steak 60	Veal Chop 40
Sirloin (for 2) 1 75	Porterhouse (for 2) ..2 25	Hamburg Steak......60	Ham 40
Sirloin (for 3) 2 50	Porterhouse (for 3) ..3 50	Filet Mignon......75	Bacon 40
Sirloin (for 4) 3 25	Porterhouse (for 4) ..4 75	English Mutton Chop ..75	Kidneys, brochette 60
Tenderloin (for 1)......90	Club Steak (for 5)......4 00	Mutton Chops (2) 60	Calf's Brains 50
Tenderloin (for 2)......1 75	Steak à la minute......75	Lamb Chops (2)......60	Liver and Bacon 50
Tenderloin (for 3)......2 50	Entrecote à la minute ..75	Lamb Chop, Virg.Ham 60	Sweetbreads 65

Garniture—Plain in Casserole with Potatoes, for one 25, with vegetables 50
Mushroom, Béarnaise or Bordelaise Sauce, for one 15

THE HOTEL ST. FRANCIS COOK BOOK

399

INDIVIDUAL PORTIONS, SERVED TO ONE PERSON ONLY
VEGETABLES

Asparagus 40	Lima Beans 20	Fried Egg Plant 25	Onions 20
Artichokes 25	Red Kidney Beans........20	Boiled Rice............15	Squash 20
Peas............20	Flageolet Beans 25	Succotash............20	Stuffed Pepper (1)........30
French Peas............25	Stewed Corn............20	Spinach 20	Macaroni or Spaghetti..20
String Beans............20	Stewed Tomatoes 20	Carrots 20	Spaghetti, Milanaise 25
French String Beans.. 25	Stuffed Tomatoes (1)..40	Beets............20	Cauliflower au gratin.....50
French Carrots 25	French Asparagus 1 25	Mashed Turnips 20	Cauliflower, Hollandaise 50

POTATOES

Boiled or Baked 20
Fried 20
Mashed 20
German Fried............30
Saratoga 20
Sauté 30
Lyonnaise 30
Croquettes 30
Delmonico 30
Au Gratin 30
Julienne 30
Duchesse............30
Parisienne 30
St. Francis............30
Maître d'Hotel 30
Browned Hashed....30
Soufflé 40
Alsacienne 35
Bénédictine 35
Anna 40
Stuffed (1)............25
Sweet, fried or sauté 30
Sweet, Southern....40

Specialties, Continued

★Broiled Fresh Mushrooms 60
★Parsnips in Cream 25

★Chateau Potatoes 30

★Peach Pie 15   ★Mince Pie 20
★Strawberry Blanc Mange 30
★Apple Pudding, soufflée 25

★Crushed Strawberry Parfait 30
★Strawberries a la Ritz 60
★Coupe St. Jacques 50
★Tutti Frutti 30

★Fresh Strawberries with Cream 40

★Dishes Indicated by a Star are Ready

SALADS

Crab............75
Fruit (1) 40
Celery Victor 35
St. Francis 40
Waldorf............40
Endives 50
Lettuce or Romaine 30
Watercress 30
Escarole or Chicory ..30
Potato............30
Cucumber 40
Tomato............40
Lettuce-Tomato 40
Artichoke 35
Chiffonnade 40
Combination 40
Celery Root, Field and
   Beet Salad............40
Chicken 75
Lobster............75
Cosmopolitan 50
Pepper or Egg (for1)10

DESSERT

Wine Jelly 20	French Pastry (each)....10	Caramel or Cup Custard 25	Marrons Glacées............40
Charlotte Russe 30	Macaroons 30	Fruit Cake 30	Omelette Surprise 1 25
Alsatian Wafers 25	Lady Fingers 15	Assorted Cakes 25	Omelette Soufflée....1 00

ICE CREAMS AND ICES

Coupe St. Jacques 50	Biscuit Tortoni or Glacé 30	Café Parfait............30	Peach Ice Cream 25
Peach Melba............60	Lalla Rookh 30	Sorbet au Marasquin..30	Vanilla Ice Cream............25
Baked Alaska (for one) 60	Viviane Cup 40	Lemon Water Ice............25	Chocolate Ice Cream........25
Meringue Panachée....35	Roman Punch............30	Raspberry Water Ice....25	Coffee Ice Cream 25
Meringue Glacée 30	Nesselrode Pudding 40	Neapolitan Ice Cream....30	Pistache Ice Cream........25

FRUIT

Fresh Strawberries with Cream 40

California Grapefruit ½ 30	Baked Apples, cream....25	Brandied Peaches 40	Preserved Fruits 25
Grapefruit Supreme 75	Bananas 15	Compote of Fresh Fruit 25	Marmalade 25
Apples (1) 15	Bananas with cream........25	Stewed Prunes 20	Guava Jelly 25
Oranges (1) 15	Orange Juice....25 50 75	Apple Sauce............15	Bar le Duc Jelly............50
Sliced Oranges 25	Grapefruit Juice............50	Apple Sauce, with cream 25	Honey 20, ...in Comb. 25

F. E. Garritt's Individual Fruit Preserves (assorted) 25

CHEESE

Olympic Club 25	Roquefort............25	Gorgonzola............25	Petaluma Cream 25
Camembert............25	Schloss 25	Mac Laren 25	Chester 25
Neufchâtel 25	Brie or Edam............25	Gruyère 25	English Cheddar 30
Limburger 25			

COFFEE, ETC.

Pot of Coffee or Tea with Cream, for one 20   Chocolate or Cocoa 25   Demi Tasse 10   Café Turc 25
Special Coffee 25   Malted Milk, cup 25   Special Bottled Milk 15   Cream, small pitcher 10
Butter, Sweet or Salted, with Rolls or Bread, per cover, 10 cents

Some banquet menus are included here as well.

Selections from The Hotel St. Francis Menu Files

Hotel St. Francis, Mexican Dinner, May 23, 1917:

Ecrevisses, Gourmet (Cold)
Abalone Chowder
Salted Jordan Almonds
Boiled Striped Bass, Hollandaise
Potatoes Nature
Pilaff Mexicaine
Roast Imperial Squab
Asparagus Tips
Salade de Saison
Fancy Ice Cream
Wafers
Demi Tasse

Note the abalone, a California specialty.

Hotel St. Francis, Californian Dinner, March 31, 1917:

California Oysters
Clear Green Turtle, Sherry
Salted Almonds
Sand Dabs, Meuniere
Sweetbreads Braise, with Peas
Broiled San Francisco Jumbo Squab
Chateau Potatoes
Cold Fresh Asparagus, Mustard Sauce
Cafe Parfait
Assorted Cakes
Demi Tasse

California oysters and sand dabs and a classic French presentation together.

For all the glamorous dinners and celebrations for which he was aptly noted one might think he lived in a rarefied atmosphere, kind of a culinary Olympus. Nothing could be further from the truth. For all his accomplishments and accolades in haute cuisine, Victor also was noted for many other culinary events.

There was a famous raisin festival held in Fresno that seemed to always create quite a stir. An announcement in the *San Francisco Call* published on April 28, 1910,[6] was addressed to "Bakers and confectioners — all of you in California between the north side of the Tehachapi and the Oregon line-" to submit their best recipes for raisin bread for the upcoming raisin festival in Fresno. A sterling silver cup was to be awarded for the best loaf "baked by any housewife or cook, not a professional baker or confectioner, in the territory." Only California raisins could be used and entrants were urged to "see what you can do with one of the finest delicacies California produces." There was also a professional category that also received a sterling silver cup.

Mr. L. J. Scroffy, February 4, 1916:
Fresh Caviar
Celery Olives Almonds
Terrapin Maryland
Wild Rice
Virginia Ham Glacé, Ferrari
Faison Truffles
Salad de Saison
Pudding Glacé, Diplomate
Mignardises
Coffee

Maryland terrapin and Virginia ham.

Bagmen of Bagdad, December 30, 1915:
Toke Points
Green Turtle Soup
Celery Olives Almonds
Terrapin Maryland
Noisette of Lamb, Colbert
Haricot Panachée
Potatoes Rissolée
Champagne Punch
Breast of Duck, Currant Jelly
Fried Hominy
Cold Asparagus, Mustard Sauce
Pudding Glacé
Assorted Cakes
Coffee

Toke points and Maryland terrapin.

The three judges were "at the top of their profession" and were "Ernest Abrogast, Chef of the Palace Hotel; Victor Hirtzler, chef of the St. Francis Hotel. Arthur Logan, chef of the Hotel Stewart."

On Saturday, April 30, the cups were awarded to Mrs. E. Schweitzer for the best in the non-professional category and to "Paddy" Woods of the Yerba Buena Naval Training Station. That this was an important event may be judged by the size of the sterling silver cups. The photo in the *Call* shows them on pedestals, appearing about two feet tall. The awards were given four columns on page three.

For Victor, this would have been another accolade — to be selected as a judge for this event. The way the chefs are mentioned in the paper, it is clear that each one of them had a sterling reputation in the San Francisco food world at that time.

At a later date[7] he said he would produce 100 loaves of a winning raisin bread loaf recipe to demonstrate the quality of California raisins and how non-professional bakers could produce extraordinary results using this California ingredient.

On another occasion, Victor was selected for an impressive thank-you by the Swiss

Mr. Colum, June 28, 1919:
Canape Caviar with Cocktail
Toke Points
Green Turtle Soup
Almonds Olives
Lobster Newburg
Ham Glacé, Champagne Sauce
Timbale of Spinach
Iowa Corn Bread
Vol au Vent Toulouse
Kirsch Punch
Guinea Hen
Potatoes Chateau
Salad
Ice Cream Cakes
Coffee

Toke points, Lobster Newburg making its way from Delmonico's in New York

to San Francisco and Iowa corn bread.

Mr. Mulcahy, February 26, 1918:
Toke Points Mignonette
Clear Bortsch in Cups
Celery   Olives   Almonds
Ecrevisses Voltaire
Noisette of Lamb with Fresh Mushrooms
Peas Etuvé—Pommes Lorette
Breast of Duck
Fried Hominy
Endive, Victor Dressing
Asparagus Glaceé
Assorted Cakes
Cafe Marcel

Toke points, classical French preparation paired with fried hominy.

Rifle Club. He had prepared a banquet for their 50th anniversary and apparently had done such an outstanding job that the group felt he should receive some special recognition. On the front page of the *Call*[8] the article states that Victor received a "loving cup," "which stands a half a foot high and is of silver." The inscription commends Victor for his "valuable service to the golden jubilee." That a chef would prepare an excellent banquet is not unique. But Victor obviously went above and beyond, exceeding all expectations, to receive this impressive award. But the article also states that "Hirtzler was wholly surprised that he should be so signaled out for special recognition and was at a loss to express his gratitude."

Despite his reputation as theatrical French chef there remained a sense of modesty about how he saw himself in his chosen profession. The tenor of the article makes clear that he was genuinely touched and moved by this award.

He would also write articles for various groups in order to promote certain foods, especially those foods grown or harvested in California. In an article entitled "The Avocado for the Table"[9] Victor talks about the avocado being a "new" food item and that such products in the "hand of an expert chef" enable the creation of new dishes to expand the library of culinary creations. (Remember that Chef Ranhofer was the first American chef to include this fruit on his restaurant menus.) Remarking on the versatility of this "new" fruit, "the fruit is indeed adapted to a variety of preparations to which most fruits do not so readily lend themselves."

He gives examples of avocados "as a cocktail," "as a sandwich," and as "Avocado en surprise," which is the flesh pureed, the stone removed and replaced with some cooked egg yolk colored with soy sauce and seasoned and shaped to look like a stone and replaced in the skin with the pureed and mayonnaise bound fruit.

Additional preparations for California avocados include molded in a cold meat or poultry salad in aspic, prepared as a dessert with sweetened whipped cream, made into a soup, added to a fish to be planked in the oven (roasted on a piece of wood as done by the Native Americans of the Northwest) as well being served as a vegetable, stuffed and served as a separate course and as a dessert sliced and "macerated with brandy, white wine, and sugar."

The are also ice creams, puddings, avocados cooked with pineapple and rice, doused with a vanilla syrup and served with a sweetened meringue and in a nod to the idea of American cuisine once again, Avocado Queen Liliuokalani named after the last reigning monarch of Hawaii. The dish is a trompe l'oeil of a peeled avocado with an angelica piece for a stem, the stone removed and replaced with a "stone" of praline ice and served on a genoise with anisette syrup and garnished with sweetened whipped and crushed praline.

Here, if there was ever a question, is a master chef developing a food product of California and making these newly developed recipes available to everyone in order to further the development of California and American cuisine.

But Victor also influenced California and American cuisines in another way: by the hiring and training of younger culinary professionals whose influences and effects are still with us.

A pair of articles by writer Ernest Beyl[10] talk about how his father came to the United States from Alsace and eventually ended up in San Francisco. Via a network of Alsatian chefs, Chef Joseph Beyl was introduced to Victor Hirtzler and hired as a commis at the St. Francis. Over the years, he developed considerable skills and Hirtzler, before returning to Europe, recommended Joseph for his own chef position at the Hotel Californian in Fresno. He was hired and continued as a chef for many years, returning to San Francisco in 1930 to be the chef at the then prestigious Alexander Hamilton Hotel. And according to Joseph Beyl he was awarded the position largely due to his association with Chef Victor Hirtzler and this great chef's mentoring of his young assistant's talent.

In an article in *Saveur Magazine*[11] Ernest Beyl reminisces about his father's association with Chef Hirtzler. Joseph Beyl related that, "after a while he taught me everything. How to make stocks and sauces ... how to prepare and serve various buffet items. He taught me fancy desserts." Ernest Beyl concludes this wonderful article by writing, "Throughout his life, my dad was fond of saying that things came easy for him — thanks to Victor Hirtzler."

From a professional standpoint, it would be impossible to calculate how many culinary professionals were developed and influenced by Victor and his star protégé over the years. But the cumulative effect has to be immense, and this type of professional interaction left its mark on American cuisine over the decades.

To get a glimpse of what it was like in Victor's kitchen at the St. Francis we have an article by one Mable Beeson,[12] who was writing an article focused on holiday dining, specifically Christmas Day, and paid a call to the St. Francis.

She writes:

"Perhaps you would like to go right down into the kitchen and see the chef at home," suggests Manager Wills of the St. Francis.
"Would I?
"Wouldn't you?"

Clearly this was a special event for the writer, and already in 1905 Victor was considered a bit of a celebrity in San Francisco. Beeson further describes a scene of the "family meal" after breakfast and before lunch when the kitchen staff "are seated and the babel of strange tongues, complimenting, criticizing, expostulating, creates the pleasing impression of a sudden journey (perhaps via wishing carpet route) to a foreign land."

"A very aristocrat of cooks is this Mr. Victor Hirtzler." After a brief recapitulation of his career, she asks, "Will he, I wonder, bear himself haughtily, as befits one who has served royalty?" She says that he was approachable, excited to see her and had already written a special holiday menu for her to look at.

As befits the founder of California cuisine and major contributor to American cuisine, Victor stated that "every dish is a real creation. We are studying for new effects all the time. Never must we be satisfied, or, voila, we are no longer of use." This encapsulates an aspect of all great chefs — the desire to continue striving to improve on his or her craft and to always demand excellence of oneself.

This was quite a menu — a dinner in the grand style for the busiest day of the culinary year. Each course was paired with a wine and some of the recipes were printed later on in the article.

A grand Buffet Russe accompanied by Chablis had Toke Point Oysters, shrimp bisque, hors d'oeuvres varié paired with sherry and terrapin Jockey Club Style with Schloss Johanissberg. Champagne was served with filet of sole, new potatoes, breast of chicken with truffles and artichoke jardinière.

The meat was Saddle of Lamb Provençale, petit pois, mousseline of frog's legs, roasted wild duck and salad that called for a red Burgundy. Assorted desserts, petits fors sec and Tartellets a l'Eccosaise, and cheese and fruits served with assorted liqueurs and brandies rounded out this impressive feast.

Here again is a chef who is at the top of his game, well known to the point of being a celebrity, clearly showing off some American food on his most important menu of the year, and yet approachable and excited about his food and his profession even after so many years in the business.

Victor remained at the St. Francis until 1926. But after prohibition was enacted he seemed not to have the same joy in what he was doing. He returned to Alsace for a holiday in 1926 and never left his home to come back to America.

In 1915 he had married Regina Caspary from Beaver Dam, Wisconsin, whose family owned a saloon, a bottling company and a wagon making business. He left his estate to her.

His obituary, published on February 12, 1931, in the *Oakland Tribune* has a heading: "Famous Chef Hirtzler Dies." It goes on to say he died in his old home in Strasbourg, France. There is also a sense that he was of a previous generation and almost forgotten in San Francisco at the time of his death. "To patrons of restaurants of today, Hirtzler's name means little." It says after 23 years at the St. Francis and one year at the Mark Hopkins, he went to Strasbourg "for a holiday."

He died at age 61, having spent his life from the age of 13 in the best kitchens of the world.

During his career he was noted as one of the world's finest chefs who was able to establish the significance of the West Coast of America and especially California as an area of distinctive and memorable food items. His efforts did much to secure the reputation of the St. Francis as one of the world's great hotels, and by extension, San Francisco as the "Paris of the West."

His dramatic and theatrical personality led to the creation of a genre of chefs known as celebrity chefs who are able to command a following for their food and antics. They attract people and publicity to secure their reputations and the reputations of the establishments that employ them. Victor had the skills, and then some, to back up the reputation.

He was a champion of American foods and cuisine taking their place alongside traditional European foods and cuisines with equal validity and quality. His influence is still with us in some of the items he created, but more in the way he shaped American cuisine for generations to come.

His career in San Francisco was a culinary one. But how he created his public persona and the way in which he suffused the hotel and the entire city with his presence made him a new category of chef. We would now call Chef Hirtzler a celebrity chef, and his hotel, the St. Francis, was the first true "collectible hotel" in the Western United States. They were made for each other.

With a flair for the dramatic and a keen understanding that so much of successful food service depends upon theatricality, he was constantly "out of the kitchen," roaming the hotel in his outlandish garb and greeting hotel guests in a much-exaggerated French accent that had "chef" written all over it.

How can his influence be overstated? So much of what he did and how he ran his kitchens is now part of our everyday culinary lives that it can be difficult to realize that Victor, as he liked being called, *made* these traits of our modern culinary lives a part of our daily existence.

What was unusual and indigenous for Amelia Simmons, Ms. Leslie and Mrs. Randolph has become accepted as *American* by the most refined diners in the country. The early exposition of Creole food by Lafcadio Hearn made its way across the country to take its place along with the classic foods of France and Germany on elegant and everyday menus.

Mrs. Fisher's book, published just before Chef Hirtzler went to San Francisco, made a dramatic impression on the people of the city and explored some of the wonders of deep South cooking.

Within a short time span, items produced and invented by Chef Ranhofer at Delmonico's would find their way into mainstream American cooking and indeed around the world.

As a celebrity chef, Chef Victor was called upon for his endorsements. This is one of them. Image courtesy of St. Francis Hotel/Starwood Resorts, Kelly Chamberlin.

No longer would someone like Dickens denigrate American cuisine, for here is shown the maturity and sophistication of American diners, the influence of great chefs and cookbook writers and the inclusion of extraordinary native American food items and styles of cooking.

American cuisine displayed its full integration and inclusion with the great cuisines of the world at the time that Victor produced the *Hotel St. Francis Cook Book.*

Enjoy! Bon Apetit! Guten Apetit! These salutations to enjoy one's food show the melting pot that is reflected in the American population and the seamless blend of native food and regional cooking based on influences from Africa to the Far East. This melting pot has given us American cuisine.

Fortunately we have Victor's *Hotel St. Francis Cook Book,* some newspaper articles and cross-references from other food writers and cookbook authors that testify to his skill a chef. We have American cuisine and California cuisine, which testify to his influence and place in American culinary history as a cornerstone of our foundation of American cuisine.

CHAPTER 9

Thank You and What's Next

The authors represented in this book were quite different from each other, yet also alike in many ways. Tracing the use of American food products is one way of discerning a commonality. Noting that all the authors lived in the United States and wrote for an American audience is another. Focusing on the audience each author reached with his or her work is yet a third.

Taken as a whole, these wonderful people, from 1798 to 1919, had profound effects on American cuisine. And I hope that I have shown how each contributed to making the whole greater than the sum of its parts, from the first mention of "cramberry" to writing about Petaluma cream cheese.

The authors selected made American ingredients known and documented their use in recipes ranging from daily household meals to the absolute pinnacle of fine dining in world renowned establishments. They wove a seamless tapestry of traditional European foods, methods and beverages with the "new" items found in a new country. In hindsight, it seems like a logical progression that was inevitable. Certainly without the contributions of these authors American cuisine would not be the same as it is now. By documenting the food in their books we now have a written account of the evolution of a national cuisine.

The immense new country all but cried out for regional cuisines that could make use of local products, both occurring naturally and cultivated by farmers according to climate, soil conditions and weather, much as one might find in Italy or France. And there was a harkening back to tradition with the development of the new regionalism of cooking methods, familiar spices and herbs and familiar main ingredients. Each of our authors, Simmons, Randolph, Leslie, Fisher and Hearn, was able to express a particular aspect of how our country was developing in a culinary sense and sometimes in a social sense as well, simply because the choice of recipes and foods reflected the growing of America as a country.

In the cases of Ranhofer and Hirtzler, we have two world-class, internationally recognized chefs, living and working in the United States and bringing these "new" ingredients into the realm of classical cooking. These chefs made even more new food items known, and through their usage and influence, made items such as avocados and abalone and sand dabs part of a larger whole. It was also an integration of both classical European cuisines with American ingredients and American preparations that helped elevate American cuisine to be on a par with its older, more traditional forebears.

Delmonico's immensely influenced how foreign visitors perceived America. In a very real way Delmonico's restaurants and the food prepared by Chef Ranhofer *were* America to many visitors, with Charles Dickens probably being the most notable.

In the institution of the St. Francis Hotel, the influence of Victor Hirtzler and the hotel itself created a sense of arrival for the city of San Francisco. And both the hotel and the man did much to secure its reputation as the Paris of the West. The opening of the hotel was like a debutante ball with the hotel coming out instead of a young lady. But the hotel created a sense of place for the city itself so that the event became, in a real sense, a coming out party for the city as well.

Both of these chefs recognized and placed American foods and recipes on the same menus as traditional haute cuisine, thus giving validity and prestige by association to our new American cuisine. Each in his own way influenced generations of professional chefs in the cultivation of a national cuisine and the development of the profession of chef. It was not until 1980 that chef was actually recognized as a profession and not categorized as a household servant.

Chef Ranhofer drew on almost all aspects of American regional foods while maintaining his schooling in classical techniques and traditional preparations: the best of both worlds. Chef Hirtzler established the idea of California cuisine and by extension, the recognition of local foods of the Northwest as special to the point where their places of origin would be stated on a menu. By including place names for foods found outside California, from Alaska to Massachusetts, he recognized what we have largely since forgotten: that certain places have the ability to create foods so special and unique as to deserve individual recognition. A European idea made its way to our shores via these exceptional culinarians.

As I write this, we may be on the cusp of a new old tradition: the emphasis on local foods as deserving of our attention, our time and money. While there are many benefits to our industrial growing of crops, it comes at a disastrously high price in terms of environmental destruction, dependence on petroleum imports for fertilizer and run-off pollution that ruins waterways and ocean fishing grounds.

Slow Food and locally grown food movements are gaining traction in our society. With an average travel distance of 1,500 miles for food products to reach an American table, we can no longer afford to do business as usual. The costs are too great. Sustainable agriculture has the potential to restore much of the lost quality and diversity of our American bounty. A brief look at what is now available compared to what was available in markets in 1900 shows a monumental decrease in products offered as a result of easy to grow crops that could be adopted to industrial methods, rather than selection of foods based on where they would grow the best.

With industrial agriculture comes a lack of diversity of species under cultivation that creates paucity in the variety of foods we eat. In most supermarkets for example, maybe four or five different apples are sold. In France, Calvados, the apple brandy, is made with over 120 different kinds of apples. Many heirloom varieties that were common are now in danger of extinction or are only available in a handful of orchards around the country. Many varieties can be found in areas where there are farms that grow so-called heirloom varieties.

The same situation seems to apply to most fruits and vegetables we eat. How many different varieties of broccoli are available in food stores? Peaches? Tomatoes? Fortunately, heirloom tomatoes are making a bit of a comeback.

On the diversity side we now have large numbers of artisan bread bakers, cheese makers, wineries, micro and craft brewers and micro distillers. And there are many specialty food companies that produce food products with recognizable ingredients printed on the label that the consumer does not need a degree in organic chemistry to understand.

After many years in food service it never ceases to impress me how personal food is for most people. So many times in the last three decades I heard comments about over-cooking "my steak," undercooking "my vegetables," "this is not what my mother made," etc. Sometimes it seemed that the chef planned to ruin a certain person's meal in advance, so personally did the guest perceive his or her food.

I think this type of connectedness extends to food we buy for home use. There is some-thing reassuring about being able to see where your tomatoes or corn or squash comes from and actually meet the person who grew this food. As I said earlier, a country's culture is largely defined by its music, literature and cuisine. We started well with the food but have strayed into the world of industrial production and removal from our sources of foods, veg-etable and animal. This disconnect is, hopefully, slowly turning around. There seems to me something so elemental about "knowing" that your food is part of the same land as you are — almost as if we share the same identity, or at least a portion of an identity.

As we usher in, hopefully, this dawning of the next phase of American cuisine, we will still experience the influences of the people in this book even as we do now. But maybe we will better recognize the people who got us to where we are today.

I encourage readers to try their food and get to know them a bit. They were all extraor-dinary individuals and your life will be richer and fuller for having known them. Let them into your minds and hearts and you will come to know our American cuisine.

Part Two

Historical Recipes, with Notes for the Modern Cook

CHAPTER 10

American Cookery
(Amelia Simmons)

Roasted and Stewed Meats

To Roast Beef

To Roaſt Beef.

THE general rules are, to have a briſk hot fire, to hang down rather than to ſpit, to baſte with ſalt and water, and one quarter of an hour to every pound of beef, though tender beef will require leſs, while old tough beef will require more roaſting ; pricking with a fork will determine you whether done

C

or not ; rare done is the healthieſt and the taſte of this age.

The general rules are, to have a brisk hot fire, to hang down rather than to spit, to baste with salt and water, and one quarter of an hour to every pound of beef, though tender beef will require less, while old tough beef will require more roasting; pricking with a fork will determine you whether done or not; rare done is the healthiest and the taste of this age.

When roasted over a brisk fire and hung, the meat will tend to rotate due to air currents. A high heat will produce a Maillard reaction (crusting and browning) as well as some caramelization. Basting with salt water evaporates the water and the salt starts to form a crust, which helps to seal in juices. There are Eastern recipes that call for salt-crusted chicken with a solid coffin of salt around the bird that accomplish that very deed. The crust formed by brushing is much thinner.

If the modern cook wanted to try this method, he or she could buy a cooking tool for roasting a "standing rib roast." This somewhat old-fashioned device roasts the prime rib vertically, rather than horizontally, which is the modern method. If the reader has the advantage of a convection oven that can pulse the air circulation, this is the best modern adaption for replicating this method of roasting.

For those of you who have old houses with still functioning cooking fireplaces, tie the string over the swinging bar that juts out over the fire bed. Make sure the fire does not actually touch the meat itself. It is also a good idea to truss the meat first to retain shape, promote even cooking and have the muscle seams bind together. Soak the string first in water as you would a bamboo skewer for a kabob, then hang it from the bar.

Testing for doneness with a fork is a standard method in professional kitchens to see the juice's color as well as to check the internal temperature. If you have a meat thermometer simply insert it as far as possible to the center of the meat and when an internal temperature of 125° to 130° is reached, the meat is rare to medium rare.

John C Hammond

AMERICAN COOKERY,

OR THE

ART OF DRESSING

VIANDS, FISH, POULTRY, AND VEGETABLES,

AND THE

BEST MODES OF MAKING

PASTES, PUFFS, PIES, TARTS, PUDDINGS,

CUSTARDS AND PRESERVES,

AND ALL KINDS OF

CAKES,

FROM THE IMPERIAL

PLUMB TO PLAIN CAKE.

ADAPTED TO THIS COUNTRY,

AND ALL GRADES OF LIFE.

By AMELIA SIMMONS,

AN AMERICAN ORPHAN.

Published according to Act of Congress.

HARTFORD:

Printed for SIMEON BUTLER,

NORTHAMPTON.

1798.

Roast Lamb

Roast Lamb.

Lay down to a clear good fire that will not want stirring or altering, baste with butter, dust on flour, baste with the dripping, and before you take it up, add more butter and sprinkle on a little salt and parsley shred fine; send to table with a nice sallad, green peas, fresh beans, or a colliflower, or asparagus.

Lay down to a clear good fire that will not want stirring or altering, baste with butter, dust on flour, baste with the dripping, and before you take it up, add more butter and sprinkle on a little salt and parsley shred fine; send to the table with a nice salad, green peas, fresh beans, or a colli-flower, or asparagus.

Notice that lamb is separate from mutton and that the vegetables served with the lamb are more in the way of spring vegetables — peas, asparagus or fresh beans. Lamb is generally reserved for an animal under two years of age, so Simmons would most likely have been referring to what we would now call a spring lamb, around five months old, or a regular lamb, under 12 months.

If a whole lamb were to be roasted, it would most likely have been on a spit or in a rotisserie pan that could collect the drippings. Here, what is most likely indicated is leg or loin. Space requirements would have meant some butchering of the carcass and tough cuts, the head, neck and fore quarter, would require a different cooking method than classic roasting. Simmons was not an unwise cook — she would not have roasted a shoulder or neck.

Pre-heat oven or gas grill with lid to 350°.

Place lamb leg, bone in, on a rack inside a pan just large enough to contain it. Brush all over with soft or melted butter and sprinkle with flour well seasoned with salt and fresh ground pepper. As the lamb roasts, baste with the pan juices about every 20 minutes.

When a meat thermometer is inserted into the thickest part of the leg and reads 135°, remove the lamb from the oven and allow to rest, covered with foil, for about 20 minutes.

Before serving, brush with butter and sprinkle with finely chopped and wrung out fresh parsley. (If the parsley is still wet it will be lumpy rather than individual pieces.) Carve at the table or if carving in the kitchen, place on a warmed serving platter.

To make a pan juice to serve with the lamb: Pour off excess fat after removing lamb. Add ½ cup finely chopped onions, half that amount each of finely chopped carrots and celery. When lightly browned, add one medium tomato, seeded, chopped fine, and two cloves of crushed garlic. When the aroma of the garlic hits your nose, sprinkle the pan with flour and stir to absorb all liquid. Cook for one or two minutes, deglaze with eight ounces red wine and stir well to incorporate the flour-vegetable mix. When the mix comes to a simmer and thickens, add some beef or lamb broth, boil for about two minutes, and adjust consistency to your taste and season with salt and pepper. Strain into a sauceboat and add finely chopped parsley and stir to incorporate.

To serve with roasted asparagus: after the lamb is removed from the oven or grill, place cleaned and trimmed asparagus on a shallow pan, sprinkle with olive oil and salt and pepper. Roast until al dente, about four to five minutes depending on the size of the stalks.

To Stuff and Roast a Turkey, or Fowl

One pound soft wheat bread, 3 ounces beef suet, 3 eggs, a little sweet thyme, sweet marjoram, pepper and salt, some add a gill of wine; fill the bird therewith and sew up, hang down to a steady solid fire, basting frequently with salt and water, and roast until a steam emits from the breast, put one third of a pound of butter into the gravy, dust flour over the bird and baste with the gravy; serve up with boiled onions and cramberry sauce, mangoes, pickles or celery.

2. Others omit the sweet herbs, and add parsley done with potatoes.

3. Boil and mash three pints potatoes, wet them with butter, add sweet herbs, pepper, salt, fill and roast as above.

> *To stuff and roast a Turkey, or Fowl.*
>
> One pound soft wheat bread, 3 ounces beef suet, 3 eggs, a little sweet thyme, sweet marjoram, pepper and salt, and some add a gill of wine ; fill the bird
>
> ———
>
> therewith and sew up, hang down to a steady solid fire, basting frequently with salt and water, and roast until a steam emits from the breast, put one third of a pound of butter into the gravy, dust flour over the bird and baste with the gravy ; serve up with boiled onions and cramberry-sauce, mangoes, pickles or celery.
>
> 2. Others omit the sweet herbs, and add parsley done with potatoes.
>
> 3. Boil and mash 3 pints potatoes, wet them with butter, add sweet herbs, pepper, salt, fill and roast as above.

This is the first recorded recipe in an American cookbook using cranberries. Simmons does not take the time to spell out a recipe for the cranberry sauce, which more than likely means that this particular food pairing was at least in the infancy of a tradition. It follows hard on several hundred years of using all sorts of fruits to go with meats and seafood as well, a holdover from medieval and renaissance cooking.

Note also that she states "soft wheat bread." Other recipes specify grating bread for the stuffing. Here we have a fresh product. Wheat was not the only grain used for making bread in colonial times — barley, oats and rye were also quite common.

Again Simmons specifies hanging the bird rather than spitting it and basting with salt water as for the beef. There is then a leap to the gravy section, once again assuming a fair amount of cooking knowledge for her readers. Serving with cranberry sauce, yes. But mangoes? That such an exotic ingredient could be stated with no further explanation gives some idea of the trade that was already flourishing in the United States. And as for pickles and celery, sounds like a turkey dinner growing up on my grandparents' farm in then rural New Jersey!

Pick a free range, grass-fed 8 to 10 pound turkey. Clean, save the giblets, dry the inside. Preheat your oven to 350°.

Break up or cut into cubes a one-pound loaf of whole wheat bread, or white bread if you like. Place in a bowl.

Finely chop or grind 3 ounces of beef suet and add to the bowl. Use of bland cooking oil will not give the same flavor and richness.

Wash and finely chop 2 tablespoons of fresh thyme, 2 tablespoons of fresh marjoram and add to the bowl.

Beat 3 large eggs with a gill of Madeira (depending upon the source this would be either 2 or 4 ounces). Start with 2 ounces of wine. Simmons does not state the type of wine but Madeira was at this time known as the "Wine of America." Pick a basic Sercial Madeira. DO NOT use grocery store "cooking wine."

Add the egg/wine mix; stir well but do not press together.

Season the stuffing with salt and pepper. Test the seasoning by taking a small piece and frying it. If it is too dry, add more Madeira; make the final adjustments for salt and pepper.

Place in a roasting pan or follow suggestions for *Roast Beef.* The turkey is done when a meat thermometer reads 165° in the joint between the thigh and carcass. Remember to baste with salt water, using one tablespoon of salt per cup of water.

When done, take the bird from the oven and allow it to rest 20 minutes, covered with foil.

As Simmons does not give a cranberry sauce recipe, try this modern version.

MODERN "CRAMBERRY" SAUCE

Place one pound of fresh cranberries in a non-reactive saucepot. Add 1 cup sugar, ½ cup honey or "tree sweetenin" (now called maple syrup), juice of one orange and juice of one lemon. Slowly bring to a simmer and cook until berries pop open. Allow to cool, place in the refrigerator, serve within one week. For a sweeter sauce, add more honey or maple syrup. When hot it will be runny. When cool it will thicken.

For an adventurous 18th-century cook, mashed potatoes (still a somewhat novel ingredient) could also be used. Follow receipt #3 as copied below.

MASHED POTATOES

To the boiled potatoes in the original recipe,
Add one stick, 4 ounces, of butter
3 eggs
2 ounces of heavy cream
2 tablespoons each of fresh thyme, marjoram and one of parsley, chopped fine. Salt and pepper to taste. Make a test as for the bread stuffing.

If you choose the potato stuffing, add one more egg. Both stuffings can be baked in casseroles rather than being stuffed into the bird. In the potato stuffing the taste of the fresh herbs is particularly delicious.

To Stuff and Roast a Goslin [Goose]

To ſtuff and roaſt a Goſlin.
Boil the inwards tender, chop them fine, put double quantity of grated bread, 4 ounces butter, pepper, ſalt, (and ſweet herbs if you like) 2 eggs moulded into the ſtuffing, parboil 4 onions and chop them into the ſtuffing, add wine, and roaſt the bird.
The above is a good ſtuffing for every kind of Water Fowl, which requires onion ſauce.

Boil the inwards [giblets] tender, chop them fine, put double quantity of grated bread, 4 ounces butter, pepper, salt, (and sweet herbs if you like) 2 eggs moulded into the stuffing, parboil 4 onions and chop them into the stuffing, add wine, and roast the bird.
The above is good for every kind of Water Fowl, which requires onion sauce.

If goose is not available, try this with roast duck; it works just as well. Use one 8 to 9 pound goose or two or three ducks to equal the same weight.

Boil, cool and finely chop giblets and place in a bowl.
Parboil 4 small onions or 8 pearl onions and finely chop and add to giblets.
Add 4 cups grated bread. Do not use canned breadcrumbs. Simply take a one-pound loaf of bread, allow it to stale and grate on a box grater using the largest holes.
Beat 2 large eggs with 2 ounces Sercial Madeira, mix well, adjust seasonings and make a test. When satisfied with the seasoning, stuff the bird(s) and roast.
As both goose and duck are much more fatty than turkey or chicken, forgo basting. Test for doneness as above at 165° and allow to rest.

SOUBISE SAUCE

Here again Simmons provides no recipe for an onion sauce, as it would have been commonplace for the well-trained cook. This is an updated version of a classic Soubise Sauce.

Add one pint whole milk and one pint heavy cream to a non-reactive saucepot. Simmer 30 minutes with a half onion with one bay leaf studded to it with two cloves. After 40 minutes remove from fire, strain and cool.

While the liquid is simmering, finely chop 2 medium onions and sauté in 2 ounces of clarified butter or neutral oil, such as canola oil. Keep the flame very low; the onions will get soft and the sugars will develop in them. Do not allow the onions to turn brown. This may take about 45 minutes. This cannot be rushed.

Sprinkle about two tablespoons of flour over the onions when sweet, stir to absorb the oil or butter and cook about one minute but do not allow any color to develop.

Slowly add the strained and cooled milk, whisking so that no lumps form. When completely added, allow sauce to simmer about 30 minutes until there is no starch feel or taste to the sauce. Either strain out the onions or press them through a food mill. The former gives a smoother, more elegant texture. The latter will have tiny pieces of onion still in the sauce.

Return to the fire and correct seasoning to taste with white pepper, salt and a slight grating of nutmeg. Serve with roasted goslin.

To alamode a round

Take fat pork cut in slices or mince, season it with pepper, salt sweet marjoram and thyme, cloves, mace, nutmeg, make holes in the beef and stuff it the night before cooked; put some bones across the bottom of the pot to keep from burning, put in one quart of Claret wine, one quart water and one onion; lay the round on the bones, cover close and stop it round the top with dough; hang on in the morning and stew gently two hours; turn it and stop tight and stew two hours more; when done, grate a crust of bread on the top and brown it before the fire; scum the gravy and serve in a butter boat, serve it with the residue of the gravy in the dish.

> To alamode a round.
> Take fat pork cut in slices or mince, season it with pepper, salt sweet marjoram and thyme, cloves, mace and nutmeg, make holes in the beef and stuff it the night before cooked; put some bones across the bottom of the pot to keep from burning, put in one quart Claret wine, one quart water and one onion; lay the round on the bones, cover close and stop it round the top with dough; hang on in the morning and stew gently two hours; turn it, and stop tight and stew two hours more; when done tender, grate a crust of bread on the top and brown it before the fire; scum the gravy and serve in a butter boat, serve it with the residue of the gravy in the dish.

This is Simmons' version of a classic braised or stewed beef. A full beef top round will weigh about 13 to 15 pounds, so get a smaller cut of about 5 pounds, rolled and tied. Use grass fed beef.

Fine dice 8 ounces of fat back.
Add the following 6 ingredients:
4 or 5 grinds of fresh pepper
2 teaspoons of salt
2 tablespoons each fresh marjoram and thyme
¼ teaspoon ground cloves
½ teaspoon freshly grated mace
½ teaspoon freshly grated nutmeg
Slit the meat in 6 or 7 places, force seasoning/fat mix into the meat and refrigerate overnight.
Take a large non-reactive pot with a tight fitting lid and place some beef bones on the bottom to form a rack. If you cannot get beef bones, use a metal rack. The bones will produce better tasting gravy.
Add the liquid:

1 quart red wine and 1 quart water.

Place the beef in the pot and bring to a simmer, reduce heat to about 185° for the liquid and cover tightly. This is where Simmons says to "stop it round the top with dough" to make a tight seal.

Cook slowly about 45 minutes to one hour, turn and finish cooking until fork tender.

Remove the meat and keep warm.

Boil the liquid in the pot, skim the scum on top, mix about 1 tablespoon flour with some wine and slowly add to liquid, whisking constantly. When the liquid comes back to the boil it will thicken. If too loose, thicken more, adjust seasoning and strain into a gravy boat.

If you want a crust on the top of the beef, butter some fresh breadcrumbs, pat on the top of the beef after removing from the pan and brown under a broiler.

Simmons does not state which round to use, but for a traditional alamode a top or bottom round could be used. The bottom round is more flavorful.

Pies

A Stew Pie

> **A Stew Pie.**
> Boil a shoulder of Veal, and cut up, salt, pepper, and butter half pound, and slices of raw salt pork, make a layer of meat, and a layer of biscuit, or biscuit dough into a pot, cover close and stew half an hour in three quarts of water only.

Boil a shoulder of veal, and cut up, salt, pepper, and butter half pound, and slices of raw salt pork, make a layer of meat and a layer of biscuit, or biscuit dough into a pot, cover close and stew half an hour in three quarts of water only.

This recipe is a combination of two different types of food; a stew and a meat pie, both often used from colonial times to the present. Here the veal shoulder, a tougher cut that requires a moist cooking method, is fully cooked by itself and then placed in a baking dish to have a top crust added, in this case of biscuits. Following the veal recipe is a recipe for buttermilk biscuits, but if you have one you like better use it. This would also have been a way of using left over, stale biscuits by grating them on the top of the "stew pie" to brown just before serving.

Shoulder of veal is flavorful but requires moist cooking, braising or stewing. Here again Simmons makes the choice for a lesser cut of meat. The name tells us that this is a combination dish, a cross between a stew and meat pie, so popular in colonial times and still very much so in England.

After trimming excess fat, simmer the shoulder in water to cover with a cheese cloth bag (sachet) made with:

1 bay leaf
2 whole cloves
1 whole allspice
1 quarter of a cinnamon stick
½ a medium peeled onion
1 tablespoon of black peppercorns whole
Your favorite selection of "sweet herbs"
Simmer until the veal is tender, 45–60 minutes. Pierce with a fork and it should slide off slowly back into the pot. If the veal is cubed, it will take less time.
When done, remove, cool and cut into 1 to 1½ inch pieces and place in baking dish of choice.

Bring the cooking liquid to a boil after removing the sachet, skim the top, reduce by ½ and lower the heat. Heat some heavy cream, about ¼ the amount of the reduced broth, and add to now simmering reduced veal broth. If you want to use just the broth, thicken a little with a mixture of flour and white wine. Check for seasoning.

Pour this over the veal in the baking dish. Top with your favorite biscuit dough and bake at 400°F, uncovered, until the biscuits are done.

If you do not have your own biscuit recipe, try this one based on a recipe from the *Professional Chef* published by the Culinary Institute of America, which has long been a champion of American cuisine.

Sift together in a large bowl (all baking recipes are best measured with a scale)
All purpose flour: 4½ cups / 18 ounces
Salt: scant one tablespoon / ½ ounce
Baking powder: 3 tablespoons / 1.5 ounces
Sugar: 12 tablespoons / 6 ounces
Add
Eggs, beaten: 3 each, large eggs
Buttermilk: ¾ cup / 6 ounces
Mix until it is blended but still shaggy. Dust your table, roll out ½ inch thick and cut with round or square cutters. Place on top of the veal stew, brush the tops with milk, bake until medium brown, 400°F until done.

The next couple of recipes are for meat pies, a lingering holdover from traditional English cooking. Pies were useful and convenient in 18th-century America. With the main meal of the day often at midday, having an already baked pie on hand for supper was definitely a time and labor saver. If prepared for the evening meal, the leftovers, already "packaged" in their own crust, could be portioned and taken to the fields the next day or packed in some sort of transport container and taken on the road. With ingredients often cooked twice and preserved with sugar and or vinegar or wine for added acid, the chance for spoilage and food poisoning were greatly reduced.

Two savory or entrée pies are included. One is for tongue and the other for beef. Note that the Thanksgiving Mince Pie is a direct descendant of these colonial meat pies. This genre is present in modern-day America in the form of filled toaster pastries and other culinary delicacies.

The savory pie has since given way to strictly sweet dessert pies, with the exception of "pot pies." Here again is an example of American culinary heritage, passed from medieval times to the Renaissance to traditional English cooking to the colonies to our modern times.

Tongue Pie

One pound of neat's tongue, one pound apple, one third of a pound of Sugar, one quarter of a pound of butter, one pint of wine, one pound of raisins, or currants, (or half of each) half ounce of cinnamon and mace—bake in paste No. 1, in proportion to size.

Often used in early American cooking and still widely used elsewhere in the world, tongue has a texture similar to ham and depending upon how it is cured or smoked, a rich flavor. Tongue is available from specialty meat suppliers and some gourmet or oriental market chains. Use calf's tongue, here specified as neat's tongue. Beef tongue is good also, but considerably larger.

If the tongue is precooked simply make sure it is peeled. If not cooked, season some water with herbs and spices of your choice and simmer the tongue until fork tender. Remove, cool and peel the tough outer skin.

Medium dice:

1 pound of meat with

1 pound of peeled and cored tart baking apples.

Mix together in a bowl with:

¾ cup of sugar

1 stick of butter broken to pieces

1 pint of Sercial Madeira

Add 8 ounces each raisins and currants previously soaked in the Madeira

1 tablespoon each ground cinnamon and mace.

Season the filling with salt and fresh ground pepper.

Line a suitably sized baking dish with dough, add the filling, top with dough and poke a few holes in the top to allow steam to escape. Brush with milk or eggs, decorate the top if you like, and bake in a 400° oven until medium dark brown.

> *Tongue Pie.*
> One pound neat's tongue, one pound apple, one third of a pound of Sugar, one quarter of a pound of butter, one pint of wine, one pound of raisins, or currants, (or half of each) half ounce of cinnamon and mace—bake in paste No. 1, in proportion to size.
> *Minced Pie of Beef.*
> Four pound boiled beef, chopped fine, and salted; six pound of raw apple chopped also, one pound beef suet, one quart of wine or rich sweet cyder, one ounce mace, and cinnamon, a nutmeg, two pounds raisins, bake in paste No. 3, three fourths of an hour.

Minced Pie of Beef

Four pound boiled beef, chopped fine, and salted; six pound of raw apple chopped also, one pound beef suet, one quart of wine or rich sweet cyder, one ounce mace, and cinnamon, a nutmeg, two pounds of raisins, bake in paste No. 3, three fourths of an hour.

This recipe is reduced by half and will make about three 9-inch pies. Use your favorite pie-crust, a store-bought version or try one of Simmons'. She specifies Number 3.

Chop fine or coarse grind and mix together in a large bowl:

Cooked beef leftovers: 2 pounds

Tart apples, peeled and cored: 3 pounds

Beef suet: 1 pound

Madeira or apple cider: 1 pint

Mace: One tablespoon ground

Cinnamon: One tablespoon ground

Whole nutmeg: Grate half the nutmeg

Raisins: One pound soaked overnight in the cider or Madeira from above.

Place the filling in pie plates lined with dough and bake in a 400° oven about 45–60 minutes. Decorate the top crust to your liking after poking a couple of holes in it to allow steam to escape. For a darker color brush the tops with two beaten eggs mixed with ¼ cup water.

In a small section called "Observations," Simmons notes that meat pies require "a hotter and brisker oven than fruit pies...." With savory meat pies there was not a problem of the sugar boiling to the over-caramelized state. Oven temperatures were difficult to ascertain with accuracy. A pie with less or little sugar was more likely to have a more pleasing consistency than one where the sugar syrup continued to boil and reduce. She states that "as it is difficult to ascertain with precision the small articles of spicery," everyone may "relish as they like." So use spice guidelines as just that. The rose-water was a commonplace flavoring at this time and it still adds a distinctive flavor and aroma to modern recipes. Simmons also states that other fruit may be used for pies and "Every species of fresh fruit such as peas, [pears?] plums, raspberries, blackberries, may be only sweetened."

A buttered apple Pie

Pare, quarter and core tart apples, lay in paste No. 3. cover with the same; bake half an hour, when drawn, gently raise the top crust, add sugar, butter, cinnamon, mace, wine or rose-water.

For a 9-inch pie, figure on 2½ pound of finished apples.

Line a pie tin with your favorite pie dough.

In a bowl mix 2½ pounds tart, pared, cored and thinly sliced apples.

Toss with:

1 cup sugar

2 ounces all purpose flour

1 tablespoon ground cinnamon

½ teaspoon ground mace

A pinch of salt

1 ounce of rose-water

Dot with 2 ounces of butter.

> *A buttered apple Pie.*
> Pare, quarter and core tart apples, lay in paste
> **No. 3. cover with the same;** bake half an hour,
> when drawn, gently raise the top crust, add sugar,
> butter, cinnamon, mace, wine or rose-water q : f :

Brush the edges of the dough on the rim of the pan with egg, top with a top crust, make a few holes for steam venting, brush with milk and sprinkle sugar on top. Bake in a 400° oven, about one hour. If you have a baking stone preheat and bake on it.

Puddings, Custards, and Cakes

This highlights the first use of cornmeal in an American published cookbook. As one of the staples of Native American cooking, corn was readily adopted by the colonists for everything from bread to pudding to pancakes to whiskey. It was used in a similar fashion to how oats were used in traditional English recipes, with additions of molasses, and pear lash as a leavening agent — another of Simmons' groundbreaking recipe techniques referred to earlier.

There is also another combination recipe of early America, a "pudding dumpling." This is similar to old central European fruit dumplings where a fruit is wrapped in a sweet dough and either steamed or poached until the fruit and dough are cooked, and the dessert is served with a sauce.

While it is not likely, given Simmons' lack of formal education, that she would have known of Czech fruit dumplings, one may conclude that this simple but very tasty dessert again made its way over the centuries to England and then to America.

A Nice Indian Pudding.

No. 1. 3 pints scalded milk, 7 spoons fine Indian meal, stir well together while hot, let stand till cooled; add 7 eggs, half pound raisins, 4 ounces butter, spice and sugar, bake one and half hour.

The night before, soak half pound of raisins in 4 ounces Madeira.

3 pints milk, scalded in a large pot

7 tablespoons fine-ground corn meal. Add to milk, stirring constantly with a whisk to avoid lumps. When this thickens, as if you are cooking cream of wheat, remove from the stove and pour into a bowl. Allow mix to cool for about 30 minutes.

Beat together:

7 eggs and

½ cup sugar and stir into corn meal base.

Melt:

One stick of butter and stir into egg and sugar mix.

Drain raisins and add to pudding.

Place in a baking dish or mold and bake one and one half hours as per Simmons. Or you can test for doneness by inserting a skewer into the center of the pudding.

> *A Nice Indian Pudding.*
>
> **No. 1.** 3 pints scalded milk, 7 spoons fine Indian meal, stir well together while hot, let stand till cooled; add 7 eggs, half pound raisins, 4 ounces butter, spice and sugar, bake one and half hour.
>
> **No. 2.** 3 pints scalded milk to one pint meal salted; cool, add 2 eggs, 4 ounces butter, sugar or molasses and spice q: f: it will require two and half hours baking.
>
> **No. 3.** Salt a pint of meal, wet with one quart milk, sweeten and put into a strong cloth, brass or bell metal vessel, stone or earthen pot, secure from wet and boil 12 hours.

When it comes out moist with no cornmeal sticking to it, pudding is done.

Allow the pudding to cool, spoon into individual serving dishes, warm, and serve with a scoop of vanilla ice cream on top or top with whipped cream.

Pudding No. 2 uses molasses as a sweetener and fewer eggs so it requires more time in the oven.

Pudding No. 3 is more like a steamed pudding or dumpling. If you want to try it, take a look at the cooking time. This was easy if there was a fire in the cooking/warming fireplace all day long.

Potatoe Pudding. Baked

No. 2 One pound boiled potatoes marshed [mashed], three quarters of a pound butter, 3 gills milk or cream, the juice of one lemon and the peal grated, half a pound of sugar, half nutmeg, 7 eggs (taking out whites), 2 spoons rose-water.

Once again, this is a recipe for a new food product just getting well known in 1796/8.

Boil one pound all-purpose potatoes and put through a ricer or food mill making sure there are no lumps.

Cream 1 cup sugar with

3 sticks of butter

Add to the well-creamed mix:

One half nutmeg, freshly grated

2 teaspoons rose-water

Add the zest and juice of one lemon.

> *Potatoe Pudding.* **Baked.**
>
> No. 1. One pound boiled potatoes, one pound sugar, half a pound butter, 10 eggs.
>
> No. 2. One pound boiled potatoes marshed, three quarters of a pound butter, 3 gills milk or cream, the juice of one lemon and the peal grated, half a pound sugar, half nutmeg, 7 eggs (taking out 3 whites,) 2 spoons rose-water.

Mix well and add the 7 yolks one at a time, incorporating well.

Add 3 gills milk or cream (12 ounces), with the potatoes and mix alternately until all ingredients are well blended.

Pour into a buttered baking dish and bake about 1 hour at 350° or until done.

A Crookneck, or Winter Squash Pudding.

Core, boil, and skin a good squash, and bruise it well; take 6 large apples, pared, cored and stewed tender, mix together; add 6 or 7 spoonsful of dry bread or biscuit, rendered fine as meal, half pint of milk or cream, 2 spoons of rose-water, 2 do. wine, 5 or 6 eggs beaten and strained, nutmeg, salt and sugar to your taste, one spoon flour, beat all smartly together, bake.

The above is a good receipt for Pompkin, Potatoes or Yams, adding more moistening or milk and rose-water, and to the two latter a few black or Lisbon currants, or dry whortleberries scattered in, will make it better.

This is a classic flavor combination of squash and apples. Here is a version for butternut squash, but also try acorn or Hubbard squash. Crookneck squash, yellow squash, gives off lots of moisture. The consistency is better for the cold weather squashes.

Pick a nicely colored butternut squash. Peel it after cutting off the ends, cut it in half and scoop out the seeds. Cut the squash into chunks and steam, boil or roast until soft all the way through.

While the squash is cooking:

Peel, core and cut up the 6 apples. Use a firm apple — Northern Spy, Rome, Pippin, Arkansas Black. Stew in a little water or apple juice until soft.

In a bowl, combine the squash and apples; they should be about the same weight, 2 pounds each.

Process some stale bread or biscuits in a food processor until very fine.

Sift and measure 6 tablespoons. No food processor? Use the fine side of a box grater and sift.

Sift and add one tablespoon of flour to the crumbs.

Beat together in a separate bowl:

6 eggs

1 cup cream

2 teaspoons of rose-water

Two ounces of Madeira

Grating of ¼ nutmeg

1 teaspoons salt

½ cup sugar (depending upon how sweet the apples are)

> *A Crookneck, or Winter Squash Pudding.*
>
> Core, boil and skin a good squash, and bruize it well; take 6 large apples, pared, cored, and stewed tender, mix together; add 6 or 7 spoonsful of dry bread or biscuit, rendered fine as meal, half pint milk or cream, 2 spoons of rose-water, 2 do. wine, 5 or 6 eggs beaten and strained, nutmeg, salt and sugar to your taste, one spoon flour, beat all smartly together, bake.
>
> The above is a good receipt for Pompkins, Potatoes or Yams, adding more moistening or milk and rose water, and to the two latter a few black or Lisbon currants, or dry whortleberries scattered in, will make it better.

Beat all smartly, i.e. sufficiently to blend all together and make a smooth batter. Strain so that if any egg whites are not fully incorporated they will not streak white when the pudding is baked.

Add to squash-apple mix and bake in a buttered dish at 350°F about 1 hour.

If you want to make the version with potatoes or yams, whortleberries are blueberries. Simmons asks for dried berries, so make sure they are plumped the night before. Also, if you like any other dried fruit, use that. She would.

Pompkin.

No. 1 One quart, stewed and strained, 3 pints cream, 9 beaten eggs, sugar, mace, nutmeg and ginger, laid into paste No. 7 or 3, and with a dough spur, cross and checquer it, and baked in dishes three quarters of an hour.

Measure the pumpkin puree; there should be 1 quart

Add 3 pints cream

Beat together:

9 eggs

1 cup sugar

> *Pompkin.*
>
> No. 1. One quart stewed and strained, 3 pints cream, 9 beaten eggs, sugar, mace, nutmeg and ginger, laid into paste No. 7 or 3, and with a dough spur, cross and checquer it, and baked in dishes three quarters of an hour.
>
> No. 2. One quart of milk, 1 pint pompkin, 4 eggs, molasses, allspice and ginger in a crust, bake 1 hour.

1 tsp ground mace
1 tsp freshly ground nutmeg
2 tsp powdered ginger
Mix with pumpkin and add a pinch of salt.
Pour into 2 9" pre-baked pie shells.
Bake in a 350° oven about 45 to 60 minutes.
On a separate baking sheet, roll out your dough of choice and cut in strips with a fluted cutter, brush with egg wash, sprinkle with sugar and bake until brown. When you remove the pie from the oven and it is still somewhat soft, place decorative strips on top of the pie and cool. This is so that the strips bake completely. If placed on the pie before baking, the undersides will not bake.

Johnny Cake, or Hoe Cake.

Scald 1 pint of milk and put to 3 pints of indian meal, and half pint of flower — bake before the fire. Or scald with milk two thirds of the indian meal, or wet two thirds with boiling water, add salt, molasses and shortening, work up with cold water pretty stiff, and bake as above.

This is a classic of early American cookery as written down by Simmons. These cakes were also known as journey cakes and were a type of colonial hardtack that would keep 'til the cows came home.

Place 3 pints of fine ground corn meal in a bowl and
Mix in 1 cup of flour.
Add 1 pint scalded milk and stir well. This will be stiff and fairly tasteless.

> *Johny Cake, or Hoe Cake.*
> Scald 1 pint of milk and put to 3 pints of indian meal, and half pint of flower—bake before the fire. Or scald with milk two thirds of the indian meal, or wet two thirds with boiling water, add salt, molasses and shortening, work up with cold water pretty stiff, and bake as above.

Season as you like with salt and pepper for more flavor.
  OR
Place two pints of fine corn meal in a bowl.
Boil one pint of milk to which has been added:
2 teaspoons salt,
¼ cup lard
¼ cup molasses.
Stir well and add flour to make a stiff, pliable dough.
Use griddles or, if you have a fireplace, go buy a hoe that is unpainted, light a fire or use a camp fire, place the hoe with the handle stick up and "griddle cook" the cakes on the hoe. Cook one side well then the other. This is the equivalent of hardtack, a dry, hard biscuit used for food when there were no restaurants or ways of preserving food on long journeys.

Indian Slapjack.

One quart of milk, 1 pint of indian meal, 4 eggs, 4 spoons of flour, little salt, beat together, baked on gridles, or fry in a dry pan, or baked in a pan which has been rub'd with suet, lard or butter.

> *Indian Slapjack.*
> One quart of milk, 1 pint of indian meal, 4 eggs, 4 spoons of flour, little salt, beat together, baked on gridles, or fry in a dry pan, or baked in a pan which has been rub'd with suet, lard or butter.

In a bowl mix together:
1 pint of fine corn meal
4 tablespoons flour
1 teaspoon salt
Add

4 eggs beaten with
1 quart milk.

Grease a griddle or frying pan and cook like a pancake. This is dense and almost crumbly cracker in consistency. Try adding about two or three tablespoons oil and 1 teaspoon baking powder for a more "modern" version.

Cookies

One pound sugar boiled slowly in half pint water, scum well and cool, add two tea spoons pearl ash dissolved in milk, then two and half pound pounds flour, rub in 4 ounces butter, and two large spoons finely powdered coriander seed, wet with above; make roles half an inch thick and cut to the shape you please; bake fifteen or twenty minutes in a slack oven—good three weeks.

Some changes have been made to update this recipe to make it viable in a modern kitchen.

Pre-heat oven to 325°F
Sift together in a bowl:
2 pounds and 2 cups flour
2 teaspoons baking powder
Pinch of salt.
Add to this
2 cups sugar and stir well to blend.
Add
8 ounces melted butter to
1 pint warm milk
Add liquid to flour mix until a dough is formed that will hold together and can be rolled into logs, or roll about ½ inch thick. Cut the log or cut the sheet into desired shapes.

Place on a baking pan lightly greased or on a silicon baking sheet (better).
Brush tops with milk and sprinkle with sugar.
Bake at 300°–325°

Plumb Cake.

Mix one pound currants, one drachm nutmeg, mace and cinnamon each, a little salt, one pound of citron, orange peel candied, and almonds bleach'd, 6 pound of flour, (well dry'd) beat 21 eggs, and add with 1 quart new ale yeast, half pint of wine, three half pints cream and raisins, q: f:

This recipe is reduced by half, and is updated for modern kitchens. It is like a holiday cake, and if you want to make a full size batch to bake and wrap for holiday presents, make the original batch. If you want to use "emptins," make your own by mixing a one pound (pint) of bottle conditioned ale, preferable from Belgium as these still have yeast in the bottle, with one pound of water and a handful of hops and two tablespoons of honey. Boil then cool the mixture. Allow to stand, covered, with a couple of small holes in the plastic wrap at room temperature for about three days. It will bubble up. Stir it down, add 1 cup ale as before, mix well, stand at room temperature another day, and refrigerate.

For use, measure the amount you need the day before, place in a bowl and cover with plastic wrap with a couple of holes in it. (To be safe, add 1 packet of instant yeast mixed in ½ cup of flour just before using your *emptins* in a recipe. Remember all yeast reacts differently in different situations.)

Preheat oven to 350°
Plump the currants and raisins the night before in Madeira.
Drain and reserve.
In a large bowl, mix:
1 cup each citron, candied orange peel and blanched almonds, finely chopped.
Add to the fruits:
2 teaspoon each ground nutmeg, mace and cinnamon
Add ¼ teaspoon salt and mix all well.
If using *emptins*, use a large mixer at slow speed.
Add 1 pint *emptins* and mix with
10 eggs, added one at a time, incorporating each before adding another.
Add 4 ounces of Madeira starting with the wine used to soak the dried fruits. Mix well.
Alternately add:
4 cups flour and ½ cup of cream until 12 cups of flour and 1½ cups of cream have been added.
Allow the dough to mix for about 10 minutes, add the raisins a few at a time.
When dough is well kneaded and does not look shaggy, stop the mixer and allow it to rise 1 hour. Punch down and shape as desired — free form, in a pan or fancy mold.
Allow it to rest about 20 minutes. Brush the top with milk, sprinkle with sugar and bake until done, about 45 to 60 minutes.
If the top is getting too brown, cover with foil and continue baking until done.
Professional Tip: When kneading the dough, if after 2 or 3 minutes it looks dry, add some milk. Simmons call for flour "well dry'd" and your flour may be too "well dry'd."

Also, note there is no added sugar or fat in this recipe. It works as is. If a richer dough is desired, add 1 cup of sugar to the candied fruit and almonds. If butter is to be added, allow the dough to rise in the mixing bowl. Soften 1 stick of butter, place on top of the dough, and turn on the mixer. Continue mixing until the butter is mixed into the dough. Then proceed to finish the recipe. This is done to prevent the yeast from getting surrounded with fat and hence made unable to activate and make the dough rise. The candied fruits and nuts also work to prevent the dough from rising properly.

PLAIN CAKE.

Nine pound of flour, 3 pound of sugar, 3 pound of butter, 1 quart emptins, 1 quart milk, 9 eggs, 1 ounce of spice, 1 gill of rose-water, 1 gill of wine.

Much less expensive than the "Plumb Cake," this is also simpler to make. It is more like a traditional pound cake. This is scaled to ⅓ original size.

Pre-heat oven to 325°F
In a large mixer cream together:
1 pound butter
2 cups sugar
2 tablespoons of spice mix of your choice

Pinch of salt
¼ cup rose-water.
Scrape the bowl and make sure all ingredients are well blended.
Add:
3 eggs, adding one at a time, until each is completely incorporated.
Add:
¾ pint *emptins,* and mix until it is completely incorporated.
Add, alternating until used up:
12 cups flour and
1 quart whole milk.
Scrape the bowl after each addition to make sure ingredients are well blended.
Knead about 10 minutes on slow speed.
Cover, allow it to rise one hour, punch down, shape, rest 30 minutes, covered, and bake
    until done, about 45–60 minutes.

What Simmons did for American cuisine is shown above with the recipes selected. These are recipes that produced good food, and with a little refinement of technique that Simmons took for granted, can be made to be exceptional in modern kitchens.

Remember the newness of it all — the first ever use of cranberries, corn meal, turkey, potash, all in one book from a semi-literate independent woman in 1796/98. If you ever eat cake, cookies, pancakes, cornbread, cranberry sauce, have a well-cooked roast or pumpkin pie, thank Simmons.

CHAPTER 11

The Virginia Housewife (Mary Randolph)

Soups

Asparagus Soup

Makes about 2½ to 3 quarts of soup

Wash and trim the tips from two pounds of asparagus and refrigerate the tops.

Peel the stalks. Simmer the peeled stalks until quite soft in 2 quarts of chicken broth. When soft, remove the asparagus from the water and puree in a blender. Strain the puree into a bowl to remove any fibrous material.

While the asparagus is cooking:

In a large soup pot, slowly render one or two pieces of smoked

> #### ASPARAGUS SOUP.
>
> TAKE four large bunches of asparagus, scrape it nicely, cut off one inch of the tops, and lay them in water, chop the stalks and put them on the fire with a piece of bacon, a large onion cut up, and pepper and salt; add two quarts of water, boil them till the stalks are quite soft, then pulp them through a sieve, and strain the water to it, which must be put back in the pot; put into it a chicken cut up, with the tops of asparagus which had been laid by, boil it until these last articles are sufficiently done, thicken with flour, butter and milk, and serve it up.

bacon until they are crisp. Remove the pieces and reserve for another use.

Sauté 1 medium onion, finely diced, in the bacon fat until it is soft, about 5 or 6 minutes.

Sprinkle about 2 tablespoons of flour over the onions until all the fat is absorbed and the roux has the texture of loose peanut butter.

Simmer 2 minutes.

Add the asparagus cooking liquid and pureed asparagus; simmer until the starchy taste of the flour is gone, 20 to 30 minutes.

Reheat for service, add about 1 cup hot milk or cream to the soup and check the seasoning.

While reheating, cut the reserved tips of asparagus the same length by cutting the stalk ends. Bring a small amount of salted water to a boil and blanch the asparagus tips until al dente and a vibrant green. Drain and garnish the soup with the tips.

Soup with Bouilli

Buy an uncured beef brisket, about 4 or 5 pounds.

Cook the brisket so it makes the broth for the soup:

Place the beef in a large soup pot and add 3 quarts of water.

Simmer about two hours until the beef is almost fork tender.

Remove beef and cool.

While the beef is cooking, cut in medium dice the following and add to the simmering broth after the beef is removed:

2 medium onions

3 medium carrots

1 small purple top turnip

1 cup of celery stalks.

Simmer until al dente and add

2 tablespoons each of finely chopped parsley and thyme.

Slice the beef into rectangles 2 × 1 inches. Place on a pan, brush with beaten egg (a pastry brush will do if you do not have a suitable feather), sprinkle with fresh bread-crumbs and brown in a pre-heated broiler.

Adjust seasoning on the soup and thicken with a little *beurre manie* if desired, but do not make it too thick.

Place browned beef strips in bowls, ladle seasoned broth over the beef and serve it up!

Professional Tip: Beurre manie is equal parts whole butter and flour kneaded together and added just before service if a soup or sauce needs a little thickening. A roux has the same equal proportions but is cooked first. Always add a cold roux to a hot liquid to avoid lumps; same for a beurre manie.

Many of the soup recipes in this book call for boiling meat or fowl or fish first. This makes a broth. If bones are used instead of meat it makes a stock. Think about how people cooked in earlier times and did not have refrigeration and it becomes clear why broths rather than stocks were used most often.

Oyster Soup

This is a great example of how times have changed. When Mrs. Randolph wrote this recipe, oysters were so common and so cheap that they were an everyday food. To make the soup as written would be prohibitively expensive now, as oysters are not very common and are extremely expensive. What follows is the making of a broth that is used as the basis for a type of oyster stew.

SOUP WITH BOUILLI.

TAKE the nicest part of the thick brisket of beef, about eight pounds, put it into a pot with every thing directed for the other soup; make it exactly in the same way, only put it on an hour sooner, that you may have time to prepare the bouilli; after it has boiled five hours, take out the beef, cover up the soup and set it near the fire that it may keep hot. Take the skin off the beef, have the yelk of an egg well beaten, dip a feather in it and wash the top of your beef, sprinkle over it the crumb of stale bread finely grated, put it in a Dutch oven previously heated, put the top on with coals enough to brown, but not burn the beef; let it stand nearly an hour, and prepare your gravy thus:— Take a sufficient quantity of soup and the vegetables boiled in it; add to it a table-spoonful of red wine, and two of mushroom catsup, thicken with a little bit of butter and a little brown flour; make it very hot, pour it in your dish, and put the beef on it. Garnish it with green pickle, cut in thin slices, serve up the soup in a tureen with bits of toasted bread.

OYSTER SOUP.

WASH and drain two quarts of oysters, put them on with three quarts of water, three onions chopped up, two or three slices of lean ham, pepper and salt; boil it till reduced one-half, strain it through a sieve, return the liquid into the pot, put in one quart of fresh oysters, boil it till they are sufficiently done, and thicken the soup with four spoonsful of flour, two gills of rich cream, and the yelks of six new laid eggs beaten well; boil it a few minutes after the thickening is put in. Take care that it does not curdle, and that the flour is not in lumps; serve it up with the last oysters that were put in. If the flavour of thyme be agreeable, you may put in a little, but take care that it does not boil in it long enough to discolour the soup.

Make the poaching liquid:

Simmer 2 medium onions, medium dice with

½ cup ham scraps, dry cure if you have it

1 rib celery medium dice

Add:

1 quart water and 1 quart white wine

Make a sachet with:

12 peppercorns and half a lemon.

Simmer 30–45 minutes.

Strain and reserve.

Place one quart of freshly shucked oysters with their juice in a saucepot.

Add enough broth to cover, poach about one to two minutes. Do not overcook!!!

Make a liaison with:

6 egg yolks and

8 ounces of cream.

Temper the mix by adding a little of the hot liquid and stirring constantly. When the bowl for the liaison feels more than warm turn off the heat under the broth, slowly pour in the tempered liaison, season with salt and fresh pepper but do not boil.

If, as Mrs. Randolph suggests, you like thyme, add about one or two teaspoons of chopped fresh thyme when poaching the oysters.

Serve very hot.

Professional Tip: A liaison is a mix of egg yolks and cream used to enrich a soup. The eggs and cream are mixed together and made warm by the addition of some of the warm soup. The warmed eggs and cream are then added back into the soup. The liquid may not be boiled after the addition; the liquid will curdle and there will be floating scrambled egg yolks that are now a lightly opaque ugly mess.

DO NOT OVERCOOK THE OYSTERS

Okra Soup

OCHRA SOUP.

GET two double handsful of young ochra, wash and slice it thin, add two onions chopped fine, put it into a gallon of water at a very early hour in an earthen pipkin, or very nice iron pot; it must be kept steadily simmering, but not boiling: put in pepper and salt. At 12 o'clock, put in a handful of Lima beans; at

2*

half-past one o'clock, add three young cimlins cleaned and cut in small pieces, a fowl, or knuckle of veal, a bit of bacon or pork that has been boiled, and six tomatos, with the skin taken off; when nearly done, thicken with a spoonful of butter, mixed with one of flour. Have rice boiled to eat with it.

Take 8 ounces of okra, wash, trim the ends and slice about ½ inch thick. Reserve.

Boil 1 quart of salted water and add the okra, simmer about 20 minutes, strain out the okra and discard the water.

Bring 2 quarts of chicken or ham stock to a simmer,

Add the blanched okra

Add:

1 yellow squash and

1 zucchini (Cymlins) sliced,

Add to the soup 1 medium onion diced small.

When the vegetables are done but still have texture, add the rendered bacon from the previous recipe.

Add

6 peeled and seeded tomatoes cut the same size as the squash.

Thicken with *beurre manie* if desired and adjust seasoning.

Professional Tip: Parboiling the okra will reduce some of the sliminess. The beurre manie will thicken the soup nicely.

To peel and seed a tomato: Remove the little core at the top and make an "X" through the skin on the bottom. Place in boiling water 30 seconds. Remove with a slotted spoon and plunge into ice water for about one minute. The skin will start to peel back by itself. Remove it; it comes off easily. Stand the tomato with the core side on a board, cut in quarters.

Carefully slice horizontally and remove core flesh and seeds. Discard seeds and dice core flesh and outer flesh.

Catfish Soup

If you do not catch your own catfish, filets are available in many stores; some specialty markets may even carry whole fish. Note that Mrs. Randolph does not say to remove the bones. This is because so much flavor is in the bones. Classic fish stock is made with bones and a white *mirepoix,* onions and celery. Making the soup with the bones as well as flesh was a way of extracting maximum flavor from a well-chosen fresh ingredient. The method here is updated as to procedure and modern cooking techniques.

> CATFISH SOUP,
>
> *An excellent dish for those who have not imbibed a needless prejudice against those delicious fish.*
>
> TAKE two large or four small white catfish that have been caught in deep water, cut off the heads, and skin and clean the bodies; cut each in three parts, put them in a pot, with a pound of lean bacon, a large onion cut up, a handful of parsley chopped small, some pepper and salt, pour in a sufficient quantity of water, and stew them till the fish are quite tender but not broken; beat the yelks of four fresh eggs. add to them a large spoonful of butter, two of flour, and half a pint of rich milk; make all these warm and thicken the soup, take out the bacon, and put some of the fish in your tureen, pour in the soup, and serve it up.

Fish stock: Get fresh fish bones, but not from salmon or mackerel. Best are snapper, sole, flounder, etc. Place in a pot after rubbing the bottom with butter, with 1 gallon of water for every 8 pounds of bones.

For the white *mirepoix:*

1 medium onion cut in quarters,

1 stalk of celery cut small and

A sachet of half dozen black peppercorns and a small pinch of thyme and two lemon slices.

Add 6 slices raw bacon and place on a low heat. Bring slowly to a gentle simmer, about 175° F, skim the scum as it rises, and simmer about 45 minutes.

Do not allow it to boil. Keep the heat moderate, around 170°. Remove the stock from the stove, strain and cool quickly. If not to be used entirely, it can be refrigerated for three days or frozen, sealed, for about two months.

For the soup:

Cut up 4 catfish filets, 1½ to 2 pounds total, into about 6 pieces each.

Poach in enough fish stock to cover and add two slices lean bacon to the poaching liquid. Do not boil. Poach at 170°.

Remove the fish from the poaching liquid and reserve.

In a 3 quart sauce pot, sauté:

2 slices of bacon until rendered.

Remove and reserve. Pour out bacon fat, strain it, wipe the pot and add rendered and strained bacon fat.

Dice:

1 medium onion small and sauté until clear. Do not brown.

Sprinkle the onion and bacon fat with about 2 tablespoons of flour until the bacon fat is

absorbed and cook 2 minutes. The roux should have the consistency of cream peanut butter. Add 8 ounces cooled fish stock and stir until smooth. Never add a hot liquid to a hot roux. Adding a cooled stock will prevent the soup or sauce from getting lumpy.
Add:

½ cup white wine and

2 quarts fish stock and poaching liquid. Bring to a simmer for 20 minutes until the starch taste and feel are gone. Adjust the seasoning.

Place in a bowl and whisk together the liaison:

4 ounces cream and

4 egg yolks.

Temper with some of the fish soup by adding a little at a time to the egg yolk mix. When the bottom of the bowl is a bit more than warm, slowly pour back into the soup pot, stirring constantly and do NOT allow it to boil.

Warm the fish pieces or return to the finished soup and ladle the soup into heated bowls. Serve immediately. If you cannot find catfish or do not like catfish, use fresh water perch or pike or muskie, remembering that the latter two fish will have more bones and the flesh will be firmer. Fresh water bass can also be used if they are a good size.

Meats

Beef à la Mode

A round of beef, an entire one, is well over 30 pounds so this might be large for many people. Buy a top round roast and cut a slit in it for stuffing. Using a long blade knife such as a carving knife, start with a small insertion and work it back and forth, pressing inwards as you go. Keep the hand without the knife on top of the meat to hold it so all five fingers are still attached when the meat is stuffed. Beef marrowbones are available in most stores.

Remove the marrow, about two ounces, and poach in red wine about 30 minutes.

Remove and dice fine and place in a bowl.

Add:

2 or 3 garlic cloves, mashed to a paste

1 tablespoon each fresh thyme and fresh parsley finely chopped

¼ teaspoon ground nutmeg

Pinch of ground cloves

Salt and pepper to taste

2 egg yolks.

Mix all well together and test a piece by frying in a small pan. Adjust the seasoning if needed and stuff the beef. If the stuffing falls apart while making a test, add some fresh

> ### BEEF A-LA-MODE.
> TAKE the bone from a round of beef, fill the space with a forcemeat made of the crumbs of a stale loaf, four ounces of marrow, two heads of garlic chopped with thyme and parsley, some nutmeg, cloves, pepper and salt, mix it to a paste with the yelks of four eggs beaten, stuff the lean part of the round with it, and make balls of the remainder; sew a fillet of strong linen wide enough to keep it round and compact, put it in a vessel just sufficiently large to hold it, add a pint of red wine, cover it with sheets of tin or iron, set it in a brick oven properly heated, and bake it three hours; when done, skim the fat from the gravy, thicken it with brown flour, add some mushroom and walnut catsup, and serve it up garnished with forcemeat balls fried. It is still better when eaten cold with sallad.

bread crumbs, just enough to bind it. (Always make a test of a stuffing or forcemeat or sausage before final cooking to know what it will taste like when fully cooked.)

Take a large pot and heat it well. Add some cooking oil, sear the meat on all sides and remove from the pot.

Add

1 small onion finely chopped

1 small carrot chopped

1 small stalk of celery finely chopped and brown slowly in the pot.

Add

1 teaspoon tomato paste, stir well and cook about one minute.

Deglaze with

1 pint red wine, scraping the pan well.

Return the meat to the pot and add enough red wine to come up about ¼ of the way on the beef.

Bring to a simmer on the stovetop. Put a lid on it, and place in a 350°F oven about 90 minutes to 2 hours.

Take the remaining stuffing and scoop out small, meatball shapes and refrigerate.

When the internal temperature of the meat is 165°, remove it from the pot and keep it warm.

Bring the liquid to a boil, reduce by about half, and thicken with a slurry made from 2 ounces of flour and 2 ounces of red wine. Add a little to the simmering liquid. When the liquid boils, it is thickened. Adjust the consistency to your liking.

Add catsups if you have made them and adjust seasonings.

Bring to a boil for one minute, strain into an ice gravy boat.

Fry the little stuffing balls in hot oil while the gravy is reducing, and drain on brown paper before serving. Pour melted butter with finely chopped parsley over the stuffing balls just before service.

Professional Tip: Deglazing is adding a liquid to a hot pan to release the bits of food that stick to the pan during high heat cooking. It releases the food from the pan, develops color and adds flavor to the sauce.

Fricando of Beef

How this is prepared depends upon the cut of meat used. Mrs. Randolph suggests stewing, which is good for a tougher cut of meat; what might be used for pot roast or a regular stew-chuck, brisket or bottom round works well for stewing. For a more tender cut, top round, the method can change to a quicker cooking method. Here is an updated version of this recipe which sounds like a traditional steak house variation for a beef tenderloin steak.

Select your beef and cut as instructed, 6 × 2 × 1 inches. Use about 2 pounds for 6 servings.

Render one piece of bacon for each "steak" and remove the bacon when crisp and reserve.

Season the steaks with salt and pepper and dredge in seasoned flour to coat.

Sear them brown on all sides and reserve. Be careful to keep the fire from getting too hot and burning the fat or the flour.

Strain the fat and wipe any dry flour or loose bacon bits from your pan and return half the bacon fat. Save the rest.

Sauté until golden:

1 medium onion diced

1 small carrot.

Add

1 tablespoon tomato paste, tomato puree or tomato ends.

Deglaze with

8 ounces red wine and add about 1 pint brown stock or broth.

> A FRICANDO OF BEEF.
>
> Cut a few slices of beef six inches long, two or three wide, and one thick, lard them with bacon, dredge them well, and make them a nice brown before a brisk fire; stew them half an hour in a well seasoned gravy, put some stewed sorrel or spinage in the dish, lay on the beef, and pour over a sufficient quantity of gravy; garnish with fried balls.

Boil 10 minutes, reduce the heat and add the meat.

Simmer at 170° until fork tender, remove the meat and keep it warm, raise the heat and reduce the liquid by half. Strain, adjust seasoning and thicken if desired with a *beurre manie.*

Slice the meat nicely, place some "gravy" on a hot plate and serve with spinach, sorrel, greens or other green vegetable of choice.

See above for the fried balls. This is a good meal for German-style bread dumplings.

If you are using a tender cut of beef, such as a top round, the steaks may be cooked medium rare and simply reheated in the sauce.

Professional Tip: Larding is an antiquated cooking technique of stuffing fat into a long hollow needle and pushing the fat through the meat, drawing out the needle and leaving the fat. This was done to provide moisture and flavor for inferior meat and is no longer used.

Veal Chops

VEAL CHOPS.

TAKE the best end of a rack of veal, cut it in chops, with one bone in each, leave the small end of the bone bare two inches, beat them flat, and prepare them with eggs and crumbs, as the cutlets, butter some half-sheets of white paper, wrap one round each chop, skewer it well, leaving the bare bone out, broil them till done, and take care the paper does not burn; have nice white sauce in a boat.

This is one of the few recipes Mrs. Randolph has for veal — simple, elegant and quite tasty — and it would be at home in any high-end restaurant today.

Get 6 chops, 10 to 12 ounces each, dressed so no meat or fat is left on the rib bones. This is called Frenching the chops. Trim any excess fat from the outside of the eye and pound to flatten slightly.

Season the meat with salt and pepper.

Dredge in seasoned flour.

Dip the chops in a bowl with 2 eggs beaten with a little water.

Dip in fresh breadcrumbs. (This is known as standard breading procedure.)

Coat both sides of each chop and shake off any excess breading.

Sauté the veal in clarified butter about two minutes each side or until nicely browned. Finish cooking them in a 350° oven. They are done when a meat thermometer registers 140°.

In the sauté pan, pour out the grease, wipe out any breadcrumbs and return the pan to the heat and add 1 ounce fresh clarified butter.

Sauté:

½ a medium onion, diced fine, until soft.

Deglaze with:

6 ounces dry white wine, scraping all the good pieces of *fond* from the bottom of the pan. Reduce the wine until almost dry.

Add

8 ounces chicken broth and reduce by half.

Add

8 ounces cream and reduce by half.

Check for seasoning, strain, and just before serving, add some freshly chopped tarragon leaves.

Professional Tip: Fond is the term for the tasty bits of brown left in a sauté pan after the item is removed. *Fond* adds color and flavor to pan sauces. Be careful not to burn the *fond* or the sauce will be bitter. For some added flavor, pull the tarragon leaves from the stems early on and add the stems to the white wine and leave them in the sauce until it is strained.

Veal Olives

This is Mrs. Randolph's version of a classic Italian dish, Veal Saltimbocca.

Cut 1½ ounce pieces from a loin of veal, allowing three pieces for each person.

Place the slices on plastic wrap and fold more plastic wrap over the meat. Pound slightly until the pieces are quite thin. Do not tear the meat.

Season the scaloppini with salt and pepper and lay a thin slice of ham on each.

Roll the veal pieces and secure with toothpicks to keep them from opening while cooking.

Roll the pieces in melted butter and then fresh breadcrumbs, place them on a rack on a cookie sheet and bake in a 400° oven until golden.

VEAL OLIVES.

TAKE the bone out of the fillet and cut thin slices the size of the leg, beat them flat, rub them with the yelk of an egg beaten, lay on each piece a thin slice of boiled ham, sprinkle salt, pepper, grated nutmeg, chopped parsley, and bread crumbs over all, roll them up tight, and secure them with skewers, rub them with egg and roll them in bread crumbs, lay them on a tin dripping pan, and set them in an oven; when brown on one side, turn them, and when sufficiently done, lay them in a rich highly seasoned gravy made of proper thickness, stew them till tender, garnish with forcemeat balls and green pickles sliced.

Serve with a sauce of choice or simply brown some butter, add a squirt of fresh lemon juice and some finely chopped parsley and pour over the veal at service time.

Professional Tip: For flavor, try using paper-thin slices of dry cured Virginia ham in place of the storebought boiled ham. This dish can also have some sautéed mushrooms with Madeira to accompany it. Try using a duxelle of mushrooms on top of the ham slices before rolling them.

A duxelle is finely chopped or ground mushrooms, sautéed with shallots, deglazed with Madeira and cooked until the liquid evaporates from the mushrooms. Season with salt and pepper, and add some fresh thyme at the end. This is a great recipe.

Pie of Sweetbreads and Oysters

Sweetbreads are the thymus gland in a calf. They are classics in French cuisine and were always considered a "gourmet" item here in the United States. Modern Americans are not fond of organ and specialty meats, which is a shame, because they run the flavor gamut — from delicate as in sweetbreads, to full flavored and rich in the case of kidneys, heart and tongue.

The sweetbreads require blanching, peeling and chilling with a weight to make them easy to slice into consistent size pieces. Mrs. Randolph stipulates making a pie. This adaption will give the same tasting result, but will maintain the individuality of the ingredients while creating a harmonious whole.

For 4 people.

Prepare up to three days ahead:

Buy a pair of sweetbreads and wash them thoroughly. Place them in salted water and poach at 170°F. Use a cooking thermometer to check the temperature. Make sure the sweetbreads are completely covered. Poach about 15 minutes or until the thermometer inserted laterally into the center registers 155°F.

When they are done, remove them and place in a container with a heavy weight on top of them to keep them flat. Cover with plastic wrap and chill at least 24 hours.

TO MAKE A PIE OF SWEETBREADS AND OYSTERS.

BOIL the sweetbreads tender, stew the oysters, season them with pepper and salt, and thicken with cream, butter, the yelks of eggs and flour, put a puff paste at the bottom and around the sides of a deep dish, take the oysters up with an egg spoon, lay them in the bottom, and cover them with the sweetbreads, fill the dish with gravy, put a paste on the top, and bake it. This is the most delicate pie that can be made. The sweetbread of veal is the most delicious part, and may be broiled, fried, or dressed in any way, and is always good.

Remove them from the refrigerator when ready to use. Gently peel the white membrane-like film without crumbling the sweetbreads. Slice into regular tiny medallions and reserve.

Poach 24 oysters about 2 minutes in a little white wine, about 8 ounces, with a finely minced shallot and a sprig of fresh thyme. Remove the oysters when they just start to curl on the edges. **Do not overcook the oysters.**

Strain the cooking liquid and reduce it by half.

Add 4 ounces of heavy cream and simmer about five minutes reducing by ⅓. Adjust for salt and pepper and a pinch of cayenne.

In a bowl lightly beat:

2 egg yolks. Take a little of the sauce and temper the yolks. When tempered, return to the saucepot. *Do not boil the sauce or the end result will be oyster flavored scrambled egg yolks.*

Add oysters and sweetbreads to the sauce until just heated through. Ladle the oysters and sweetbreads into 4 puff pastry shells. Pour the sauce into the shells to moisten and serve. Any extra sauce may be served in a sauceboat on the side.

Top the pastry shells with decoratively cut shapes made from puff pastry.

Serve with sautéed spinach and roasted tomatoes.

Steaks of Leg of Mutton

Buying a boneless leg of lamb, and separating it into the large muscles most easily completes this recipe. These can then be charbroiled whole or, as Mrs. Randolph says, are also quite nice when cut as for veal cutlets.

STEAKS OF A LEG OF MUTTON.

CUT off the flank, take out the bone, and cut it in large slices half an inch thick, sprinkle some salt and pepper, and broil it, pour over it nice melted butter with capers; a leg cut in the same way and dressed as directed for veal cutlets, is very fine. It is also excellent when salted as beef, and boiled, served up with carrots or turnips.

A shoulder of mutton is best when roasted, but may be made into cutlets or in a harrico.

One leg will serve about 8 to 10.

Broil to your liking and make a sauce of 8 ounces lightly browned butter, two dozen capers and a squeeze of fresh lemon juice just before serving.

Serve very hot. For summertime, serve with grilled vegetables. For cold weather, try roasted root vegetables or a vegetable stew, both well seasoned.

Seafood

In early Virginia fresh and saltwater fish were in abundant supply. Oysters were considered quite ordinary, sturgeon was so plentiful that it was effortlessly caught and bass were everywhere. I heard a story one time that there was a law that prohibited serving oysters to slaves more than six days per week.

To Roast a Shad

Shad are ancient fish that live most of their lives in the ocean, returning to their birth stream to spawn. Shad season runs in the spring and the fish is found all along the East Coast from the tidewater to New England. It can be somewhat of an acquired taste. The shad roe are almost more popular than the fish itself.

Their bone structure is tricky with an extra set of lateral bones; have the fishmonger sell the fish already filleted.

Mrs. Randolph recommends roasting on a board, something most likely learned from Native Americans — think planked salmon, a famous dish from the Pacific Northwest. Try it.

Make an oyster stuffing, the same as for turkey. Season it

> ### TO ROAST A SHAD.
>
> FILL the cavity with good forcemeat, sew it up, and tie it on a board of proper size, cover it with bread crumbs, with some salt and pepper, set it before the fire to roast; when done on one side, turn it, tie it again, and when sufficiently done, pull out the thread, and serve it up with butter and parsley poured over it.

very well and lay it on the bottom filet of fish. Bring up the top filets and secure with wooden skewers that have been soaked in water overnight.

Cover the fish with fresh breadcrumbs, drizzle with melted butter and bake at 350°F about 15 to 20 minutes. There is no need to turn in a modern oven. To roast it on a plank, get a cedar plank, soak it overnight in water, and place the shad on it and roast as above.

Serve with brown butter flavored with fresh lemon juice and chopped fresh parsley.

One medium shad will serve two as an entrée.

To Caveach Fish

This is Mrs. Randolph's version of ceviche, which most people will remember as being made with raw fish and a vibrant acid, mostly lime juice, and various seasonings, often quite spicy. Here the fish is cooked then pickled. More properly, this dish is an escabiche, or pickled fish that is first cooked.

Take 2 pounds of any firm-fleshed fish — snapper, grouper, cobia — and cut the filets into slightly larger than bite-size pieces.

Make a *court bouillon* with:

8 ounces white wine and 8 ounces fish stock (or water) seasoned with salt and pepper.

Slice 1 small lemon and

1 fresh fennel stem and add to the *court boullion.*

Boil the *court bouillon* about five minutes to develop flavors first and then lower the temperature to 170°.

> ### TO CAVEACH FISH.
>
> CUT the fish in pieces the thickness of your hand, wash it and dry it in a cloth, sprinkle on some pepper and salt, dredge it with flour, and fry it a nice brown; when it gets cold, put it in a pot with a little chopped onion between the layers, take as much vinegar and water as will cover it, mix with it some oil, pounded mace, and whole black pepper, pour it on, and stop the pot closely. This is a very convenient article, as it makes an excellent and ready addition to a dinner or supper. When served up, it should be garnished with green fennel, or parsley.

Poach the fish pieces in the 170° *court boullion.*

Do not overcook the fish. Remove the fish when done and place in a glass bowl or dish.

Prepare a marinade with:

4 ounces cider vinegar
1 ounce water
1 whole mace
12 peppercorns
2 thinly sliced fennel stems.

Adjust the salt and white pepper. Add some cayenne if the dish is to be spicy hot, or some thinly sliced hot chili pepper, jalapeno or Serrano.

If a more acidic taste is desired, add one ounce of fresh lemon juice.

Add a drizzle of olive oil.

Taste to make sure it is not too acidic; pour the marinade over fish to cover. Refrigerate overnight or for two days.

When ready to serve, bring the preparation to room temperature and remove the fish from marinade, place on small plates, garnish and pour a touch of the marinade onto the plate to lightly surround the fish. This makes a great first course and can be flavored to any degree of heat or with any herbs available. Serve with hot, crisp crusted bread drizzled with olive oil.

Fried Oysters

This simple preparation allows the briny taste of fresh oysters to shine. Note that Mrs. Randolph says oysters are a "proper garnish for calves' head, or most made dishes." This implies that other foods were considered more important than oysters and that they were good enough to go with other foods, but maybe not on their own.

TO FRY OYSTERS.

TAKE a quarter of a hundred of large oysters, wash them and roll them in grated bread, with pepper and salt, and fry them a light brown; if you choose, you may add a little parsley, shred fine. They are a proper garnish for calves' head, or most made dishes.

Make them as she says, and garnish with your favorite sauce or condiment. Use fresh breadcrumbs. Figure on 6 pieces for an appetizer portion.

Scalloped Oysters

This is an easy dish that screams for the freshest oysters possible. Use the amount as specified above: 6 pieces for an appetizer, 12 for an entrée portion. If making the entrée, serve with a simple green salad and a vinaigrette dressing made with a soft vinegar, such as rice wine vinegar. A great wine for this oyster extravaganza is a Chablis Premier or Grand Cru.

TO SCOLLOP OYSTERS.

WHEN the oysters are opened, put them in a bowl, and wash them out of their own liquor; put some in the scollop shells, strew over them a few bread crumbs, and lay a slice of butter on them, then more oysters, bread crumbs, and a slice of butter on the top; put them into a Dutch oven to brown, and serve them up in the shells.

Shuck the oysters and retain the juice. It can be used for oyster sauce or oyster stew or shellfish chowder. Butter the shell, place an oyster in it, dust with fresh breadcrumbs and add a small pat of butter, sprinkle with salt, fresh ground pepper and cayenne. Repeat for all your oysters and shells. Allow three shells, six oysters, for an appetizer. Place in a hot oven, 400°, and remove when brown. Serve immediately with a splash of brown butter with finely chopped parsley added.

To Make a Curry of Catfish

Most likely what will be available in the market will simply be catfish filets. Allow six-ounce portions for entrée service. Mrs. Randolph does not indicate a garnish, but feel free to use a traditional garnish of a chutney, cucumber salad, yogurt, etc. Best served with long grain rice or boiled parsley potatoes.

For 6 servings

Select a dish that will hold six, six-ounce filets. To the dish add:

2 medium onions, sliced thin

A mixture of 3 parts water and 1 part lager beer to cover the fish.

Bring to a simmer, 170°, and add the filets on top of the onions. Poach until done, being careful not to overcook them.

Remove the filets, boil down the sauce by half and puree in a blender.

> **TO MAKE A CURRY OF CATFISH.**
>
> TAKE the white channel catfish, cut off their heads, skin and clean them, cut them in pieces four inches long, put as many as will be sufficient for a dish into a stew pan with a quart of water, two onions, and chopped parsley; let them stew gently till the water is reduced to half a pint, take the fish out and lay them on a dish, cover them to keep them hot, rub a spoonful of butter into one of flour, add a large teaspoonful of curry powder, thicken the gravy with it, shake it over the fire a few minutes, and pour it over the fish; be careful to have the gravy smooth.

Return the liquid to the fire and thicken with a *beurre manie* made with two parts butter, one part flour and one part curry powder. Stir this into the simmering, pureed liquid until it thickens.

If serving the curry in a large dish, check the sauce for seasoning and strain the sauce over the fish filets and serve immediately. If serving on individual plates, make sure the plates are hot, place fish on plate and spoon a little of the sauce between the fish and the rim of the plate. Garnish the fish with finely chopped parsley and pass the remaining sauce separately.

If a more pronounced curry flavor is desired, a teaspoon of Thai yellow curry paste may be stirred into the sauce after it starts to thicken. Allow the sauce to come to a simmer and adjust seasonings as needed.

To Pitchcock Eels

In 1736 an Englishman by the name of Richard Bradley wrote that to spitchcock an eel was to grill or fry pieces of eel with some breadcrumbs and herbs. Mrs. Randolph omits the "s" but it seems to be the same method. Eel is quite tasty, especially smoked and served with a spicy

> **TO PITCHCOCK EELS.**
>
> SKIN and wash your eels, then dry them with a cloth, sprinkle them with pepper, salt, and a little dried sage, turn them backward and forward, and skewer them; rub a gridiron with beef suet, broil them a nice brown, put them on a dish with good melted butter, and lay around fried parsley.

dipping sauce. Eels were a staple of Western European food for centuries, and here we see the tradition carried on in Virginia. Remember: Eels are fish.

If eel filets can be found already skinned, buy those. If you catch your own, cut off the heads and tails, grab them with non-slip gloves, and take a pair of pliers and skin tail to head, or where the head was. Gut and wash them thoroughly. Pat dry and filet along the backbone, or for better flavor, cook on the bone.

Season the eels with salt and pepper. Dredge them in well-seasoned flour to which has been added finely chopped sage to taste. Depending upon how large the pieces are, insert wooded skewers to have them retain their shape.

Grill them on a preheated cast iron griddle or skillet. If you have beef suet, melt it in the skillet. If not, use clarified butter and grill them nice and brown on both sides.

For service, make some brown butter with chopped parsley, and pour over just before service.

Fowl and Poultry

TO BOIL A TURKEY WITH OYSTER SAUCE.

GRATE a loaf of bread, chop a score or more of oysters fine, add nutmeg, pepper and salt to your taste, mix it up into a light forcemeat with a quarter of a pound of butter, a spoonful or two of cream, and three eggs; stuff the craw with it, and make the rest into balls and boil them; sew up the turkey, dredge it well with flour, put it in a kettle of cold water, cover it, and set it over the fire; as the scum begins to rise, take it off, let it boil very slowly for half an hour, then take off your kettle and keep it closely covered; if it be of a middle size, let it stand in the hot water half an hour, the steam being kept in, will stew it enough, make it rise, keep the skin whole, tender, and very white; when you dish it, pour on a little oyster sauce, lay the balls round, and serve it up with the rest of the sauce in a boat.

N. B. Set on the turkey in time, that it may stew as above; it is the best way to boil one to perfection. Put it over the fire to heat, just before you dish it up.

TO MAKE SAUCE FOR A TURKEY.

As you open the oysters, put a pint into a bowl, wash them out of their own liquor, and put them in another bowl; when the liquor has settled, pour it off into a sauce pan with a little white gravy, and a teaspoonful of lemon pickle—thicken it with flour and a good lump of butter; boil it three or four minutes, put in a spoonful of good cream, add the oysters, keep shaking them over the fire till they are quite hot, but don't let them boil, for it will make them hard and appear small.

To Boil a Turkey With Oyster Sauce

Start with a 12 to 15 pound turkey; best would be free range and an heirloom variety. These are more flavorful than farm raised commercial turkeys and will give a taste closer to what Mrs. Randolph was used to.

For the giblets, simmer the heart and gizzard to make a broth and sauté the liver for a snack or cook for the cat.

Rinse and dry the inside of the bird, making sure there are no blood clots, etc.

Allow a one-pound loaf of artisan bread to stale. Grate with the coarsest side of a box grater.

Drain and chop, finely:
    24 oysters, reserving the liquor.
Add to the grated bread.

In a separate bowl mix:
    2 tablespoons cream
    3 eggs and seasonings to taste.
Add in 1 stick (4 ounces) melted butter, salt and pepper.

Pour over breadcrumb-oyster mix.

Toss with a lifting motion of your hands. Do not mash the stuffing.

Break off a small piece, roll into a ball and poach it. Taste for seasoning and adjust to taste.

Stuff the cavity but do not cram the stuffing in there.

Close the opening with butcher's twine.

Place the turkey in a large pot to which has been added:

1 large onion sliced

2 stalks of celery sliced and

1 carrot sliced.

Cover with cold water and place on the stove on the largest burner.

Bring to a simmer with tiny bubbles showing on the side of the pot. Skim the scum and allow bird to simmer until a thermometer registers 160° when inserted in the joint between the thigh and carcass.

Turn off the heat and cover tightly. In about 20 to 30 minutes check the temperature again, it should be at 165° or slightly higher.

With the leftover stuffing, make little stuffing balls and either poach them or fry them.

While the bird is poaching, make the sauce.

Open enough oysters to make a pint, placing them in a strainer set over a bowl to catch the liquor.

Reserve and refrigerate the oysters.

Pour off the liquid into a small saucepot, making sure no sand gets into the pot.

Reduce the liquor by one half.

Add 1 cup cream and reduce by one half.

Thicken to a desired consistency with a little *beurre manie,* and when the sauce cones to a simmer, add the oysters but do not allow the liquid to come to a hard boil. Poach the oysters in the sauce for about two minutes. They are done when they barely curl at the edges.

Season the sauce with salt, white pepper, a grating of fresh lemon zest and a teaspoon of fresh lemon juice.

Remove the turkey while the sauce is simmering, drain and carve as usual and pass the sauce in a sauceboat.

The turkey is not roasted, so it will not be brown. It is poached and will be wonderfully juicy and tender. Mrs. Randolph knew what she was about. Be careful not to allow the poaching liquid to boil: It must be kept between 170° and 180°. Pay attention to the oysters and do not let them overcook. They will become rubbery if overcooked.

To Make a Dish of Curry After the East Indian Manner

The method here is modified for more modern cooking methods.

Take two broiling chickens and separate legs, thighs, wings, and cut the breast down the middle, open the carcass and separate the two halves of the breast, bone in, from the backbone. Cut each breast half in two pieces on a diagonal. Heat some oil in a large stew pot.

Season all the chicken pieces with salt and pepper. Brown well all over in the hot oil, removing each piece as it browns. Do not put too many pieces in at one time as they will not brown properly.

When all the pieces are browned, pour off the oil, reduce the heat to low/medium, and add:

TO MAKE A DISH OF CURRY AFTER THE EAST INDIAN MANNER.

Cut two chickens as for fricassee, wash them clean, and put them in a stew pan with as much water as will cover them; sprinkle them with a large spoonful of salt, and let them boil till tender, covered close all the time, and skim them well; when boiled enough, take up the chickens, and put the liquor of them into a pan, then put half a pound of fresh butter in the pan, and brown it a little; put into it two cloves of garlic, and a large onion sliced, and let these all fry till brown, often shaking the pan; then put in the chickens, and sprinkle over them two or three spoonsful of curry powder; then cover the pan close, and let the chickens do till brown, often shaking the pan; then put in the liquor the chickens were boiled in, and let all stew till tender; if acid is agreeable, squeeze the juice of a lemon or orange in it.

1 stick unsalted butter.

When it stops foaming, add to it:

1 medium onion, quartered and sliced.

When the onion is soft, after about 5 minutes, add:

2 cloves of garlic, or more to taste, crushed to a paste. When the garlic gives off aroma, add:

3 tablespoons of curry powder or more to taste as if making a roux.

Stir until the butter is absorbed, adding more curry powder or flour if needed.

Deglaze the pot with 12 ounces lager beer or chicken stock or a mixture, scraping to get the tasty brown pieces off the bottom, stirring all the time. Make sure your broth and beer are room temperature so lumps do not form.

Bring the liquid to a simmer, return the chicken pieces, cover and braise until done. The chicken may be braised on the stovetop or in a 350° oven. The chicken is done when a leg or thigh is removed and the juices run clear when pierced with a fork.

Serve with plain white rice and garnishes of sliced cucumber, plain yogurt, assorted chutneys and flat bread. This method makes a nice homey-style chicken curry.

Chicken Pudding, a Favorite Virginia Dish

The chicken is parcooked, poached, until almost done, then baked in a batter that could also be used for frying. Follow Mrs. Randolph's instructions. The chickens may be roasted as well. If the chickens are poached, the poaching liquid may be reduced by half for a mild chicken broth. The following will serve 8 people for dinner.

CHICKEN PUDDING, A FAVOURITE VIRGINIA DISH.

BEAT ten eggs very light, add to them a quart of rich milk, with a quarter of a pound of butter melted, and some pepper and salt; stir in as much flour as will make a thin good batter; take four young chickens, and after cleaning them nicely, cut off the legs, wings, &c. put them all in a sauce pan, with some salt and water, and a bundle of thyme and parsley, boil them till nearly done, then take the chicken from the water and put it in the batter, pour it in a deep dish, and bake it; send nice white gravy in a boat.

Cut up the chickens or have your butcher cut them into 8 pieces each: 2 legs, 2 thighs, 2 portions of breast with the wing attached and 2 bottom two thirds of the breast without the wing.

Leave the bones in.

Make the poaching liquid:

Place all chicken parts from four chickens in a large pot.

Cover with cold water and add a sachet of:

2 sprigs thyme

6 peppercorns

2 cloves garlic

2 small shallots

2 sprigs of parsley.

Tie the sachet with some twine and drop it into the poaching liquid, leaving a piece of the twine outside the pot to pull out the sachet later.

Slowly bring to a simmer, using a meat thermometer to hold the poaching liquid at 170°F. Poach about 20 to 25 minutes. Pull out a leg. There should still be a little pink on the bone.

While the chicken is poaching, prepare the batter.

In a large bowl beat:

10 eggs until uniformly golden colored.

Add:

1 quart of whole milk or 1 pint whole milk and 1 pint half and half.

Season this with salt and fresh ground white pepper, some fresh grated nutmeg and mace. Stir in:

¼ pound melted butter.

Add ¾ cup flour, more or less, stirring with a whisk to make sure there are no lumps. The batter should be only moderately thick, almost like a batter for a cake.

If the batter seems too thin, add a little more flour. This is quite similar to the classic French dessert batter for a *clafouti*.

When the chicken is done, remove the sachet and remove the chicken, place in a large baking dish, pour the batter over the chicken pieces (which are no more than two layers deep), making sure the batter gets between all the pieces.

Bake the pie at 375° until golden and the batter has risen to cover the chicken.

To make a sauce for the chicken:

Take 1 quart of poaching liquid and reduce by ½.

In another pot, melt:

2 tablespoons of butter over medium low heat.

Finely chop:

1 medium onion

1 stalk of celery and sauté both in the butter until soft.

Sprinkle about 3 tablespoons flour over the veggies. Stir to make sure there are no lumps. Cook the roux about two or three minutes. The roux should be about the consistency of peanut butter or a little looser.

Add 1 cup of room temperature milk, making a paste in the pot with a small amount of the milk, stirring to make sure there are no lumps. Add the remaining milk slowly, whisking constantly.

Add 1 cup of the reduced chicken stock and simmer the sauce for 45 minutes.

Adjust the seasoning, strain and enrich with 4 ounces hot heavy cream. Adjust the seasonings.

To serve, bring the baking dish to the table with appropriate serving utensils and serve the sauce on the side in a nice sauceboat.

No need for an added starch as the batter already contains the starch. Serve with a green salad or sautéed spinach or greens.

Other Receipts

Okra and Tomatoes

Here are two recipes for okra, one with tomatoes and one by itself. Can there be a more vivid link to the influence of Caribbean and West African cooking than these recipes?

Buy 1 pound of tomatoes and 1 pound of fresh okra. Peel the tomatoes and slice the okra in ½ inch-thick slices.

Melt some butter or oil in a sauté pan and sauté:

1 medium onion, chopped fine, about 5 minutes.

Add the okra and tomatoes and season with salt and pepper or to taste.

Reduce the heat and slowly simmer about 30 to 45 minutes or until the okra is soft and has thickened the stew.

Tomatoes give off lots of liquid, so additional stock or water may not be needed.

> **OCHRA AND TOMATOS.**
>
> Take an equal quantity of each, let the ochra be young, slice it, and skin the tomatos; put them into a pan without water, add a lump of butter, an onion chopped fine, some pepper and salt, and stew them one hour.

Gumbo — A West India Dish

GUMBO—A WEST INDIA DISH.

GATHER young pods of ochra, wash them clean, and put them in a pan with a little water, salt and pepper, stew them till tender, and serve them with melted butter. They are very nutritious, and easy of digestion.

For the okra by itself, follow the directions above, including sautéing the onion. If the okra is too slimy, parboil it for about 10 minutes in salted water before making the gumbo. While sautéing the okra with the onion add some gumbo file powder to thicken the dish.

Omelette Soufflé

OMELETTE SOUFFLE.

BREAK six eggs, beat the yelks and whites separately till very light, then mix them, add four table spoonsful of powdered sugar, and a little grated lemon peel; put a quarter of a pound of butter in a pan; when melted, pour in the eggs and stir them; when they have absorbed the butter, turn it on a plate previously buttered, sprinkle some powdered sugar, set it in a hot Dutch oven, and when a little brown, serve it up for a desert.

This is a classic French-inspired dish — a simple, quick and nutritious dessert.

Separate 6 eggs.

Butter a 1 quart soufflé dish or 4 individual soufflé dishes and dust with granulated sugar, dumping out the excess sugar. The sugar crystals act like little ball bearings to help the soufflé rise while baking.

Sift 2 tablespoons of powdered sugar into the 6 egg yolks and whip until light and lemon-colored and the whisk leaves a track.

Using a clean whisk, beat the whites to soft peaks, and sift in 2 tablespoons of powdered sugar.

Stir a spoonful of beaten whites into the yolks to lighten them, fold in the remaining whites and pour into the soufflé dish or individual dishes.

Bake the soufflé in a 350° oven until risen and lightly browned. Serve immediately.

A sauce or melted jam may be served along with the soufflé.

Oyster Catsup

All most people think about when the word ketchup is said, is a tomato-based product loaded with high fructose corn syrup, tomatoes and vinegar. A catsup, or ketchup, was a common seasoning agent that could be made from any number of vegetables, fruits or, in this case, oysters. Follow proper canning procedures from the jar manufacturer to be safe

OYSTER CATSUP.

GET fine fresh oysters, wash them in their own liquor, put them in a marble mortar with salt, pounded mace, and cayenne pepper, in the proportions of one ounce salt, two drachms mace, and one of cayenne to each pint of oysters; pound them together, and add a pint of white wine to each pint; boil it some minutes, and rub it through a sieve; boil it again, skim it, and when cold, bottle, cork, and seal it. This composition gives a fine flavour to white sauces, and if a glass of brandy be added, it will keep good for a considerable time.

or make enough to last a week or two and if you still have some left over, freeze it. If oyster catsup sounds too exotic, look at any oriental foods shelf in a modern supermarket. Oyster sauce will most likely be on the shelves.

Buy a pint of oysters with their liquor and pulse in a blender for one or two seconds, or use a mortar and pestle.

Add seasonings: salt, mace and cayenne.

A drachm is roughly ¼ of a teaspoon. By weight it is one eighth of an ounce. If you have a scale that will weigh accurately, use that. Add all the ingredients to a non-reactive pot.

Add the wine, 1 pint, to the pot and boil it. After 1 or 2 minutes strain it and simmer 3 or 4 minutes and skim any scum that rises to the surface.

When cool, add an ounce of brandy and refrigerate.

Tomato Catsup

A peck is a quarter of a bushel, dry measurement. It is pretty much an archaic term now, but was in use for several hundred years both in England and the United States. Commercial suppliers sometimes still indicate this on a wholesale carton or bag.

Buy a peck of tomatoes, which can be found so packaged at many farm stands.

Wash them well and take out the core.

Cut them in quarters or sixths and add to a large pot. Keep the fire low and add 2 tablespoons of salt.

Cook them until they get soft, start to lose their shape and much of the liquid has evaporated. Strain them through a food mill, discard the skins and seeds and return the paste to the fire.

While the tomatoes are cooking, fine dice: ½ cup yellow onion.

Add ¼ teaspoon ground mace, or if you have blade mace, make a sachet with an eighth of an ounce, add a tablespoon of whole black pepper, tie the sachet and add to the pot.

> ### TOMATO CATSUP.
>
> GATHER a peck of tomatos, pick out the stems, and wash them; put them on the fire without water, sprinkle on a few spoonsful of salt, let them boil steadily an hour, stirring them frequently; strain them through a colander, and then through a sieve; put the liquid on the fire with half a pint of chopped onions, half a quarter of an ounce of mace broke into small pieces; and if not sufficiently salt, add a little more—one table-spoonful of whole black pepper; boil all together until just enough to fill two bottles; cork it tight. Make it in August, in dry weather.

Cook until virtually all liquid is gone, but do not scorch the tomato catsup.

Adjust seasoning after removing the sachet. This can be made spicier by adding cayenne, more pungent by adding some cider vinegar, etc. But do not add any sugar. This is a condiment, not a dessert.

Mushroom Catsup

Get a peck of mushrooms — plain old button mushrooms work well.

Take off the stems and reserve. Wipe the mushroom and chop coarsely.

Add them to a pot over moderate heat and cook until they are just about covered in their own liquid.

Take them from the fire, pass through a food mill and return to the pot.

Add

2 tablespoons salt

3 cloves of garlic crushed to a paste

2 teaspoons of ground cloves, and cook until reduced by ½.

Cool and place in a container in the fridge or freeze for later use. This is an intensely flavored condiment and

> ### MUSHROOM CATSUP.
>
> TAKE the flaps of the proper mushrooms from the stems—wash them, add some salt, and crush them; then boil them some time, strain them through a cloth, put them on the fire again with salt to your taste, a few cloves of garlic, and a quarter of an ounce of cloves pounded, to a peck of mushrooms; boil it till reduced to less than half the original quantity—bottle and cork it well.

you will be surprised at the amount you get from a ¼ bushel of mushrooms. You really cook the mushrooms down to their essence.

Walnut Catsup

TO MAKE WALNUT CATSUP.

GATHER the walnuts as for pickling, and keep them in salt and water the same time; then pound them in a marble mortar—to every dozen walnuts, put a quart of vinegar; stir them well every day for a week, then put them in a bag, and press all the liquor through; to each quart, put a tea-spoonful of pounded cloves, and one of mace, with six cloves of garlic—boil it fifteen or twenty minutes, and bottle it.

The best walnuts are younger, smaller ones. Mrs. Randolph suggests taking them when a pin can just pierce the flesh. If you do not have your own trees, try to buy as fresh as possible.

Make a salt solution of:
¼ cup of salt to 2 cups of water and pour it while boiling over the nuts. Keep in the refrigerator 9 days, and repeat the boiling salted water step after three days and after 6 days. Use about one pound walnuts.

Take the nuts and grind them coarsely or use a mortar and pestle. Place them in a bowl and cover them with sherry vinegar and refrigerate, for one week, stirring every day. This is the base for the catsup.

For 1 quart of base, add 6 garlic cloves, crushed to a paste, a rounded teaspoonful of ground cloves and 1 rounded spoonful of ground mace.

Cook until it boils and reduces by ⅓ to ½.

Cool and place in fridge, or for a smoother catsup, strain through a food mill and then cheesecloth.

To Dress Salad

TO DRESS SALAD.

To have this delicate dish in perfection, the lettuce, pepper grass, chervil, cress, &c. should be gathered early in the morning, nicely picked, washed, and laid in cold water, which will be improved by adding ice; just before dinner is ready to be served, drain the water from your salad, cut it into a bowl, giving the proper proportions of each plant; prepare the following mixture to pour over it: boil two fresh eggs ten minutes, put them in water to cool, then take the yelks in a soup plate, pour on them a table spoonful of cold water, rub them with a wooden spoon until they are perfectly dissolved; then add two spoonsful of oil: when well mixed, put in a teaspoonful of salt, one of powdered sugar, and one of made mustard; when all these are united and quite smooth, stir in two table spoonsful of common, and two of tarragon vinegar; put it over the salad, and garnish the top with the whites of the eggs cut into rings, and lay around the edge of the bowl young scallions, they being the most delicate of the onion tribe.

There is not much that I can add to this. If you are lucky enough to have your own garden or a good farmer's market nearby, just go for it.

An Apple Custard

This little recipe is deceptively good. My guess is the pippin apple here is the Newtown pippin, which was reportedly a favorite of George Washington, another familiar Virginia native.

In a pot, put 1 pound of sugar and one pint of water. This makes a *simple syrup* in which you will poach the apples. While this is heating, get 12 whole cloves and put them in a sachet to steep in the syrup.

Get twelve pippins, pare and peel them, slice them about ¼ inch thick. Adjust the heat of the syrup to a simmer and add the apple slices. Poach, and when soft, carefully remove the apple slices to a baking dish and discard the cloves.

Make the custard:

Scrape a vanilla bean into a quart of milk and throw in the bean, too.

Add 4 ounces of sugar to the pot.

Bring to a boil.

In a bowl have:

6 eggs lightly beaten with

4 ounces of sugar.

Slowly pour the vanilla milk into the eggs, stirring constantly so you do not get scrambled eggs.

When complete, pour the custard over the apple slices and rinse and save the vanilla bean.

Place baking dish in a larger container and pour hot water halfway up the sides of the baking dish.

Bake at 300° until a skewer inserted in the center of the baking dish comes out clean.

Remove immediately from the water bath and cool on a rack.

Allow to set up for several hours.

Serve with whipped cream or a gingerbread spice cookie.

I do have to warn you, you will not want to share this with anyone. So tell your family and friends the author is an idiot, the recipe was a dud and stash the custard for yourself for later on when you are alone.

AN APPLE CUSTARD.

PARE and core twelve pippins, slice them tolerably thick, put a pound of loaf sugar in a stew pan, with a pint of water and twelve cloves: boil and skim it, then put in the apples, and stew them till clear, and but little of the syrup remains—lay them in a deep dish, and take out the cloves; when the apples are cold, pour in a quart of rich boiled custard—set it in water, and make it boil till the custard is set—take care the water does not get into it.

Pumpkin Pudding

Reading this, most readers will realize this is what we now call pumpkin pie. If you make your own crust, line a pie plate and dust with flour. Cover the raw dough with foil and weight down with dried beans and bake for 12 minutes in a 400° oven. Remove from the oven, carefully remove foil and replace in the oven for another 5 to 6 minutes. If the shell is not prebaked it will always be soggy.

Take one quart of pumpkin puree and add to it:

6 well-beaten eggs.

Stir in:

8 ounces whole milk

4 ounces of brandy and

6 ounces of sugar.

Spice to your liking with ginger, allspice, nutmeg — whatever your favorite flavor profile is.

This should make enough for 2 9-inch pies.

PUMPKIN PUDDING.

STEW a fine sweet pumpkin till soft and dry; rub it through a sieve, mix with the pulp six eggs quite light, a quarter of a pound of butter, half a pint of new milk, some pounded ginger and nutmeg, a wine glass of brandy, and sugar to your taste. Should it be too liquid, stew it a little drier, put a paste round the edges, and in the bottom of a shallow dish or plate—pour in the mixture, cut some thin bits of paste, twist them, and lay them across the top, and bake it nicely.

Place in a 300° oven and test for doneness as for apple custard.

If you think the melted butter is needed, then add it.

Doughnuts

Use instant yeast.

Sift:

1 pound of flour with ½ cup (4 ounces) of brown sugar.

Add:

1 tablespoon of instant yeast

DOUGH NUTS—A YANKEE CAKE.

DRY half a pound of good brown sugar, pound it, and mix it with two pounds of flour, and sift it; add two spoonsful of yeast, and as much new milk as will make it like bread: when well risen, knead in half a pound of butter, make it in cakes the size of a half dollar, and fry them a light brown in boiling lard.

---

1 teaspoon salt

1¼ cup of room temperature milk. If this is too stiff, add two or three ounces more. Flours have variable moisture contents.

Allow to rise about 45 minutes then mix in:

1 stick of softened butter.

The yeast needs some time to rise before the butter is added or the fat will surround the yeast and prevent the dough from rising. Think brioche.

Knead to a smooth dough and let rise until almost doubled.

Punch down, roll and cut into desired sizes and shapes and fry in 350° fat. When still warm, roll in cinnamon sugar.

These can be made into crullers or cut large and filled with jam or custard.

Rice Waffles

Boil:

1 cup of white rice in

2 cups of milk until completely soft. Feel free to add some lemon rind, orange rind, vanilla, almond extract, etc. to your taste.

Remove from the pot when done, mash, and stir in:

1½ cups flour

1 teaspoon of salt

½ teaspoon baking powder.

Mix together:

2 ounces melted butter

2 well-beaten eggs and about

1 to 2 cups of whole milk. Add the milk last and adjust thickness to your liking.

RICE WOFFLES.

BOIL two gills of rice quite soft, mix with it three gills of flour, a little salt, two ounces melted butter, two eggs beaten well, and as much milk as will make it a thick batter—beat it till very light, and bake it in woffle irons.

Cook in a waffle iron. Serve with soft butter and maple syrup, cane syrup or whatever you like.

CONSUMER ALERT: Eating these waffles at breakfast may cause you to never leave the breakfast table!

Ice Cream

Well, let that be a lesson to you indolent cooks! Following are a few selections of Mrs. Randolph's ice creams.

VANILLA CREAM

The following version gives a slightly different texture than Mrs. Randolph's ice cream.

Take:

1 quart whole milk and

1 quart heavy cream. Place in a non-reactive pot with:

5 ounces of white sugar and 1 split vanilla bean, seeds scraped into the pot.

VANILLA CREAM.

BOIL a Vanilla bean in a quart of rich milk, until it has imparted the flavour sufficiently—then take it out, and mix with the milk, eight eggs, yelks and whites beaten well; let it boil a little longer; make it very sweet, for much of the sugar is lost in the operation of freezing.

Place on the stove and bring to a near boil.

In a large bowl, beat well:

8 whole eggs with

5 ounces sugar.

Temper the mixture and return to the fire.

Cook until the mixture coats the back of a spoon, strain through a fine mesh strainer into a clean bowl set in an ice water bath and chill as rapidly as possible to prevent any bacterial growth.

Chill in the refrigerator overnight.

When cold, freeze according to manufacturer's freezer directions.

Professional Tip: A la nappe means to cook until the point when a liquid will leave a track as described above. To nappé a food item on a plate means to coat with a sauce.

QUINCE CREAM

Use the same base as for vanilla but add 8 ounces quince puree to the strained ice cream base and omit 8 ounces of milk. Quince is a vastly under-appreciated fruit. Mostly seen in the fall and late summer, they taste like apples that have sophistication and culture. A slight citrus taste with hints of tropical fruits makes this one of the most delicious fruits around. They must be cooked, are highly astringent when raw and should be completely soft, pureed and strained before adding to the ice cream base. Freeze as above.

PEACH CREAM

Make it the same way as for the quince cream but do not cook the peaches. Make sure to use only ripe fruit. Following Mrs. Randolph's directions: "Put them in a china bowl, sprinkle with some sugar and chop them very small with a silver spoon — if the peaches be sufficiently ripe they will become a smooth pulp."

ALMOND CREAM

No need to shell the almonds yourself. Buy some nice blanched, sliced almonds in the market. Four ounces of almonds will suffice for one quart of ice cream base. There are two ways to do this. Pick yours.

1. Make the vanilla base as above but omit the vanilla. Strain the hot ice cream base over the sliced almonds in a clean bowl and refrigerate overnight. Macerating the almonds like this will extract lots of flavor.

2. Take the 5 ounces of sugar that is to

OBSERVATIONS ON ICE CREAMS.

IT is the practice with some indolent cooks, to set the freezer containing the cream, in a tub with ice and salt, and put it in the ice house; it will certainly freeze there; but not until the watery particles have subsided, and by the separation destroyed the cream. A freezer should be twelve or fourteen inches deep, and eight or ten wide. This facilitates the operation very much, by giving a larger surface for the ice to form, which it always does on the sides of the vessel; a silver spoon with a long handle should be provided for scraping the ice from the sides as soon as formed; and when the whole is congealed, pack it in moulds (which must be placed with care, lest they should not be upright,) in ice and salt, till sufficiently hard to retain the shape—they should not be turned out till the moment they are to be served. The freezing tub must be wide enough to leave a margin of four or five inches all around the freezer, when placed in the middle—which must be filled up with small lumps of ice mixed with salt—a larger tub would waste the ice. The freezer must be kept constantly in motion during the process, and ought to be made of pewter, which is less liable than tin to be worn in holes, and spoil the cream by admitting the salt water.

ALMOND CREAM.

POUR hot water on the almonds, and let them stand till the skins will slip off, then pound them fine, and mix them with cream: a pound of almonds in the shells, will be sufficient for a quart of cream—sweeten and freeze it. The kernels of the common black walnut, prepared in the same way, make an excellent cream.

be tempered with the egg yolks and process with the four ounces of almonds to a fine powder. Cook as for the vanilla custard. The almonds will strain out when you strain the base.

These recipes are by no means all that await the curious cook. My goal is to show how much we use today, and how much that is associated with Southern cooking — its history and influences and techniques — is presented for us here, so elegantly yet forcefully, by Mrs. Randolph. How I would love to have been at one of her dinner parties!

Throughout her early life, Mrs. Randolph lived the life of the landed aristocracy, but her responsibilities as a plantation owner's wife were legion. Her personal land professional integrity made her strive for quality and was a driving force throughout her life.

After losing their fortune, Mr. and Mrs. Randolph found success in another arena, thanks in large measure to her enormous cooking skills and her innate sense of hospitality. As the author of the first true American regional cookbook, she indeed led the way for generations to follow.

It speaks volumes that her book is still in print and readily available. You should get to know this woman. She was truly a first lady of American cuisine.

CHAPTER 12

Directions for Cookery (Miss Leslie)

Soups

Veal Soup

Make a white veal stock with cut-up leg or shin bones. Calves' feet add lots of flavor and gelatin if you can find them.

Use 8 pounds of bones for each gallon of stock.

Add the bones to a tall, narrow stock-pot and cover with cold water.

Slowly bring to a simmer, skimming the scum as it rises.

While the stock is coming to a simmer, cut up:

2 medium onions

2 stalks of celery and add to the broth.

Make a sachet with:

12 black peppercorns

1 sprig thyme

1 small bay leaf.

> **VEAL SOUP.**
>
> The knuckle or leg of veal is the best for soup. Wash it and break up the bones. Put it into a pot with a pound of ham or bacon cut into pieces, and water enough to cover the meat. A set of calf's feet, cut in half, will greatly improve it. After it has stewed slowly, till all the meat drops to pieces, strain it, return it to the pot, and put in a head of celery cut small, three onions, a bunch of sweet marjoram, a carrot and a turnip cut into pieces, and two dozen black pepper-corns, with salt to your taste. Add some small dumplings made of flour and butter. Simmer it another hour, or till all the vegetables are sufficiently done, and thus send it to table.
>
> You may thicken it with noodles, that is paste made of flour and beaten egg, and cut into long thin slips. Or with vermicelli, rice, or barley ; or with green peas, or asparagus

Simmer the soup 6 to 8 hours. Do not let it come to a full boil.

Strain and discard bones and *mirepoix*.

FOR THE SOUP:

Reduce the stock volume by 25 percent. This concentrates flavor and improves the texture.

Cut into small dice:

2 or 3 stalks of celery

1 large carrot cut the same size

1 small rutabaga cut the same size as the celery and carrots.

After about 10 minutes, add:

3 medium onions peeled and cut the same as the vegetables above.

Simmer until vegetables are done but still have good texture, as if you were cooking pasta al dente. Season with salt and pepper.

Add 1 bunch of marjoram, leaves only, washed and minced. Add this to the soup just before service and simmer one or two minutes.

For a thickened soup add several pieces of *beurre manie,* or as Miss Leslie suggests, feel free to add barley, rice, vermicelli or peas and asparagus tops.

Professional Tip: The best way to cook the vegetables is separately so that they retain their individual flavors and textures. Just ladle some of the stock into a smaller pot and simmer in order until they are done.

Rich Brown Soup

Miss Leslie here is making a highly spiced beef broth. Modern tastes may not appreciate the 48 cloves stuck in the meat. In this more modern version, the cloves are reduced and the technique for the end result is adapted to a modern stove.

RICH BROWN SOUP.

TAKE six pounds of the lean of fresh beef, cut from the bone. Stick it over with four dozen cloves. Season it with a tea-spoonful of salt, a tea-spoonful of pepper, a tea-spoonful of mace, and a beaten nutmeg. Slice half a dozen onions; fry them in butter; chop them, and spread them over the meat after you have put it into the soup-pot. Pour in five quarts of water, and stew it slowly for five or six hours; skimming it well. When the meat has dissolved into shreds, strain it, and return the liquid to the pot. Then add a tumbler and a half, or six wine glasses of claret or port wine. Simmer it again slowly till dinner time. When the soup is reduced to three quarts, it is done enough. Put it into a tureen, and send it to table.

Purchase 6 pounds of lean beef, preferably chuck or bottom round or shin meat or oxtail for flavor. Cut the meat into tranches if in one piece, about 1 inch thick.

When the meat is cut:

Heat 4 tablespoons of oil in a large Dutch oven or rondeau.

When hot, season the meat with salt and fresh ground pepper, and brown well on all sides, removing the pieces as they brown and holding them on the side. Do not overcrowd the pan or the temperature of the oil will go down too much and the meat will be greasy.

When all the meat is brown, discard the oil and add 6 tablespoons of butter and reduce heat.

Slice 4 medium onions thinly and sauté slowly until well browned in the butter. This can take more than 30 to 40 minutes. Keep the heat low or the butter will burn. The idea is to generate color and develop the sugars in the onions. Be patient.

When sufficiently brown, return the beef and mix well with the onions.

When well blended, add:

12 ounces of red wine and scrape all the brown bits off the bottom of the pot. Allow the wine to reduce by about one half its volume.

Add four quarts of beef broth and make a sachet with:

1 nutmeg

6 cloves

12 whole black peppercorns and

1 piece of mace.

Simmer for about 90 minutes or until reduced by ¼ its original volume.

Remove the sachet, strain the soup and return the liquid to the pot. Discard the solids. Adjust for salt and pepper and serve.

Professional Tip: After simmering the beef, the nutrients and flavor are in the broth. If you cannot discard the beef, return it to the broth. This is quite flavorful and harkens back to Middle Ages cooking techniques for its flavor. Serve with crusty bread and a green salad for lunch or a light supper in cold weather.

Should you choose to use one large piece of beef as Miss Leslie instructs, and you choose to return the meat back to the soup pot, make sure all 48 cloves, or however many cloves you choose to use, are present and accounted for, as ingesting a whole clove is decidedly unpleasant and can be hazardous to your health. Also, if you want more clove flavor, feel free to increase the number of cloves in the sachet if that is how you are making the soup.

If you want a little flavor variation in the soup, for the sachet use whole allspice instead of black peppercorns.

Venison Soup

Venison was a staple of early American cooking with professional hunters supplying more settled areas with meat and feathered game. Much of the game has disappeared but the deer are still with us. If you hunt, or know someone who does, use the leg meat for this, or even the fore quarter — although that will require more cooking. Venison can be purchased in specialty stores and online. It is expensive.

Heat ¼ cup oil in a soup pot.

Cut the venison into a uniform shape and size. Season it with salt and pepper and brown well all over. Remove from the pot. Remember not to add too much at one time or the meat will get greasy.

Add more oil if needed and brown:

1 large onion, diced.

Add 1 pound of ham scraps or a ham hock of equal weight, and simmer for two or three minutes.

Sprinkle about ¼ cup of flour mixed with:

> ### VENISON SOUP.
>
> TAKE four pounds of freshly killed venison cut off from the bones, and one pound of ham in small slices. Add an onion minced, and black pepper to your taste. Put only as much water as will cover it, and stew it gently for an hour, keeping the pot closely covered. Then skim it well, and pour in a quart of boiling water. Add a head of celery cut into small pieces, and half a dozen blades of mace. Boil it gently two hours and a half. Then put in a quarter of a pound of butter, divided into small pieces and rolled in flour, and half a pint of port or Madeira wine. Let it boil a quarter of an hour longer, and then send it to table with the meat in it.

1 teaspoon of ground mace over the onions and ham, making sure all the oil is absorbed. Your roux should be the consistency of creamy peanut butter, just a little runny. Reduce heat and cook until the roux is medium brown. DO NOT BURN THE ROUX.

Deglaze the pot with:

4 or 5 ounces of dry Madeira. Scrape all the bits and pieces off the bottom of the pot. Make sure there are no lumps.

Add 2 quarts of beef broth or venison stock, reduce the heat and slowly bring to a simmer.

Allow the soup to simmer two hours, skimming the scum as it rises to the top.

In a separate sauté pan, sauté:

2 stalks of celery diced small until soft, and reserve.

When the meat is tender, check to see if it needs skimming again. If not, add the celery and simmer about two minutes and adjust seasoning.

Serve in hot bowls. If a little richness is desired, just before serving stir in some whole butter, about 2 ounces, after the heat is turned off.

Professional Tip: Do not make the soup too thick; remember it is a soup not a stew. Adding flour to fat with vegetables or other ingredients already in a pot makes it a *compound roux.*

Catfish Soup

CAT-FISH SOUP.

CAT-FISH that have been caught near the middle of the river are much nicer than those that are taken near the shore where they have access to impure food. The small white ones are the best. Having cut off their heads, skin the fish, and clean them, and cut them in three. To twelve small cat-fish allow a pound and a half of ham. Cut the ham into small pieces, or slice it very thin, and scald it two or three times in boiling water, lest it be too salt. Chop together a bunch of parsley and some sweet marjoram stripped from the stalks. Put these ingredients into a soup kettle and season them with pepper: the ham will make it salt enough. Add a head of celery cut small, or a large table-spoonful of celery seed tied up in a bit of clear muslin to prevent its dispersing. Put in two quarts of water, cover the kettle, and let it boil slowly till every thing is sufficiently done, and the fish and ham quite tender. Skim it frequently. Boil in another vessel a quart of rich milk, in which you have melted a quarter of a pound of butter divided into small bits and rolled in flour. Pour it hot to the soup, and stir in at the last the beaten yolks of four eggs. Give it another boil, just to take off the rawness of the eggs, and then put it into a tureen, taking out the bag of celery seed before you send the soup to table, and adding some toasted bread cut into small squares. In making toast for soup, cut the bread thick, and pare off all the crust.

This soup will be found very fine.

Eel soup may be made in the same manner: chicken soup also.

For modern cooks, catfish is found in markets already cut into filets. This makes the preparation easier but less tasty. The reasons for this are that farm-raised catfish are fed grains and an otherwise bland diet and they are not wild. In Miss Leslie's recipe, two things will work to provide better flavor — the fish are wild caught and they are cooked bone in. Both add lots of flavor to soups. As to the basic taste of the fish, farm-raised fish simply do not compare to their wild cousins — not just catfish, any variety.

Take about 2 quarts of fish stock and simmer:

1½ pounds of dry cure ham, medium dice, for about 30 minutes. Some scum will rise, so skim it off. Taste for saltiness — if too salty add a little stock; if too bland leave it alone until the soup is finished.

While simmering the ham, make a sachet of:

2 tablespoons of celery seed and tie it closed. Let it simmer in the pot with the ham and fish stock.

While the fish stock and ham are simmering, make a Béchamel Sauce with:

2 quarts of whole milk. Do not make it too thick. When done, strain and reserve warm. Check the stock temperature. At 170°F carefully add the fish pieces cut into 2-ounce pieces and gently poach about 7 or 8 minutes. Do not let the water boil and do not let the fish overcook.

Gently remove the fish filets when done and reserve, being careful not to break them.

Remove the sachet with the celery seed and add the Béchamel Sauce to the soup. Bring to a simmer and let cook about 10 minutes. Taste for saltiness and adjust accordingly.

Take 1 bunch of parsley and the leaves from 1 bunch of fresh marjoram and chop them finely. Add to the soup and simmer 2 to 3 minutes.

In a separate bowl:

Temper 4 egg yolks and add back into the soup, being careful not to boil again or you will have catfish-flavored scrambled egg yolks.

Place 2 or 3 pieces of fish in each soup bowl and ladle the soup over them and serve immediately. You can follow Miss Leslie's advice and make the *paysanne* cut croutons or make some toasted garlic bread and serve on the side.

Professional Tip: This makes a bit more than one gallon of soup. As a soup course, plan on 6 to 8 ounces per serving. As an entrée soup, served with bread and maybe a salad, figure on 12 to 16 ounces per serving.

Here is Miss Leslie holding court on quality — from where the fish are caught to tempering the eggs. Fish living near the shore would have been bottom feeding on all manner of detritus, from raw sewage to rotting animal parts. Hence, get the fish from the deep-water part of the river away from the river banks.

The use of the Béchamel to me is easier and more consistent than using *beurre manie.* The cook ahead of time establishes the consistency. Remember when Miss Leslie was writing this book and what she had to work with — a large fireplace with limited access to the fire and fewer and larger cooking vessels. Pots in colonial times were expensive and many households did not have a surfeit of pots and pans. Note also her instructions for croutons: here she indicates another classical French cut, *paysanne,* which is square cut and about ⅛" thick to ¼" thick.

Try this soup with any other fish. For salmon you may use dill for a fresh herb. For grouper, try using allspice in a sachet rather than celery seed for a more "islandie" flavor. For bass, use fennel seed in the sachet and sauté some fennel bulb diced fine and add to the soup at service time. Play with your food. Use what you have and what you like. If you follow Miss Leslie's technique you will have a good soup. And good cooking is all about technique.

Lobster Soup

This is one of the best soups from our early cooking heritage — luxurious and bursting with the flavor of lobster. Lobster was not uncommon when this book was written. Now it is quite expensive so my updating uses a lobster stock and less whole lobster but the taste and texture are the same.

Simmer three lobster bodies in three quarts of white veal stock. You may be able to get lobster bodies from a good fish store. If not, and if you are not inclined to make a white veal stock, buy the three two-pound lobsters, all females. On the underside of the lobster body there are two little legs called swimmers. On a female they are soft, on a male they are hard.

Bring four quarts of water to a boil.

Kill the lobsters by inserting the tip of a large chef's knife between the eyes on the top of the lobster's head. Insert quickly and press all the way to the cutting board. This kills the lobster instantly.

Plunge the deceased lobsters in the boiling water and cook 8 minutes. Remove from the water with tongs and cool in a shallow dish. Pour off the cooking water.

When cool, remove the lobster meat from the tail, claws, legs and the coral, which is the red part in the lobster body.

Push the coral through a fine stainless steel strainer into a bowl.

Add an equal amount of leg meat and trimmings and mash all with a pestle.

Season with lemon zest, a pinch of cayenne pepper, nutmeg and ground mace.

For each four ounces of lobster/coral mix, add one egg yolk and season with salt and white pepper, fresh ground.

Shape the dumplings, *quenelles* in French, and poach one to make sure the seasoning is okay and that the dumplings hold together. If they tend to fall apart, add 2 or 3 teaspoons of fresh breadcrumbs. Test again.

Bring your stock to a simmer, whether white veal or lobster. Ladle about one pint of the soup into a separate smaller pot and poach the dumplings. Thicken the soup with a little roux, but not too much. Let it simmer about 20 minutes; adjust the salt and pepper.

Place a dumpling or two in each heated bowl and the lobster meat cut into pieces of a size
that will fit on a soup spoon. Ladle the soup over the garnish.

Serve immediately.

For richness add a little cream just before serving and about two ounces of Madeira. This
soup is not the color of lobster bisque. If you want a pinkish color, reserve some of the
strained coral and add to the soup just before serving.

Fish and Seafood

To Boil Fresh Salmon

TO BOIL FRESH SALMON.

SCALE and clean the fish, handling it as little as possible.
and cutting it open no more than is absolutely necessary.
Place it on the strainer of a large fish-kettle and fill it up with
cold water. Throw in a handful of salt. Let it boil slowly.
The length of time depends on the size and weight of the fish.
You may allow a quarter of an hour to each pound; but experience alone can determine the exact time. It must however
be thoroughly done, as nothing is more disgusting than fish
that is under-cooked. You may try it with a fork. Skim it
well or the colour will be bad.

The minute it is completely boiled, lift up the strainer and
rest it across the top of the kettle, that the fish may drain,
and then, if you cannot send it to table immediately, cover it
with a soft napkin or flannel several folds double, to keep it
firm by absorbing the moisture.

Send it to table on a hot dish. Garnish with scraped horseradish and curled parsley. Have ready a small tureen of lobster sauce to accompany the salmon.

Take what is left of it after dinner, and put it into a deep
dish with a close cover. Having saved some of the water
in which the fish was boiled, take a quart of it, and season it
with half an ounce of whole pepper, and half an ounce of whole
allspice, half a pint of the best vinegar, and a tea-spoonful of
salt. Boil it; and when cold, pour it over the fish, and cover it
closely again. In a cold place, and set on ice, it will keep a
day or two, and may be eaten at breakfast or supper.

If much of the salmon has been left, you must proportion a
larger quantity of the pickle.

Boil salmon trout in a similar manner.

This is literally starting from scratch,
or rather scaling. The cook is instructed
on cleaning, handling, poaching (boiling), what to do when the fish is done,
how to keep it warm and how to serve—
even what sauce to use to accompany the
fish. When dinner is over, Miss Leslie
even instructs how to save the leftovers in
a safe manner.

For a modern kitchen, fish poaching pans are available with racks inside.
Poach the fish in a *court boullion*. If
poaching a whole fish ask your fish mon-
ger to scale it for you. If you do scale it
at home, fill a sink or large pan with cold
water and use the back of a paring knife
running the length of the fish from the
tail to the head. This keeps the scales
from flying all over the kitchen. They are
impossible to clean up if you make a
mess early on.

If you do not want to poach a
whole fish, filet each side and poach one
or both after scaling. Watch your *court
boullion* temperature; it should be no
more than 170°. The fish is done when
it loses its raw appearance. If you see
white appearing on the flesh of the fish
it is overcooked. It is easier to portion
the fish when raw and figure on a portion of 6 to 8 ounces per person as an entrée. As a
first course, 3 to 4 ounces is a good portion. Remember, a first course is just that and there
will be several following courses. The idea is to balance size of portion in relationship to
the entire meal. We are dining, not feeding.

There are two more recipes for salmon—both are baked but in very different styles.
For the first use a smallish fish and after cleaning and scaling, grab the tail and pull it under
the open cavity and through the mouth of the fish. This is a classic method of presenting

the fish for a French *Truite au Bleu* and again shows the French influence on Miss Leslie's cooking. If this looks too weird for you simply bake the fish whole or sectioned in sides, dotting with butter, salt and pepper. Try a 350° oven for about 12 to 15 minutes, depending upon the size of the fish.

For the second method we are looking at individual portions basted with a pungent sauce of anchovies and "catchup." The end result is almost a cross between a fish baked in parchment and a baked, basted fish. Try it in a parchment paper — it is easy, requires no attention and keeps the fish wonderfully moist.

Make the sauce by pureeing in a blender 8 ounces of ruby port, two anchovy filets, two tablespoons of ketchup or salsa or a favorite red-colored condiment. Strain through a fine strainer into a small saucepot and heat to simmering for about 10 minutes. Adjust seasoning if needed, turn off the heat and whisk in whole butter.

Place each piece of fish on a square of parchment paper that has been folded in half and opened. Place the fish below the fold. Season the fish with salt and white pepper and spoon about a teaspoon of the sauce over each piece of fish. Place a small round of lemon on the fish and a small piece of butter on top of the lemon. Fold the top half over the bottom half and seal the edges by making a tight fold. Place on a baking sheet and into a 350° oven for about 15 to 18 minutes. When done, place on plates and open the parchment at the table. Serve additional sauce on the side if desired.

Halibut Cutlets

The best results for this recipe use beaten egg white rather than yolk, fresh bread crumbs and fresh lard for frying. Storebought lard is not good, so if you have access to fresh, rendered, lard use it. If not, rendered beef fat gives a wonderful flavor. If you want to live until morning, try using canola or safflower oil instead. These cutlets are wonderful sautéed in oil until light brown, finished in a 350° oven with a pan sauce of brown butter, lemon juice and finely chopped flat leaf parsley or, better yet, finely julienned fresh fennel.

HALIBUT CUTLETS.

Cut your halibut into steaks or cutlets about an inch thick. Wipe them with a dry cloth, and season them with salt and cayenne pepper. Have ready a pan of yolk of egg well beaten, and a large flat dish of grated bread crumbs.

Put some fresh lard or clarified beef dripping into a frying pan, and hold it over a clear fire till it boils. Dip your cutlets into the beaten egg, and then into the bread crumbs. Fry them of a light brown. Serve them up hot, with the gravy in the bottom of the dish.

Salmon or any large fish may be fried in the same manner.

Halibut cutlets are very fine cut quite thin and fried in the best sweet oil, omitting the egg and bread crumbs.

Oyster Pie

Several of Miss Leslie's recipes call for oysters and most say to not overcook them. Many people overcook fish, especially oysters, clams, lobster and shrimp. If you have ever dined in a restaurant and ordered shrimp scampi you probably know what I mean — where shrimp are cooked to the doneness of little pink marbles.

This dish works well served in individual soufflé dishes. Make the puff paste or buy some, remembering that virtually all commercial puff paste is made with shortening, not butter. This leaves a pasty, oily feel in your mouth and contains highly saturated oils such as palm oil and palm kernel oil. Make it yourself. Miss Leslie would.

Roll out the dough ⅛ inch thick, keeping it as cool as possible. Select a cutter to match the size of your serving dish(es) and decorate nicely. Brush with beaten egg yolk and bake in a 400° oven until nicely risen. Do not underbake or the tops will collapse.

While the dough is baking you can complete the dish.

Go to a good fish store and order a container of select oysters packed in their liquor or order in the shell, figuring 12 pieces for an entrée, 6 for a first course.

Place the oyster liquid in a small saucepan and poach the oysters. They are done when they just start curling on the edges.

Remove the oysters and reduce the liquor by about 25 percent. Season the liquid with cayenne, a little salt, nutmeg and a little ground mace. For each serving you will need two ounces of sauce for a first course, 3 ounces for an entrée.

> ### OYSTER PIE.
>
> MAKE a puff-paste, in the proportion of a pound and a half of fresh butter to two pounds of sifted flour. Roll it out rather thick, into two sheets. Butter a deep dish, and line the bottom and sides of it with paste. Fill it up with crusts of bread for the purpose of supporting the lid while it is baking, as the oysters will be too much done if they are cooked in the pie. Cover it with the other sheet of paste, having first buttered the flat rim of the dish. Notch the edges of the pie handsomely, or ornament them with leaves of paste which you may form with tin cutters made for the purpose. Make a little slit in the middle of the lid, and stick firmly into it a paste tulip or other flower. Put the dish into a moderate oven, and while the paste is baking prepare the oysters, which should be large and fresh. Put them into a stew-pan with half their liquor thickened with yolk of egg boiled hard and grated, enriched with pieces of butter rolled in bread crumbs, and seasoned with mace and nutmeg. Stew the oysters five minutes. When the paste is baked, carefully take off the lid, remove the pieces of bread, and put in the oysters and gravy. Replace the lid, and send the pie to table warm.

For every cup of sauce in the pot, add about 4 tablespoons of dry bread crumbs made from French bread. Do not use breadcrumbs that are made from bread that contains sugar, eggs or spices. Simmer a few minutes. If a finer texture is desired puree the thickened sauce in a blender and strain through a fine strainer into a clean pot.

Bring the sauce to a simmer, temper four ounces cream and two egg yolks in a separate bowl, turn the heat as low as possible and return to the pot. Do not let it boil. Check seasoning. Return the oysters until heated through and portion into whatever serving dish you are using. Top with a pre-baked lid that fits the top of the serving dish(es) and serve immediately.

Stewed Lobster

The recipe is pretty straightforward, but what is important here is the fact that this is a book for all American households and cooks of all abilities. For the success of this book on such a large scale these were recipes that were not for special occasions nor for wealthy people. Product availability and price would have figured into what choices were made for inclusion. That lobster was readily available in Philadelphia speaks to the abundance and variety of items in everyday use in Miss Leslie's time.

Cook the lobster as for the lobster soup and mix, for each four ounces of lobster, the yield from a one-pound lobster and:

⅛ teaspoon each of ground nutmeg and mace

a pinch of salt and cayenne to cut the richness.

Take 8 ounces of lobster stock and add 4 ounces of white wine and reduce by half. Add the lobster and reheat, check for seasoning. This will provide liquid for 4 appetizer servings (double the amount for an entrée serving). Use 4 ounces of lobster per person.

Swirl in or whisk in 2 ounces of butter for each serving of 4 ounces of lobster.

Serve in a shallow heated dish covered breadcrumbs drizzled with melted whole butter and brown under a broiler, unless you have a red-hot shovel handy.

Soft Crabs

Is there anything that speaks of Mid-Atlantic food more than soft shell crab? Now mostly farm-raised, these crabs are available year-round with the traditional season being from mid–May to the end of June or a little beyond. For those of you not familiar with these critters you should be. Miss Leslie simply fries them in hot fat after cleaning them. They are much improved by a few simple steps. In her "gravy," if done exactly as written, the cook would end up with melted lard floating on top of some milk. I do suspect that Miss Leslie was anticipating a certain knowledge level from her readers and that she surmised they would add a starch to bind the sauce.

Try this adaption.

Figure 2 crabs per person if they are hotel primes.

Make a seasoned flour of:

1 cup of flour with 2 teaspoons salt, one teaspoon white pepper, ½ teaspoon cayenne pepper.

If your crabs are live, soak them in milk overnight before cleaning.

Clean as Miss Leslie advises, then dip in beaten egg whites and dredge in the seasoned flour.

Melt clarified butter in a sauté pan over moderate heat and sauté about two minutes per side depending upon size. Do not overcook.

Pour off excess butter and keep the crabs warm.

Deglaze the pan when done sautéing with about 4 ounces white wine or dry Madeira. Add the Madeira and wine "off the fire" then return the pan to the heat. (Do not pour alcohol in any form into a pan that is still in contact with a flame or hot cooking surface. Lift the pan and turn slightly away from the stove.) Reduce by ¾ and add

4 ounces heavy cream. Reduce this by ½ and adjust seasoning, adding finely chopped parsley just before service.

If you like fried parsley, fry a little on the side. If you do not want a cream sauce as Miss Leslie suggests, simply add some whole butter when done sautéing and brown it, adding a little lemon juice and chopped parsley. If you want to make hoagies, cut some rolls

---

STEWED LOBSTER.

HAVING boiled the lobster, extract the meat from the shell, and cut it into very small pieces. Season it with a powdered nutmeg, a few blades of mace, and cayenne and salt to your taste. Mix with it a quarter of a pound of fresh butter cut small, and two glasses of white wine or of vinegar. Put it into a stew-pan, and set it on hot coals. Stew it about twenty minutes, keeping the pan closely covered lest the flavour should evaporate. Serve it up hot.

If you choose, you can send it to table in the shell, which must first be nicely cleaned. Strew the meat over with sifted bread-crumbs, and brown the top with a salamander, or a red hot shovel held over it.

SOFT CRABS.

THESE crabs must be cooked directly, as they will not keep till next day.

Remove the spongy substance from each side of the crab, and also the little sand-bag. Put some lard into a pan, and when it is boiling hot, fry the crabs in it. After you take them out, throw in a handful of parsley, and let it crisp; but withdraw it before it loses its colour. Strew it over the crabs when you dish them.

Make the gravy by adding cream or rich milk to the lard, with some chopped parsley, pepper and salt. Let them all boil together for a few minutes, and then serve it up in a sauce-boat.

in half and spread with your favorite spicy sandwich spread and eat while the crabs are still hot. If you have not had soft-shell crabs, you probably are new to hoagies as well!

Meats

Also included here are recipes for stewed beef, beef à la mode, beef pudding (sliced beef wrapped in a dough, tied and boiled for three hours), the method for stewing beef and how to stew a round of beef, beef bouilli (another French influence for a decade of American cooks), beef hash, cakes, heart and tripe.

Pepper Pot

PEPPER POT.

TAKE four pounds of tripe, and four ox feet. Put them into a large pot with as much water as will cover them, some whole pepper, and a little salt. Hang them over the fire early in the morning. Let them boil slowly, keeping the pot closely covered. When the tripe is quite tender, and the ox feet boiled to pieces, take them out, and skim the liquid and strain it. Then cut the tripe into small pieces; put it back into the pot, and pour the soup or liquor over it. Have ready some sweet herbs chopped fine, some sliced onions, and some sliced potatoes. Make some small dumplings with flour and butter. Season the vegetables well with pepper and salt, and put them into the pot. Have ready a kettle of boiling water, and pour on as much as will keep the ingredients covered while boiling, but take care not to weaken the taste by putting too much water. Add a large piece of butter rolled in flour, and lastly put in the dumplings. Let it boil till all the things are thoroughly done, and then serve it up in the tureen.

Soak four pounds of tripe overnight in cold water in the refrigerator. Change the water several times. Drain. Blanch the tripe in boiling salted water until tender. Discard the water, cool the tripe and cut into 1½ inch squares. What you are most likely to find is honeycomb tripe.

If using beef bones, simmer them in about three gallons of water with a sachet of:
10 whole peppercorns cracked, more if you like it more peppery
2 cloves of garlic
1 medium bay leaf
4 ounces of parsley, fresh
1 sprig of fresh thyme
1 sprig fresh marjoram or savory.
Bring to a simmer on the stovetop, cover tightly and place in 300° oven for about 2 hours or lower the heat and simmer on the stovetop.

While the soup is cooking peel and quarter an onion and slice not too thinly. There should be about 8 ounces of sliced onion.

Peel and slice one or two medium potatoes, and reserve in water to prevent from browning. You should have about 8 ounces of sliced potatoes.

Remove the tripe and beef bones. Strain the soup and reserve the liquid. Degrease the liquid and bring back to a simmer. Add the vegetables and cook until tender, about 10 to 12 minutes.

Pick the meat when the beef bones are cool enough and reserve the meat.

Make a spätzle batter and cook in the simmering soup. When they float they are done.

Add the meat and tripe back in, adjust seasoning and serve very hot.

Veal Knuckle

For 6 entrées.

Try the veal the way Miss Leslie writes, remembering what was said before about the limitations of cooking in fireplaces. Or you can try this updated version, which adds some nice color while preserving the flavors of the original. Veal knuckle is a large piece of veal, sometimes known as the shank. Most often it will be cut across the bone into semi-circular pieces of 12 to 16 ounces. It is this more modern cut I use here. If you can find an entire shank simply adjust the cooking time and the size of the pot. A whole shank can be problematic when cutting at the dinner table but it is impressive. The meat is done when it literally separates from the bone, much as well made barbecue ribs do, and it should be that tender.

Season the 6 pieces of veal with salt and fresh-ground black pepper.

Dredge the pieces in seasoned flour, shake off any excess.

Heat oil in a stew pot (rondeau) and when hot, brown the meat on both sides to a medium dark brown color, but do not burn them.

Remove the meat from the pot and reserve.

If most of the oil is absorbed, add enough to barely cover the bottom. Reduce the heat to moderate.

Add and brown 2 onions, peeled, quartered and thinly sliced. Be patient.

Sprinkle about 4 tablespoons of flour over the onions when they are brown, just enough to absorb the fat, and make a compound roux that is the consistency of runny peanut butter.

Cook for two or three minutes.

Deglaze the pot with 6 ounces of white wine and make a smooth sauce. Scrape all the nice brown bits off the bottom of the pot, the *fond.*

Bring to a simmer, return the veal pieces carefully, and add brown veal stock until the pieces are just covered.

Bring to a slow simmer and add a sachet with 6 sprigs of parsley and three sprigs of marjoram and 6 whole peppercorns. Tie the sachet and tie it to a pot handle, cover the pot and braise in the oven for 2 to 2½ hours or until the meat starts to separate from the bone.

Remove the sachet, place veal on a platter or individual heated plates, adjust the seasoning in the pan sauce and add 1 bunch of chopped fresh parsley and leaves from two sprigs of freshly chopped marjoram.

Pour some sauce over the veal and pass the rest.

TO STEW A KNUCKLE OF VEAL.

Lay four wooden skewers across the bottom of your stew-pan, and place the meat upon them; having first carefully washed it, and rubbed it with salt. Add a table-spoonful of whole pepper, the leaves from a bunch of sweet marjoram, a bunch of parsley leaves chopped, two onions peeled and sliced, and a piece of butter rolled in flour. Pour in two quarts of water. Cover it closely, and after it has come to a boil, lessen the fire, and let the meat only simmer for two hours or more. Before you serve it up, pour the liquid over it.

This dish will be greatly improved by stewing with it a few slices of ham, or the remains of a cold ham.

Veal when simply boiled is too insipid. To stew it is much better.

VEAL CUTLETS.

The best cutlets are those taken from the leg or fillet. Cut them about half an inch thick, and as large as the palm of your hand. Season them with pepper and salt. Grate some stale bread, and rub it through a cullender, adding to it chopped sweet marjoram, grated lemon-peel, and some powdered mace or nutmeg. Spread the mixture on a large flat dish. Have ready in a pan some beaten egg. First dip each cutlet into the egg, and then into the seasoning on the dish, seeing that a sufficient quantity adheres to both sides of the meat. Melt in your frying-pan, over a quick fire, some beef-dripping, lard, or fresh butter, and when it boils lay your cutlets in it, and fry them thoroughly; turning them on both sides, and taking care that they do not burn. Place them in a covered dish near the fire, while you finish the gravy in the pan, by first skimming it, and then shaking in a little flour and stirring it round. Pour the gravy hot round the cutlets, and garnish with little bunches of curled parsley.

You may mix with the bread crumbs a little saffron.

Veal Cutlets

For 6 entrées.

As Miss Leslie says, the best cutlets come from the loin or the leg. If using leg cutlets, pound the cutlets to about ⅛ inch thick, being careful not to tear the meat. If using veal loin, the meat can be a little thicker but not much. Loin of veal is about three times the price of leg of veal.

Season the meat with salt and white pepper. Each cutlet should weigh about 4 ounces.

Make your own breadcrumbs by using stale French bread, no sugar or other sweeteners allowed, and as Miss Leslie says "Grate some stale bread, and rub it through a cullender." The breadcrumbs need to be quite fine.

Make about one cup of breadcrumbs and season with:

½ teaspoon white pepper, ground

1 tablespoon finely chopped fresh marjoram leaves

1 teaspoon grated fresh lemon zest

½ teaspoon powdered mace.

Mix well.

In a separate bowl, beat 6 eggs with a little water.

Dip the cutlets in the beaten egg, then the seasoned breadcrumbs, "seeing that a sufficient quantity adheres to both sides of the meat."

Heat some oil in a sauté pan and brown the cutlets on both sides and when medium brown place them on a pan an finish cooking them in the oven. If you are deep frying, make sure your fat temperature does not go higher than 350° or the meat will be brown on the outside and rare on the inside.

While the veal is finishing in the oven, pour off the remaining fat, deglaze with some brown veal stock and reduce to sauce consistency. Adjust the seasoning and it strain into a sauceboat.

Place the meat on a platter or on heated plates and serve the sauce on the side.

Professional Tip: Cooking the veal this way makes a pan sauce as Miss Leslie instructs, it's just that the procedure is a little different. The sauce is a reduction sauce, although if you want to thicken it with a *beurre manie,* feel free to do so.

Also, feel free to deglaze with Madeira, white wine, red wine or even a tawny port. If using the port add some more fresh lemon zest just before serving. Also, if you use the port, you may think about adding some cranberries and cooking them ahead of time in 1 cup of water and 1 cup of sugar, just until the skins burst. Strain them out of the poaching liquid and simmer in the sauce for about two minutes before serving.

Veal Patties

This is a wonderful dish for a luncheon or a casual supper. If there is leftover veal from a roast or trimmings from making the cutlets, use them. If need be, go to the store and get some ground veal or even a shoulder and grind it after trimming off all the fat. Use the largest die if you grind it.

Serves 6 as a light supper served with a side salad.

Take 1 pound of ground or finely minced veal and:

8 ounces of ham, preferably dry cure with some fat on it. Remember veal is lean.

Sauté in butter until warmed through.

Season with salt and ground white pepper.

Remove the veal with a slotted spoon and save any juices that might run off.

Sprinkle a little flour on the butter, stirring well and add about 4 ounces of brown veal stock, stirring with a whisk to make sure there are no lumps.

Let it cook for about 3 minutes and add:

4 ounces, 1 jill, heavy cream and stir with the whisk. While the sauce is coming to a simmer, add:

⅛ teaspoon cayenne pepper

¼ teaspoon fresh grated nutmeg

Finely grated zest of one lemon

1 tablespoon of fresh lemon juice.

Return the meat with any collected juices, bring to a simmer for 2 or 3 minutes, adjust the seasoning and ladle into puff paste shells, pre-baked and warmed, which are sitting on hot plates. If you want a vegetable in addition to a salad, orange glazed carrots would be tasty.

VEAL PATTIES.

MINCE very fine a pound of the lean of cold roast veal, and half a pound of cold boiled ham, (fat and lean equally mixed.) Put it into a stew-pan with three ounces of butter divided into bits and rolled in flour, a jill of cream, and a jill of veal gravy. Season it to your taste with cayenne pepper and nutmeg, grated lemon-peel, and lemon-juice. Set the pan on hot coals, and let the ingredients simmer till well warmed, stirring them well to prevent their burning.

Have ready baked some small shells of puff-paste. Fill them with the mixture, and eat the patties either warm or cold.

Professional Tip: This is a multi-layered taste treat. Make your own puff pastry and savor all the flavors going on here. Sweet brown veal stock, tangy lemon juice, aromatic lemon zest, spicy nutmeg and cayenne pepper and rich cream to balance the lemon. Miss Leslie was no slouch.

Calf's Liver

When prepared properly, calf's liver is tender and flavorful. Many people overcook it, which dries it out and makes it tough with a texture of thick, stubborn cardboard. Most likely you will find the liver already sliced in the supermarket. If you have a regular butcher you patronize, have him or her slice the liver into 4-ounce cutlets, about ⅛ to a ¼ inch thick. One cutlet per person is ample as it will be a large slice, about 4 ounces.

Season the liver with salt and pepper.

Dredge it in seasoned flour that has fresh thyme leaves mixed in. Shake off any excess.

TO FRY CALF'S LIVER.

CUT the liver into thin slices. Season it with pepper, salt, chopped sweet herbs, and parsley. Dredge it with flour, and fry it brown in lard or dripping. See that it is thoroughly done before you send it to table. Serve it up with its own gravy.

Some slices of cold boiled ham fried with it will be found an improvement.

You may dress a calf's heart in the same manner.

Heat clarified butter in a sauté pan and gently place the cutlets in the pan, laying the meat away from you towards the far side of the pan. Do not overcrowd the pan. Turn the meat after about two minutes or when nicely browned. Sauté the second side the same way. When nicely brown on the outside but still a little pink inside, remove from the pan and keep warm.

For the "gravy" Miss Leslie recommends, try this pan sauce.

For 6 servings.

After sautéing the veal, pour off any old butter, wipe the pan with a dry cloth to remove any bits of flour that may burn.

Add some more clarified butter.

When hot, add 1 ounce of julienne ham slices per person and heat thoroughly.

Add ½ ounce of sliced mushrooms per person if you like.

When the ham is hot, deglaze the pan off the fire with 2 ounces of Madeira, scraping the *fond* from the bottom of the pan.

Reduce by ¾.

Add 1 ounce of brown veal stock or beef broth per person and reduce by ¾.

Adjust the seasoning, adding some more fresh thyme leaves, finely chopped if you like.

Swirl in about 2 ounces total whole butter to lightly thicken the sauce and give it a shine.

For a simpler sauce, after finishing the veal, deglaze with brown veal stock and reduce by ¾, figuring 2 ounces of stock per person.

Cutlets à la Maintenon

Miss Leslie suggests neck chops, but I would stick with chops from the rack or loin chops. Allow 2 double chops per person.

Have your butcher cut 12 double chops, chops with two rib bones and about ¾ of an inch thick. Ask to have the "cap meat" removed so what you have is the eye of the chop. Scrape the bones clean so there is nothing that will burn while roasting.

Here Miss Leslie uses a French technique of cooking, *en papillote,* an item wrapped in a type of parchment paper. This prevents juices from escaping and retains the flavors of whatever is in the paper envelope with the meat. This technique is often used with fish. Modern cooks have the advantage of being able to use a modern oven. The adaption will preserve the flavors of Miss Leslie's recipe.

For 6 persons.

Add a mixture of 50 percent clarified butter and 50 percent canola oil to a sauté pan and, after seasoning the chops with salt and fresh-ground pepper on both sides, sear the meat so it has a nice brown crust on both sides. Do not allow anything in the pan to burn.

When seared, remove the chops to a prep table. Move the pan and its drippings and *fond* off the heat. This is for your sauce.

Pre-heat your oven to 350°

Make the coating for the chops.

Hard-boil 6 eggs, making sure the yolks do not turn green.

Remove the yolks when cool and finely grate them into a bowl using a box grater.

Add to the yolks 1 tablespoon each:

Finely chopped parsley, marjoram, fresh rosemary, summer savory.

Finely grate one small onion into the mixture, again using the box grater.

Season with salt, pepper and nutmeg to taste.

Add about 2 tablespoon of fresh breadcrumbs to the mix and make a test by cooking a teaspoon in butter. Adjust consistency and seasoning.

For each two chops, cut a heart-shaped piece of parchment paper. Fold it in half, open it and place two chops side by side abutting the crease separating the top and bottom halves of the heart. Starting at the "top of the heart, fold overlapping creases until you go all the way to the bottom of the heart."

As you make these hearts, place each of the six in a baking sheet. When all are ready, place in a 350° oven for about 20 minutes. This is approximate as all ovens are different and cooking times will vary. Twenty minutes will give around a medium rare.

For service remove from the paper and place two chops on each pre-heated plate.

For the sauce, make the basic Madeira sauce from the calf's liver recipe before, only use the mushrooms this time. Reheat the searing pan and deglaze the pan used for searing the chops.

Professional Tip: This recipe shows the profound influence French cuisine had on Miss Leslie. As a result, two generations, thousands of women, were in turn influenced by

French food as well. The influence is rarely stated directly, but the names, cooking techniques and seasonings all point to a serious Francophile. This in turn had a lasting influence on American cuisine — many times filtered, but still there.

To Roast a Loin of Pork

If you buy a rack of pork, or an entire loin in the market, it will have been skinned. There should be a nice white fat covering at least ¼ to ½ inch thick. Separate the front end of the loin, the side closest to the shoulder, and save for another use.

This will serve 10 to 12 people with leftovers.

Make the stuffing.

Peel and fine dice 1 medium onion and sauté in oil until soft.

When soft, remove with a slotted spoon and put in a bowl.

Add the finely chopped leaves of 4 sprigs of fresh sage.

Add 8 ounces of cubed stale bread or grate 8 ounces on a box grater. Add to the bowl.

Add 4 egg yolks and mix well.

Season with salt and pepper.

Make a test for seasoning. If it seems too dry, remember it will absorb juice as the pork cooks. If you must add some liquid, add a little veal or chicken stock or some Madeira or white wine.

Follow Miss Leslie's instructions of slitting between the ribs and inserting the stuffing. In her version it is spitted and roasted in front of a fire. If you have an outdoor grill or an indoor rotisserie, do the same. Or it can be roasted in the oven at 350° until a meat thermometer registers 155° when inserted into the center of the loin.

Make your favorite gravy and serve with fresh applesauce, mashed potatoes and turnips sweetened with maple syrup.

> ## PORK, HAM, &c.
>
> ### GENERAL REMARKS.
>
> In cutting up pork, you have the spare-rib, shoulder, griskin or chine, the loin, middlings and leg; the head, feet, heart and liver. On the spare-rib and chine there is but little meat, and the pieces called middlings consist almost entirely of fat. The best parts are the loin, and the leg or hind-quarter. Hogs make the best pork when from two and a half to four years old. They should be kept up and fed with corn at least six weeks before they are killed, or their flesh will acquire a disagreeable taste from the trash and offal which they eat when running at large. The Portuguese pork, which is fed on chestnuts, is perhaps the finest in the world.
>
> If the meat is young, the lean will break on being pinched, and the skin will dent by nipping it with the fingers; the fat will be white, soft, and pulpy. If the skin or rind is rough, and cannot be nipped, it is old.
>
> Hams that have short shank-bones, are generally preferred. If you put a knife under the bone of a ham, and it comes out clean, the meat is good; but quite the contrary if the knife appears smeared and slimy. In good bacon the fat is white, and the lean sticks close to the bone; if it is streaked with yellow, the meat is rusty, and unfit to eat.
>
> Pork in every form should be thoroughly cooked. If the least under-done, it is disgusting and unwholesome.

We have two different pies following. One is for fresh pork with apples and the other is for a ham with chicken and mushrooms. They are similar but have entirely different texture and flavor profiles.

In the first, there is a goodly amount of moisture and a vibrant flavor of the classic partner for pork, apples. There are many versions of this type of dish in different cuisines and this is similar to one from Normandy. Apples by this time were very popular and found throughout the states. If you are not familiar with pippins, they are great apples for baking, with a nice tartness even when fully ripe. They also have a much firmer texture than Macintosh or delicious apples, and make the best pies.

The ham pie is almost like an Italian *torta* and should have a nice layered appearance when baked. I make a couple of suggestions that are compatible with the flavor profile in the original recipe.

For the pork pie, serve baked sweet potatoes and creamed onions or salsify.

For the ham, try scalloped potatoes made with some blue cheese and serve with a crisp salad or corn succotash.

Pork Pie

PORK PIE.

Take the lean of a leg or loin of fresh pork, and season it with pepper, salt, and nutmeg. Cover the bottom and sides of a deep dish with a good paste, made with a pound of butter to two pounds of flour, and rolled out thick. Put in a layer of pork, and then a layer of pippin apples, pared, cored, and cut small. Strew over the apples sufficient sugar to make them very sweet. Then place another layer of pork, and so on till the dish is full. Pour in half a pint or more of water, or of white wine. Cover the pie with a thick lid of paste, and notch and ornament it according to your taste.

Set it in a brisk oven, and bake it well.

Serves 8 to 10 people.

Buy a 4 to 5 pound pork shoulder with the blade bone removed or a similar size piece of fresh pork leg. Trim off as much fat as possible and cut the meat into 1½ inch cubes.

Make a seasoning mixture of 2 tablespoons of salt, 1 tablespoon of fresh ground white pepper, ¼ teaspoon fresh grated nutmeg. Mix together well. Feel free to add some mace if you like it more aromatic or some cayenne if you like a little heat. Toss the cubed pork with the spice mixture and reserve.

Pre-heat your oven to 400°.

Peel, core and slice 2½ pounds Pippin or Northern Spy apples. Toss them in a bowl with 8 ounces of sugar and a touch of cinnamon if you like.

Roll the pastry about ⅛ inch thick and roll it onto the rolling pin. Drape it into a baking dish large enough to hold all the pork and apples. Have enough dough so that you do not have to pull on it to fully line the dish. Brush the edge of the dough with beaten egg.

Assemble the pie as Miss Leslie instructs and make a nice decorative top. Place in the 400° oven for 20 minutes and reduce the heat to 350°.

Insert a meat thermometer into the center of the dish and when it registers 155°, the pie is done. Remove from the oven and allow it to sit for about 15 to 20 minutes.

Bring it to the table in the serving dish.

Ham Pie

HAM PIE.

Cover the sides and bottom of a dish with a good paste rolled out thick. Have ready some slices of cold boiled ham, about half an inch thick, some eggs boiled hard and sliced, and a large young fowl cleaned and cut up. Put a layer of ham at the bottom, then the fowl, then the eggs, and then another layer of ham. Shake on some pepper, and pour in some water, or what will be much better, some veal gravy. Cover the pie with a crust, notch and ornament it, and bake it well.

Some mushrooms will greatly improve it.

Small button mushrooms will keep very well in a bottle of sweet oil—first peeling the skin, and cutting off the stalks.

Serves 8 to 10 people.

Pre-heat the oven to 400°.

Use the same dough as for the pork pie.

Slice 1 pound of ham, preferably dry cure, thinly and layer ½ of it on the dough.

Slice and arrange on the ham 6–8 hard-boiled eggs, covering all the ham.

Thinly slice some roasted or poached chicken, about 8 ounces, mixing white and dark meat over the eggs.

Season this layer with fresh ground pepper.

Layer over the chicken 2 cups mushrooms simmered in Madeira until fully cooked then drained and sliced or diced small. Season this layer with some salt and fresh ground pepper.

Top off the pie with the remaining sliced ham and finally the top layer of dough. When rolling the top layer, cut a small circle in the center to allow steam to escape. Decorate the top nicely. Brush with beaten egg and place in the oven for 20 minutes. Carefully slide the pie out and into the center hole pour the leftover Madeira from the cooked mushrooms. There should be about 1 cup of liquid. If more liquid is needed, use a reduced or thickened brown veal or beef stock.

Finish baking for another 30 to 40 minutes.

Remove from the oven when a meat thermometer reaches 155° when inserted into the center of the pie. Allow the pie to set up for 15 to 20 minutes and serve with Madeira sauce on the side.

Glazed Ham

Try this for a brunch or Sunday night supper. This can be done with a bone-in ham or a boneless one as well. Use your best quill feather so the egg and cream are evenly brushed on and the crumb crust is undisturbed. No good quill feathers left? Use a brush. When coated place in a 400° oven until nicely browned. The amounts of the three ingredients will vary by the size of the ham.

Have fun.

> **TO GLAZE A COLD HAM.**
>
> WITH a brush or quill feather go all over the ham with beaten yolk of egg. Then cover it thickly with pounded cracker, made as fine as flour, or with grated crumbs of stale bread. Lastly go over it with thick cream. Put it to brown in the oven of a stove, or brown it on the spit of a tin roaster, set before the fire and turned frequently.
>
> This glazing will be found delicious.

Venison, &c.

Miss Leslie is talking about wild hunted venison which was abundant and hunted by professionals along with a variety of other game animals, birds and water fowl. Much of what was available then is not now, and all venison sold in markets is farm raised. In the case of New Zealand venison, the deer are free range in the truest sense in that they are unconfined, freely roam a large area and are killed and inspected before dressing and shipment. Venison is lean in comparison with domesticated animals, has a wonderful dark color and can be roasted, grilled or done to the same degree as beef or lamb. It tastes like "game" and has a firmer texture than other animals.

Venison bones make a rich, flavorful stock of which Miss Leslie makes good use. Her directions for roasting a saddle or haunch of venison are extensive. I will summarize leaving out most measurements and focus on her technique. The sauce recipe is a bit more detailed.

Miss Leslie advocates covering the loin with a paper covered with a rolled paste of flour and water and the fat side facing the fire. She specifies a spit for roasting. If that option is available, use it. Otherwise roast in an oven preheated to 350°. As it is roasting, baste it with a mixture of 8 ounces of a full-bodied red wine mixed with 4 ounces of whole butter. Venison does ot have a thick fat coating like a sirloin or a prime rib and benefits from basting often.

About 10 or 15 minutes before removing from the spit or the oven, brush with whole butter, softened, mixed with ½ the amount of flour to make a nice crust.

Cook the rack to 130° on a meat thermometer when inserted into the center of the meat.

Allow the roast to stand about 10–15 minutes. If you have frilly decorations for the ends of the bones, feel free. Serve the venison on a pre-heated platter and carve at the table or place two ribs per portion on each of six dinner plates.

For the sauce:

Take 1 to 2 pounds of venison scrap, heat some oil in a saucepot and brown the meat well. When well browned, reduce the heat, add 3 pints of brown stock (Miss Leslie asks for water), and add a sachet made with three cloves, three blades of mace, ½ whole nutmeg. Reduce this over moderate heat until reduced to 1 pint or less. Skim the fat and strain through a fine mesh strainer into a clean saucepot.

Over moderate to slow heat, melt 4 ounces of currant jelly into the reduction sauce. When melted, add 4 ounces of a full-bodied red wine and reduce by ¼ to ⅓ volume. Miss Leslie calls for thickening the sauce with a *beurre manie.* It can be finished by swirling in 2 to 3 ounces of whole butter just before serving, after the heat is turned off. Adjust the seasoning for salt and cayenne. With the sweetness of the jelly and the brown stock, a nice hit of cayenne will leave a fun tingle on your tongue. Sweet balances hot, which is why Miss Leslie calls for the cayenne in the first place.

Serve with sautéed Brussels sprouts and walnuts, diced pears and roasted potatoes and wild mushroom ragout.

This is a special meal and should be served with a good wine, so break out the good stuff.

What follows are recipes for kid ("They are best three to four months old") to hare ("If a hare is old do not roast it, but make soup of it") to rabbit stew, fricassee and fried rabbit.

Professional Tip: Miss Leslie uses classical techniques to produce a quality product. So many of her directions underscore a deep understanding of the food products she worked with and how to achieve the best results using what we would now call primitive cooking methods and equipment.

The use of a reduction sauce for flavor concentration, protecting the leaner venison from drying out, specifications for selecting other meats with quality — always foremost in her thoughts and directions — are hallmarks of her book.

Poultry, Game, &c.

Chicken Curry

This will serve 6 to 8 people. Two roaster chickens would be best for this dish, unless you can find older hens that used to lay eggs and are now known as fowls. They should be about 5 to 6 pounds. Follow Miss Leslie's recipe for the curry paste but use 1 teaspoon of

---

POULTRY, GAME, &c.

GENERAL REMARKS.

In buying poultry choose those that are fresh and fat. Half-grown poultry is comparatively insipid; it is best when full-grown but not old. Old poultry is tough and hard. An old goose is so tough as to be frequently uneatable. When poultry is young the skin is thin and tender, and can be easily ripped by trying it with a pin; the legs are smooth; the feet moist and limber; and the eyes full and bright. The body should be thick and the breast fat. The bill and feet of a young goose are yellow, and have but few hairs on them; when old they are red and hairy.

Poultry is best when killed over night, as if cooked too soon after killing, it is hard and does not taste well. It is not the custom in America, as in some parts of Europe, to keep game, or indeed any sort of eatable, till it begins to taint; all food when inclining to decomposition being regarded by us with disgust.

When poultry or game is frozen, it should be brought into the kitchen early in the morning of the day on which it is to be cooked. It may be thawed by laying it several hours in cold water. If it is not thawed it will require double the time to cook, and will be tough and tasteless when done.

In drawing poultry be very careful not to break the gall, lest its disagreeable bitterness should be communicated to the liver.

cloves rather than whole cloves. If you are using cardamom seeds make sure they are finely ground. They will also be more flavorful if lightly toasted first. The easiest way to do this is to peel and coarsely chop the 8 medium onions, add the spice and onions to the bowl of a large food processor and puree until smooth.

Add some clarified butter to a large pan and brown the chicken pieces well. Do a few pieces at a time so the pan does not lose too much heat and make the chicken greasy. As the pieces are browned, transfer them to a large, deep baking dish that will hold all the pieces and the liquid.

After the chicken is happily in the large pot or baking dish, reduce the heat, add the onion-curry paste mixture and sauté 2 to 3 minutes. Add a little butter if the pan looks dry. Sprinkle lightly with flour to absorb any butter, stir and cook 1 to 2 minutes, deglaze the pan with chicken stock, stirring to make sure there are no lumps. Bring this to a boil for 1

minute, adjust seasoning if needed and pour over the chicken in the baking dish, making sure there is sufficient liquid to cover all chicken pieces. Cover tightly and braise about 30 to 45 minutes.

Follow Miss Leslie and serve with boiled rice. You may also like to serve some chutney, sliced cucumber salad, some yogurt, coconut or any other garnish that suits your fancy. Finish the meal with a nice jasmine rice pudding garnished with caramelized mangoes.

CHICKEN CURRY.

TAKE a pair of fine fowls, and having cut them in pieces, lay them in salt and water till the seasoning is ready. Take two table-spoonfuls of powdered ginger, one table-spoonful of fresh turmeric, a tea-spoonful of ground black pepper; some mace, a few cloves, some cardamom seeds, and a little cayenne pepper with a small portion of salt. These last articles according to your taste. Put all into a mortar, and add to them eight large onions, chopped or cut small. Mix and beat all together, till the onions, spices, &c. form a paste.

Put the chickens into a pan with sufficient butter rolled in flour, and fry them till they are brown, but not till quite done. While this is proceeding, set over the fire a sauce-pan three parts full of water, or sufficient to cover the chickens when they are ready. As soon as the water boils, throw in the curry-paste. When the paste has all dissolved, and is thoroughly mixed with the water, put in the pieces of chicken to boil, or rather to simmer. When the chicken is quite done, put it into a large dish, and eat it with boiled rice. The rice may either be laid round on the same dish, or served up separately.

This is a genuine East India receipt for curry.

Lamb, veal, or rabbits may be curried in the same manner.

Roasted Game Birds

In these all-purpose directions Miss Leslie covers the most prominent game birds people in our age are still likely to find. Traditional stuffings of citrus fruit or bread and egg are intermingled with the classic French technique of larding the breast meat with bacon. She further makes use of the trimmings for making a brown stock for her "gravy" made with red wine and orange juice.

For this sauce, use the same technique as in the venison recipe, and here the addition of some currant jelly would be a nice touch. If there are cranberry preserves available in your kitchen, add a couple of tablespoons as it will go well with the orange juice.

Serves 6.

Each person should have 8 to 10 ounces of bird per person, before cooking. If there is an eight-ounce serving of a bone-in bird there will be about four to five ounces of meat per person. Make the stock from the bones and trimmings by sautéing them in a little oil. When completely brown, deglaze with some veal stock or chicken stock. Add a little liquid, scrape the *fond* from the pan bottom, and add enough stock to cover the birds by about 1 inch. To this, add 4 to 8 ounces of a full-bodied red wine and simmer the sauce for about 2 hours. This is probably more time than it actually takes as even game birds are now farm-raised but you will gain some additional flavor and it will make your kitchen smell great. If time is short about 45 to 60 minutes after the wine is added is sufficient.

Thirty minutes before service, strain the sauce, reduce by half and adjust the seasoning. For texture simply swirl in 4 ounces of whole butter rather than thickening with flour. Make sure the pot is off the heat when the butter is swirled in — otherwise it will simply melt and not bind the sauce. Figure on 2 to 3 ounces of sauce per person.

For the birds, if roasting is decided upon, preheat the oven to 350°, brush the birds with canola oil and roast until the juices run clear. As all the birds listed are different sizes, they all have different cooking times. A thermometer inserted at the thigh and carcass joint should read 165° to be absolutely safe. Serve with pear compote, spaetzle and braised cabbage or red cabbage. With game birds, nothing beats a quality red Burgundy or New World pinot noir from a good year.

> TO ROAST PHEASANTS, PARTRIDGES, QUAILS, OR GROUSE.
>
> PICK and draw the birds immediately after they are brought in. Before you roast them, fill the inside with pieces of a fine ripe orange, leaving out the rind and seeds. Or stuff them with grated cold ham, mixed with bread-crumbs, butter, and a little yolk of egg. Lard them with small slips of the fat of bacon drawn through the flesh with a larding needle. Roast them before a clear fire.
>
> Make a fine rich gravy of the trimmings of meat or poultry, stewed in a little water, and thickened with a spoonful of browned flour. Strain it, and set it on the fire again, having added half a pint of claret, and the juice of two large oranges. Simmer it for a few minutes, pour some of it into the dish with the game, and serve the remainder in a boat.
>
> If you stuff them with force-meat, you may, instead of larding, brush them all over with beaten yolk of egg, and then cover them with bread-crumbs grated finely and sifted

Sauces, Vegetables and Condiments

In Miss Leslie's book, immediately following the game birds is a section on plain sauces (lobster, anchovy, celery, nasturtian [*sic*], white and brown onion, mushroom, egg, bread, mint, and a host of herb and fruit sauces). It is a measure of her expertise the breadth of sauces listed and reading them gives one the feeling that Miss Leslie is writing down just some of what she knows. There is even a small section on storebought sauces with detailed serving directions for all sauces.

> TOMATA CATCHUP.—Gather the tomatas on a dry day, and when quite ripe. Peel them, and cut them into quarters. Put them into a large earthen pan, and mash and squeeze them till they are reduced to a pulp. Allowing half a pint of fine salt to a hundred tomatas, put them into a preserving kettle, and boil them gently with the salt for two hours, stirring them frequently to prevent their burning. Then strain them through a fine sieve, pressing them with the back of a silver spoon. Season them to your taste with mace, cinnamon, nutmeg, ginger, and white or red pepper, all powdered fine.
>
> Put the tomata again over the fire with the spices, and boil it slowly till very thick, stirring it frequently.
>
> When cold, put it up in small bottles, secure the corks well, and it will keep good a year or two.

Tomata Catchup

This is a scaled-down version as most people do not have a "preserving kettle" large enough for 100 tomatoes. Use only fully ripened tomatoes picked at the end of the season. The idea is to create a concentrated flavor and that needs ripe fruit. Peel 25 very ripe tomatoes and cut them in quarters.

Sprinkle ¼ cup of Kosher salt over the tomatoes and get them started on a slow fire. Stir slowly and they will give up their juice in time.

Simmer for 2 hours stirring often.

While they are simmering assemble your spices:

Mace 2 teaspoons

Cinnamon 6 teaspoons

Nutmeg 2 teaspoons

Ginger 2 teaspoons

White pepper 4 teaspoons

Cayenne pepper 1 teaspoon.

Puree the tomatoes in a food mill and return the puree to the low heat with your spices added. (A food processor will make a smoother puree but the food mill produces a more desirable texture.) Bring the mixture to a boil and taste for seasoning and adjust as desired. Simmer until the mixture is somewhere between tomato puree and tomato paste.

Fill regular canning jars following manufacturer's procedure.

Lemon Catchup

Wash 9 lemons, remove the stems, slice thinly and remove seeds.

In a coffee or spice grinder, grind together:

4 tablespoons mustard seed

½ ounce black peppercorns

½ ounce coarsely chopped whole nutmeg

¼ ounce blade mace

¼ ounce whole cloves.

Use the whole spices ground fresh as the flavor profile will be much more pronounced than if you use spice powders in jars. This is our version of the mortar and pestle, which works very well also.

Peel and slice:

2 ounces of fresh horseradish and grate on the medium grate of a box grater.

Add all this to the lemons in a non-reactive sauce pot and add:

3 ounces Kosher salt.

Pour in 1 quart of champagne or white wine vinegar then slowly bring to a simmer, stirring often.

Let it simmer 20 to 30 minutes and transfer to a large glass container or other non-reactive storage vessel and refrigerate, covered, three weeks, stirring every day.

Process all through a food mill after three weeks and jar and refrigerate or bring to a boil for 10 minutes and jar as instructed for the tomato catchup.

Professional Tip: I would not use Meyer lemons for this, as they are lower in acid than other varieties. If a less pronounced tartness is desired use rice vinegar rather than a champagne or wine vinegar.

LEMON CATCHUP.—Cut nine large lemons into thin slices, and take out the seeds. Prepare, by pounding them in a mortar, two ounces of mustard seed, half an ounce of black pepper, half an ounce of nutmeg, a quarter of an ounce of mace, and a quarter of an ounce of cloves. Slice thin two ounces of horseradish. Put all these ingredients together. Strew over them three ounces of fine salt. Add a quart of the best vinegar.

Boil the whole twenty minutes. Then put it warm into a jar, and let it stand three weeks closely covered. Stir it up daily.

Then strain it through a sieve, and put it up in small bottles to flavour fish and other sauces.

This is sometimes called lemon pickle.

Both of these are intensely flavored and not sweetened. They truly aid in bringing out and enhancing the flavors of your cooking. Remember, a catchup, catsup or now, a ketchup, is a condiment of Asian origin and does not need any sugar. Miss Leslie also lists many recipes for flavored vinegars, different mustards and a spice blend called "kitchen pepper."

Vegetables

Miss Leslie includes some basic directions for cooking and keeping instructions for vegetables we still use on a regular basis such as potatoes, cabbage, cauliflower, parsnips, turnips, squashes (a.k.a. cymlings as for Mrs. Randolph), pumpkin (no longer considered unusual), eggplant and many others. Miss Leslie also includes a short segment on salad greens and chestnuts.

There follows a section on pickling and another on sweetmeats, another method of preserving seasonal bounty. The preserved fruits run the gamut from peaches to pineapples to quinces.

Fruits

Reading Miss Leslie's instructions remind me of watching my grandmother, who lived on a small family farm and preserved all of her vegetables and fruits for the winter. She and my grandfather had very little money and often would not buy large amounts of store food.

Here are two recipes. For the peaches, the reason for cracking and boiling the pits is that, like bitter almonds, they contain a bitter acid, prussic acid. Apricot pits have the same acid. This acid gives definition to the flavor but must be used sparingly as it is classified as poisonous. For modern cooks, it is best to use pure almond extract.

In Miss Leslie's time cranberries were no longer considered unusual. Their inclusion in Miss Leslie's book demonstrates that they were very much a part of American cuisine at the time.

Cranberry Preserve

TO PRESERVE CRANBERRIES.—The cranberries must be large and ripe. Wash them, and to six quarts of cranberries allow nine pounds of the best brown sugar. Take three quarts of the cranberries, and put them into a stew-pan with a pint and a half of water. Cover the pan, and boil or stew them till they are all to pieces. Then squeeze the juice through a jelly-bag. Put the sugar into a preserving kettle, pour the cranberry juice over it and let it stand till it is all melted, stirring it up frequently. Then place the kettle over the fire, and put in the remaining three quarts of whole cranberries. Let them boil till they are tender, clear, and of a bright colour, skimming them frequently. When done, put them warm into jars with the syrup, which should be like a thick jelly.

Follow Miss Leslie's directions as this is a simple and very good cranberry preserve. For procedure, after cooking the mashed cranberries and water, strain the water directly into a clean pot and add the sugar into the water. There is less chance of burning the sugar. When the berries are added bring the pot to a boil and simmer until the whole berries just pop open. Turn off the heat and fill your jars according to the manufacturer's exact directions. Cranberries have a lot of pectin and will set up quickly once they start getting cool.

Peach Preserve

Except for the peach pits, follow her directions, but omit the final boiling of the syrup after the peaches are out. Use superfine sugar and you should not have to skim the scum with modern sugar. Again, jar as to manufacturer's specifications. Her ratio of 1:1 for sugar and fruit by weight is still a good measure for making your own preserves.

Pastry, Puddings, Etc.

Miss Leslie makes a great point right from the get-go, saying "All paste should be made in a very cool place." With too much heat, making a puff pastry or flaky pie dough is almost impossible. The flakiness comes from the separation of layers of fat and flour. If the temperature is too high the separation will not be achieved. With a dough that receives several turns, this is especially true. Also, her comments on the saltiness of butter rings true today as most bakers and pastry chefs insist on unsalted butter for consistency in taste and texture. Here again she is right on the money, saying, "As pastry is by no means an article of absolute necessity, it is better not to have it at all, than to make it badly, and of inferior ingredients."

Her first Best Plain Paste is a version of what is called a 3-2-1 dough. This means that by weight, there are 3 parts flour to 2 parts butter to 1 part cold water. Miss Leslie divides and rolls in most of the butter to make the dough flakier. The recipe below will give good results. Although her directions are for rolling the paste 1" thick for pie shells, most modern cooks would not favor that idea. We are more accustomed to thinner dough.

PRESERVED PEACHES.

TAKE large juicy ripe peaches; free-stones are the best, as they have a finer flavour than the cling-stones, and are much more manageable both to preserve, and to eat. Pare them, and cut them in half, or in quarters, leaving out the stones, the half of which you must save. To every pound of the peaches allow a pound of loaf-sugar. Powder the sugar, and strew it among your peaches. Cover them and let them stand all night. Crack half the peach-stones, break them up, put them into a small sauce-pan and boil them slowly in as much water as will cover them. Then when the water is well flavoured with the peach-kernels, strain them out, and set the water aside. Take care not to use too much of the kernel-water; a very little will suffice. Put the peaches into a preserving kettle, and boil them in their juice over a quick fire; (adding the kernel-water,) and skimming them all the time. When they are quite clear, which should be in half an hour, take them off, and put them into a tureen. Boil the syrup five minutes longer, and pour it hot over the peaches. When they are cool, put them into glass jars, and tie them up with paper dipped in brandy laid next to them.

THE BEST PLAIN PASTE.

ALL paste should be made in a very cool place, as heat renders it heavy. It is far more difficult to get it light in summer than in winter. A marble slab is much better to roll it on than a paste-board. It will be improved in lightness by washing the butter in very cold water, and squeezing and pressing out all the salt, as salt is injurious to paste. In New York and in the Eastern states, it is customary, in the dairies, to put more salt in what is called fresh butter, than in New Jersey, Pennsylvania, and Delaware. This butter, therefore, should always undergo the process of washing and squeezing before it is used for pastry or cakes. None but the very best butter should be taken for those purposes; as any unpleasant taste is always increased by baking. Potted butter never makes good paste. As pastry is by no means an article of absolute necessity, it is better not to have it at all, than to make it badly, and of inferior ingredients; few things being more unwholesome than hard, heavy dough. The flour for paste should always be superfine.

You may bake paste in deep dishes or in soup plates. For shells that are to be baked empty, and afterwards filled with stewed fruit or sweetmeats, deep plates of block tin with broad edges are best. If you use patty-pans, the more flat they are the better. Paste always rises higher and is more perfectly light and flaky, when unconfined at the sides while baking. That it may be easily taken out, the dishes or tins should be well buttered.

A Nice Plain Paste

Into a deep bowl sift:

3 pints of flour, 24 ounces by weight.

Divide 1 pound of butter into 4 pieces.

Work the first quarter of butter into the dough and when the pieces of butter are about pea-sized, add a little less than 8 ounces of water.

Mix these ingredients into a ball of dough, but do not overdo it.

Flour a pastry board or table and roll out ⅛" thick and spread ¼ of the butter on the dough; fold over the other half and roll the dough out to ⅛" thick.

Repeat these two steps until the last 2 quarters of butter are rolled into the dough.

For easiest working of the dough, allow it to rest about 2 to 3 hours in the refrigerator. The gluten in the flour will relax and a cooler dough is easier to roll.

Use the dough as you need it, but remember not to use too much flour for dusting or the dough will be tough. There are also recipes for suet dough, dough made with ½ lard and ½ butter, a more common paste for home use or tops of pies as well as a paste made with beef drippings.

For a classic French puff pastry, Miss Leslie uses a variation of what is called 6-three folds, where one large piece of butter is rolled into the dough and folded into thirds 6 times. Her method works well, and is not all that different from a more modern paste.

Fine Puff Paste

Take 1 pound of butter, no need to wash it, and divide into quarters. Cut off 1 quarter and divide the remaining three quarters into 2 equal pieces each, all the while keeping the butter cold.

In a bowl, place 4 cups all purpose flour, sifted, and add the 1 quarter of the butter. Blend the flour and butter until they have the consistency of very coarse cornmeal.

Add 12 ounces of very cold water all at once and work the dough just until the water is absorbed, there is no dry flour on the bottom of the bowl and the dough itself looks like a shaggy dog that is barely holding itself together. Take the dough out of the bowl and shape it into a nice rectangle then place on a pan and cover with plastic wrap or a clean towel. Refrigerate the dough 20 to 30 minutes.

Take out the dough, flour a work surface and roll the dough to about ⅛" thick, keeping it a rectangle. Take one of the 6 pieces of butter the same temperature and consistency as the dough. Spread the butter over ⅔ of the dough. Make a letter fold by folding the unbuttered third over the middle third, then the right-side third over the other two. This is a three-fold.

Roll gently to even the thickness of the dough, cover and refrigerate 20 to 30 minutes. Repeat 5 more times until all the reserved pieces of dough are rolled in the puff paste. It is best to allow the dough to rest in the refrigerator overnight before using it.

Professional Tip: This is a variation on the classic French method of making puff paste. The dough can be used for tarts, pastries, strudels, pot-pies, savory hors d'oeuvres, etc.

Sweet Paste

Follow Miss Leslie with the only caveat being not to add very much milk. Mix the dough and see if it needs any added liquid. This is her version of the French Pate Brisée, which the Germans call Mürbteig. It is very rich and expensive when compared to pie dough. When you bake it blind, make sure you line the tart pan with foil and fill to the rim with dried beans. Bake about 10 minutes at 350°, remove from the oven, carefully remove the foil and beans and bake another 5 to 6 minutes until it is nicely browned. If you are going to bake something in the shell, bake up to the removal of the beans, allow to cool, then fill and bake.

Orange, Lemon, and Quince Puddings

These three recipes are so well written, they can be followed as they are, with the following hints:

- The orange and lemon puddings are custards and should be baked in water baths, with the water coming halfway up the baking dish, in a 350°oven.
- A wine glass was listed as 2 ounces, ¼ cup. Use an off dry wine if using a white wine such as Riesling. If using a brandy, Spanish brandy has a nice sweet flavor profile.
- The quince pudding works well in a pan lined with a half-baked sweet paste. In this case, no need for a water bath.
- Add just a pinch of salt to all recipes.

Farmer's Rice Pudding

Here again follow Miss Leslie. Definitely test the rice before removing from the oven. This sets up best if chilled overnight. Feel free to alter the spices to your taste. Try this with a flavorful rice such as jasmine and add a little rose-water or orange flower water.

Indian Pudding

This is a little different than Simmons' recipe. Make it as Miss Leslie writes except for the following:

Stir the milk and meal until it thickens, making sure it does not stick to

---

SWEET PASTE.—Sift a pound and a quarter of the finest flour, and three ounces of powdered loaf-sugar into a deep dish. Cut up in it ten ounces of the best fresh butter, and rub it fine with your hands. Make a hole in the middle, pour in the yolks of two beaten eggs, and mix them with the flour, &c. Then wet the whole to a stiff paste with half a pint of rich milk. Knead it well, and roll it out.

This paste is intended for tarts of the finest sweetmeats. If used as shells, they should be baked empty, and filled when cool. If made into covered tarts, they may be iced all over, in the manner of cakes, with beaten white of egg and powdered loaf-sugar. To make puffs of it, roll it out and cut it into round pieces with the edge of a large tumbler, or with a tin cutter. Lay the sweetmeat on one half of the paste, fold the other over it in the form of a half-moon, and unite the edges by notching them together. Bake them in a brisk oven, and when cool, send them to table handsomely arranged, several on a dish.

Sweet paste is rarely used except for very handsome entertainments. You may add some rose water in mixing it.

ORANGE PUDDING.

GRATE the yellow part of the rind, and squeeze the juice of two large, smooth, deep-coloured oranges. Stir together to a cream, half a pound of butter, and half a pound of powdered white sugar, and add a wine-glass of mixed wine and brandy. Beat very light six eggs, and stir them gradually into the mixture. Put it into a buttered dish with a broad edge, round which lay a border of puff-paste neatly notched. Bake it half an hour, and when cool grate white sugar over it.

You may add to the mixture a Naples biscuit, or two finger biscuits, grated.

———

LEMON PUDDING—May be made precisely in the same manner as the above; substituting lemons for oranges.

QUINCE PUDDING.—Take six large ripe quinces; pare them, and cut out all the blemishes. Then scrape them to a pulp, and mix the pulp with half a pint of cream, and half a pound of powdered sugar, stirring them together very hard. Beat the yolks of seven eggs, (omitting all the whites except two,) and stir them gradually into the mixture, adding two wine glasses of rose water. Stir the whole well together, and bake it in a buttered dish three quarters of an hour. Grate sugar over it when cold.

A FARMER'S RICE PUDDING.—This pudding is made without eggs. Wash half a pint of rice through two cold waters, and drain it well. Stir it raw into a quart of rich milk, or of cream and milk mixed; adding a quarter of a pound of brown sugar, and a table-spoonful of powdered cinnamon. Put it into a deep pan, and bake it two hours or more. When done, the rice will be perfectly soft, which you may ascertain by dipping a tea-spoon into the edge of the pudding and taking out a little to try. Eat it cold.

A BAKED INDIAN PUDDING.—Cut up a quarter of a pound of butter in a pint of molasses, and warm them together till the butter is melted. Boil a quart of milk; and while scalding hot, pour it slowly over a pint of sifted Indian meal, and stir in the molasses and butter. Cover it, and let it steep for an hour. Then take off the cover, and set the mixture to cool. When it is cold, beat six eggs, and stir them gradually into it; add a table-spoonful of mixed cinnamon and nutmeg; and the grated peel of a lemon. Stir the whole very hard; put it into a buttered dish, and bake it two hours. Serve it up hot, and eat it with wine sauce, or with butter and molasses.

PLAIN PANCAKES.—Sift half a pound or a pint of flour. Beat seven eggs very light, and stir them gradually into a quart of rich milk. Then add by degrees the flour, so as to make a thin batter. Mix it very smooth, pressing out all the lumps with the back of a spoon. Set the frying-pan over the fire, and when it is hot, grease it with a spoonful of lard. Then put in a ladle full of the batter, and fry it of a light brown, turning it with care to prevent its breaking. Make each pancake large enough to cover the bottom of a dessert plate; greasing the pan every time. Send them to table hot, accompanied by powdered sugar and nutmeg mixed in a small glass bowl. Have wine with them also.

the bottom of the pot. When the milk is thoroughly absorbed, allow it to bubble up for a minute or two, all the while stirring to prevent it from scorching.

Bake at 350° in a water bath until done. Test by inserting a toothpick into the center of the pudding. It should be clean but moist when the pudding is done.

Try this with maple syrup or vanilla ice cream in addition to Miss Leslie's suggestions, all of which are good.

Plain Pancakes

This recipe is for classic French crepes. Follow Miss Leslie but spray the crepe pan after each crepe is done, turning them once. Make them thin then take them out of the pan and place on plastic wrap or parchment paper. Make the batter a day ahead and let it rest overnight. When ready to make this batch add a pinch of salt and two table-spoons of melted butter. Stir well and strain into a clean bowl making sure there are no lumps. Make all of them at once and freeze what you do not need. They are good for dessert filled and rolled or with jam spread between the crepes. They are good for breakfast when served with maple syrup. They can be used for a light entrée when filled with a savory filling.

Following these recipes are many for various puddings, some ice creams, types of blanc mange (made with isinglass, which is made from the bladders of fish and was also used for clarifying beer, ale and wine) and instructions for making coloring for confectionary.

These preceding recipes demonstrate how Miss Leslie was able to have a lasting influence on American cuisine. From a standpoint of simplicity and frugality the rice pudding demonstrates low cost, good taste and good nutrition. There was a plethora of "frugal cookbook" authors in the 19th century and while Miss Leslie's book went far beyond that narrow scope, she nevertheless was able to include this facet of American cooking within the larger context of her book. The Indian Pudding harkens back to the founding of the colonies and shows the longevity and influence Native American foods had and still have on our eating habits. The recipe for the crepes shows what a profound influence French food had on her writing and, by way of her books, on American food in her time as well as ours. Is there anyone who has not had a crepe or is not at least familiar with the product? This is due in large measure to the fact that this was the largest-selling cookbook of the 19th century and had a corresponding influence on American food.

Washington Cake

This is Miss Leslie's idea of a pound cake, versions of which are still found in modern baking books. It harkens back to traditional English cakes.

In a mixing machine bowl or large bowl if you are using a hand held mixer, cream together:
1 pound of butter and
1 pound of sugar until they are light and fluffy. The lightness indicates that air has been incorporated into the fat.

Sift together in a second bowl:
4 cups (1 pound) of all-purpose flour
1 teaspoon of baking powder
½ teaspoon salt
1 freshly-grated nutmeg
1 scant tablespoon of ground cinnamon.

Add to the sugar/butter mix:
6 large eggs, one at a time. When each is incorporated, scrape the bowl with a rubber spatula, AFTER turning off the mixer.

Mix together 2 ounces each of Madeira and two ounces of brandy with 1 pint whole milk. Reserve.

After all six eggs have been added, add:
⅓ of the flour alternately with the mixed liquids, scraping the bowl after each addition. Repeat this twice more until all the flour and liquid have been added.

> WASHINGTON CAKE.—Stir together a pound of butter and a pound of sugar; and sift into another pan a pound of flour. Beat six eggs very light, and stir them into the butter and sugar, alternately with the flour and a pint of rich milk or cream; if the milk is sour it will be no disadvantage. Add a glass of wine, a glass of brandy, a powdered nutmeg, and a table-spoonful of powdered cinnamon. Lastly, stir in a small tea-spoonful of pearl-ash, or sal-aratus, that has been melted in a little vinegar; take care not to put in too much pearl-ash, lest it give the cake an unpleasant taste. Stir the whole very hard; put it into a buttered tin pan, (or into little tins.) and bake it in a brisk oven. Wrapped in a thick cloth, this cake will keep soft for a week.

Scrape the batter into several buttered and floured loaf pans, round cake pans or square baking pans. Fill a pan ⅔ full with batter and bake in a 325°–350° oven until a skewer inserted in the center comes out clean. Do not over bake.

Remove from the oven, let cool 5–10 minutes and turn out on a cooling rack.

Professional Tip: Note the use of pearl ash as in the recipes of Amelia Simmons. Modern baking powders had not yet been invented, but her admonition to not use too much "lest it give the cake an unpleasant taste" holds true for baking powder even now. If you have ever eaten a cake or biscuit that had an out-of-balance amount of baking powder and gotten a bitter taste, that is the reason.

Make sure the butter and sugar are well creamed. If not, the cake will be dry and have an unpleasant crumb texture.

Moravian Sugar Cake

There were many German immigrants who settled in the Philadelphia area, and are still there — think Mennonites and Amish. The so-called Pennsylvania Dutch were originally from Germany, some from Switzerland. A wonderful tradition of German-American baking

MORAVIAN SUGAR CAKE.—Cut up a quarter of a pound of butter into a pint of rich milk, and warm it till the butter becomes soft; then stir it about in the milk so as to mix them well. Sift three quarters of a pound of flour (or a pint and a half) into a deep pan, and making a hole in the middle of it, stir in a large table-spoonful of the best brewer's yeast in which a salt-spoonful of salt has been dissolved; and then thin it with the milk and butter. Cover it, and set it near the fire to rise. If the yeast is sufficiently strong, it will most probably be light in two hours. When it is quite light, mix with the dough a well-beaten egg and three quarters of a pound more of sifted flour; adding a table-spoonful of powdered cinnamon, and stirring it very hard. Butter a deep square baking pan, and put the mixture into it. Set it to rise again, as before. Mix together five ounces or a large coffee-cup of fine brown sugar; two ounces of butter; and two table-spoonfuls of powdered cinnamon. When the dough is thoroughly light, make deep incisions all over it, at equal distances, and fill them with the mixture of butter, sugar and cinnamon; pressing it hard down into the bottom of the holes, and closing the dough a little at the top to prevent the seasoning from running out. Strew some sugar over the top of the cake; set it immediately into the oven, and bake it from twenty minutes to half an hour, or more, in a brisk oven, in proportion to its thickness. When cool, cut it into squares. This is a very good plain cake; but do not attempt it unless you have excellent yeast.

is centered in this area and was something Miss Leslie would have been familiar with. This is the cake my grandmother made when I was growing up and her maiden name was Schützinger. This is a yeast dough. Follow the modern adaption for a more reliable result. Note also that Miss Leslie calls for brewer's yeast, which is a continuation of the "emptins" of Amelia Simmons.

Make the starter:
Warm 1 pint of milk but do not go over 110°.
In a large bowl, sift 3 cups (12 ounces) of all-purpose flour with:
2 teaspoons instant yeast and make a well in the center.
Stir to make a smooth paste, cover and allow to rise in a warm place about 1 hour until light and doubled in volume.
Place starter on a mixing machine on low speed and add:
1 beaten egg and mix until incorporated.
Add 1 teaspoon salt.
Add 1 stick (4 ounces) softened unsalted butter and mix until incorporated.

Add an additional 3 cups (12 ounces) all-purpose flour sifted with 1 scant tablespoon of ground cinnamon.

Mix until a smooth dough is formed. Turn out into a buttered baking pan and fit it to the pan. Proof a second time, covered, until an indentation stays when the dough is lightly pressed.

While the dough is rising, make the butter topping.

Cream together:
2 ounces of butter
5 ounces light brown sugar
2 tablespoons ground cinnamon.

Make indentations in the risen cake in lines and rows, spaced equi-distant from each other. Deposit a small amount of the butter/brown sugar mix into each indentation until the mixture is used up. Sprinkle the entire cake with granulated sugar and bake in a 350° oven until done, heeding Miss Leslie: bake "twenty minutes to half an hour, or more, in a brisk oven, in proportion to its thickness."

Professional Tip: This is a yeast dough with a long tradition in Germany, Austria and Switzerland. It is natural that the tradition came to America with the immigrants, and natural that even English traditions would be influenced by the food and that after Miss Leslie's book, this influence extended all the way into 20th-century America.

Coconut Jumbles

No need to grate a coconut by hand. Make sure you buy unsweetened grated coconut for this cookie. Follow Miss Leslie and for the coconut make the amount 8 ounces by weight. Do not use a volume measurement as different shreds will produce different weights for the same volume. For rose-water, 2 teaspoons. Cut the dough into equal pieces, form into little ropes and circle to join the ends. Bake them on a silicon pan liner or parchment paper at 350°–375°, maybe 10–12 minutes, depending upon how thick the ropes were rolled. If the dough is too wet to roll, add some flour until it is of rolling consistency; if too stiff add a little milk.

> COCOA-NUT JUMBLES. — Grate a large cocoa-nut. Rub half a pound of butter into a pound of sifted flour, and wet it with three beaten eggs, and a little rose water. Add by degrees the cocoa-nut, so as to form a stiff dough. Flour your hands and your paste-board, and dividing the dough into equal portions, make the jumbles with your hands into long rolls, and then curl them round and join the ends so as to form rings. Grate loaf-sugar over them; lay them in buttered pans, (not so near as to run into each other,) and bake them in a quick oven from five to ten minutes.

Doughnuts

Is there anything that speaks more of America's love affair with sweet things more than doughnuts? Another link to a German-Central European tradition, these are generally still made in season in north Germany, specifically the winter. These can be eaten plain, rolled in cinnamon sugar, drizzled with melted chocolate or a white icing, and even filled.

Notice that Miss Leslie does not call for salt. I added this for several reasons: taste, dough texture, controlling fermentation. Use instant yeast.

Follow Miss Leslie with the following changes:

Instead of using brewer's yeast, use two tablespoons of instant yeast.
In the second bowl of flour, add 1-teaspoon salt.
In the second bowl, warm the milk to 100°.

You may have to flour the rolling surface heavily. Fry in oil or melted shortening at 340°. Turn when brown on the underside and brown the second side. Make a test to see how long your frying really takes. In baking, items are done when they are done, and not before and not after. When you make these the second time, you will know how long on each side.

Some Breakfast Items

Buckwheat Cakes

Buckwheat is a type of grass that originated in Asia. The unusual name comes from the Dutch *boecweite* that, I am told, means "beech mast" as the grains are supposedly shaped like the masts of Dutch ships of the mid–15th century. It is a dark grain, earthy and citrusy with a slightly bitter aftertaste and is probably best known as the grain of the Russian specialty, blini, which are one of the traditional accompaniments for caviar.

For modern cooking follow Miss Leslie with a couple of updates:
To every quart of flour (16 ounces) add 2 ounces of corn meal.
Use 2 teaspoons of instant yeast rather than brewer's yeast.
Moisten with 12 ounces of warm water to make the batter. If it is too loose, add a little corn meal. If it is too dry, add a little more liquid.

Add 1 teaspoon of salt and 1 tablespoon of sugar when the water is added by dissolving both in the water.

For a more tender cake, add 2 ounces of melted butter after the batter has risen and is ready for baking.

No need for the pearl-ash.

Serve with butter and maple syrup or cinnamon-spiced honey.

If you want to add eggs to the batter, add before the water is added.

Two eggs should be sufficient; they add nutrition, structure, moisture and cost.

Sally Lunn

This classic American bread should be eaten at one sitting. If not, freeze the remainder. It stales easily.

Follow Miss Leslie but add these updates:

Place in a mixing bowl the milk warmed to 90°, 1-tablespoon instant yeast, and the flour. On top of the flour add the remaining ingredients and turn on the mixer and mix about 6 minutes on slow speed. It should rise in about 1 hour

Butter a square baking pan, a loaf pan or try the individual pieces on the griddle. Bake the bread in a 350° oven until done.

> A SALLY LUNN.—This cake is called after the inventress. Sift into a pan a pound and a half of flour. Make a hole in the middle, and put in two ounces of butter warmed in a pint of milk, a salt-spoonful of salt, three well-beaten eggs, and two table-spoonfuls of the best fresh yeast. Mix the flour well into the other ingredients, and put the whole into a square tin pan that has been greased with butter. Cover it, set it in a warm place, and when it is quite light, bake it in a moderate oven. Send it to table hot, and eat it with butter.
>
> Or, you may bake it on a griddle, in small muffin rings, pulling the cakes open and buttering them when brought to table.

Miss Leslie gives further instructions on making several kinds of yeast, butter, cheese, hot chocolate, coffee and tea. There is an entire chapter on "Domestic Liquors, Etc." Included are recipes for beers made from spruce, ginger, molasses and sassafras. Wines made from fruits include gooseberry, currant, raspberry, elderberry, elderflower and cider. There are assorted shrubs, mead, a variety of cordials and all types of flavoring syrups. A little further on are instructions for punches, sherbets and small beers.

In her section on preparations for the sick there are various jellies made for people with eating problems and people who need items that are nutritious and easy to digest. There are also a variety of remedies for everything from an overdose of laudanum to mosquito bites.

There is also a large section on perfumes and cosmetics, ink and almond paste. There are a few additional recipes for custard, ice cream and some odds and ends.

Miss Leslie's literary writing added immeasurably to the available titles for children — but her stories are not soft. There is an emotional growth associated with many of her stories that some modern readers might find difficult to absorb.

Her bestsellers were her cookbooks, and through them she had a profound influence on several generations of American cooks and cookery.

High standards and an insistence on cleanliness and sanitation are marks of a dedicated professional, and certainly Miss Leslie was that. Get to know the lady through her cooking. The soul of a nation is expressed in its food and arts and language. In language and food, American culture has a true champion in Miss Leslie.

CHAPTER 13

What Mrs. Fisher Knows About Old Southern Cooking (Mrs. Abby Fisher)

Breakfast Breads

Breakfast Cream Cake

This recipe is a version of a popover, which is an individual serving of Yorkshire Pudding.

Pre-heat oven to 425.°
In a large bowl beat together:
4 large eggs
½ cup heavy cream
1 cup whole milk.
Add and stir until there are no lumps:
2 cups flour, sifted twice.
Preheat muffin pans with a small amount of melted beef fat, lard or oil. When the fat is smoking hot, remove the pan from the oven and slowly pour the mixture into the cups.
Cream cakes will puff up and turn dark golden brown.

> 8   Breakfast Cream Cake.
>
> Four eggs beat light, one gill of cream to a tea-cup of sweet milk, one pint of flour, sifted, half teaspoonful of salt; mix cream, milk, and eggs together, well stirred, then add flour gradually until thoroughly mixed. Have your baking cups hot when put to bake. Requires ten minutes to bake in hot oven.

Waffles

Sift together in a large bowl:
3 cups all-purpose flour
1 teaspoon baking soda
1 teaspoon salt.
In a separate bowl beat together:
2 large eggs with
2 cups buttermilk or 1 cup milk and
   1 cup plain yogurt.
Add egg mixture to flour mixture and
   stir well to eliminate lumps. Let stand about 20 minutes. Melt and add:
1 tablespoon unsalted butter.
Use waffle iron of choice but make sure the iron is hot.

> 4   Waffles for Breakfast.
>
> Two eggs beat light, one pint of sour milk, to one and a half pint of flour, one teaspoonful of soda sifted with the flour, one tablespoonful of butter, teaspoonful of salt, well mixed, and then add the eggs. Always have your irons perfectly hot and well greased. In baking, melt butter before mixing in flour. Place them in a covered dish and butter them on sending to the table.

Professional Tip: I recommend buttermilk here, as the sour milk from Mrs. Fisher's time is almost impossible to make. Raw milk is needed for that and modern pasteurized milk will spoil before it sours. Buttermilk has sufficient acid to react with the baking soda. A 50 percent mixture of milk and yogurt works as well but will make the batter a bit thicker. Note also there is no sugar in this recipe. The sweetness will come from whatever topping is added later.

Breakfast Corn Bread

This bread has a wonderful texture and is a unique version of a Southern staple.

Boil a ½ cup white rice in 3 cups of water until fully tender and completely soft. Drain. Add rice to the bowl of a food processor or a large mixing bowl, then add:
1½ cups corn meal, white or yellow
1 teaspoon salt.
Blend well until it looks more white than yellow.
While the machine is running add:
1 tablespoon melted butter
3 large eggs
¼ cup of whole milk.
Add the above ingredients and stir or run the processor until incorporated.
This produces a dense corn bread. If you prefer a lighter one, add
2 teaspoons of baking powder with the dry ingredients.

7	Breakfast Corn Bread,

One tea-cup of rice boiled nice and soft, to one and a half tea-cupful of corn meal mixed together, then stir the whole until light; one teaspoonful of salt, one tablespoonful of lard or butter, three eggs, half tea-cup of sweet milk. The rice must be mixed into the meal while hot; can be baked either in muffin cups or a pan.

Bake the bread in greased muffin cups or a baking pan in a 400° oven until done.

Professional Tip: Here again there is no sweetening added to the batter. Serve with soft unsalted butter and a variety of honeys or preserves.

Croquettes

Mrs. Fisher next has a section on croquettes, which shows what must have been a popular and versatile item. There are croquettes for lamb, chicken, meat, crab, liver, oyster and fish. There is also an item called a *vigareet,* that is a croquette made from lamb or veal with the addition of brains to the mixture.

Crab Croquettes

If fresh crabs are available, count on two to three ounces of meat per medium-sized fresh blue crabs. To boil them, bring a large quantity of water to a boil, add salt and whatever other seasonings are preferred. Put several crabs in at one time, boil rapidly for about five to six minutes, remove and repeat until all your crabs are boiled. Cool, crack and pick the meat and don't forget the legs. If putting live crabs in boiling water seems cruel, hold a crab down and plunge the point of a chef's knife between the eyes from above the crab. Press through to the cutting board. This kills the crab instantly.

30	Crab Croquettes.

Have crabs well boiled in salt and water, then pick them clean from the shell; chop fine; take the large end of a piece of celery and grate into the crab; chop with crab a small piece of onion fine; mix half a teacup of fine powdered cracker into crab; season with pepper and salt, also the least bit of fine red pepper, as crabs should be seasoned high to be nice. Have your lard hot, and fry just before wanted at table. Beat two eggs, dip croquettes in the egg, roll in powdered crackers before frying; make them oblong shaped.

If fresh crabs are not available, consider buying canned, pasteurized crabmeat in one-pound cans. Make sure the meat is picked over to remove any leftover cartilage or shell.

1 pound of crabmeat
1 small stalk celery, grated (¼ cup)
1 medium onion, grated (½ cup)
½ cup cracker meal
1 egg (not in Mrs. Fisher's recipe)

Mix all the ingredients together, add a little more cracker meal if too loose, a little cream if too dry. Make a test to check for seasoning by sautéing a little bit of the crab mix in a small pan.

Beat two eggs well, shape croquettes as desired, dip in eggs and roll in cracker meal.

Preheat deep fat to 350° and fry just before ready to serve.

Soups

Beef Soup and Oxtail Soup

These two soups are together for the simple reason that they are essentially the same. The beef soup is really a simple beef broth, or clear soup. The best meats for this are beef shin meat or bottom round. The flavor can be developed by adding, for the 6 pounds of meat, 1 pound onions, peeled and cut up; half pound celery stalks cut up; half pound carrots cut up and a sachet of a dozen peppercorns and herbs of choice. If raw meat is used, the broth will be a pale grey color, or what is known as a white broth, which is akin to a white stock made with unroasted bones.

> 38   Beef Soup.
>
> Six pounds of meat to two and one-half gallons of water. Boil to one gallon and one-half; then strain all meat out from the bouillon. Season with pepper and salt.
>
> 39   Ox-Tail Soup.
>
> Can be made from the same bouillon of beef as seen in No. 38, in the following manner. Take two quarts of bouillon to two ox-tails; boil down to three pints. You can put in either ochra or vermicelli. Season with salt and pepper. Skim all grease off while boiling. Have the butcher unjoint the ox-tail.

Bring slowly to a simmer, skimming the scum as it rises. Strain as directed and season very well.

The oxtail soup starts with the above broth and adds a specified amount of oxtails, disjointed. Follow directions as above.

For better flavor, always roast the bones, meat and, in this case, the oxtails.

If the addition of okra is desired, add ½ pound sliced okra about 15 minutes before service.

Oyster Gumbo Soup

Here is a simple example of how West African influences insinuated themselves into the vernacular of Southern, and by extension American, cuisine. Gumbo, referred to here, is not okra, but gumbo file, or powder, which is ground and powdered dried leaves of the sassafras tree. The word "gumbo" itself is of Angolan origin, *kingumbo,* which came into use in the 19th-century jargon of Southern cooks, from coastal Carolina to New Orleans. It can refer to a soup cum stew or, in these directions, a seasoning long in use by Native Americans, to thicken a soup or stew. To this day, many people are familiar with the term and the food as prepared throughout the decades by Mrs. Fisher and others like her. In her

> **43   Oyster Gumbo Soup.**
>
> Take an old chicken, cut into small pieces, salt and black pepper. Dip it well in flour, and put it on to fry, over a slow fire, till brown; don't let it burn. Cut half of a small onion very fine and sprinkle on chicken while frying. Then place chicken in soup pot, add two quarts water and let it boil to three pints. Have one quart of fresh oysters with all the liquor that belongs to them, and before dishing up soup, add oysters and let come to a boil the second time, then stir into soup one tablespoonful of gumbo quickly. Dish up and send to table. Have parsley chopped very fine and put in tureen on dishing up soup. Have dry boiled rice to go to table with gumbo in separate dish. Serve one tablespoonful of rice to a plate of gumbo.

book, the cuisine was made available to a much wider audience than a small collection of plantations in the deep South, or even the relatively large city of San Francisco.

Buy a roasting chicken and cut it into 10 pieces — 2 legs, 2 thighs, 2 wings with the tips removed, and each side of the breast cut into 2 pieces.

Lay the chicken pieces in a large pan and season well with salt and pepper and allow to come to room temperature.

Make a seasoned flour mixture with:

2 cups all purpose flour, or cake flour is better

Salt, pepper, and a goodly pinch of cayenne pepper.

Dredge the chicken pieces in the seasoned flour and shake off excess.

Heat oil or fresh lard in a large cast iron skillet. Keep heat at medium and add the chicken pieces, three or four at a time. Do not crowd the pan or the temperature of the fat will cool too much and the chicken will be greasy.

Cook well on both sides until medium brown and crispy, making sure no fine particles of flour burn on the bottom of the pan.

When all the pieces are crispy and brown, place in a large soup pot.

Drain oil and wipe out the skillet. Add a little more oil.

Fine dice one medium onion and sauté until soft, then add to the pot with the chicken.

Add two quarts of water or chicken broth, bring to a simmer, and simmer until reduced by 25 percent, or to 1½ pints.

When opening fresh oysters, make sure to save the liquid, or if buying shucked oysters, make sure their liquid is included.

Add one quart of oysters and juice to the chicken, return to a simmer but do not boil or the oysters will be tough.

When the gumbo returns to a simmer, add the tablespoon of file powder but do not boil or the liquid will get stringy. Adjust the seasoning.

Serve immediately with a dish of plain boiled rice.

Corn and Tomato Soup

This is a pretty color and must be well seasoned.

1 gallon beef broth or stock

4 pounds of tomatoes, very ripe. Feel free to use a mix of varieties.

6 ears of corn

Salt, pepper, fresh thyme, fresh sage.

> **47   Corn and Tomato Soup.**
>
> Take a fresh beef bone, put on to boil with one gallon of water, and when boiling skim the grease off. Cut corn from cob and scald tomatoes with boiling water. Skin them and put both vegetables into soup, the corn ten minutes before dinner. Cut tomatoes in small pieces and let them boil in soup at least one hour.

Bring to a simmer one gallon of rich beef stock or broth and simmer with a sachet of two sprigs fresh thyme and two of fresh sage, if desired.

Peel and seed the tomatoes, cut in a medium dice and add to the simmering stock. Simmer until thoroughly cooked and almost pureed.

While the tomatoes are simmering, scale the corn from the cobs and reserve.

Season the soup with salt and pepper, and, as Abby says, add the corn 10 minutes before service. Discard the sachet and correct seasoning. You may add a little sugar if you feel the soup is too acidic.

Pastries and Cakes

Pastry for Making Pies of all Kinds

This is a fine pastry for pies, sweet and savory, and turnovers. The ratio of fat to flour is high, which makes for a tender pastry. The balance of butter and lard provides taste and delicacy, salt sparks the flavor and then adding "enough cold water and mix[ing] with your hands so as to make the pastry hold together" prevents over-mixing and making the pastry tough or rubbery. Mrs. Fisher also says to roll the dough to the "thickness of an egg shell," which

> 48   Pastry for making Pies of all kinds.
>
> One pound of flour nicely sifted to quarter pound of butter and one quarter pound of lard, one teaspoonful of salt, fine, mixed in flour while dry; then with your hands rub the butter and lard into the flour until thoroughly mixed, then add enough cold water and mix with your hands so as to make pastry hold together, be sure not have it too wet; sprinkle flour very lightly on pastry board, and roll pastry out to the thickness of an egg-shell for the top of fruit, and that for the bottom of fruit must be thin as paper. In rolling pastry, roll to and from you; you don't want more than ten minutes to make pastry.

shows considerable refinement and is a far cry from Simmons' bottom pastry one inch thick.

Remember what Mrs. Fisher says: "You don't want more than ten minutes to make pastry." Many people work a dough to death and it then becomes tough and rubbery. Speed, delicacy and proper ratio of ingredients will make an outstanding pastry.

Sweet Potato Pie

Can there be a more appropriate recipe with which to showcase classic desserts of Southern Cooking than a sweet potato pie? Not only is a sweet potato a New World food, but this pie is still popular in the South. Slaves would have gravitated towards sweet potatoes in part because they were so similar to a West African staple, the yam. Both are tubers from a rhizome, with the sweet potato having a bit more sweetness to it.

Make the recipe as it is; with the following alterations from Mrs. Fisher's sequence:

- Grate the zest from the orange before squeezing the juice. Put the salt in when the sweet potatoes get mashed.
- Add four ounces of brown sugar, more if the potatoes are not so sweet.
- Use a ten-inch-deep pie dish and bake at 350° until a skewer inserted into the center of the pie comes out moist but not wet.

> 53   Sweet Potato Pie.
>
> Two pounds of potatoes will make two pies. Boil the potatoes soft; peel and mash fine through a cullender while hot; one tablespoonful of butter to be mashed in with the potato. Take five eggs and beat the yelks and whites separate and add one gill of milk; sweeten to taste; squeeze the juice of one orange, and grate one-half of the peel into the liquid. One half teaspoonful of salt in the potatoes. Have only one crust and that at the bottom of the plate. Bake quickly.

For a crisper crust, pre-bake the shell by filling it in the pie plate with foil and dry beans to the rim. Bake about 15 minutes at 400° and reduce the heat for the pie.

Gold Cake

60   Gold Cake.

Take one dozen eggs and separate the yelks from the white, and beat the yelks very light; one pound of butter, one pound of flour and one pound of powdered sugar; rub the butter and sugar together until creamed very light, then add the beaten yelks of the eggs to the creamed butter and sugar, and beat again until light. Take two teaspoonfuls of the best yeast powder, and sift with the one pound of flour, then add this flour to the creamed butter and eggs, with a half teacupful of sweet milk, and stir the whole hard and fast till light, then grate the peel of one lemon and squeeze the juice in the cake and stir well.

This cake is a Victorian-era creation and is often paired with a Silver Cake. They are the same cake: the gold uses egg yolks and the silver egg whites. Most modern versions substitute baking powder for yeast, which is what Mrs. Fisher specifies. Perhaps there was no baking powder available; certainly there would have been yeast or sourdough starter available on a more regular basis.

Sift together 4 cups of all-purpose flour and 2 teaspoons of instant yeast; reserve.

Separate 12 eggs making sure no yolk contaminates the whites; reserve separately.

In a large bowl beat:

1 pound unsalted butter

1 pound 10x powdered sugar, sifted until light and almost colorless.

While the butter/sugar mix is creaming, beat in a separate bowl the egg yolks until light in color and the whisk leaves a track in the yolks.

Add the yolks gradually, in three or four additions, scraping the mixing bowl after each addition.

Grate the zest of 1 lemon and add to the mixture; then squeeze the juice and reserve.

Slowly add the flour/yeast mixture in three additions, alternating with

½ cup of room temperature milk. Mix well and work the dough until it is nice and shiny.

Shape to fit in shaped pans you like that have been well buttered. Cover with plastic wrap and allow to rest for about 30 minutes at room temperature.

Place in pre-heated 350° oven and bake until golden brown, testing after 30 minutes by inserting a skewer into the center of the cake. When it comes out clean, the cake is done.

For the Silver Cake: Use the egg whites and instead of using the lemon zest and juice, flavor with 1 teaspoon of almond extract or rose-water and 1 teaspoon of peach extract.

Everything else stays the same.

Carolas

67   Carolas.

Five eggs to two cups of sugar; break eggs into the sugar and beat the whole till perfectly light. Sift one quart of flour; take one-half teacup of sweet milk and put a level teaspoonful of soda in it, without lumps; one teaspoonful of salt. Flavor with the juice of one orange, the peel of half an orange, grated, and one teaspoonful of butter. Make the dough in the same way as for light bread; roll out dough as for biscuit. Cut them out five inches by two inches, slice them two inches in the middle and stretch open a little. Have your fat boiling hot, but do not let it burn. Put carolas in hot fat, shake skillet gradually till brown. As you take them out of the fat, lay them in a pan on clean paper, so as to drain grease from them.

This is a type of cruller and can be made in a variety of shapes in addition the one Mrs. Fisher specifies. This is similar to what a modern recipe would be for the same item even though cooking techniques and equipment are light years away from what was used when these were made in Mobile.

To finish the crullers, make a mix of one cup granulated sugar and two teaspoons of ground cinnamon and dredge carolas while still warm.

Follow Mrs. Fisher here with one adjustment: sift the soda with the flour twice, grate the orange zest before squeezing the juice and for a teacup of milk figure on 6 ounces. Mix until the dough is smooth and shiny, rest for a few minutes and roll and cut as directed or shape as you wish. Fry at 350° to 375° and remove with a strainer when golden brown. Drain on paper and enjoy.

Sauces, Pickles and Preserves

Sweet Cucumber Pickles

This recipe works well with the smaller pickling gherkins. Follow Mrs. Fisher, but before layering the cucumbers with sugar, put them in a large, non-reactive container and cover.

To be safe in jarring any produce, be sure to follow manufacturer's instructions for processing.

Compound Tomato Sauce

This is a condiment Mrs. Randolph or Miss Leslie might have called "catsup." It is flavorful, spicy and intense and makes a sensational addition to stews and thick soups, or served with roasted meats or poultry. It also works well as a dipping sauce for fried calamari, but is not for the faint of heart.

Cooking until thick virtually evaporates the moisture from the vinegar and liquid rendered by the tomatoes. This also concentrates the flavors in a spectacular fashion. A half batch or even a quarter batch will be a reasonable amount for most situations. For a commercial restaurant a full batch would work well.

A peck is a quarter bushel. Adjust the amount according to the situation. For best results use summer, locally ripened tomatoes, not the supermarket tomatoes. If available, strain the sauce through a food mill for the best texture. Use cider vinegar.

It is not necessary to cook "all day." Simmer over a low heat for about two hours, take a tablespoon of the sauce and place on a plate and tilt the plate. If water runs out of the sauce, return to the fire for some additional cooking.

73　　　Sweet Cucumber Pickles.

Take as many pickles as you want to make that have already been pickled in vinegar, and slice them in four pieces lengthwise, or cut them crosswise the thickness of a silver half-dollar, and place them in an earthen jar in layers of about three inches in thickness, covering each layer of pickles all over with granulated sugar. Keep repeating the layers three inches thick and covering them with sugar until you have placed all the pickles under sugar you have cut up. Let them remain under the sugar twenty-four hours, then take them out and put them in jars. Then make a syrup in the following way: One quart of sugar to one quart of clear water, and let it boil down to one quart. You will then have one quart of pure syrup. Add one teacup of wine vinegar to one pint of syrup, then add the vinegar syrup to the pickles until they are thoroughly covered. Always use granulated sugar.

79　　　Compound Tomato Sauce.

One peck of ripe tomatoes, cut them in slices and put them in a vessel, and add one tea-cupful of salt to them, two ounces fine allspice, one ounce of fine cloves, one tablespoonful of black pepper and one of cayenne pepper, five large silver skin onions cut up fine, and the whole stand twenty-four hours; mix well together when you set to stand, then put it to cook with one quart of vinegar and let it cook all day; stir it occasionally; it must become thick before it is thoroughly cooked, then strain all skin and studs out of it through a sieve; when cool put in a demijohn, as it is will keep better than in bottles when first made.

N. B. If you don't like much pepper use half the quantity, if you like it very hot use double the quantity.

90   Brandy Peaches—No. 2.

Have the cling peach, free from decay. Peel as in preceding recipe. Weigh the peaches after peeling, or measure them in a gallon measure, so as to allow one pound of sugar to one gallon of peaches in making the syrup. Then put the sugar on the fire to make the syrup, adding enough clear water to keep the sugar from burning while melting. Let the syrup boil until it gets as thick as honey. Put your peeled peaches in a stone jar—one that is air-tight. Set the jar, with the peaches in it, in a kettle on the fire and fill the kettle (not the jar) with cold water. Then take one teacupful of syrup to one teacupful of brandy and pour it on the peaches until they are covered thoroughly with the brandy and syrup. Let the water in the kettle around the jar of peaches boil for three hours, and *no* longer. Close the jar up tight, so as to keep the heat in it while boiling. After three hours of actual boiling, lift the kettle with jar in it from the fire, and set aside to cool where a draught of air will not strike it. When thoroughly cool, pack the peaches in glass jars, and fill with brandy and syrup as directed where peaches are boiled. If not enough, use equal proportions of brandy and syrup till the peaches are covered. These brandy peaches are great appetizers, especially for invalids.

Brandy Peaches

Peaches are generally known as cling or freestone varieties. Cling peaches have fruit that is relatively difficult to separate from the pit, or stone. Freestones leave the pit much more easily. Cling peaches are often used in canning, preserving and baking as the flesh may be blemished by separating it from the pit. Once cooked, small blemishes are not noticed.

Make sure the peaches used are of good quality, ripe and are not deteriorating.

Follow Mrs. Fisher here with the following adjustments: for the syrup, put the water into the pot, then add the sugar, start on a slow fire and increase the heat after the sugar is dissolved. Take the peaches and place in a tall, stainless steel pot, such as a stock pot, and place that in a wider pot for the double boiler. Place peaches in the inner pot, measure the syrup and an equal amount of brandy and mix. Pour over the peaches, cover with plastic wrap, then aluminum foil. The plastic wrap will keep the acid of the fruit from contact with the foil. Bring the water to a simmer and cook three hours over a moderate heat, checking the water level. When done, remove the inner pot, fill the jars and top off with brandied syrup and process according to manufacturer's instructions. Alternatively, the brandied peaches could be refrigerated. If refrigerated, allow to come up to room temperature before serving.

For a type of brandy, I would select a good Spanish brandy. Spanish brandies tend to have a sweet vanilla-honey flavor and work well here and with Recipe 101.

Strawberry Jam

97   Strawberry Jam.

Must have fresh berries that are not running. Squeeze the juice from the berries through a clean linen cloth; then add one-half pint of sugar to every pint of juice and put on to boil in a porcelain kettle, and when it boils as thick as honey add the berries that you squeezed the juice from to the syrup and let it continue to boil until it gets as thick as mush, when it will be cooked enough. You can put it up in glasses or jars; put paper on the top wet with brandy, and then cover and put in a dark place. Use granulated sugar.

Note that only good quality, fresh berries are used. This jam is not a way of using fruit that is going bad. By cooking the syrup ahead and adding the berries later on, the fruit retains a superior texture. The syrup, made from the fruit juice and sugar, reduces, which concentrates the flavor of the berries even before the fruit is added.

Follow the manufacturer's instructions for putting by and make sure all utensils are perfectly clean and sterilized. A stainless steel pot is fine, but do not use aluminum — the metal will react with the acid in the juice and fruit. The juice of ½ lemon per pound of raw berries will add a nice touch.

Blackberry Brandy

Note that this recipe was a prize-winning recipe in 1879 at the State Fair and garnered a good deal of press for Mrs. Fisher; it helped establish her as a force in San Francisco's food scene. Follow Mrs. Fisher but make sure the brandy is strained before bottling. It may also be made with the following change of procedure:

Add 1 quart of water to a very large, non-reactive pot and then add the 10 pounds of sugar. Bring slowly to

> 101   Blackberry Brandy.
>
> To five gallons of berries add one gallon of the best brandy; put on fire in a porcelain kettle and let it just come to a boil, then take it off the fire and make a syrup of granulated sugar; ten pounds of sugar to one quart of water. Let the syrup cook till thick as honey, skimming off the foam while boiling; then pour it upon the brandy and berries and let it stand eight weeks; then put in bottle or demijohn. This blackberry brandy took a diploma at the State Fair of 1879. Let the berries, brandy and syrup stand in a stone jar or brandy keg for eight weeks when you take it off the fire.

a boil. Pour the hot syrup over the berries and return to the boil. Remove from the fire and allow to cool to slightly more than room temperature. Add the brandy, stir well and seal. Keep cool and strain after eight weeks.

This is more what we would now call a cordial or liqueur. It is quite sweet with intense fruit flavor balanced by the taste and alcohol of the brandy.

Savory Dishes

Jumberlie — A Creole Dish

Welcome to Mrs. Fisher's version of what is commonly called Jambalaya. There are many variations of this dish. Hers is flavorful and easy to make, just remember to season well and remember it should have a high flavor profile. Do not be shy with black pepper and cayenne. Adding chorizo as well as ham will make it spicier and a little smoky.

> 119   Jumberlie—A Creole Dish.
>
> Take one chicken and cut it up, separating every joint and adding to it one pint of cleanly-washed rice. Take about half a dozen large tomatoes, scalding them well and taking the skins off with a knife. Cut them in small pieces and put them with the chicken in a pot or large porcelain saucepan. Then cut in small pieces two large pieces of sweet ham and add to the rest, seasoning high with pepper and salt. It will cook in twenty-five minutes. Do not put any water on it.

Professional Tip: Make sure tomatoes are fully ripe and the only liquid for cooking the rice is the tomato juice and what moisture comes from the ham and chicken.

A 2½ to 3 pound chicken works well. Separate the wings, legs, thighs, and take out the backbone. Cut the breasts into two parts on each side. Place the chicken in an even layer in a pot, season well and add the ham. Then add the rice, evenly sprinkled over the chicken and ham. Place the cut up tomatoes over the rice, cover and gradually bring to a simmer. Check for doneness by sampling the rice: if it is soft the dish is done. If it seems a little dry, feel free to add some water or chicken to insure complete cooking.

For the recipe test, one cup of chicken broth was added at the beginning of cooking and it worked well.

Eggplant Stuffed

This works best with smaller eggplants. If they are available, use the small yellow ones or the vibrant Japanese eggplants.

Allow one small eggplant per person.

Slice the eggplants in half, carefully scoop out the flesh, cut in medium dice and toss in a bowl with salt and allow to stand in a colander for about 45 minutes. This will draw off most off the potential bitterness of the eggplant and cause less moisture to bleed out during cooking.

Bring some salted water to a boil, plunge the drained eggplant cubes in the water and blanch about 5 minutes. Drain and make the stuffing.

> **142   Egg Plant Stuffed.**
>
> Take out the inside of the plant and boil it in just enough water to cover it for ten minutes, and then drain or press the water all out through a cullender. Chop some ham fine, take bread crumbs and butter (one tablespoonful to one egg plant), and have equal proportions of ham, cracker and bread crumbs to the inside of the plants. Season with salt and black pepper to taste and fry it brown. Then stuff the plants full and close and put them to bake. They will bake in ten minutes, but should not be put in the oven until just before table use. They are a delicious vegetable prepared in this manner. Use a hot oven.

Make a mix of equal parts Panko breadcrumbs, cracker meal and finely diced ham. Allow 2 ounces of stuffing per eggplant per person. Mix one tablespoon melted butter per eggplant in with the dry ingredients, sauté in a skillet and adjust seasoning.

Remove from heat and add to eggplant, mix well and stuff eggplant halves. Bake until hot in a 400° oven 10–15 minutes and serve immediately.

Corned Beef Hash

> **147   Corned Beef Hash.**
>
> Take boiled corned beef and chop it very fine, four hot boiled Irish potatoes to one pound of beef, mash potatoes in the beef while hot, one slice of onion chopped with meat, half a teaspoonful of mustard mixed, two sprigs of parsley; then make into pones like a small loaf of bread, and bake brown. Season with black pepper to taste.

Allow 1 pound of potatoes for each pound of corned beef. Trim off all fat from the beef and either chop fine or grind using a coarse die. Use 2 ounces of sliced onion, finely diced, Dijon mustard and washed, finely-chopped parsley. No need to add salt to corned beef.

For a crisper exterior, brush with oil before placing in a 400° oven until well heated through. Try a grating of fresh black pepper over the pones just before service.

Note that "Irish Potatoes" is a term still in use towards the end of the 19th century. This is due in part to the desire to distinguish varieties of white potatoes from sweet potatoes, but also reflects the strong identification of the tuber and the ethnic Irish, the result of massive emigration from Ireland to America as a result of widespread starvation from the potato famine in Ireland earlier in the century. Ethnic jokes and slurs still circulate about potatoes and the Irish in the 21st century.

Circuit Hash

For this recipe, use Fordhook Lima Beans as they are the same as butter beans. Butter beans are a regional name for lima beans. Baby lima beans are not a substitute as they are a separate variety and do not have the same flavor profile as butter beans.

Follow Mrs. Fisher's recipe with these adjustments:

Peel, seed and coarsely chop the tomatoes before adding to the cooking pot.

Render the pork or melt the butter and add the tomatoes and butter beans. Tomatoes give off lots of juice, but keep an eye on the pot in case you need to add some liquid. Add about 1 tablespoon of salt and 1 teaspoon of ground white pepper when the cooking starts.

> 152   Circuit Hash.
>
> One dozen tomatoes, one quart of butter beans, one dozen ears of corn cut off from cob, quarter pound of lean and fat pork cut in fine pieces, if pork is not liked, use two tablespoonfuls of butter; put on in a sauce-pan and stew one hour.
>
> Note. Five minutes before dinner put in the corn to cook with the rest of stew.

Stew the beans until they are tender. Then add the corn as Mrs. Fisher directs; adjust the seasoning before service. This is a good side dish as well as a good vegetarian entrée.

Miscellaneous

Tonic Bitters

This is a good example of Mrs. Fisher's homemade medicinal remedies. Peruvian Bark was so called because it was first harvested in Peru and because it became a cure for malaria, as it renders out quinine. Gentian Root stimulates gastric juices and saliva, stimulates the appetite and stimulates the taste buds. Aloe is thought to aid in treatment of diabetes and lowering of low-density lipoproteins. Be careful to use the correct aloe as some types are banned by the FDA. This preparation may also be used as an aperitif for otherwise healthy persons, but is more appealing when mixed with sparkling water and a slice or orange.

This can easily be traced to ancient European traditions of making herbal medicinal preparations, usually with a very high alcohol content. These types of tonics are still readily available in Switzerland, Germany and elsewhere in Europe, sold commercially.

Pap for Infant Diet

This is the preparation that Mrs. Fisher said made possible her raising to maturity 11 children. As a cure for diarrhea, the boiled flour has become a modified starch and may bind the bowels, but I am not a medical person. I suspect that a goodly measure of why her children lived to maturity was the quality of food she made for them. And it cannot be overlooked the incredible will this woman possessed. Reading her words, I cannot help but think she was as determined with her children as she was with other aspects of her life, and that her kids benefited from this inner toughness.

> 160   Pap for Infant Diet.
>
> Take one pint of flour, sift it and tie it up in a clean cloth securely tight, so that no water can get into it; and put it in boiling water and let it boil steady for two hours, then take it out of water, and when it gets cold take outside crust from it. Whenever you are ready to nurse or feed the child, grate one tablespoonful of the boiled flour, and stir it into half a pint of boiled milk while the milk is boiling; sweeten the same with white sugar to taste. When the child has diarrhea, boil a two-inch stick of cinnamon in the pap. I have given birth to eleven children and raised them all, and nursed them with this diet. It is a Southern plantation preparation.

This remarkable book and its author give us a glimpse into a time that seems so far removed from our own that it is hard to imagine. That is one reason why Mrs. Fisher and her book are so important to our cuisine and our culture — it allows us to embrace the testimony of this woman who lived in a society so different from ours. Her unimaginable circumstances were overcome by a personality that would not be denied and we are the better for having had this woman in our country so long ago.

Thank you, Mrs. Fisher.

CHAPTER 14

La Cuisine Creole (Lafcadio Hearn)

This is a large book of over 250 pages with a table of contents at the end. Foods are arranged by category and are presented this way here. As in other chapters, some suggestions are made to allow for modern appliances and products but the recipes are true to form.

Tomato Soup With Vegetables, Very Fine

This soup is flavorful and nutritious, just the thing for a nice family meal. Cooking times are reduced to be more in tune with modern tastes. Follow Hearn's quantities to produce a soup for 12 people. Here are some serving options:

> TOMATO SOUP WITH VEGETABLES. VERY FINE
>
> Cut small, three carrots, three heads of celery, four onions and two turnips; put them into a saucepan with a tablespoonful of butter, a slice of ham and a half cup of water; let them simmer gently for an hour; then if a very rich soup is desired add to the vegetables two or three quarts of good soup stock, made by boiling a beef bone in three quarts of water until the meat is tender. Let all boil together for half an hour, and then add ten or twelve ripe tomatoes and a half-dozen whole peppers. It should cook for another hour or so. It must then be strained through a sieve or coarse cloth. Serve with toasted or fried bread cut in bits in the tureen. This is an elegant family soup, particularly nice in summer when the vegetables are fresh.

1. Hearn says to strain the vegetables before service, which produces a flavorful soup without the actual vegetables in it. The nutrients are extracted into the broth.
2. Reduce cooking times as described here and leave the vegetables in the soup for a more filling dish, more like an entrée in and of itself.
3. Remove the well cooked vegetables and carefully puree them in a blender. Return to the soup pot to have a cream of vegetable soup.

Modern quantities: Use a large soup pot or brazier. Melt the butter first, then add the onions and cook until light brown, add the carrots, white turnips and celery and do the same. Cut all vegetables in a medium dice. Add the ham cut in medium dice and brown as well.

When all the vegetables are nicely browned, deglaze with the water and reduce until almost dry. For more flavor, deglaze with a dry sherry or Madeira. Add the beef broth and simmer about 30 minutes. While the soup is simmering, peel and seed the tomatoes and cut in a medium dice. Add the tomatoes about 5 minutes before serving.

For the peppers: If using sweet peppers, cut in a medium dice and sauté with the onions at the beginning of the soup. If using hot peppers, put them in a sachet and remove before service. The sweet peppers with give a more mellow taste; the hot peppers add real bite. Adjust the seasoning and select one of the serving methods above.

Professional Tip: For added flavor, make a sachet with herbs of choice. Herbs that go well with these vegetables are thyme, basil, oregano, tarragon and marjoram.

Oyster Soup

One of the glories of New Orleans cooking is the abundance of fresh seafood. Follow Hearn for this, but for the breadcrumbs:

Take 4 ounces un-sugared French bread, slice thinly and toast medium brown.

Remove the crusts and make the breadcrumbs in a food processor and sift before adding to the soup. Use the milk or light cream and use fresh ground pepper. Taste for salt last as the oyster liquor will be salty if the oysters are fresh and there is salt in the breadcrumbs.

Gombo Filee with Oysters No. 2

Two characteristics of Creole cooking are here: the brown roux and "gombo filee." In modern spelling, gumbo file is the same ingredient as Hearn uses — dried leaves of the sassafras tree made into a powder and used as a spice and a thickener. An ancient cooking ingredient, it was used by Native Americans before Creole cooking. The brown roux can be tricky to make. It is a 50–50 mixture of fat and flour. Keep the heat low and keep

> GOMBO FILEE WITH OYSTERS, NO. 2
>
> Fry a tablespoonful of flour in a tablespoonful of lard. Let it brown slowly so as not to scorch. Boil the liquor of two quarts of oysters, and when it is boiling throw in a cupful of cut leeks or onions, a large slice of ham, some parsley, and stir in the browned flour. Let this cook fifteen minutes; then pour in two quarts of oysters. Let them boil a few minutes, season with salt and pepper; take out the parsley and sift in half a cup of dried and pounded fresh filee; if not fresh more will be required.

an eye on it. It should be a medium brown, about the shade of almost dark toast, and will be extremely hot. In professional kitchens, a hot roux is affectionately known as liquid napalm and will burn through your skin quite nicely. Be very careful when cooking roux of any color.

When brown, allow the roux to cool. Never add a hot roux to a hot liquid and vice-versa. For two quarts of oysters, use 8 ounces of ham, leeks sliced thinly as specified and tie the parsley bunch in a piece of cheese cloth and leave the string hanging over the side of the pot for easy removal later on. Do not overcook the oysters. At a simmer, cook until they start to curl, 3 to 5 minutes at most. Season well and spike it with a little cayenne as well.

Crayfish Bisque. A Creole dish

Crayfish go by several names, are related to lobsters and live primarily in fresh water. Flesh is sweet and they are small, so eating with the fingers is all but required. They turn bright red when cooked and are used extensively in classic French cuisine.

Make the stuffing for the heads:

Follow Hearn and when the crayfish are nice and red, drain off the water and cool the fish. Remove the meat from the tail, weigh it, and place in a bowl the fish and one-third its weight in milk-soaked breadcrumbs. Melt one stick of unsalted butter and add to the bowl, with the leaves of one bunch of fresh thyme finely chopped, ditto two sage leaves, one clove of garlic and one small onion finely diced.

Scrape out the foreign matter in the heads and soak as Hearn directs. If you fry them, just do as written above and keep warm.

In a clean pan:

Melt 4 ounces of butter

CRAYFISH BISQUE. A CREOLE DISH

Parboil the fish, pick out the meat, and mince or pound it in a mortar until very fine; it will require about fifty crayfish. Add to the fish one-third the quantity of bread soaked in milk, and a quarter of a pound of butter, also salt to taste, a bunch of thyme, two leaves of sage, a small piece of garlic and a chopped onion. Mix all well and cook ten minutes, stirring all the time to keep it from growing hard. Clean the heads of the fish, throw them in strong salt and water for a few minutes and then drain them. Fill each one with the above stuffing, flour them, and fry a light brown. Set a clean stewpan over a slow fire, put into it three spoonfuls of lard or butter, a slice of ham or bacon, two onions chopped fine; dredge over it enough flour to absorb the grease, then add a pint and a half of boiling water, or better still, plain beef stock. Season this with

Add 2 ounces of finely diced or cubed ham

2 medium onions finely diced.

Sauté until the onions are soft. Do not let the butter burn.

Make a *compound roux* by sprinkling a quantity of flour over the ingredients equal to the quantity of butter. Stir together well and cook 3 to 4 minutes.

Add:

1½ pints beef broth or stock, cold not hot, dissolve the compound roux, bring to a simmer and add:

Leaves of 1 bunch of thyme finely chopped

2 whole bay leaves

Salt and pepper, and simmer 30 minutes until the starchy feel and taste of the flour is gone.

Reheat the heads, place plain white rice in serving bowls, ladle in 6 ounces of soup and garnish with the crayfish heads in a nice pattern in each bowl. Plan on 12 crayfish per person.

Okra

A NICE WAY TO COOK OKRA OR GOMBO

Take a pint of young tender okra, chop it up fine, add to it half as much skinned, ripe tomatoes, an onion cut up in slices, a tablespoonful of butter, a little salt and pepper, and a spoonful of water; stew all together till tender, and serve with meat or poultry.

Trim the okra before measuring it and plunge it in boiling salted water for about 1 minute. Remove and run the okra under cold water. This reduces the sometimes objectionable sliminess of the vegetable. Peel and seed the tomatoes, collecting any juice as this is done.

Melt the butter, about 2 ounces. Sauté the onion slowly 5 minutes and sprinkle with salt and pepper. Add the okra and tomatoes and do the same. Add very little water as the tomatoes give off plenty but keep an eye on the pot. Adjust the seasoning just before service. Do not overcook.

Tomato Catsup

TOMATO CATSUP. RECIPE FOR MAKING A SMALL QUANTITY

Take a gallon of ripe tomatoes, skin them by pouring boiling water over them; let them get cold and put them in a stew pan with four tablespoonfuls of salt, and the same of ground black pepper, half a spoonful of ground allspice, and three spoonfuls of ground mustard. Throw in eight pods of red pepper, and let all stew slowly until the tomatoes are soft and tender. Thin the mixture with enough vinegar to allow the catsup to be strained through a sieve; cook it fifteen minutes, and bottle up when cold. This will last in any climate, if well boiled and made according to these directions. Keep always in a cool, dark closet or cellar. Light ruins all catsups, pickles or preserves, when they are exposed to it. This is a fine recipe.

This is a simple recipe, but note there is no sweetener added. This is a savory and spicy catsup with a real zing and zip to the taste. Jar according to manufacturer's directions when done or refrigerate for up to two weeks.

Red pepper pods can be the small dried Chinese or Thai pepper pods. Use a food mill to pass the catsup. It gives a better texture than using a food processor.

Boston Brown Bread

In a Creole cookbook? One measure of how these good cooks took what was good from just about anywhere, and put their stamp on it. For the sour milk, substitute yogurt or half yogurt and half sour cream. The texture is a little denser but sour versus spoiled milk is almost impossible to come by. Allow the first rise, punch down the bread, shape and allow a short second proof in the loaf pan for about 45 minutes.

Traditional Boston Bread is steamed, but try baking it in a well greased loaf pan in a 350° oven for about 1 hour. Use instant yeast and one teaspoon of salt mixed with the flours. This bread makes a great breakfast toast, or allow it to stale and use it for French toast, or *Pain Perdu* in Creole.

> BOSTON BROWN BREAD
>
> One and a half pints of Indian meal, half a pint of wheat flour, one cup of sweet milk, one cup of sour milk, with a teaspoonful of soda in it; three tablespoonfuls of molasses, one tablespoonful of yeast, and a pinch of salt. Put it in a warm place to rise, then let it bake steadily for four hours; warm by steaming it when wanted to use.

Italy's Buckwheat Cakes

Buckwheat is Asian in origin and belongs to the family of plants known as dock. Like other grain types of plants, the seeds are starchy and can be made into flour. It is dark and has a vaguely fruity, citrus, tang to it that finds a great flavor balance with honey or maple syrup.

Saleratus is a type of single acting baking powder. Instant yeast is substituted for the brewer's or liquid yeast. Allowing the batter to rise overnight gives added tang to the flavor.

> ITALY'S BUCKWHEAT CAKES
>
> One quart of fresh buckwheat flour, half a cup of yeast, one tablespoonful of salt, one and a half quarts (or a little less) of milk and water warmed. Beat all well with a large spoon, and pour the mixture in a tall jar, as in that it rises better than in a flaring or open crock. In the morning add a teaspoonful of soda or saleratus, just before frying the cakes. Then grease the griddle and fry them brown; eat with syrup or honey.

Follow Hearn but use two teaspoons of instant yeast and put the mix in a *large* glass or other non-reactive container. Cover with plastic wrap and poke several holes in the top. The next morning, stir down the batter and make pancakes as usual.

Want a flavored honey? Heat the honey with some orange juice and grated zest of one or two oranges and let cool and hold overnight for use the next day.

Sour Milk Doughnuts Without Yeast

In modern parlance these are known as cake doughnuts. Stir the eggs and sugar together with a ½ teaspoon of salt. Add the melted shortening and sift the baking soda with the flour and stir into the egg mixture. This will be stiff, start with a small amount of flour and add alternately with about 1 quart of buttermilk. Add the flour first, stir until smooth, then add about 1 cup of buttermilk. When the flour is incorporated and the dough is able to be rolled, stop adding the milk.

Flour a wooden surface well and roll the dough about ¾ of an inch thick. Cut

> SOUR-MILK DOUGHNUTS WITHOUT YEAST
>
> Take a quart of flour, three eggs, three-fourths of a pound of sugar, and half a cup of shortening; add a teaspoonful of soda, and mix to a soft dough with buttermilk. Roll out, cut them, and fry in boiling lard.

into desired shapes. Heat the frying fat to 350°. Fry one side and then turn the doughnuts over with a pair of wooden sticks; chopsticks are fine for this. When golden brown, remove, drain on an icing rack and serve as is, roll in cinnamon sugar or ice with a simple icing.

Genoise Cakes

This is a Creole version of classic French petits fours, although made in one rather than three layers. Cream the butter and sugar, add the eggs one at a time, add the flour, sifted twice. Add 4 ounces of brandy or Madeira

> **GENOESE CAKES**
>
> Half a pound of butter, half a pound of sugar, four eggs, half a pound of flour, a small glass of brandy or wine. Bake in a square sheet; ice it and cut into diamonds; ornament with dots or stripes of any kind of bright jelly or preserves.

wine just before baking. For a finer texture, separate the eggs, whip the egg whites separately and fold in after the flour is incorporated and bake immediately. For a less dense cake, add 2 teaspoons of baking powder when sifting the flour. Bake at 400° and remove from the oven when barely light gold in color.

German Lady Fingers

Use blanched almonds processed to a flour consistency in a food processor. With the almonds, less flour is needed than with a regular cake. Start with ½ cup sifted and add only until the batter is stiff enough to roll. Write down how much is used for future reference, but remember the amount

> **GERMAN LADIES FINGERS**
>
> Beat the yolks of five eggs with half a pound of sugar. Add half a pound of blanched almonds, cut fine or pounded. Grate the rind of a lemon, mix well, and add gradually enough sifted flour to make into a dough. Roll out and cut in strips the length and size of the forefinger; wet them with the beaten white of two eggs, and bake.

may change from time to time. Use large eggs and fresh lemon zest. Do not use extract. Beat the egg whites well before brushing on the lady fingers. For a little added color, lightly sift some powdered sugar on the lady fingers after brushing with the egg white.

Cream Cakes

This is a traditional French pâte à choux, cabbage paste, aka éclair paste. These little pastries can be piped with a pastry bag as well as dropped using a plain or a star tip. The paste is also used for éclairs and is versatile as an hors d'oeuvre as well. Pâte à choux is also good for use as a fritter batter—simply season to taste and mix in crab, shrimp or conch and deep fry. It is one of the most versatile, hence valuable, techniques in classic French cooking.

To bake, preheat the oven to 400°. When the puffs have risen and are golden brown, turn off the oven, prop the door open with something, and allow the pastries to dry out in the oven. This will assure the batter is cooked all the way through and will not collapse when removed from the oven. Fill with custard, whipped cream or cut in half, add a scoop of ice cream and cover with chocolate sauce for a "profiterole."

> **CREAM CAKES**
>
> Boil a cup of butter with a half pint of water; while it is boiling, stir in two cups of sifted flour; let it cool, and when cool, add five eggs well beaten, and a quarter of a spoonful of soda dry. Drop this mixture with a teaspoon on tins and bake in a quick oven.

Sicilian Biscuits Dropped On Tins

This is the Creole version of the Italian biscotti. If using a stand mixer, heat the sugar and eggs in a bowl in a double boiler, but not over 120°, and do not let the eggs scramble on the bottom of the bowl. Whip until cool on the mixer, fold in the flour and vanilla. Drop as Hearn suggests or use a pastry bag. This basic mix can be flavored any way under the sun — with chopped or ground nuts, rosewater, cocoa instead of 20 percent of the flour; the variations are endless.

> SICILIAN BISCUIT DROPPED ON TINS
>
> Take four eggs, twelve ounces of powdered and sifted sugar, and ten ounces of flour. Beat the eggs and sugar together in a stewpan on the fire, until the batter feels warm to the touch; remove it from the fire, and stir it thoroughly until it becomes cold; now add the flour, and flavor with vanilla. Butter some paper and place it on the baking tins, or pans. Drop the cake mixture in round or ovals on the buttered paper, and bake in a slow oven. When put in the oven sift white sugar over the biscuit.

Peaches and Cream Frozen

Be sure the peaches are ripe and blemish free. Place in a large bowl and sprinkle with about 2 ounces of sugar. Set aside. For best results use light cream, which can be difficult to find. A mixture of 1 pint milk and one pint 40 percent cream works best. Place the sugar and ¾ of the cream on the stove and bring to a simmer. Whisk the yolks and remaining cream in a bowl. When the cream comes to a boil, slowly pour over the yolks, stirring constantly. When the bowl is a bit more than warm to the touch return the mixture to the stove and cook until it thickens and coats the back of spoon. Strain into a clean bowl and chill as rapidly as possible. A water bath of half ice and half water is best. Stir every couple of minutes. The best texture is achieved by refrigerating the custard overnight and making the ice cream the next day. Follow the manufacturer's instructions. Add the peach pieces just before removing the ice cream from the machine.

> PEACHES AND CREAM FROZEN
>
> Peel and stone a quart of nice yellow peaches; put them in a bowl, sweeten them well, and chop very fine. If you have sweet cream, put to the fruit a quart of it; if you have not, take a quart of milk, sweeten it with half a pound of sugar, let it boil, and when boiling, pour it on to the beaten yolks of four eggs. When this custard cools, you may add the chopped peaches, which should be well sweetened. Pour all in the freezer and set it where it can be frozen.

A Richer Molasses Pie

This very simple pie is a variant of shoo-fly pie. Sugar was a big crop in Hearn's day and molasses is the by-product of sugar refining. For the piecrust use a regular pie dough made with all butter.

> A RICHER MOLASSES PIE
>
> One cup of molasses, one cup of sugar, four eggs, and four tablespoonfuls of butter. Mix together the sugar, butter and eggs, then stir in the molasses. Bake in a rich crust.

My Own Pudding

Right from the horse's mouth! This is a pudding much like a pastry cream. The amount of cornstarch will make a stiff pudding. A ½ cup is a more reasonable amount for modern tastes. Add a pinch of salt to the cornstarch in the mixing bowl. Add vanilla or other flavoring as desired. Bake about 20 minutes at 350°. Cool for 30 minutes, make the meringue and brown under a broiler or in a hot oven.

MY OWN PUDDING

Let a quart of milk be set on to boil; while it is getting hot, mix a cup of maizena or corn starch with enough cold water to form it into a thick batter; add to this a cup of white sugar and the yolks of four eggs; take the milk off and stir eggs, maizena, and sugar, into the milk; beat all together a few minutes, then pour the mixture into a baking dish and bake it lightly about ten minutes, or long enough only to cook the eggs; then take the pudding out, and while hot put over it a layer of jelly or jam; beat up the whites of the eggs with a cup of sugar, put this over the jelly and brown.

PEACHES AND APRICOTS IN BRANDY

Take nice smooth peaches not too ripe, put them in a vessel and cover them with weak lye; take them out in two hours, and wipe carefully to get off the down and outside skin, and lay them in cold water. Weigh the fruit, add their weight in sugar, and half a pint of water to each pound of sugar; boil and skim this syrup, put in the peaches; when the syrup is clear of scum, let them boil for twenty minutes or half an hour, then take them out and lay them on dishes to cool. Boil the syrup for an hour longer, or until reduced one-half and quite thick. When cold, put the peaches or apricots in jars, and cover them with equal quantities of the syrup and French brandy. If it is apricots, cook them very gently, or they will come to pieces in the syrup; ten minutes is long enough to stew them before bottling.

SYLLABUB

Take the juice of a large lemon, and the yellow rind pared thin; one glass of brandy, two glasses of white wine, and a quarter of a pound of powdered sugar. Put these ingredients into a pan, and let them remain one night; the next day add a pint of thick cream, and the whites of two eggs beaten together; beat them all together to a fine froth, and serve in jelly glasses.

LOUISIANA ORANGE FLOWER MACAROONS

Take a coffee cup of the freshly gathered petals of the orange, cut them with a pair of scissors into two pounds of dry, sifted white sugar; this keeps their color fresh. Beat the whites of seven eggs to a stiff froth, and add to the orange flowers and sugar. Drop this mixture on white paper in small cakes, and bake in a slow oven; do not let them brown.

Peaches and Apricots In Brandy

This is a good way to preserve fruit for non-seasonal use. It is similar to a German Rhum-Topf and versions of this recipe were made throughout New England from earliest colonial times. Rather than using lye, bring a pot of water to a rolling boil. Add the peaches a few at a time for 30 seconds, remove with a strainer and place in ice water. The skins will slip off when cool. Do not peel apricots. They fall apart easily. If there is not enough brandied syrup for all the fruit, simply make more using the same ratios as in the recipe. Seal according to manufacturer's directions.

Syllabub

This is a beverage that was found throughout colonial America and is awfully tasty. Try some for a party. It works as a dessert or as a punch, and can be any flavor.

Louisiana Orange Flower Macaroons

These are really meringues and are best made by heating an oven to 200°, putting the meringues in the oven for about 1 hour. Lift one up to see if it is dry underneath. If not, bake until it is. Be patient.

Grand Brule à la Boulanger

Hearn saw fit to include a number of New Orleans drinks in his book. This Grand Brule not only displays New Orleans top to bottom, but also highlights the penchant Hearn had for the macabre and the supernatural. His power of evocation of a mood and a setting is displayed to a masterly degree here and this power suffuses much of his writing. From Inuit folk tales to New Orleans drinks to Japanese painting, Hearn had an ability to delve into the emotion and meaning behind the underlying aspects of a culture. This penetrating ability is evident when he writes of words, paintings, folk music or food.

The laughter he describes after a silence can be either of merriment or of relief from a situation too other-worldly, however brief, to face without laughter.

Gin Fizz

This classic is still made the same; the egg white is for the foam.

Parlor Punch (Moran's)

A "little lemon juice" can be a ½ ounce, but use more if more tartness is preferred. A wine glass is three ounces. Use a tall glass or large modern wine glass.

A Note about Moran's — there is a Moran's now in New Orleans. The building was originally an import house for Spanish products, became a coffee house, was where Jean Lafitte met with Andrew Jackson (Lafitte's ghost is said to live there), was and is known as the Old Absinthe House, and is now a popular restaurant in the same location on Bourbon Street. A direct quote from their web site, www.ruebourbon.com: "The Absinthe Room where mixologist Cayetano Ferrer created the famous **Absinthe House Frappe** here in 1874" is now a

---

GRAND BRULE A LA BOULANGER

(*From a Gourmet.*)

The crowning of a grand dinner is a brule. It is the *piece de resistance*, the grandest *pousse cafe* of all. After the coffee has been served, the lights are turned down or extinguished, brule is brought in and placed in the centre of the table upon a pedestal surrounded by flowers. A match is lighted, and after allowing the sulphur to burn entirely off is applied to the brandy, and as it burns it sheds its weird light upon the faces of the company, making them appear like ghouls in striking contrast to the gay surroundings. The still-ness that follows gives an opportunity for thoughts that break out in ripples of laughter which pave the way for the exhilaration that ensues.

Pour into a large silver bowl two wineglasses of best French brandy, one half wineglass of kirsh, the same of maraschino, and a small quantity of cinnamon and allspice. Put in about ten cubes of white sugar; do not crush them, but let them become saturated with the liquor. Remove the lumps of sugar, place in a ladle and cover with brandy. Ignite it as before directed, then lift it with the contents from the bowl, but do not mix. After it has burned about fifteen minutes serve in wine glasses. The above is for five persons, and should the company be larger add in proportion. Green tea and champagne are sometimes added.

GIN FIZ—NO. 1

One-half tablespoonful of sugar, a little lemon juice, two wineglassfuls of seltzwater, one wineglassful "Tom", or Holland gin, teaspoonful of white of an egg, and ice; shake well and strain into fancy glass.

PARLOR PUNCH (MORAN'S)

One tablespoonful of white sugar, a little lemon juice, two wineglassfuls of English black tea, one wine-glassful of whiskey, one-half wineglassful of Jamaica rum, a little raspberry syrup, plenty of small ice. Shake well, and strain in fancy glass.

---

restored bar and restaurant with original fixture and a tradition of people signing dollar bills and taping them to the ceiling for when they return.

How to Mix Absinthe in Every Style

Absinthe, known as "la Fee Verte," the Green Fairy, is a legendary part of the 19th-century artistic community. Picasso, Poe, Van Gogh, Baudelaire — all were champions of this mostly misunderstood, high proof spirit. Thought to have been distilled late in the 18th century in Switzerland, it captivated people around the world by the end of the next century. It is usually distilled and bottled at 136 to 146 proof, more than 68 percent alcohol by volume. It is in a long tradition of medicinal herbal remedies, distilled to

HOW TO MIX ABSINTHE IN EVERY STYLE

Plain absinthe; half a sherry glass of absinthe; plenty of fine ice, with about two wineglassfuls of water. Put in the water, drop by drop, on top of absinthe and ice; stir well, but slowly. It takes time to make it good.

concentrate healing effects of chemical compounds found in many plants. What sets absinthe apart is the inclusion of wormwood, *Artemesia absinthium,* which tastes like anise but has a bitter aftertaste. While wormwood is a poison taken in large quantities, its percentage in absinthe formulas is so small as to make poisoning a drinker impossible. And at 136 proof, it is no wonder that so many people "had visions" under its influence. The tradition in serving absinthe was to place a cube of sugar on a perforated silver palette knife and pour the liquor over the sugar cube, lessening the bitter aftertaste. Cold water is added to dilute the spirit, which in a process called "louche," turns the liquid a milky white. The liquid typically has a slight green or yellow-green tint and its opacity is a result of flavoring oils dispersing rather than dissolving in the water.

For many years there was public hysteria about absinthe based on urban legend types of stories of it creating madness. By the early 19th century it was banned in most countries but is now distilled once again, using wormwood as one of its ingredients.

Bouille-Abaisse

This is a version of the traditional southern French seafood dish. The directions following Hearn's recipe are a bit more precise, but the result is similar.

BOUILLE-ABAISSE

Chop some onions and garlic very fine, fry them in olive oil, and when slightly colored add some fish cut up in slices; also a few tomatoes scalded, peeled and sliced, some salt, black and red pepper, thyme, sweet-bay, parsley, and half a bottle of white wine, and enough water to cover the fish. Put it over a brisk fire and boil a quarter of an hour. Put slices of toasted bread in a deep dish, place the fish on a shallow dish with some broth, and pour the balance on the bread and serve hot.

Olive oil, 4 ounces
1 medium onion, finely diced
4 peeled and seeded tomatoes cut into large dice
Salt, pepper and cayenne to taste
1 bunch fresh thyme, leaves finely chopped
1 fresh laurel leaf, known as bay leaf when dried, finely chopped
2 sprigs of flat leaf parsley
1 pint of a dry, high acid white wine
Toast for 4 soup bowls

Heat the oil, add the onions and cook over low heat until translucent.

Add the tomatoes, some salt and pepper and cayenne, stir and cook until the tomatoes start giving off some juice.

Add the herbs and stir again, deglaze with the white wine.

Lay the fish pieces on top of the vegetables and herbs. Use at least three varieties with different colored skin (and a couple of shellfish if you like).

Season the stew again to taste with salt, pepper and cayenne. Add the water to cover, bring to a simmer and reduce heat. Cook about 15 minutes or until fish is done but no white albumen is showing on the flesh of the fish.

Serve as Hearn directs. Multiple seasonings give greater depth of flavor and make each particular ingredient retain its individual flavor profile.

Hearn displayed the influences on Creole cooking from around the world in this book. His love affair with the city, its culture, languages and people seeps from the pages of his writing — whether reading the cookbook or any of his literary works on the city. He wrote about Creole traditions, Creole food, and created some of the first studies anywhere on comparative linguistics using Creole dialects for his work.

As the first Creole cookbook it made the cuisine known to the world beyond Louisiana and the results are with us today. The authenticity and genuine understanding of his writing speak across the centuries to take us with him to experience firsthand the mysteries of this great city and its unique Creole culture.

CHAPTER 15

The Epicurean (Charles Ranhofer)

Starting on page 169, Chef Ranhofer gives us *"elementary methods"* — essential skills such as how to make almond milk, borders for platters made from metal to gum paste, brine, liquid caramel, how to carve fish, partridge, roast beef ribs, tenderloin of beef and legs of ham and mutton. The reader can learn how to carve a turkey, coat aspic molds, make dozens of different dessert items, make forcemeats and stuffings — the list goes on.

Further on (page 224) begins a section on professional kitchen equipment, most of which has not changed all that much since Chef Ranhofer's time. Probably the biggest change is the method of heating for a range, which is now mostly gas or electric. In Chef Ranhofer's kitchen, gas was something new — many kitchens used wood or coal for the stoves. But many restaurants still have grills fired by wood or charcoal. On page 224 is a device our first author would recognize: an English Roaster, wherein a bird or roast is hung perpendicular to the fire. In Chef Ranhofer's "modern" version, there is an automatic device for turning the meat.

Where recipes refer to many other items a professional kitchen would have on hand in Chef Ranhofer's day, some adjustments have been made to accommodate our more modern methods of cooking.

But how to select some representative items from the book? This incredible book has around 3,500 different items. Selections were made to demonstrate how the fusion of classic French training, paired with some American ingredients and some surprisingly modern touches, made Chef Ranhofer's kitchen the palace of culinary excellence it was. Reading through this book is to experience a world of flavor and elegance unfolding in front of the reader. It is truly a "time machine" that whisks the reader to an elegant and opulent age where, at least in the case of Chef Ranhofer and the Delmonico family, cost was no object in the pursuit of excellence.

Soups

The numbers in brackets after the soup name are the number of portions for the recipe. For smaller batches simply divide by the proper divisor.

Lobster Bisque à la Portland (24)

Note that all bisques are made with a type of shellfish or crustacean. Thickened with wet crusts means using trimmed bread, softened and then pureed with the soup.

246

(196). BISQUES (Bisques).

An exquisite and delicious bisque. The ancient bisques made between the years 1700 and 1750, differed greatly from our modern bisques. They were more like stews than soups or potages and were prepared with squabs, quails, pullets and fish, the crawfish only serving as a garnish, and were basted over with a crawfish gravy. Bisques as they are made to-day, are simply a puree, thickened with rice, or thick stock, or wet crusts and accompanied by various garnishings. Bisques are divided into five classes: First, those made of clams, oysters or mussels; Second, crabs; Third, shrimps, Fourth, crawfish; Fifth, lobsters. They must be highly seasoned, although not containing much red pepper, rather clear than thick, slightly colored, and accompanied by small, simple garnishings.

(208). BISQUE OP LOBSTER A LA PORTLAND (Bisque de Bernard a la Portland),
Cut twelve pounds of lobster lengthwise in two, break the claws, sprinkle over some butter, and cook them on a baking-sheet in a hot oven for twenty-five minutes. Remove them, and suppress the largest shells, pound the meat with its equal quantity of plain boiled rice, seasoned with salt, pepper, and curry, and when all is well reduced to a paste, dilute it with broth; strain through a sieve and then a tammy, and warm up the soup without boiling; thicken it with twelve hard boiled egg-yolks pounded with four ounces of butter, and mix in also a pint of double cream, and serve as garnishing some mushrooms cut into fine Julienne and lobster quenelles. Put the soup into a tureen.
Lobster Quenelles. Cut one pound of cooked lobster meat in thin slices, add the coral and two ounces of butter; pound well and when reduced to a paste, take it from the mortar. Pound three quarters of a pound of panada, add gradually to it half a pound of butter, then the lobster paste, three eggs, one after the other, salt, pepper, nutmeg, and two tablespoons of Allemande sauce, test and rectify if necessary (No. 60). Roll this forcemeat to use for lobster quenelles, or else fill some sheeps' casings with it to make lobster boudins

Twelve pounds of lobster, 6 2-pound lobsters, split lengthwise, cracked claws
3 pounds of unsalted butter
Place the lobsters on a sheet pan or in a roasting pan, dot with butter and roast at 375°
    15 to 20 minutes, or until fully cooked but not tough and rubbery.
When done, allow to cool, strain in a colander, reserving the juice, remove the meat for
    the puree.
3 pounds soft cooked, plain white rice, 1½ pounds raw
Salt and fresh ground pepper to taste
2 tablespoons of medium hot curry powder
Puree and mix these ingredients together then strain though a fine mesh sieve or chinois.
Add to the puree:
2 quarts of lobster stock.
Mix together:
12 hard cooked egg yolks
4 ounces unsalted butter.
Slowly stir this into the reheated soup base being careful not to let it boil.
Add:
1 pint of hot 40 percent heavy cream and stir well.
Adjust seasoning.
For the quenelles (a modern adaption):

4 1-pound lobsters, boiled and cooled, meat removed, coral reserved
2 ounces of sweet butter
Puree the lobster, coral and butter and force through a fine mesh sieve.
4 ounces 40 percent cream
4 egg whites
Put the lobster/coral/butter mix in a bowl in another bowl of ice.
Stir in the four egg whites.
Whip the cream to very soft peaks, and gently fold into the base.
Season well, roll in plastic wrap as for a jellyroll, poach in 170° water.
Quenelles may also be made by using two spoons for oval shapes or any shape desired,
    and they would then be poached in highly seasoned *court bouillon* or a mix of half white
    wine and half lobster stock.

Chicken Okra Soup (24)

This is a good example of how a Frenchman uses classical training to make an American
soup with an African vegetable!

Chicken breast, 2 pounds cut into ½" squares
Dry cure ham, 8 ounces, cut into ¼" squares
Onions, 8 ounces cut into ⅛" squares
Peeled and seeded tomatoes, 2 pounds
Rice, 4 ounces, raw, cooked soft in salted water with 1 tsp of butter
Okra, 1 pound trimmed, cut into ¼" thick, crosswise
Green peppers, 4 ounces ¼" dice
Melt the butter in a large pot, sauté the onions until soft but not brown.
Add the ham, stir together and cook about 2 minutes.
Add the chicken, stir and reduce heat to low.
Add the liquid, 2 quarts veal stock, 1 of chicken stock and 1 of beef broth to the vegetables
    and chicken.
Bring to a simmer and skim off all fat.
After skimming, simmer 20 minutes, add the okra and peppers and simmer until tender.
Add the pressed tomatoes and return to a simmer for about 3 minutes.

(299). CHICKEN OKRA SOUP (Gombo de Volaille).

Prepare two pounds of the breast of chicken cut into half inch squares, half a pound of salted raw ham cut in quarter inch squares, half a pound of onions cut in eighth inch squares and two pounds or eight fine tomatoes plunged into boiling water to remove their skins; then cut in four, and slightly pressed to extract the seeds; four ounces of rice, picked, washed and cooked in salted water with half an ounce of butter, one pound of okras cut crosswise in pieces a quarter or three eighths of an inch, according to their size, four ounces of finely cut up green peppers, four quarts of broth and four ounces of butter. Put the butter into the saucepan on the fire, and when it is very hot, throw in the onions to fry colorless, add the ham and let all fry together ; then add the chicken meat; fry again slowly while stirring, till the butter is entirely clarified; then moisten with chicken broth made from the bones of the chicken, and four pounds of leg of veal, adding some beef stock. Remove all the fat from the soup, and boil for twenty minutes; put in the okras and green peppers, then continue cooking until the gumbo or okras are entirely done; add the tomatoes, boil a few minutes longer and season with salt, Worcestershire sauce and mushroom catsup. Place the rice in a soup tureen, and pour the soup over. This soup is frequently strained and served in consomme cups.

Adjust seasoning as per Chef Ranhofer.

Put some rice into each bowl or a tureen and ladle the soup over the rice.

This soup is chicken gumbo that went to college. The complex flavors of the three stocks with the Worcestershire sauce add a great depth of flavor.

Oyster Soup with Powdered Okra or Gumbo (Gumbo File) (10)

Follow Chef Ranhofer, but remember to shuck the oysters and reserve their juice first. Cook the onion and add oysters as directed with their liquor. Add the water or fish stock quickly and bring to a boil. Do not overcook the oysters.

Put the file powder in a bowl and slowly shake into the soup, stirring all the while with a whisk. Figure on 1 ounce of dry rice per person and 6 oysters.

The molded rice makes a nice presentation served on a side dish or platter. If serving the soup in bowls, feel free to put the rice in the bowl first.

---

(336), OYSTER SOUP WITH POWDERED OKRA OR GUMBO (Soupe aux Huitres en Gombo en poudre).

Mince a two ounce onion finely, fry it in two ounces of butter without letting it attain a color, then add sixty medium oysters with their juice, and the same quantity of water, season with salt and red pepper, then place the saucepan on a quick fire and remove at the first boil; skim and thicken with two spoonfuls of powdered gumbo for each quart of soup. Have some rice boiled in salted water; when done, mix in with it a little butter and set it in a buttered mold, place it in a hot oven for ten minutes and serve this separately, but at the same time as the soup, after unmolding it.

Sauces and Garnishes

Chef Ranhofer's sauces start with the preparation of what he calls broths or bouillons. These are the equivalents of what we mostly call stocks now and they serve as the basis for all manner of sauces, glazes and soups. When making a basic preparation of any kind, whether stock, broth, pastry dough or filling, remember that if the foundation ingredient is not of the best quality, the end product will always be compromised.

Chicken Essence

This is a basic item that concentrates flavors to a remarkable degree. When added to a sauce or soup the flavor profile is extraordinary. In a modern application, if used as a reduction sauce base, it will be exquisite.

Unsalted butter, 2 ounces
Veal trimmings, 1 pound, cut small

---

(387). CHICKEN ESSENCE (Essence de Volaille).

Fry one pound of sliced kernel of veal and a pound and a half of broken chicken bones in some butter without coloring them, adding two minced shallots, half a pound of minced carrots, and four ounces of onions. Moisten with one quart of white chicken bouillon (No. 188) and reduce to glaze; moisten again and reduce once more, then add a bunch of parsley garnished with two bay leaves and as much thyme, four cloves and half a bottleful of white wine; boil, skim, and cook slowly for half an hour, then strain through a napkin or silk sieve.

Chopped chicken bones, 8 ounces
Shallots, minced, 2 each
Carrots, fine dice, 8 ounces
Onions, fine dice, 4 ounces
Chicken bouillon, 1 quart (1)
Chicken bouillon, 1 quart (2)
Parsley, 1 bunch
Bay leaves, 2
Fresh thyme, 1 bunch
Cloves, whole, four
Dry white wine, 1 pint.

Melt the butter, sauté the veal and chicken but do not brown. Add the shallots, carrots, and onion and cook until the onions are wilted but have no color. Add bouillon 1, bring to a simmer and reduce to about 8 ounces. Add bouillon 2 and reduce to 1 cup then add the remaining ingredients in a sachet along with the white wine. Finish cooking and strain, chill quickly and refrigerate or freeze.

The addition of the veal to chicken-based liquid delivers layers of flavor not normally found in such a preparation. The proportions of the added vegetables are also interesting in that so much carrot is added in relation to the onion. The cloves add a spice and a degree of robust flavor to the final product.

Béchamel Sauce

This is the classic mother sauce of French cuisine from which many other sauces are derived. Most references say to use a roux, milk and an onion studded with a bay leaf and a couple of cloves. Chef Ranhofer lightened this basic sauce and added more complex flavors through the addition of additional *mirepoix*, parsley and mushroom peelings.

---

(409), BECHAMEL SAUCE (Sauce Bechamel.)

This is made by preparing a roux of butter and flour, and letting it cook for a few minutes while stirring, not allowing it to color in the slightest; remove it to a slower fire and leave it to continue cooking for a quarter of an hour, then dilute it gradually with half boiled milk, and half veal blond (No. 423). Stir the liquid on the fire until it boils, then mingle in with it a mirepoix of roots and onions (No. 419), fried separately in butter, some mushroom peelings and a bunch of parsley; set it on a slower fire and let cook for twenty-five minutes without ceasing to stir so as to avoid its adhering to the bottom; it must be rather more consistent than light. Strain it through a fine sieve then through a tammy into a vessel, and allow it to cool off while continuing to stir; set it aside for further use.

Clarified butter, 4 ounces
Bread flour, 4 ounces
Milk, 2 quarts
White veal stock, 2 quarts
Mirepoix:
Carrots, cut into ¼" squares, 4 ounces
Onions, cut into ¼" squares, 2 ounces
Turnips, white, cut into ¼" squares, 1 ounce
(These can be cooked in butter while the roux is cooking.)

Sachet:
Parsley and thyme, 1 bunch each
Bay leaf, 1
Basil, ¼ of a small bunch
Garlic, 1 clove
Cloves, whole, 2 each
Mace, blade, 1 each

Follow Chef's directions for the roux, being careful not to brown it. Use cold milk and stock when stirring into the roux, adding a little at a time to avoid lumps. When all the liquid is added, add the sachet and return to a simmer, stirring all the while. Let it simmer 30 to 45 minutes on a medium fire being careful not to scorch the sauce. Check for seasoning before straining. Strain the sauce as directed and cool rapidly.

This is a lighter version of a classic Béchamel, which is usually made with all milk. Not only does the white veal stock lighten the texture of the sauce, it adds additional flavor not traditionally found in this preparation.

Following the section on sauces is one on what are called compound butters, where various flavoring elements are mixed in with softened butter. This category includes such items as various herb butters, shrimp butter, lobster butter, maître d'hotel butter and so on. Cold sauces follow the butters with familiar items such as applesauce, cranberry sauce, mint sauce and so on. There are ten different mayonnaise and mayonnaise-based sauces with variations, five rémoulade sauces, two tartar sauces and the following.

Tomato Catsup

A familiar condiment from the earliest days of American cuisine has its day in the world's most elegant restaurant. Follow Chef Ranhofer here, for the capsicum pepper a regular green pepper is indicated as the heat follows later. Have the tomatoes peeled and seeded. A food mill makes a better, more interesting product than does a blender or a food processor.

(633). TOMATO CATSUP (Catsup de Tomates).

Boil one quart of vinegar in a saucepan, adding a quarter of an ounce of capsicum peppers, one ounce of garlic, half an ounce of shallot, all nicely peeled, and half an ounce of white ground pepper, also a coffeespoonful of red pepper, and let boil for ten minutes, then strain through a fine sieve. Mix in with this vinegar, one and a half pounds of tomatoes, reduce all together and then add the juice of three lemons, and salt to taste. Should this sauce be too thick, add more vinegar or some water; fill up the bottles, let stand till cold, then put them in a very cool place to use when needed. This sauce is excellent as a relish for cold meats fish, oysters, etc.

Aquitaine Garnish

Elegant food in this time period was replete with all manner of garnishes for each dish served. Oftentimes the garnishes could define the dish itself with the food items on the menu followed by the name of the garnish. For example, a menu might read: *Breast of Pheasant, Grilled, à la Aquitaine.* The garnish itself is as follows, and would be served with or over the main item.

There are more than 125 different garnishes in this section, each with its own ingredients

---

(640). AQUITAINE GARNISHING (Garniture à l'Aquitaine).

Have a pound of escaloped duck livers sautéd in butter; half a pound of small button mush-rooms cooked with butter, lemon juice, salt and water; a quarter of a pound of small whole truffles, cooked in Madeira wine; half a pound of pressed beef palate cut cock's-comb shape, warmed in meat glaze (No. 401) and butter. Infuse a stick of Ceylon cinnamon for ten minutes in a gill of Madeira wine; strain this through a napkin into a quart of reduced espagnole sauce (No. 414). Dress the garnishing in clusters, pour over half the sauce and serve the remainder in a separate sauce-boat. This garnishing can be used for entrées; if this be the case, mix the ingredients composing it together in a sautoire with the sauce, and dress them.

---

and preparation method, some requiring inclusion of items not part of the garnish section at all. These added items might be wines, sauces, glazes, and so on. There are also variations for many of the specified items, which raises the count measurably. All of the intricate work was part and parcel of the type of service and food offered by Chef Ranhofer and the restaurant.

Side Dishes

For the first time in an American haute cuisine cookbook, avocados make their appearance. Chef Ranhofer had known of the fruit for some time but had not been able to find a reliable supply for the New York market. What was a rare piece of culinary exotica has become an everyday staple all across America.

---

(771). ALLIGATOR PEARS (Avocats).

Originally from South America. Select the fruit when very ripe, peel off the outer green skin, and cut the pear in slices, range them on a side dish, season with salt, pepper and vinegar, and garnish around with slices of lemon cut in halves.

From pages 357 to 400 is a section, containing the avocados from above, called *Side Dishes*. (For cold side dishes go to page 367, and from there on are presented a bewildering variety of hot side dishes.) Here are found all manner of canapés, side dishes ranging from gherkins to lobster and beet salad, aka "Lobster à la Boulognaise" [*sic*]. Item 809 is of particular interest, as this the familiar lobster or shrimp rolls, a local specialty in New York and New England. Chef Ranhofer extends the category to include crawfish, sole, chicken and foies-gras. He even instructs the chef: "These rolls must not be split on the side, but make an opening on the top, reserving the cover. Empty them of their crumb, and fill the entire insides with either lobster, crawfish, shrimp, or pressed cold fried soles, cutting them in 3/16" squares...."

There are recipes for such American staples as marinated green beans, all types of sandwiches, pickled walnut as well as several varieties of marinated and pickled fish, beef tongue, truffles, tuna, turbot, sweetbreads, cannelloni, cock's comb, chicken livers, croquettes and numerous other items. The "little dishes," or "flying dishes" as they were sometimes known, received the same amount of care and diligence of preparation as entrées did. No detail was too small to be important. Apparently, the name "flying dishes" refers to the fact that, according to Chef Ranhofer, these items were not on the menu, but were passed butler-style between the early courses of the dinner.

The following example shows Chef Ranhofer's penchant for exactitude and absolute dedication to the highest standards of perfection.

---

(895). CROUSTADES À LA CASTILLANE (Croustades à la Castillane).

Fig. 221.

Prepare a very thick chestnut purée as already described in the garnishings (No. 712), with it fill some six-sided molds previously cooled in ice-water and drained before filling, when perfectly cool dip them into very hot water to unmold. Bread-crumb them in cracker dust, beaten eggs and bread-crumbs, smooth the surfaces, and mark an incision with a pastry cutter three-quarters of an inch in diameter; fry them to a fine color, remove the cover and empty out the insides to refill with beef tenderloin cut in quarter inch dice pieces and sautéd in butter with some mushrooms cut exactly the same, and a brown and Marsala wine sauce (No. 492). Instead of replacing the lid, cover the aperture with a small round celery croquette three-quarters of an inch across, that has been made with braised celery cut in small squares and mixed with velouté sauce (No. 415), and when cold bread-crumbed and fried.

Flavors and textures abound in this small dish, which relies upon three separate preparations ands specific cutting instructions and well as breading techniques. This would have been one of several canapés or side dishes as part of a 12 or 14-course dinner.

A bit later on is a large section on timbales, items not so often seen in modern kitchens. They were prepared in molds lined with aspic. Decorations were attached to the sides and bottoms of the molds and usually given another coat of aspic to protect them. When set, the molds were then filled with a mixture, or several mixtures and sealed. These are involved items requiring a large mise en place, many pieces of often custom-made equipment and highly skilled professionals to execute their preparation.

---

(976). MOSAIC TIMBALES (Timbales Mosaïque).

Fig. 231.

The timbale molds (No. 2, Fig. 137) are to be entirely decorated with small lozenges of tongue, truffle and hard boiled egg-whites, to represent a mosaic ground work. Begin by placing a ring of truffle at the bottom of the mold, inside of this a smaller ring of egg-whites, and in the center to fit in a half inch round of beef tongue; this fills the entire bottom. Decorate the sides with alternate lozenges to form squares or boxes, having all the red on one side, the black on the other, and the white on top of each square; the upper and lower row should be divided in two lengthwise; by following these directions they will form perfect mosaic squares, taking care that the points are directed outward; support this decoration with a snipe quenelle forcemeat (No. 91); set in the center a ball made of royal cream (No. 241), and finish filling the molds; poach and serve them as for No. 959. Serve a white Colbert sauce (No. 451) separately.

(977). NEAPOLITAN TIMBALES (Timbales Napolitaine).

The salpicon is composed of tongue, truffles and mushrooms, cut in three-sixteenth of an inch squares and combined with espagnole sauce (No. 414), meat glaze (No. 402) and tomato sauce (No. 549); let cool, cut some macaroni into pieces a sixteenth of an inch long, fill the empty places in each macaroni half of them with a round piece of truffle to fit it exactly, and the other half with beef tongue instead of truffles. Butter the timbale molds (No. 2, Fig. 137), lay a round piece of truffle on the bottom, and around it set the bits of macaroni, one row filled with tongue, and over this, one filled with truffles; one laid symmetrically above the other until the mold is filled. Garnish the bottom and sides with chicken quenelle forcemeat (No. 89), and a half inch ball of the salpicon in the center, fill up with more forcemeat and finish them exactly the same as for No. 959. Serve a separate sauce-boat of Neapolitan sauce (No. 507).

Fig. 232.

After the molds had set up or jelled, they would be dipped in hot water and unmolded onto plates or platters for buffet presentation. They could also serve as light courses for luncheons or dinners but were not substantial enough for more than that.

The variety of fillings and decorations were enormous and a chef would only be limited by a standard preparation that would need a pre-ordained name, but could otherwise invent new items for a specific clientele in a restaurant or for a party.

The two shown here are good representations of this all-but-lost art that was commonplace in haute cuisine restaurants in the Victorian age.

Mollusks and Crustaceans

This is probably the largest and most diverse group of animals on the planet — their ancestors go all the way to Cambrian times. The University of California Museum of Paleontology on their web site state that there are somewhere between 50,000 and 200,000 species distributed around the globe with habitats ranging from high mountain ranges to deep sea trenches. Sizes range from smaller than one millimeter (so small they live between grains of sand) to larger than 20 meters for the giant squid.

Included in this group are some species commonly used for food throughout history: scallops, clams, mussels, snails, squids and octopuses.

Chef Ranhofer devotes recipes 994 to 1061 to mollusks, with a further section on terrapins, turtles, and servable yield for them. Mollusks appear in many different incarnations including fritters, pancakes, stuffed, à la Newberg, boiled, fried, broiled — just about any way possible — with a nod to some classic European dishes (ravigote) and American specialty (soft-shell crab). Included in this group are land snails, frog's legs and, of course, lobster.

Here makes the appearance of one of the world's most famous lobster dishes, Lobster Newberg, first created by Chef Ranhofer. It was originally Lobster Wenberg, named after a rollicking sea captain who apparently got into fisticuffs one night in the restaurant and was ejected forever. Two letters changed place and a standard of world cuisine came to be known by its current name.

Lobster Newberg

Follow Chef's directions here, they are simple and straightforward. The simplicity of this dish demands the best and freshest lobster, flavorful cream and a good quality Madeira. Season well and serve piping hot in a tureen or on individual plates with a rice timbale. One caveat: Bring the lobster water to a rolling boil before committing the crustaceans to

---

(1037). **LOBSTER À LA NEWBERG OR DELMONICO** (Homard à la Newberg ou à la Delmonico).

Cook six lobsters each weighing about two pounds in boiling salted water for twenty-five minutes. Twelve pounds of live lobster when cooked yields from two to two and a half pounds of meat and three to four ounces of lobster coral. When cold detach the bodies from the tails and cut the latter into slices, put them into a sautoir, each piece lying flat and add hot clarified butter; season with salt and fry lightly on both sides without coloring; moisten to their height with good raw cream; reduce quickly to half and then add two or three spoonfuls of Madeira wine; boil the liquid once more only, then remove and thicken with a thickening of egg-yolks and raw cream (No. 175). Cook without boiling, incorporating a little cayenne and butter; warm it up again without boiling, tossing the lobster lightly, then arrange the pieces in a vegetable dish and pour the sauce over.

their final swim. Then cook the lobsters only about seven to eight minutes to prevent them from getting rubbery. Make sure clarified butter is used and be careful not to boil the sauce after the egg yolks are added.

This, obviously, is THE recipe.

Fish

Bass figures heavily here with 15 recipes: six for bluefish, even two for buffalo fish, a freshwater fish resembling carp. The once common cod gets 13 entries, including cod tongues, poached cod head, salted cod and cod fish balls. Just about all the major fish are represented in over 42 pages of recipes containing 218 different recipes.

There is even a recipe for lamprey, which is not a fish and is not accepted by Americans as a food source, although it is still popular in Spain and Portugal.

The recipe here is for kingfish, a coastal fish found off the East Coast. Depending on the species, ranges run from New York to Brazil and Argentina. They live mostly on shrimp and crabs and are quite tasty. Here is Chef Ranhofer preparing a fish in red wine, making it sound quite modern.

Kingfish à la Batelière

For this, if kingfish is not available, try using a one-pound haddock. This is not a king fish as in king mackerel. The flavor is not the same but it makes a satisfactory substitute. Chef Ranhofer cooks the fish, bone in and arranges on a platter. Trim the fish and cut in half crosswise. A one-pound fish will give about seven to eight ounces of meat; so one fish is good for two people. Use a dry red wine that is not too fruity, think red Burgundy or light pinot noir. Keep the spices in a sachet, bring to an almost simmer at 180°. Do not overcook.

If a filet is desired on the plate, simply lift the fish from the pan and keep warm. Strain the sauce and return to the fire. Remember a gill is 4 ounces or a ½ cup. Use pearl onions,

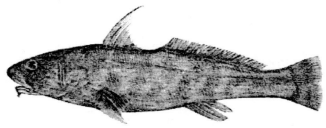

(1179). KINGFISH À LA BATELIÈRE (Kingfish à la Batelière).

Cut a half pound kingfish crosswise into two pieces; range them in a low saucepan moistening with red wine; season with salt, pepper, cloves, garlic, mushroom parings, and add one gill of

FIG. 393.

brandy, pouring it slowly over the other ingredients, set it on the fire and throw in some small onions fried and previously blanched; leave them in for ten minutes on a hot fire. Dress the fish and garnish the intersections with the small onions, strain the sauce through a tammy, add to it butter, and pour it over all; surround with heart-shaped croûtons of bread fried in butter and crawfish.

Some kingfish weigh as much as three pounds.

blanched, peeled and cooked in butter without browning for about two minutes before being added to the cooking vessel. Reduce the sauce by about ½, and swirl in ¼ pound softened unsalted butter with the heat turned off. Whisk until the butter is incorporated and the sauce has a beautiful shine.

This is a dish that would be at home in any upscale restaurant today.

Beef

As might be expected in America, beef played a major role in Chef Ranhofer's kitchen. Recipes 1313 through 1478 are devoted to beef in one incarnation or another, requiring 36 pages of text. Recipes are here with quite a variety of flavors — chipolata, bone marrow on toast (or served in the bone on a linen napkin), oxtails boiled, fried and braised, beef tongue in a variety of ways, ribs, buttocks and rumps from Bourgeoise to Flemish to Greek style, all manner of sirloin of beef, including one garnished with brain patties to one served with chicory and sweet potato soufflé.

Items that may not be expected include Salisbury Steak, albeit made with beef tenderloin; Beef Steak Hamburg Style, the precursor of the ubiquitous all–American hamburger, again made with either the tenderloin or sirloin and seasoned with kidney suet (or marrow), sautéed onion, salt, pepper and nutmeg. The Tartare version is served raw, a "flattened ball" with an indentation for a raw egg or yolk.

As might be expected there are many recipes that have classical names referring to garnish or famous persons, such as Rump à la Caréme, which pays homage to the great historical chef.

As a key to the apparently large amounts of food consumed by our ancestors, a "small beefsteak" is portioned at 12 ounces after being completely trimmed. A "regular" size steak is 20 ounces.

Chef Ranhofer created another staple of American cuisine with the following recipe. It remains one of the most popular and delicious steaks in the modern chef's repertoire.

Delmonico Sirloin Steak of Twenty Ounces Plain

Although he worked in New York most of his life, Chef Ranhofer also worked in other cities and was aware of a variety of regional cuisines, as this recipe shows. It is also instructive to note that his inclusion of the uniquely American Creole cuisine helped to make it known beyond the borders of New Orleans, much as Hearn's book did. Remember, Hearn's book was first published in New York.

It also implies that Chef Ranhofer put regional American food on a more or less equal footing with the regional cuisines of his homeland — quite a recognition coming from a professional of his stature.

(1375). DELMONICO SIRLOIN STEAK OF TWENTY OUNCES, PLAIN (Bifteck de Contrefilet Delmonico de Vingt Onces, Nature).

Cut from a sirloin slices two inches in thickness; beat them to flatten them to an inch and a half thick, trim nicely; they should now weigh twenty ounces each; salt them on both sides, baste them over with oil or melted butter, and broil them on a moderate fire for fourteen minutes if desired very rare; eighteen to be done properly, and twenty-two to be well done. Set them on a hot dish with a little clear gravy (No. 404) or maitre d'hôtel butter (No. 581).

Minced Tenderloin, Creole Style

It is a simple recipe, but note the care of presentation. The tomatoes and peppers are cooked separately as each has different requirements, and are later combined in the sauce to serve with the meat. Season highly: salt to taste, but add a fair amount of black and cayenne pepper (and maybe a touch of file powder to thicken the sauce).

(1397). **MINCED TENDERLOIN, CREOLE STYLE**, (Émincé de Filet de Bœuf à la Créole).

Cut six ounces of tenderloin of beef lengthwise, shape the slices into escalops an inch and a half in diameter, by an eighth of an inch in thickness. Sauté them in butter, when ready take the meat out and keep it warm between two dishes, adding beef stock (No. 194a) with part of its fat, some halved tomatoes peeled, pressed and fried in butter, also some green peppers sliced fine and fried in butter. Season highly, arrange the minced meat in a border of rice boiled in salted water to which half an ounce of butter has been added, and serve.

Veal

After 15 separate recipes for brains and breast, items rarely found on menus anymore, veal cutlets have their day with 11 recipes. But these are more like what we now call veal chops, and in Delmonico's kitchens the chops were larded, a technique no longer in use. But we do have the option of making some stuffed calves' ears, making sure they are very small and clean.

There are a number of dishes prepared with items rarely seen: head, feet, kidneys and liver. The following several pages contain many recipes for sweetbreads, tongue and even gristle of veal.

Mutton and Lamb

These are separate sections of the book and occupy 36 pages and an impressive 385 recipes and variations. Many of the cuts are the same for each animal and there are many traditional recipes included. Of interest are lamb fries, epigrams of lamb, from the breast, and, in a method now reserved almost exclusively for fish and seafood in modern times, Chef Ranhofer gives us lamb cutlets, chops, cooked in paper (papillote).

Pork

A scant 11 pages are devoted to pork but they include bacon, black pudding, breast, chitterlings, cutlets, feet, ham, Virginia ham, sausages, suckling pig, tenderloin and tongue.

Poultry

As might be expected, this section is large, encompassing 51 pages with 224 recipes. But they do not all taste like chicken as this category includes capon, chicken, duck, one recipe for bustard (a large ground-dwelling bird common to savannah-type grasslands in Europe and the Russian steppes), goose, gosling, guinea fowl, pigeons, pullets, a hen less than one year old, squab, wild turkey (as distinguished from domestic turkey), and spring turkey.

Many of these recipes are similar as to name and preparation and share cooking methods. There are plenty of artful, highly decorated items for elegant buffets and elaborate dining room service.

It should be remembered that the American fondness for pigeon led to the extinction of the passenger pigeon in little more than a century. In an issue of *Chambers's Journal* John James Audubon remarked in 1833 that he had seen a flock of pigeons where "the air was literally filled with pigeons; the light of noonday was obscured as by an eclipse; the dung fell in spots, not unlike melting flakes of snow; and the continued buzz of wings had a tendency to lull my senses to repose." Sadly, restaurants such as Delmonico's were largely responsible for this tragic extinction. Their population was estimated by Audubon to be around three to five billion when America was first settled. Audubon made his observation in 1833 and by 1901 the birds were extinct.

Pigeons with Green Peas

As the pigeons are long gone, squab works well for this, as does quail and even pousin or game hen.

(1969). PIGEONS WITH GREEN PEAS (Pigeons aux Petits Pois).

Truss six pigeons as for an entree (No. 178), returning the livers to their original place. Melt some chopped fat pork in a saucepan, add to it a quarter of a pound of small five-eighths inch squares of bacon and fry for a few moments, then remove them with a skimmer. Put the pigeons into this saucepan with five or six small onions for each bird, brown slightly and slowly, then add one and a half quarts of green peas, a bunch of parsley and the bacon. Two minutes later moisten with two gills of stock (No. 194a), boil for five minutes and withdraw the saucepan to a slower fire, push into the oven, and finish cooking the peas and pigeons, then drain out the birds, untruss and dress them on a dish; thicken the peas with kneaded butter (No. 579), and place them around the pigeons.

Clean and dry the birds (6) and truss and return the livers to the cavities.
Lard, 4 ounces
Bacon, cut into ⅝" squares, 4 ounces
Pearl onions, blanched and peeled, 30 each
Fresh green peas, 3 pints (if using frozen peas, leave them out until just before service)
Beef stock or broth, 1 cup
Beurre manie

Follow Chef Ranhofer all the way through. When adding the onions slowly rotate the pans so they brown evenly and develop their sugars. Ties the parsley sprig and leave the string attached so it can be removed after cooking. If finishing in the oven, preheat it to 375°; if finishing on the stovetop reduce to barely simmering.

Cook until the peas are tender, remove the birds, reduce the sauce by ⅓ and thicken to taste with *beurre manie*. If using frozen peas, add them when the birds are removed just to heat through.

Game

Chef Ranhofer's mastery extended to game dishes as well. There are countless references to the abundance of quantity and variety of game in the early United States. There were all kinds of ducks and waterfowl, bison as far east as Pennsylvania, wild boar, cousins of escaped domestic pigs brought by colonists from Europe from Florida to New England, antelope, hares and rabbits as well as all manner of game birds.

Thirty-six pages contain 1620 recipes, from "Bear Steaks Broiled" to "Woodcock Stuffed." He presents eight different varieties of duck — blackhead, brant, canvasback, mallard, redhead, ruddy and teal. Grouse, hare, larks and partridges are here with partridges taking up several pages of recipes. Plovers, quails, rabbit (as opposed to hare), snipes, thrushes, antelope and deer venison, roebuck and woodcock round out the offerings.

What appears fairly frequently is an item called a saddle, which goes from the shoulders to the end of the loin. This is a large piece and is suited for tableside service as it should be carved in the dining room; or decorated and served cold on a buffet, in which case it would be sliced, and put back together for the guest.

Venison Cutlets à la Financière

To modernize this recipe, do the following:

Rather than larding the chop (cutlet), place a strip of bacon over each chop. Heat the clarified butter in a pan, put the chops in and finish in a 400° oven.

The Financière garnish is quite involved for large pieces, but somewhat more manageable for entrées.

(2172). VENISON CUTLETS À LA FINANCIÈRE (Côtelettes de Chevreuil à la Financière).

Prepare some venison cutlets the same size as those of mutton (No. 1590); lard them on one side only, but all on the same side, with the handles on the right; put them into a buttered sautoir with the larded side uppermost and cook them in a hot oven; finally drain off the butter from the sautoir, glaze the cutlets with a brush, trim them with paper frills (No. 10) and dress in a circle on a low venison quenelle forcemeat border; fill the center with a financiere garnishing (No. 667).

For every four chops:
Mince ½ ounce of black truffles
1 ounce of button mushroom tops already peeled and cooked
Peeled and cooked sweetbreads, ¼" thick and cut with a 1" round cutter
Foie gras ¼" thick also cut in a 1" round and
1" long quenelles of venison. Warm these garnishes in Sauce Financière and arrange around the venison on a heated dinner plate.
To make the sauce:
For every 4 chops, sauté 1 ounce of ham in butter.
Add 2 ounces of mushroom peelings
½ ounce truffle peelings
one bay leaf
½ sprig fresh thyme
4 ounces of dry Madeira
and reduce by half over a slow fire.
Add:

8 ounces of white veal stock and

8 ounces of Espagnole Sauce. Reduce by ½, degrease and strain through a fine mesh sieve or chinois.

This is a simplified version that recreates the flavors with a minimum of work. Items can be prepped in advance, but it is still a challenging dish, even for seasoned professionals.

For the next 29 pages, there are numerous recipes for:

- Assorted types of hash including staples such as beef and corned beef hash, chicken hash, partridge hash, pheasant hash and even lamb hash with fried bananas.
- There are items called *pains,* which may best be described as a type of open sandwich-cum-entrée with assorted forcemeats, quenelles and sauces.
- Patties, potpies, potted dishes, quenelles, filled tart shells, savory soufflés, savory tarts, timbales and vol-au-vents, which are puff pastry shells with a variety of fillings.

Chef Ranhofer included plates of many of these items, which show some impossibly intricate décor for individual as well as larger items. The Victorian penchant for elaborate presentation and show is everywhere.

Cold Service

Cold Service describes aspics, platter presentations, items in pastry and pastry shells, chaudfroids (items glazed with a hot sauce that solidifies when cool, used to coat an item for further decoration). Elaborate, highly stylized items that would be part of a formal dinner buffet, these preparations demonstrate the art of garde manger to a very high level.

Following is an example of one dish that shows the intricacy of preparation and display — this would have been but one item on a larger, even more elaborate buffet setting. Items glazed in aspic, or jelly, are still found occasionally on modern buffets but have generally fallen from favor. They also take a monumental amount of time, and this selection, Terrine of Foie-Gras in Aspic — Whole, illustrates the final presentation and describes the many steps required for the assemblage of such an ornate item.

Terrine of Foie-Gras in Aspic — Whole

Vegetables from artichokes to turnips, an extraordinary amount of egg dishes and a smaller section on farinaceous products leads into the "Sweet Entrements." Remembering that Chef Ranhofer received his initial training in pastry, it is no surprise that there are 94 pages of desserts, including cakes, pies, tarts, assorted fruit items and small cakes. This section is separate from the "Bakery" entries that cover another six pages.

Frozen Desserts

"Ices (Glaces)" contains the frozen desserts presented at Delmonico's, and some sound as if they could have been concocted in a modern patisserie. Recipe 3450 is for an ice cream made with a choice of three infusions: cinnamon, ginger or pumpernickel rye bread. His American or Philadelphia style of ice cream is here referred to as "Ice Cream Without Cooking." Flavoring is done by macerating flavorings such as vanilla or lemon. With variations

(2413). TERRINE OF FOIES-GRAS IN ASPIC—WHOLE (Terrine Entière de Foies-Gras en Aspic).

Unmold a terrine of foies-gras: scrape it neatly with a knife on top and sides to remove all the exterior grease, and keep it on ice. Procure a mold of the same shape but an inch wider in diameter and an inch deeper; incrust it in pounded ice; decorate the bottom and sides with fanciful cuts of truffles, tongue, egg-white, and pistachios, dipping each piece into half-set jelly before fastening

Fig. 417.

them on; cover this decoration with a layer of jelly, and pour in more to lay half an inch thick in the bottom. Place the foies-gras exactly in the center and finish filling the mold with cooled-off jelly; keep on ice. Put a rice foundation bottom one inch and a half in height on a plated metal tray with a half-inch high straight edge (the rice foundation should be one inch and a half less in diameter than the tray), turn the aspic out of its mold on to the rice foundation, fastening a small basket on top secured by a skewer, and filling it with small glazed truffles. Decorate around the rice foundation with triangular jelly croûtons, as shown in the drawing.

such as orange flower water and light chocolate, Chef Ranhofer sounds positively futuristic. Certainly two of the most adventurous follow.

Rice Ice Cream with Citron, Garnished with Truffles

(3457). RICE ICE CREAM WITH CITRON, GARNISHED WITH TRUFFLES Crème de Riz et au Cédrat, Garnie de Truffes).

Place eight egg-whites in a tinned basin with twelve ounces of sugar and four tablespoonfuls of rice flour; stir well together, adding a quart of boiling milk; cook without boiling on a slow fire, remove and when cold put in a pint of cream; pass through a sieve, freeze and then add half a pound of very finely shredded citron peel and half a pint of blanched rice cooked in syrup. Have it molded in a low Madeleine mold, and garnish around with imitation truffles prepared as follows:

Truffle Ice Cream.—This cream can only be made with fresh truffles. Brush over half a pound of fresh, fragrant truffles; peel, slice and infuse in a pint of boiling cream for thirty minutes. Drop twelve egg-yolks in a tinned basin with ten ounces of sugar; mix well together and then add one quart of cream, including that in which the truffles are being infused; cook the preparation without boiling, and add the truffles after pounding and passing them through a sieve. Freeze and mold in molds imitating whole truffles coated with chocolate; pack in ice. Chop up the truffle peelings very finely, mixing in a few vanilla seeds; dry in the open air, pass through a sieve and roll the unmolded imitation truffles in this powder. Use these truffles to decorate the above ice cream.

White Coffee Ice Cream

Once again, the following recipe sounds more modern than old-fashioned. The trick with this is to roast the beans until they are a little less that cinnamon colored — think very pale beige. The roasting should be enough to barely bring the flavoring compounds to the surface of the bean without adding noticeable color. Note that there are two versions of this ice cream, one with yolks and one with whites.

There are numerous punches, ices, puddings and elaborate presentations for each, depending upon its name. Punches are types of frozen desserts in which ice cream, sometimes sorbets, and additional flavoring ingredients as well as meringue may be added and then refrozen in a particular mold. See the following.

(3460). WHITE COFFEE ICE CREAM (Crème au Café Blanc).

Roast very slowly, either in a roaster or in a frying pan, half a pound of good coffee beans, not having them too dark. Boil a pint of milk and pour it over the roasted coffee laid in a saucepan, cover tightly and keep it on the side of the range for half an hour. Put twenty egg-yolks in a saucepan or a tinned copper basin with twelve ounces of powdered sugar and a quarter of a vanilla stick; beat well together and dilute with three pints of milk and the infused coffee; stir this cream on a slow fire to thicken without boiling, and as soon as the preparation has attained the correct consistency transfer it to a well tinned metal vessel and stir occasionally while cooling; strain it twice, the last time through an exceedingly fine sieve. Try a small part in a freezer packed in ice to discover its consistency, and if too thin add some thirty-two degree syrup, and raw cream if too thick. Freeze by working it until firm and smooth.

Virgin Coffee Cream is prepared with egg-whites instead of yolks, exactly the same way, the proportions being, half a pound of coffee, one quart of milk, sixteen egg-whites instead of the yolks, ten ounces of sugar, a quart of cream and a quarter of a vanilla stick.

(3513). NENUPHAR PUNCH—LILIES (Punch Nénuphar).

Place in a vessel the peel of one lemon, the peel of half an orange, half an ounce of coriander seeds and a small piece of Ceylon cinnamon, also four drops of extract of citron; set it in a heater or expose to the sun for four hours in a hermetically closed earthen vessel; afterward pass it through a filter and add a quart of syrup at thirty-two degrees. Mix the whole well and bring the composition to sixteen degrees, coloring to a light pink; strain through a very fine sieve and freeze. When the ice begins to congeal pour in three gills of kirsch and maraschino and half its volume of Italian meringue (No. 140). Use this ice for filling some gum paste Nenuphar lilies and serve at once.

Nenuphar Punch — Lilies

Gum paste is a mixture of powdered sugar and gum tragacanth and is used primarily for flower decorations for fancy cakes and display pieces. Here, each person gets the punch served in individual lilies.

Chef Ranhofer also includes recipes on how to make large display pieces for dessert buffets in the shapes of swans, Roman helmets, rabbits, pineapples and so on. Iced drinks also are included as are confectionary items. Included here are even templates for making large sugar or chocolate pieces with which to decorate a buffet or dessert table.

CHAPTER 16

The Hotel St. Francis
Cook Book (Victor Hirtzler)

Most of Victor's recipes give quantities and methods, and in the instances where something needs filling in, additional instructions are given.

January 3, Luncheon

Chicken salad, Victor. Cut the breast of a boiled soup hen or boiled chicken in half-inch squares, add one-half cup of string beans cut in pieces one inch long, a cup of boiled rice, one peeled tomato cut in small squares and one sliced truffle. Season with salt, fresh-ground black pepper, a little chives, chervil, parsley, one spoonful of tarragon vinegar and two spoonsful of best olive oil. Mix well and serve on lettuce leaves.

For four servings use two breasts of a roasting chicken or fowl, if available. Poach at 170°, blanche and shock haricot verts until bright green and tender/crisp. Be sure to seed the tomato and slice the truffle thinly. If truffles are not available, use tops from button mushrooms poached in white wine and for the salad oil use substitute one spoonful of olive oil with truffle oil.

January 9, Dinner

Bisque of California oysters. Put one pint of California oysters, with their juice, in a pot and bring to the boiling point. Then skim, and add one pint of cream sauce, one-half pint of milk, a bouquet garni, and boil for ten minutes. Remove the bouquet garni, strain the broth through a fine sieve and return to the pot. Heat a pint of cream and strain into the soup, add three ounces of sweet butter, and season to taste.

Serves 6 to 8.

This shows a melding of classical technique with a California ingredient. Bisques are shellfish soups enriched with cream. They do not have the main ingredient, i.e. lobster, crab, oyster, in the soup itself. Rather, it is a concentration of the flavor of the main ingredient.

Make a basic Béchamel Sauce without an onion pique:

Melt 2 ounces of butter

Add 2 ounces of flour and cook for a few minutes with no color.

Add 1 pint of whole milk, stirring to avoid lumps.

Simmer gently about 30 minutes. Strain and cool rapidly.

This is a neutral, basic cream sauce that is added to the oysters and their liquid above.
For the bouquet garni: Tie in a piece of cheesecloth — one 1" piece of celery, one 1" piece of white of leek, one small bunch of parsley stems, one small bay leaf, two whole cloves, a small sprig of thyme, and one clove of garlic (optional). Leave a string attached so it can be easily removed.

Follow as above and after straining and adding cream, adjust the seasoning, adding just a pinch of cayenne with the salt and white pepper.

Whisk in the unsalted butter with the heat turned off and do not re-boil.

February 4, Dinner

> **Broiled Alaska black cod.** This Alaskan fish is brought from the north frozen, and is very fine, being rich and fat. Broiling is the best way of preparing it, as it needs a quick fire to cook the oil in the fish. Season well, and serve with maitre d'hotel sauce made with plenty of lemon juice.

Procure 4 six-ounce filets of Alaskan black cod. Brush with oil and sprinkle with salt and pepper. Broil in an overhead broiler or on a charcoal grill. Do not overcook. Sauce or maître d'hotel butter: Soften ¼ pound sweet butter, add the juice of 1 lemon and 1 tablespoon of finely chopped parsley, salt and white pepper. Roll in wax paper and chill well. Slice in ½ ounce pieces and place on top of grilled fish. For a liquid sauce, melt the butter and serve at room temperature so the butter stays melted and coats the fish.

March 23, Supper

> **Eggs Pocahontas.** Fry six strips of bacon, and two dozen California, or one dozen Blue Point, oysters. Scramble ten eggs and mix with the above. Season well.

Serves 6.

For a light supper, serve this with a green salad and sourdough bread toast.

April 20, Luncheon

> **Candied sweet potatoes.** Boil four sweet potatoes, remove the skins, and cut in egg shapes. Put in sauté pan with two ounces of butter, and roast slowly. When nearly brown add a spoonful of powdered sugar and continue roasting till sugar and potatoes are brown.

Serves 8 as a side dish.

The vegetable cut here is a classic tourné. Do this before cooking the sweet potatoes — it is much easier and they are less likely to crumble. From the earliest days of a young country to the showpiece of the West, this shows an acceptance and refinement of a truly American food item.

May 3, Luncheon

> **Suprême of oysters, St. Francis.** For about eight people. Use twenty California oysters or seven Eastern oysters for each person. Serve like an oyster cocktail in grapefruit suprême glasses in the following sauce: Mix one cup of tomato ketchup, a short cup of cream, one teaspoonful of Worcestershire sauce, one teaspoonful of lemon juice, season with salt, a dash of tobasco, and paprika. The cream should be added last. Keep the sauce on ice until needed.

Follow the recipe as given and note that California and the St. Francis descriptors appear together. They may also be served on the half shell. The sauce, minus the cream, can be made a day ahead for better flavor.

June 7, Dinner

> **Boiled Tahoe trout, sauce mousseline.** Put two Tahoe trout in a vessel in cold water, add one-half glassful of white wine vinegar, half of an onion and half of a carrot sliced, a bouquet garni, and a small handful of salt. Bring to a boil, and set on side of the range for twenty minutes. Serve on a platter on a napkin, garnished with small round boiled potatoes, lemons cut in two, and parsley in branches. Serve sauce mousseline separate. The potatoes may be served separate if desired.

A small handful of salt should be about 1 to 2 tablespoons. Choose a shallow pan and bring the liquid to a simmer at 170° and then add the fish, making sure they are completely covered. Do not overcook. Sauce Mousseline is equal parts Hollandaise Sauce and whipped cream, with the cream gently folded into the Hollandaise. If it is put under a broiler to lightly brown, it becomes Glaçage Royale.

On this day's menu are to be found: Baked Beans, Boston style; Brown bread; Soft clam soup Salem; Vol au vent Tolouse; Stuffed Capon Antoine; Peas à la Française.

July 7, Dinner

> **Potage Honolulu.** Put on the fire a soup hen, in three quarts of water; season with a tablespoonful of salt, and bring to a boil. Then add one bouquet garni, three onions, three green peppers, and three-quarters of a pound of rice. When the hen is boiled soft remove it, with the bouquet garni and the peppers. Strain the rice, onions and broth through a fine sieve, and put back in the casserole. Bring to a boil, and bind with the yolks of two eggs mixed with a cup of cream. Season well with salt and Cayenne pepper, and add three canned red peppers cut in small squares, before serving.

Start with 1 quart of stock and this will serve 8 guests.
To make this a bit easier, use a pre-made chicken stock or broth and simmer with the ingredients specified. Tie the peppers into the sachet for easy removal. Puree the soup in a blender or food processor. Return to the fire and bring to a boil for a couple of minutes. Lower the heat or turn it off. Mix the yolks and cream, temper, and return

to the pot. Season the soup according to directions. Drain and pat the canned red peppers dry and cut in ¼" dice.

July 20, Dinner

> **Crab Gumbo.** Put two ounces of butter, one chopped onion and one chopped green pepper in a casserole and simmer until done. Then add two quarts of fish broth and one-half cup of rice, and boil very slowly for fifteen minutes. Then add three peeled tomatoes cut in small dices, one spoonful of Worcestershire sauce, the meat of two whole crabs, and a can of okra; or one pound of fresh okra cut in pieces one inch long. Cook slowly for twenty minutes, season well with salt and pepper, and sprinkle with a little chopped parsley.

Cut the onions and peppers in ¼" dice, the same as for the tomatoes. Use fresh okra, blanched for about 10 minutes in boiling slated water. This will serve 10 to 12 guests. Season well.

August 2, Dinner

> **Pumpkin pie.** Make a custard with five eggs, two ounces of sugar, one pint of pumpkin pulp, one pony of molasses, three ounces of melted butter, one pinch of grated nutmeg, one pinch of cinnamon and one pinch of allspice. Mix to a custard, and finish like a custard pie.

To round out the custard, stir in 6 ounces heavy cream and bake as usual, making sure the crust is pre–baked until a light golden color is reached.

From Amelia Simmons to Victor Hirtzler, Native American food for the early colonists to the dining elite in 20th-century San Francisco. Quite a journey.

September 5, Dinner

> **New beets, Californienne.** Put in a sauté pan two ounces of butter, three cloves, one teaspoonful of tarragon vinegar, one-half teaspoonful of sugar, and some fresh-cooked and peeled, small beets. Simmer for a few minutes.

Pre–boil the beets with the skin on, peel, cool and cut in ¼" dice. Use whole butter but do not let it get too dark.

September 7, Dinner

> **Sand dabs, Gaillard.** Season four sand dabs with salt and pepper, put
>
> in a buttered pan, lay four raw oysters on top of each fish, add one-half glass of white wine, cover with buttered paper, and cook in oven for ten minutes. Then remove the paper and pour one pint of cream sauce over the fish. Sprinkle with two chopped hard-boiled eggs, put a few bits of butter on top, and bake in oven until brown.

Serves 4 as an entrée, 8 as a first course.

For best results use the smaller California oysters. Season the fillets well and make sure the skin is removed before cooking. This works well in individual casseroles.

October 9, Luncheon

> **Cranberry water ice.** Cook the berries in a very small quantity of water in a granite or porcelain lined kettle, as otherwise the berries will become discolored. Then strain the cooked berries through a hair-sieve, making a thin purée. To every quart of berries add the juice of two lemons. For each quart of berries dissolve a pint of sugar in a cup of water, and add to the purée. Taste to see if sweet enough. Freeze in the same manner as other water ices. Serve as an ice, for dessert, or between courses; although the latter manner of serving ices is going out of vogue.

Use a stainless steel pot and freeze according to manufacturer's directions. This is a wonderful warm weather dessert.

Remember Amelia Simmons and her "Cramberry" sauce?

November 4, Dinner

> **Celery Victor. (Salad).** Wash six stalks of large celery. Make a stock with one soup hen or chicken bones, and five pounds of veal bones, in the usual manner, with carrots, onions, bay leaves, parsley, salt and whole pepper. Place celery in vessel and strain broth over same, and boil until soft. Allow to cool in the broth. When cold press the broth out of the celery gently with the hands, and place on plate. Season with salt, fresh-ground black pepper, chervil, and one-quarter white wine tarragon vinegar to three-quarters of olive oil.

Make a stock of half chicken and half beef or veal broth, which can be purchased. These items or their ingredients are always available in a high quality professional kitchen. Follow the recipe and make sure the chervil is fresh and that a best quality tarragon vinegar is used with best quality oil. This is a simple salad and needs great ingredients to shine.

December 14, Dinner

> **Louisiana gumbo filé.** Two chickens, one quart of large oysters, one quart of cooked shrimps, six bell peppers, four large onions, one quart of tomatoes, one-half pound of butter, two bunches of celery, one small bunch of parsley, one-quarter teaspoonful of tobasco sauce, and black pepper and salt to suit.
>
> First.—Cut the chicken the same way as for fricassée, and wipe dry.
>
> Second.—Cut onions and brown in butter, and strain.
>
> Third.—Fry chicken brown in strained butter, then set to one side.
>
> Fourth.—Add two tablespoonsful of flour to strained-butter and brown gradually. When a rich brown add two quarts of boiling water, then add the tomatoes. Now bring to boiling point and strain through a fine strainer.

Fifth.—Place strained liquor in a large stew pan and add one teaspoonful of salt and a half teaspoonful of black pepper, then add the chicken. Should the liquor not sufficiently cover the chicken add more hot water to about two inches above. Then add the bell peppers and celery without cutting up. Boil over slow fire until chicken can be picked off the bones with fork. Then remove chicken and strip meat from bones and cut in small pieces, remove the celery and bell peppers, and replace chicken. Add the shrimps, oysters and tobasco sauce. Boil for ten minutes. Then gradually add sufficient "filé powder" to bring to a rich creamy consistency. Add to each plate two large tablespoonsful of boiled rice. Serve immediately.

Boiled rice. Wash one-half pound of rice and soak in cold water for an hour. Cook over hot fire in four quarts of boiling water for fifteen minutes, or until the grains can be mashed between the fingers. Strain through a colander.

Do this step-by-step and have all ingredients ready ahead of time. Clean and peel the shrimp and when opening the oysters, save the juice, strain it and add to the pot. Do not cook the gumbo too long after the oysters are added.

Recipes from the entire year show the influence of California and other place-of-origin food products and how food items, shown earlier in their initial incarnations, made their way into mainstream American cuisine.

Appendix

Fisher, Mrs. Abby

Breakfast Breads
Breakfast Cornbread
Breakfast Cream Cake
Waffles

Croquettes
Crab Croquettes

Miscellaneous
Pap for Infant Diets
Tonic Bitters

Pastries and Cakes
Carolas
Gold Cake
Pastry for Making Pies of All
Kinds
Sweet Potato Pie

Sauces, Pickles and Preserves
Blackberry Brandy
Brandy Peaches
Compound Tomato Sauce
Strawberry Jam
Sweet Cucumber Pickle

Savory Dishes
Circuit Hash
Corned Beef Hash
Eggplant Stuffed
Jumberlie — A Creole Dish

Soups
Beef Soup and Oxtail Soup
Corn and Tomato Soup
Oyster Gumbo Soup

Hearn, Lafcadio

Breads, Pastries, Drinks, Miscellaneous
Boston Brown Bread
Bouille-Abaisse
CreamCakes
Genoise Cakes
German Lady Fingers
Gin Fizz
Grand Brule à la Boulanger
How to Mix Absinthe in Every
Style
Italy's Buckwheat Cakes
Louisiana Orange Flower Mac-
aroons
My Own Pudding
Parlor Punch Moran's
Peaches and Apricots in Brandy
Peaches and Cream Frozen
A Richer Molasses Pie
Sicilian Biscuits Dropped on
Tins
Sour Milk Doughnuts Without
Yeast
Syllabub

Soup
Crayfish Bisque, a Creole Dish
Gombo File with Oysters No.
Oyster Soup
Tomato Soup with Vegetables,
Very Fine

Vegetables and Condiments
Okra
Tomato Catsup

Hirtzler, Victor

Beef
Delmonico Steak if Twenty
Ounces
Minced Tenderloin, Creole Style

Cold Items
Cranberry water ice
Rice Ice Cream with Citron,
Garnished with Truffles
Terrine of FoieGras in Aspic-
Whole
White Coffee Ice Cream

Fish
Boiled Tahoe Trout, sauce mous-
seline
Broiled Alaska Black Cod
Kingfish à la Bateliére

Miscellaneous
Candied Sweet Potatoes
Celery Victor
Chicken Okra Soup
Chicken Salad, Victor
Eggs Pocahontas
Lobster Bisque à la Portland
Louisiana Gumbo File
New Beets, Californienne
Oyster Soup with Powdered
Okra or Gumbo
Potage Honolulu
Pumpkin Pie
Sand dabs, Gaillard
Supréme of Oysters, St. Francis

Mollusks and Crustaceans
Bisque of California Oysters

Crab Gumbo
Lobster Newberg

Poultry and Game

Pigeons with Green Peas
Venison Cutlets à la Financière

Sauces and Garnishes

Aquitaine Garnish
Béchamel Sauce
Chicken Essence
Tomato Catsup

Side Dishes

Alligator Pears
Crouetades à la Castelaine
Mosaic Timbales
Neapolitan Timbales

Leslie, Miss Eliza

Fish and Seafood

To Boil a Fresh Salmon
Halibut Cutlets
Oyster Pie
Soft Crabs
Stewed Lobster

Fruits

Cranberry Preserve
Peach Preserve

Meats

Calf's Liver
Chicken Curry
Cutlets à la Maintenon
Glazed Ham
Ham Pie
Pepper Pot
Pork Pie
To Roast a Loin of Pork
Roasted Game Birds
Veal Cutlets
Veal Knuckle
Veal Patties
Venison

Pastry, Puddings, etc.

Buckwheat Cakes
Coconut Jumbles
Doughnuts
Farmer's Rice Pudding
Fine Puff Paste
Indian Pudding
Moravian Sugar Cake
A Nice Plain Paste
Orange, Lemon and Quince Puddings

Plain Pancakes
Sally Lunn
Sweet Paste
Washington Cake

Sauces, Vegetables and Condiments

Lemon Catchup
Tomata Catchup

Soups

Rich Brown Soup
Catfish Soup
Lobster Soup
Veal Soup
Venison Soup

Randolph, Mary

Fowl and Poultry

To Boil a Turkey with Oyster Sauce
Chicken Pudding, a Favorite Virginia Dish
To Make a Dish of Curry After the East Indian Manner

Ice Cream

Almond Cream
Peach Cream
Quince Cream
Vanilla Cream

Meats

Beef à la mode
Fricando of Beef
Pie of Sweetbreads and Oysters
Steaks of Leg of Mutton
Veal Chops
Veal Olives

Other Recipes

An Apple Custard
Doughnuts
To Dress a Salad
Gumbo — a West Indian Dish
Mushroom Catsup
Okra and Tomatoes
Omelette Soufflé
Oyster Catsup
Pumpkin Pie
Rice Waffles
Tomato Catsup
Walnut Catsup

Seafood

To Caveach a Fish
Fried Oysters

To Make a Curry of Catfish
To Pitchcock Eels
To Roast a Shad
Scalloped Oysters

Soups

Asparagus Soup
Catfish Soup
Okra Soup
Oyster Soup
Soup with Bouilli

Ranhofer, Charles

Beef

Delmonico Steak if Twenty Ounces
Minced Tenderloin, Creole Style

Cold Items

Nenuphar PunchLilies
Rice Ice Cream with Citron, Garnished with Truffles
Terrine of FoieGras in Aspic-Whole
White Coffee Ice Cream

Fish

Kingfish à la Bateliére

Mollusks and Crustaceans

Lobster Newberg

Poultry and Game

Pigeons with Green Peas
Venison Cutlets à la Financière

Sauces and Garnishes

Aquitaine Garnish
Béchamel Sauce
Chicken Essence
Tomato Catsup

Side Dishes

Alligator Pears
Crouetades à la Castelaine
Mosaic Timbales
Neapolitan Timbales

Soups

Chicken Okra Soup
Lobster Bisque à la Portland
Oyster Soup with Powdered Okra or Gumbo

Simmons, Amelia

Pies

A Buttered Apple Pie
Minced Pie of Beef
A Stew Pie
Tongue Pie

Puddings, Custards and Cakes

Cookies

A Crookneck, or Winter Squash Pie
Johnny Cake or Hoe Cake
Indian Slapjack
A Nice Indian Pudding
Plain Cake
Plumb Cake
Pompkin
Potatoe Pudding Baked

Roasts

To à la mode a Round
To Roast Beef
Roast Lamb
To Stuff and Roast a Turkey or Fowl
To Stuff and Roast a Goslin

Notes

Prologue

1. Super, p. 32.
2. *Ibid.*, p. 43.
3. Spenser, p. 11.
4. *Ibid.*, p. 14.
5. Carlin, p. 145.
6. *Ibid.*, p. 146.
7. *Ibid.*, p. 38.
8. Sperber, pp. 106–116.
9. Smith, *Eating History*, p. 52.
10. *Ibid.*, p. 53.

Chapter 1. Native American Foods

1. Volo, p. 272.
2. Grew, p. 37.
3. *Ibid.*, p. 36.
4. Mann, p. 109.
5. Cohen, pp. 65–69.
6. *The Cambridge World History of Food*, Vol. 2, p. 1265.
7. Krondl, np..
8. *The Cambridge World History of Food*, Vol. 1, pp. 97–111.
9. Mann, p. 369–378.
10. Jensen, p. 423.
11. Hillard, p. 35.
12. Pilcher, p. 31.

Chapter 2. Amelia Simmons

1. Ashliman.
2. Divine, et al., p. 34.
3. *Ibid.*, p. 93.
4. *Ibid.*, pp. 115–117.

Chapter 3. Mary Randolph

1. Cummings, p. 11.
2. www.infoplease.com/ce6/history.
3. Boorstin, p. 103.
4. www.Monticello.org.

5. *Ibid.*
6. www.history-magazine.com/natroad.
7. Virginia Women in History, www.lva.virginia.gov.
8. http://www.arlingtoncemetery.net/maryrand.htm.
9. http://digital.lib.msu.edu/projects/cookbooks/html/authors/author_randolph.html.
10. Anonymous, ca. 1838.

Chapter 4. Miss Leslie

1. Divine et al., p. 278.
2. *The Pennsylvania Magazine of History and Biography*, Vol. 74, No. 4 (Oct., 1950), pp. 512–527.
3. Allibone, p 1086.

Chapter 5. Mrs. Abby Fisher

1. Wagner, pp. 42–43.
2. Fisher, p. 72.
3. "A Slave's Family Rent Asunder," p. 6.
4. Wagner, p. 44.
5. *Ibid.*, pp. 44–45.
6. *Ibid.*, p. 45.
7. *Ibid.*, p. 49.

Chapter 6. Lafcadio Hearn

1. EyeWitness to History.
2. Montoya.
3. Larson.

Chapter 7. Chef Ranhofer

1. Faas, p. 115.
2. Krondl, np..
3. *The New York Times*, July 26, 1891.
4. Andrews, pages?.
5. Davidson, pages?.
6. *The New York Times*, March 23, 1879.
7. Andrews.
8. Feeding America.

9. *The New York Times*, May 16, 1882.

10. Ibid, February 7, 1895.

11. Ibid, January 30, 1894.

12. *St. Paul Globe*, April 3, 1898.

13. *Salt Lake City Herald*, November 13, 1894.

14. *New York Daily Tribune*, May 30, 1907.

15. *The New York Times*, October 11, 1899, obituary.

16. Davidson, *American Heritage*.

Chapter 8. Chef Victor Hirtzler

1. Civitello, pp. 277–278.

2. *San Francisco Call*, nd.

3. *San Francisco Call*, April 29, 1910.

4. *Oakland Tribune*, May 19, 1912.

5. *San Francisco Call*, February 20, 1904.

6. *San Francisco Call*, March 20, 1904.

7. *Ogden Standard*, April 24, 1918.

8. *San Francisco Call*, September 19th, 1910.

9. California Avocado Association, 1917 Annual Report, 3:51–54.

10. Beyl, *Northside Magazine*.

11. Beyl, *Saveur*.

12. *San Francisco Call*, nd.

Bibliography

Books

Allibone, S. Austin. *A Critical Dictionary of English Literature and British and American Authors, Living and Deceased, From the Earliest Accounts to the Latter Half of the Nineteenth Century, Containing Over Forty-Six Thousand Articles (Authors), with Forty Indexes of Subjects.* Detroit: Gale Research, 1965.

Abramson, Julia. *Food Culture in France.* Westport, Connecticut: Greenwood Press, 2007.

Ambrose, Stephen. *The Men Who Built the Transcontinental Railroad 1863–1869.* New York: Simon & Schuster, 2000.

Audubon, J.J. *Ornithological Biography.* 5 vols. Edinburgh, 1831–39.

Berzok, Linda Murray. *American Indian Food.* Westport, Connecticut: Greenwood Press, 2005.

Boorstin, Daniel J. *The Americans: The Colonial Experience.* New York: Random House, 1958.

Bullock, Mrs. Helen. *The Williamsburg Art of Cookery.* Williamsburg: Reitz Press, 1938.

Carlin, Martha, and Joel Rosenthal, eds. *Food and Eating in Medieval Europe.* London: Hambledon Press, 1998.

Civitello, Linda. *Cuisine and Culture: A History of Food and People,* 2nd edition. Hoboken, New Jersey: John Wiley and Sons, 2007.

Crosby, Alfred W. Jr. *The Columbian Exchange, Biological and Cultural Consequences of 1492.* Westport, Connecticut: Praeger Publishers, 2003.

Cummings, Richard Ashborn. *The American and His Food.* Chicago: University of Chicago Press, 1940–41. Reprint, New York: Arno Press, 1970.

Curtis, Wayne. *And a Bottle of Rum: A History of the New World in Ten Cocktails.* New York: Three Rivers Press, 2007.

Dalby, Andrew. *Empire of Pleasures: Luxury and Indulgence in the Roman World.* London: Routledge, 2000.

De Blij, H.J. *Atlas of North America.* New York: Oxford University Press, 2005.

De Voe, Thomas Farrington. *The Market Assistant, Containing a Brief Description of Every Article of Human Food Sold in the Public Markets of the Cities of New York, Boston, Philadelphia, and Brooklyn.* New York: Hurd and Houghton, 1867.

Divine, Robert A., et al. *America Past and Present.* Glenview, Illinois: Scott, Foresman, 1984.

Eden, Trudy. *Cooking in America, 1590–1842.* Westport, Connecticut: Greenwood Press, 2006.

Edwards, Clarence. *Bohemian San Francisco: Its Restaurants and Their Most Famous Recipes.* San Francisco: P. Elder, 1914.

Edwards, John. *The Roman Cookery of Apicius.* London: Rider Books, 1988.

Epstein, Norrie. *The Friendly Shakespeare.* New York: Viking, 1992.

Faas, Patrick. *Around the Roman Table.* New York: Palgrave MacMillan, 2003.

Fernandez-Arnesto, Felipe. *Near a Thousand Tables, a History of Food.* New York: Free Press, 2002.

Fisher, Mrs. Abby. *What Mrs. Fisher Knows about Old Southern Cooking, Soups, Pickles, Preserves Etc.* San Francisco: Women's Co-operative Printing Office, 1881.

Flandrin, Jean-Louis, and Massimo Montanari. *The Rise of the Restaurant, Food: a Culinary History.* New York: Columbia University Press, 1999.

Forte, Angelo, Richard Oram, and Frederick Petersen. *Viking Empires.* New York: Cambridge Press, 2005.

Grew, Raymond, ed. *Food in Global History.* Boulder: Westview Press, 1999.

"Food and Counter Culture: A Study of Bread and Politics," Warren Belasco, Chapter 14, pp. 273–288.

Hart, John S. *Female Prose Writers of America.* Philadelphia: E.H. Butler, 1866.

Hearn, Lafcadio. *La Cuisine Creole, A Collection of Culinary Recipes.* Second Edition. New Orleans: F.F. Hansell & Bro., 1885.

Hilliard, Sam Bowers. *Hog Meat and Hoecake, Food*

Supply in the Old South. Carbondale: Southern Illinois University Press, 1972.

Hirsch, Arthur Henry. *The Huguenots of South Carolina.* Columbia: University of South Carolina Press, 1999.

Hirtzler, Victor. *The Hotel St. Francis Cookbook.* Chicago: Hotel Monthly Press, 1919.

Hoff, Archie Corydon. *Dainty Sweets; ices, creams, jellies, preserves by the world famous chefs.* Los Angeles: International Publishing, 1913.

Homer. *The Odyssey.* Translated by A.T. Murray. Cambridge, Massachusetts: Loeb Classical Library, 1919, I.

Hurt, Douglas. *American Agriculture.* West Lafayette, Indiana: Purdue University Press, 2002.

Kertzer, David I., and Marzio Barbagli, eds. *Family Life in the Long Nineteenth Century.* New Haven, Connecticut: Yale University Press, 2002.

Kiple, Kenneth F., and Kriemhild Coneè Ornelas, eds. *The Cambridge World History of Food,* Volumes 1 and 2. New York: Cambridge University Press, 2000.

Krondl, Michael. *Around the American Table.* New York: New York Public Library, 1995.

Larousse Gastronomique. Revised and updated by Clarkson Potter. New York: Clarkson Potter, 1999.

Leslie, Miss (Eliza). *Directions for Cookery, in Its Various Branches.* Tenth Edition. Philadelphia: E. L. Carey & A. Hart, 1840.

Mann, Charles C., *1491, New Revelations of the Americas Before Columbus.* New York: First Vintage Books, 2006.

Mariani, John. *America Eats Out.* New York: William Morrow, 1991.

McWilliams, James. *A Revolution in Eating, How the Quest for Food Shaped America.* New York: Columbia University Press, 2005.

Nathan, Rhoda, ed. *Nineteenth-Century Women Writers of the English Speaking World.* Westport, Connecticut: Greenwood Press, 1986.

Oliver, Sandra. *Food in Colonial and Federal America.* Westport, Connecticut: Greenwood Press, 2005.

Pilcher, Jeffrey. *Food in World History.* New York: Routledge, 2006.

Pollan, Michael. *In Defense of Food.* New York: Penguin Press, 2008.

Randolph, Mrs. Mary. *The Virginia Housewife or, Methodical Cook.* Baltimore: Plaskitt, & Cugle, 1838.

Ranhofer, Charles. *The Epicurean, A Complete Treatise of Analytical and Practical Studies on the Culinary Art.* New York City: Author, 1894.

Revel, Jean-Francois. *Culture and Cuisine — A Journey Through the History of Food.* Translated by Helen Lane. New York: Doubleday, 1982.

Richie, Carson I. A. *Food in Civilization: How History Has Been Affected by Human Tastes.* New York: Beaufort Books, 1981.

Scully, Terrence, ed. *The Viandier of Taillevent.* Ottawa: University of Ottawa Press, 1988.

Shaffer, Lynda Norene. *Native Americans Before 1492, The Mound Building Centers of the Eastern Woodlands.* Armonk, New York: M E Sharpe, 1992.

Simmons, Amelia. *American Cookery, or the Art of Dressing Viands, Fish, Poultry, and Vegetables.* Hartford, Northampton: Simeon Butler, 1798.

Sinclair, Mick. *San Francisco, A Cultural and Literary History.* Oxford, United Kingdom: Signal Books, 2004.

Smith, Andrew. *Eating History.* New York: Columbia University Press, 2009.

Smith, Andrew F., ed. *The Oxford Encyclopedia of Food and Drink in America.* Volumes 1 and 2. Oxford: Oxford University Press, 2004.

Soyer, A. *Pantrophean, The History of Food and Its Preparation from the Earliest Ages of the World.* Boston: Ticknor, Reed, and Fields, 1853.

Spenser, Colin. *British Food, an Extraordinary Thousand Years of History.* New York: Columbia University Press, 2002.

Sperber, Jonathan. *The European Revolutions 1848–1851.* Cambridge: Cambridge University Press, 2005.

Stavely, Keith, and Kathleen Fitzgerald. *America's Founding Food, the Story of New England Cooking.* Chapel Hill: University of North Carolina Press, 2004.

Sturtevant, William, ed. *Handbook of North American Indians.* Vol. 3. Washington, DC: Smithsonian Institution, 2006.

Super, John A. *Food, Conquest and Colonization in Sixteenth Century Spanish America.* Albuquerque, New Mexico: University of New Mexico Press, 1988.

Thomas, Lately. *Delmonico's, a Century of Splendor.* Boston: Houghton Mifflin, 1967.

Thompson, Katherine, and Hilary Mac Austin, eds. *The Face of Our Past.* Bloomington, Indiana: Indiana University Press, 1999.

Turner, Jonathan. *Human Institutions: a Theory of Societal Evolution.* Lanham, Maryland: Rowman & Littlefield Publishers, 2003.

Volo, James, and Dorothy Volo. *Family Life in 17th and 18th Century America.* Westport, Connecticut: Greenwood Press, 2006.

Wagner, Tricia Martineau. *African Women of the Old West.* Guilford, Connecticut: TwoDot, 2007.

Warnes, Andrew. *Hunger Overcome? Food and Resistance in Twentieth-Century African American Literature.* Athens, Georgia: University of Georgia Press, 2004.

Whitney Publication, American Cookery, 1920.

Williams, Susan. *Food in the United States, 1820s–1890,* Westport, Connecticut; London: Greenwood Press, 2006.

Magazines, Internet Sources, Newspapers

Andrews, Peter. "Delmonico's." *American Heritage Magazine* 31/5 (August/September 1980).

Ashliman, D.L., ed. "Vikings in America." http://www.pitt.edu/~dash/vinland.html.

Beyl, Ernest. "Another Unlikely Hero in the Gastronomic Trenches." *Northside Magazine*, January 2010.

_____. "My Father the Sous Chef." *Saveur Magazine* 72 (January/February 2004).

_____. "Victor Hirtzler, Alsatian Superstar Chef." *Northside Magazine*, February 2010.

Brown, Dale Mackenzie. "The Fate of Greenland's Vikings." *Archaeology*, February 28, 2000. http://www.archaeology.org.

California Avocado Association, Trade Group Newsletter.

California Historical Society. http://californiahistoricalsociety.org.

Center for Columbia River History. http://www.ccrh.org.

Clayton, H.J. "Clayton's Celebrated California Salad Dressing." Seasonal Chef. http://www.seasonalchef.com/clayton.htm.

Cohen, Marc Nathan. "Cambridge." In *Pre-historic Hunter Gatherers: The Emergence of Cultural Complexity*. Theoretical papers and essays, conference publication, Orlando Academic Press, 1985.

Conrad, Jon, M. "Open Access and Extinction of the Passenger Pigeon in North America, Natural Resource Modeling." *InterScience* 18/4 (2005): 501–519.

Davidson, Marshall. "A Royal Welcome for the Russian Navy." *American Heritage* 11/4 (June 1960). http://americanheritage.com.

EyeWitness to History. http://www.eyewitnesstohistory.com.

Internet Search Archive. http://www.archive.org/index.php.

Jensen, Joan M. "Native American Women and Agriculture." *Sex Roles* 3/5 (October 1977).

Ladies' Literary Portfolio (June 24, 1829): I, 28.

Larson, Susan. "Creative Writing Teacher Anne Gisleson Finds Comfort in Non-Fiction." *New Orleans Times-Picayune*, February 25, 2009.

Library of Virginia. "Virginia Women in History." http://www.lva.virginia.gov/public/vawomen/.

Montoya, Maria. "Book Review of *The Sound of Building Coffins*." *New Orleans Times-Picayune*, March 4, 2009.

"The National Road." *History Magazine*. http://www.history-magazine.com/natroad.html.

Newfoundland and Labrador Heritage. "Irish Monks and the Voyage of St. Brendan." http://www.heritage.nf.ca/exploration/brendan.html.

New York Daily Tribune

New York Times

Oakland Tribune (Oakland, California)

Ogden Standard (Ogden, Utah)

Parsons, Russ. "Our Own Escoffier." *Los Angeles Times*, December 15, 1999.

Saint Paul Globe

Salt Lake City Herald

"A Slave's Family Rent Asunder." *The Independent*, May 29, 1862.

Smithsonian Institution. http://www.si.edu/encyclopedia.

Thomas Jefferson Foundation. "Jefferson's West." http://www.monticello.org/jefferson/lewisandclark/louisiana.html.

University of California Museum of Paleontology. "The Mollusca, an Introduction." http://www.ucmp.berkeley.edu/taxa/inverts/mollusca/mollusca.php.

Utah Education Network. http://www.uen.org/.

Recipe Index

Subject Index

LaVergne, TN USA
02 February 2011
214850LV00003B/101-294/P

9 780786 458691